Critical Race Theory

Essays on the Social Construction and Reproduction of "Race"

Series Editor

E. Nathaniel Gates

Benjamin N. Cardozo School of Law
Yeshiva University

GARLAND PUBLISHING, INC.
New York & London
1997

Contents of the Series

Cultural and Literary Critiques of the Concepts of "Race"

Edited with introductions by
E. Nathaniel Gates

Benjamin N. Cardozo School of Law
Yeshiva University

GARLAND PUBLISHING, INC.
New York & London
1997

Library of Congress Cataloging-in-Publication Data

Cultural and literary critiques of the concepts of "race" / edited with
    introductions by E. Nathaniel Gates.
        p.   cm. — (Critical race theory ; 2)
    Includes bibliographical references.
    ISBN 0-8153-2601-7 (alk. paper). — ISBN 0-8153-2599-1 (set)
    1. Race. 2. Racism. I. Gates, E. Nathaniel. II. Series.
GN269.C85 1997
305.8—dc21   97-2000
                                                          CIP

Printed on acid-free, 250-year-life paper
Manufactured in the United States of America

Contents

Volume Introduction

The power of metaphor to reproduce or reinforce a racialized order of dominion is made palpable in the process of dominant groups representing themselves, as well as subaltern, racialized others, to the larger world. The production of such representations seeks to establish a set of guiding images and principles, a virtual archive of information, detailing what it means to be normative, as well as what it means to embody social and cultural alterity. Actual individuals, as mere objects of such representations, are invoked only as the enactors or repositories of these conjured images. The set of representations thus confabulated aims to cabin those it depicts within the constraints of certain predetermined representational limits. By delimiting their imaginative repertoire it aspires to demarcate their "nature."

In corollary fashion, the depictions of the spaces occupied by dominant groups are valorized, while those inhabited by racialized others are systematically devalued and estranged. Their reservations, ghettos, prisons, plantation quarters, colonies, and townships are represented as sites of disorder and danger. Their cultural productions are likewise depicted differentially, continually disclosed as the cultural expressions of unassimilable others: "Native artifacts," not art; objects for display in a museum of natural history, not an art museum; "primitive emotional discharge," not sublime or mystical religious expression; and "black music," as opposed to music.

Because racialized representations are thus able to depict and evaluate their objects simultaneously, they wield enormous epistemological power. This power to depict and (de)value racialized others is also the power to designate, identify, and in an important sense, (re)constitute them. The practice of depicting racialized others and endowing them with value also has the effect of constraining their autonomy, of extending a potent form of control and dominion over them. In exercising this control, racialized representation seeks to establish the contours of the self images of its objects, to furnish, in effect, the ground for the construction or modification of their senses of self.

Because the successful imposition of a racial designation or identity requires a detailed depiction of the racialized other, the more detailed the image produced in a racialized representation, the more effectively it shapes its representational object. The racialized image is, therefore, informative in the richest sense of that term. By providing an exhaustive compendium of the other's racialized "nature" and possibilities, it reconfigures how she is perceived, as well as her perceptions.

Like racialized others, who are constrained to discover themselves in distorted representations that are deeply imbricated in relationships of social dominion, the producers of racialized representations also act within complex social milieus. The political economy and culture that govern their life-worlds inevitably impinge upon the images, techniques, and categories they employ in their productive processes. The processes of fabricating the images, tropes, and metaphors that sustain "race" as a symbolic system are thus characterized by a clever sleight of hand. Although they depend upon the premises of prevailing, "common sense," racial mythologies, these processes don simultaneously the protective cloak of selected learned disciplines — disciplines with a purportedly universal and formal character that confers both authority and legitimation. This is accomplished by exploiting all of the putative racial knowledge implicit in such disciplines as law, history, and biology.

Actual representations of racialized others are, however, in no sense uniform or static. Quite the contrary, they are dynamic and undergo significant transformation over time. The explanations offered for the essential alterity of any group of racialized others, the characteristics attributed to them, and the evaluations of those characteristics, are all adjusted periodically. For example, over the course of some five-hundred-odd years, European-American representations of the American Indigenes have demonstrated remarkable plasticity. Although emphasis upon skin color differentials has remained a constant distinguishing feature of such representations, other elements have proven to be historically variable. Similarly, the evaluative content of the racialized representations of American Indigenes has by no means been consistently negative. Indeed, there are innumerable instances in which the qualities attributed to or identified with the so-called "Indian" have been wholly positive.

The individuals who constitute the objects of racialized representation, i.e., those who have been created or culturally realized as racialized others, also change over time. Hence, when analyzing representations of racialized others, it is necessary to remain alert to their social and historical status, to their heterogeneity and dynamism, as well as to their more constant features. The analytical implication of this fact is that one cannot simply assume the existence of an uncomplicated process of representational reproduction whereby contemporary representations are mechanistically inherited from the past. Rather, contemporary representations should always be regarded as the product of a historical legacy of active transformations, each made in light of prevailing social circumstances.

Although the current racial categories and representations of contemporary social and cultural others derive their status as self-evident "common sense" from what we know to be a biologistic fallacy, modern social history suggests that there is often a considerable lag time between the abandonment of untenable scientific postulates and the evisceration of their cultural impact. Consequently, scientifically depassed, yet culturally resonant, naturalistic notions of "race" continue to be pressed into the service of new projects of representation and cultural construction. In an effort to realign perceptions and expand the boundaries that currently constrict the representations of subaltern, racialized others, the critical essays and reviews assembled in this volume explore and critique the continuing hold of racial tropes and metaphors.

Cultural and Literary Critiques of the Concepts of "Race"

James Baldwin's writing is an enduring menace to white supremacy. In his novels and plays and particularly in his essays (*The Fire Next Time, Nobody Knows My Name, Notes of a Native Son*), he has written eloquently and prophetically about American racism—and in so doing he has told white folks more than they ever wanted to hear (and certainly more than they could have figured out on their own) about the utter fraudulence of their self-congratulatory notion that they are "white" and therefore superior. In Baldwin's uncompromising view, "white" is a lie. Here he tells the truth about that truthlessness—and the corrupt political leadership that is its inevitable result.

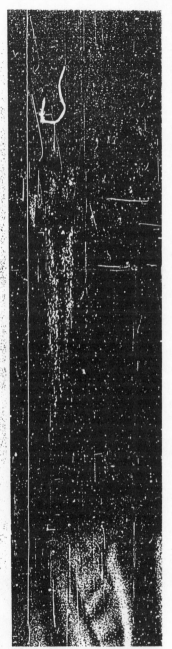

On Being White ...And Other Lies

The crisis of leadership in the white community is remarkable—and terrifying—because there is, in fact, no white community.

This may seem an enormous statement—and it is. I'm willing to be challenged. I'm also willing to attempt to spell it out.

My frame of reference is, of course, America, or that portion of the North American continent that calls itself America. And this means I am speaking, essentially, of the European vision of the world—or more precisely, perhaps, the European vision of the universe. It is a vision as remarkable for what it pretends to include as for what it remorselessly diminishes, demolishes or leaves totally out of account.

There is, for example—at least, in principle—an Irish community: here, there, anywhere, or, more precisely, Belfast, Dublin and Boston. There is a German community: both sides of Berlin. Bavaria and Yorkville. There is an Italian community: Rome, Naples, the Bank of the Holy Ghost, and Mulberry Street. And there is a Jewish community, stretching from Jerusalem to California to New York. There are English communities. There are French communities. There are Swiss consortiums. There are Poles: in Warsaw (where they would like us to be friends) and in Chicago (where because they are white we are enemies). There are, for that matter, Indian restaurants, and Turkish baths. There is the underworld—the poor (to say nothing of those who intend to become rich) are always with us—but this does not describe a community. It bears terrifying witness to what happened to everyone who got here, and paid the price of the ticket. The price was to become "white." No one was white before he/she came to America. It took generations, and a vast amount of coercion, before this became a white country.

It is probable that it is the Jewish community—or more accurately, perhaps, its remnants—that in America has paid the highest and most extraordinary price for becoming white. For the Jews came here from countries where they were not white, and they came here, in part, *because* they were not white; and incontestably—in the eyes of the Black American (and not only in those eyes) American Jews have opted to become white, and this is how they operate. It was ironical to hear, for example, former Israeli prime minister Menachem Begin [CONTINUED ON PAGE 92]

By James Baldwin

2

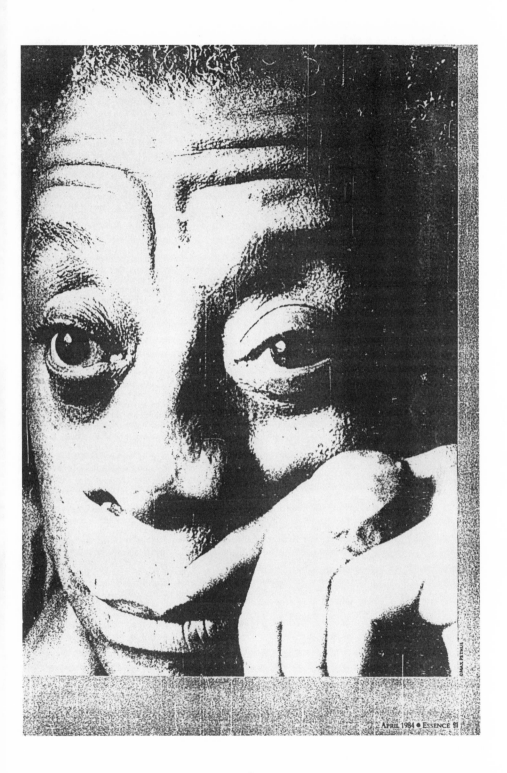

3

declare some time ago that "the Jewish people bow only to God" while knowing that the state of Israel is sustained by a blank check from Washington. Without further pursuing the implication of this mutual act of faith, one is nevertheless aware that the Jewish translation into a white American can sustain the state of Israel in a way that the Black presence, here, can scarcely hope—at least, not yet—to halt the slaughter in South Africa.

And there is a reason for that.

America became white—the people who, as they claim, "settled" the country became white—because of the necessity of denying the Black presence, and justifying the Black subjugation. No community can be based on such a principle—or, in other words, no community can be established on so genocidal a lie! White men—from Norway, for example, where they were *Norwegians*—became white: by slaughtering the cattle, poisoning the wells, torching the houses, massacring Native Americans, raping Black women.

This moral erosion has made it quite impossible for those who think of their lives as white in this country to have any moral authority at all—privately, or publicly. The multitudinous bulk of them sit, stunned, before their TV sets, swallowing garbage that they know to be garbage, and—in a profound and unconscious effort to justify this torpor that disguises a profound and bitter panic—pay a vast amount of attention to athletics: even though they know that the football player (the Son of the Republic, *their* sons!) is merely another aspect of the money-making scheme. They are either relieved or embittered by the presence of the Black boy on the team. I do not know if they remember how long and hard they fought to keep him off it: I know that they do not dare have any notion of the price Black people (mothers and fathers) paid and pay. They do not want to know the meaning, or face the shame, of what they compelled—out of what they took as the necessity of being white—Joe Louis or Jackie Robinson or Cassius Clay (aka Muhammad Ali) to pay. I know that they, themselves, would not have liked to pay it.

There has never been a labor movement in this country, the proof being the absence of a Black presence in the so-called father-to-son unions. There are, perhaps, some niggers in the window; but Blacks have no power in the labor unions.

Just so does the white community, as a means of keeping itself white, elect, as they imagine, their political (!) representatives. No nation in the world, including England, is represented by so stunning a pantheon of the relentlessly mediocre. I will not name names—I will leave that to you

But this cowardice, this necessity of justifying a totally false identity and of justifying what must be called a genocidal history, has placed everyone now living into the hands of the most ignorant and powerful people the world has ever seen: And how did they get that way?

By deciding that they were white. By opting for safety instead of life. By persuading themselves that a Black child's life meant nothing compared with a white child's life. By abandoning their children to the things white men could buy. By informing their children that Black women, Black men and Black children had no human integrity that those who call themselves white were bound to respect. And in this debasement and definition of Black people, they debased and defined themselves.

And have brought humanity to the edge of oblivion: because they think they are white. Because they think they are white, they do not dare confront the ravage and the lie of their history. Because they think they are white, they cannot allow themselves to be tormented by the suspicion that all men are brothers. Because they think they are white, they are looking for, or bombing into existence, stable populations, cheerful natives and cheap labor. Because they think they are white, they believe, as even no child believes, in the dream of safety. Because they think they are white, however vociferous they may be and however multitudinous, they are as speechless as Lot's wife—looking backward, changed into a pillar of salt.

However—! White being, absolutely, a moral choice (for there *are* no white people), the crisis of leadership for those of us whose identity has been forged, or branded, as Black is nothing new. We—who were not Black before we got here either, who were defined as Black by the slave trade—have paid for the crisis of leadership in the white community for a very long time, and have resoundingly, even when we face the worst about ourselves, survived and triumphed over it. If we had not survived, and triumphed, there would not be a Black American alive.

And the fact that we are still here—even in suffering, darkness, danger, endlessly defined by those who do not dare define, or even confront, themselves—is the key to the crisis in white leadership. The past informs us of various kinds of people—criminals, adventurers and saints, to say nothing, of course, of popes—but it is the Black condition, and only that, which informs us concerning white people. It is a terrible paradox, but those who believed that they could control and define Black people divested themselves of the power to control and define themselves. ◆

James Baldwin's latest book, Evidence of Things Not Seen (about the slaying of 29 Black children in Atlanta), will be published later this year.

4

WHITE

BY RICHARD DYER

THIS IS AN ARTICLE about a subject that, much of the time as I've been writing it, seems not to be there as a subject at all. Trying to think about the representation of whiteness as an ethnic category in mainstream film is difficult, partly because white power secures its dominance by seeming not to be anything in particular, but also because, when whiteness *qua* whiteness does come into focus, it is often revealed as emptiness, absence, denial or even a kind of death.

It is, all the same, important to try to make some headway with grasping whiteness as a culturally constructed category. 'Images of' studies have looked at groups defined as oppressed, marginal or subordinate – women, the working class, ethnic and other minorities (e.g., lesbians and gay men, disabled people, the elderly). The impulse for such work lies in the sense that how such groups are represented is part of the process of their oppression, marginalisation or subordination. The range and fertility of such work has put those groups themselves centre-stage in both analytical and campaigning activity, and highlighted the issue of representation as politics. It has, however, had one serious drawback, long recognised in debates about women's studies. Looking, with such passion and single-mindedness, at non-dominant groups has had the effect of reproducing the sense of the oddness, differentness, exceptionality of these groups, the feeling that they are departures from the norm. Meanwhile the norm has carried on as if it is the natural, inevitable, ordinary way of being human.

Some efforts are now being made to rectify this, to see that the norm too is constructed, although only with masculinity has anything approaching a proliferation of texts begun. Perhaps it is worth signalling here, before proceeding, two of the pitfalls in the path of such work, two convolutions that especially characterise male writing about masculinity – guilt and me too-ism. Let me state that, while writing here as a white person about whiteness, I do not mean either to display the expiation of my guilt about being white, nor to hint that it is also awful to be white (because it is an inadequate, limiting definition of being human, because feeling guilty is such a burden). Studies of dominance by the dominant should not deny the place of the writer in relation to what s/he is writing about it, but nor should they be the green light for self-recrimination or trying to get in on the act.

Power in contemporary society habitually passes itself off as embodied in the normal as opposed to the superior[1]. This is common to all forms of power, but it works in a peculiarly seductive way with whiteness, because of the way it seems rooted, in common-sense thought, in things other than ethnic difference. The very terms we use to describe the major ethnic divide presented by Western society, 'black' and 'white', are imported from and naturalised by other discourses. Thus it is said (even in liberal text books) that there are inevitable associations of white with light and therefore safety, and black with dark and therefore danger, and that this explains racism (whereas one might well argue about the safety of the cover of darkness and the danger of exposure to the light); again, and with more justice, people point to the Judaeo-Christian use of white and black to symbolise good and evil, as carried still in such expressions as 'a black mark', 'white magic', 'to blacken the character' and so on.[2] I'd like to look at another aspect of commonsensical conflations of black and white as natural and ethnic categories by considering ideas of what colour is.

I was taught the scientific difference between black and white at primary school. It seemed a fascinating paradox. Black, which, because you had to add it to paper to make a picture, I had always thought of as a colour, was, it turned out, nothingness, the absence of all colour; whereas white, which looked just like empty space (or blank paper), was, apparently, all the colours there were put together. No doubt such explanations of colour have long been outmoded; what interests me is how they manage to touch on the construction of the ethnic categories of black and white in dominant representation. In the realm of categories, black is always marked as a colour (as the term 'coloured' egregiously acknowledges), and is always particularising; whereas white is not anything really, not an identity, not a particularising quality, because it is everything – white is no colour because it is all colours.

This property of whiteness, to be everything and nothing, is the source of its representational power. On the one hand, as one of the people in the video *Being White*[3] observes, white domination is reproduced by the way that white people 'colonise the definition of normal'. Paul Gilroy similarly spells out the political consequences, in the British context, of the way that whiteness both disappears behind and is subsumed into other identities. He discusses the way that the language of 'the nation' aims to be unifying, permitting even socialists an appeal in terms of 'we' and 'our' 'beyond the margins of sectional interest', but goes on to observe that:

there is a problem in these plural forms: who do they include, or, more precisely for our purposes, do they help to reproduce blackness and Englishness

[1] cf, Herbert Marcuse, *One Dimensional Man*, Boston, Beacon Press, 1964.

[2] cf, Winthrop Jordan, *White over Black*, Harmondsworth, Penguin, 1969; Peter Fryer, *Staying Power*, London, Pluto, 1984.

[3] Made by Tony Dowmunt, Maris Clark, Rooney Martin and Kobena Mercer for Albany Video, London.

as mutually exclusive categories? . . . why are contemporary appeals to 'the people' in danger of transmitting themselves as appeals to the white people?[4]

On the other hand, if the invisibility of whiteness colonises the definition of other norms – class, gender, heterosexuality, nationality and so on – it also masks whiteness as itself a category. White domination is then hard to grasp in terms of the characteristics and practices of white people. No one would deny that, at the very least, there are advantages to being white in Western societies, but it is only avowed racists who have a theory which attributes this to inherent qualities of white people. Otherwise, whiteness is presented more as a case of historical accident, rather than a characteristic cultural/historical construction, achieved through white domination.

The colourless multi-colouredness of whiteness secures white power by making it hard, especially for white people and their media, to 'see' whiteness. This, of course, also makes it hard to analyse. It is the way that black people are marked as black (are not just 'people') in representation that has made it relatively easy to analyse their representation, whereas white people – not there as a category and everywhere everything as a fact – are difficult, if not impossible, to analyse *qua* white. The subject seems to fall apart in your hands as soon as you begin. Any instance of white representation is always immediately something more specific – *Brief Encounter* is not about white people, it is about English middle-class people; *The Godfather* is not about white people, it is about Italian-American people; but *The Color Purple* is about black people, before it is about poor, southern US people.

This problem clearly faced the makers of *Being White*, a pioneering attempt to confront the notion of white identity. The opening vox pop sequence vividly illustrates the problem. Asked how they would define themselves, the white interviewees refer easily to gender, age, nationality or looks but never to ethnicity. Asked if they think of themselves as white, most say that they don't, though one or two speak of being 'proud' or 'comfortable' to be white. In an attempt to get some white people to explore what being white means, the video assembles a group to talk about it and it is here that the problem of white people's inability to see whiteness appears intractable. Sub-categories of whiteness (Irishness, Jewishness, Britishness) take over, so that the particularity of whiteness itself begins to disappear; then gradually, it seems almost inexorably, the participants settle in to talking with confidence about what they know: stereotypes of black people.

Yet perhaps this slide towards talking about blackness gives us a clue as to where we might begin to see whiteness – where its difference from blackness is inescapable and at issue. I shall look here at examples of mainstream cinema whose narratives are marked by the fact of ethnic difference. Other approaches likely to yield interesting results include: the study of the characterisation of whites in Third World or diaspora cinema; images of the white race in avowedly racist and fascist cinema; the use of the 'commutation test'[5], the imaginary substitution of black

[4] Paul Gilroy, *There Ain't No Black in the Union Jack*, London, Hutchinson, 1987, pp 55-56. See also the arguments about feminism and ethnicity in Hazel Carby, 'White Woman Listen! Black Feminism and the Boundaries of Sisterhood' in Centre for Contemporary Cultural Studies, *The Empire Strikes Back*, London, Hutchinson, 1982, pp 212-23.

[5] John O Thompson, 'Screen Acting and the Commutation Test', *Screen* Summer 1978, vol 19 no 2, pp 55-70.

for white performers in films such as *Brief Encounter*, say, or *Ordinary People* (if these are unimaginable played by black actors, what does this tell us about the characteristics of whiteness?) or, related to this, consideration of what ideas of whiteness are implied by such widespread observations as that Sidney Poitier or Diana Ross, say, are to all intents and purposes 'white'. What all these approaches share, however, is reference to that which is not white, as if only non-whiteness can give whiteness any substance. The reverse is not the case – studies of images of blacks, Native Americans, Jews and other ethnic minorities do not need the comparative element that seems at this stage indispensable for the study of whites.

***

The representation of white *qua* white begins to come into focus – in mainstream cinema, for a white spectator – in films in which non-white characters play a significant role. I want to look at three very different examples here – *Jezebel* (USA, Warner Brothers, 1938), *Simba* (GB, Rank Studios, 1955) and *Night of the Living Dead* (USA, 1969). Each is characteristic of the particular genre and period to which it belongs. *Jezebel* is a large-budget Hollywood feature film (said to have been intended to rival *Gone with the Wind*) built around a female star, Bette Davis; its spectacular pleasures are those of costume and decor, of gracious living, and its emotional pleasures those of tears. *Simba* is a film made as part of Rank's bid to produce films that might successfully challenge Hollywood at the box office, built around a male star, Dirk Bogarde; its spectacular pleasures are those of the travelogue, its emotional ones excitement and also the gratification of seeing 'issues' (here, the Mau-Mau in Kenya) being dealt with. *Night of the Living Dead* is a cheap, independently-produced horror film with no stars; its spectacular and emotional pleasures are those of shock, disgust and suspense, along with the evident political or social symbolism that has aided its cult reputation.

The differences between the three films are important and will inform the ways in which they represent whiteness. There is some point in trying to see this continuity across three, nonetheless significantly different, films. There is no doubt that part of the strength and resilience of stereotypes of non-dominant groups resides in their variation and flexibility – stereotypes are seldom found in a pure form and this is part of the process by which they are naturalised, kept alive.[6] Yet the strength of white representation, as I've suggested, is the apparent absence altogether of the typical, the sense that being white is coterminous with the endless plenitude of human diversity. If we are to see the historical, cultural and political limitations (to put it mildly) of white world domination, it is important to see similarities, typicalities, within the seemingly infinite variety of white representation.

All three films share a perspective that associates whiteness with

[6] See T E Perkins, 'Rethinking Stereotypes' in Michele Barrett et al (eds), *Representation and Cultural Practice*, New York, Croom Helm, pp 135-59; Steve Neale, 'The Same Old Story', *Screen Education* Autumn/Winter 1979/80, nos 32-33, pp 33-38. For a practical example see the British Film Institute study pack, *The Dumb Blonde Stereotype*.

order, rationality, rigidity, qualities brought out by the contrast with black disorder, irrationality and looseness. It is their take on this which differs. *Simba* operates with a clear black-white binarism, holding out the possibility that black people can learn white values but fearing that white people will be engulfed by blackness. *Jezebel* is far more ambivalent, associating blackness with the defiance of its female protagonist – whom it does not know whether to condemn or adore. *Night* takes the hint of critique of whiteness in *Jezebel* and takes it to its logical conclusion, where whiteness represents not only rigidity but death.

What these films also share, which helps to sharpen further the sense of whiteness in them, is a situation in which white domination is contested, openly in the text of *Simba* and explicitly acknowledged in *Jezebel*. The narrative of *Simba* is set in motion by the Mau-Mau challenge to British occupation, which also occasions set pieces of debate on the issues of white rule and black responses to it; the imminent decline of slavery is only once or twice referred to directly in *Jezebel*, but the film can assume the audience knows that slavery was soon ostensibly to disappear from the southern states. Both films are suffused with the sense of white rule being at an end, a source of definite sorrow in *Simba*, but in *Jezebel* producing that mixture of disapproval and nostalgia characteristic of the white representation of the ante-bellum South. *Night* makes no direct reference to the state of ethnic play but, as I shall argue below, it does make implicit reference to the black uprisings that were part of the historical context of its making, and which many believed would alter irrevocably the nature of power relations between black and white people in the USA.

The presence of black people in all three films allows one to see whiteness as whiteness, and in this way relates to the existential psychology that is at the origins of the interest in 'otherness' as an explanatory concept in the representation of ethnicity.[7] Existential psychology, principally in the work of Jean-Paul Sartre, had proposed a model of human growth whereby the individual self becomes aware of itself as a self by perceiving its difference from others. It was other writers who suggested that this process, supposedly at once individual and universal, was in fact socially specific – Simone de Beauvoir arguing that it has to do with the construction of the male ego, Frantz Fanon relating it to the colonial encounter of white and black. What I want to stress here is less this somewhat metaphysical dimension[8], more the material basis for the shifts and anxieties in the representation of whiteness suggested by *Simba*, *Jezebel* and *Night*.

The three films relate to situations in which whites hold power in society, but are materially dependent upon black people. All three films suggest an awareness of this dependency – weakly in *Simba*, strongly but still implicitly in *Jezebel*, inescapably in *Night*. It is this actual dependency of white on black in a context of continued white power and privilege that throws the legitimacy of white domination into question. What is called for is a demonstration of the virtues of whiteness that would justify continued domination, but this is a problem if whiteness is

[7] See Frantz Fanon, *Black Skin, White Masks*, London, Pluto, 1986; Edward Saïd, *Orientalism*, London, Routledge and Kegan Paul, 1978; Homi K Bhabha, 'The Other Question – the Stereotype and Colonial Discourse', *Screen* November-December 1983, vol 24 no 6, pp 18-36.

[8] See Benita Parry, 'Problems in Current Theories of Colonial Discourse', *Oxford Literary Review*, vol 9, nos 1-2, 1987, pp 27-58.

also invisible, everything and nothing. It is from this that the films' fascinations derive. I shall discuss them here in the order in which they most clearly attempt to hang on to some justification of whiteness, starting, then, with *Simba* and ending with *Night*.

'Simba'

Simba is a characteristic product of the British cinema between about 1945 and 1965 – an entertainment film 'dealing with' a serious issue.[9] It is a colonial adventure film, offering the standard narrative pleasures of adventure with a tale of personal growth. The hero, Alan (Bogarde), arrives in Kenya from England to visit his brother on his farm, finds he has been killed by the Mau-Mau and stays to sort things out (keep the farm going, find out who killed his brother, quell the Mau-Mau). Because the Mau-Mau were a real administrative and ideological problem for British imperialism at the time of the film's making, *Simba* also has to construct a serious discursive context for these pleasures (essentially a moral one, to do with the proper way to treat native peoples; toughness versus niceness). It does this partly through debates and discussions, partly through characters clearly representing what the film takes to be the range of possible angles on the subject (the bigoted whites, the liberal whites, the British-educated black man, the despotic black chief) but above all through the figure of the hero, whose adventures and personal growth are occasioned, even made possible, through the process of engaging with the late colonial situation. The way this situation is structured by the film and the way Alan/Bogarde rises to the occasion display the qualities of whiteness.

Simba is founded on the 'Manicheism delirium' identified by Frantz Fanon as characteristic of the colonialist sensibility[10]; it takes what Paul Gilroy refers to as an 'absolutist view of black and white cultures, as fixed, mutually impermeable expressions of racial and national identity, [which] is a ubiquitous theme in racial "common sense" '[11]. The film is organised around a rigid binarism, with white standing for modernity, reason, order, stability, and black standing for backwardness, irrationality, chaos and violence. This binarism is reproduced in every detail of the film's *mise-en-scène*. A sequence of two succeeding scenes illustrates this clearly – a meeting of the white settlers to discuss the emergency, followed by a meeting of the Mau-Mau. The whites' meeting takes place in early evening, in a fully lit room; characters that speak are shot with standard high key lighting so that they are fully visible; everyone sits in rows and although there is disagreement, some of it hot-tempered and emotional, it is expressed in grammatical discourse in a language the British viewer can understand; moreover, the meeting consists of nothing but speech. The black meeting, on the other hand, takes place at dead of night, out of doors, with all characters in shadow; even the Mau-Mau leader is lit with extreme sub-Expressionist lighting that dramatises and distorts his face; grouping is in the form of a broken, uneven

[9] See John Hill, *Sex, Class and Realism*, London, British Film Institute, 1986, chaps 4 and 5.

[10] Frantz Fanon, op cit, p 183.

[11] Paul Gilroy, op cit, p 61; see Errol Lawrence, 'In the Abundance of Water the Fool is Thirsty: Sociology and Black Pathology', in Centre for Contemporary Cultural Studies, op cit, pp 95-142.

Binarism in *Simba*'s *mise-en-scène*: white culture (above) and black culture (below).

circle; what speech there is is ritualised, not reasoned, and remains untranslated (and probably in no authentic language anyway), and most vocal sounds are whooping, gabbling and shrieking; the heart of the meeting is in any case not speech, but daubing with blood and entrails and scarring the body. The return to whiteness after this sequence is once again a return to daylight, a dissolve to the straight lines of European fencing and vegetable plots.

The emphasis on the visible and bounded in this *mise-en-scène* (maintained throughout the film) has to do with the importance of fixity in the stereotyping of others – clear boundaries are characteristic of things white (lines, grids, not speaking till someone else has finished and so on), and also what keeps whites clearly distinct from blacks. The importance of the process of boundary establishment and maintenance has long been recognised in discussions of stereotyping and representation.[12] This process is functional for dominant groups, but through it the capacity to set boundaries becomes a characteristic attribute of such groups, endlessly reproduced in ritual, costume, language and, in cinema, *mise-en-scène*. Thus, whites and men (especially) become characterised by 'boundariness'.[13]

Simba's binarism is in the broadest sense racist, but not in the narrower sense of operating with a notion of intrinsic and unalterable biological bases for differences between peoples.[14] It is informed rather by a kind of evolutionism, the idea of a path of progress already followed by whites, but in principle open to all human beings – hence the elements in the binarism of modernity versus backwardness. Such evolutionism raises the possibility of blacks becoming like whites, and it is the belief in this possibility that underpins the views of the liberal characters in the film, Mary (Virginia McKenna) and Dr Hughes (Joseph Tomelty), the latter pleading with his fellow settlers at the meeting to 'reason', not with the Mau-Mau but with the other Africans, who are not beyond the reach of rational discussion. The possibility is further embodied in the character of Peter Karanja (Earl Cameron), the son of the local chief (Orlando Martins), who has trained to be a doctor and is now running a surgery in the village. The film is at great pains to establish that Peter is indeed reasonable, rational, humane, liberal. It is always made quite clear to the viewer that this is so and the representatives of liberalism always believe in him; it is the whites who do not trust him, and one of Alan's moral lessons is in learning to respect Peter's worth. It seems then that part of the film is ready to take the liberal evolutionist position. Yet it is also significant that the spokespeople for liberalism (niceness and reason) are socially subordinate; a woman and an Irish doctor (played for comic eccentricity most of the time), and that liberalism fails, with its representatives (Mary, Peter and now won-over Alan) left at the end of the film crouched in the flames of Alan's farm, rescued from the Mau-Mau in the nick of time by the arrival of the white militia, and Peter dying from wounds inflicted on him by the Mau-Mau (represented as a black mob). Although with its head, as it were, the film endorses the possibility of a black person becoming 'white', this is in fact deeply disturbing, setting in motion the anxiety attendant on any loosening of the fixed visibility of the colonised other. This anxiety is established from the start of the film and is the foundation of its narrative.

As is customary in colonial adventure films, *Simba* opens wth a panoramic shot of the land, accompanied here by birdsong and the sound of an African man singing. While not especially lush or breathtaking, it is peaceful and attractive. A cry of pain interrupts this mood and we see the man who has been singing stop, get off his bicycle and walk towards

[12] e.g., Homi Bhabha, op cit; Richard Dyer, 'Stereotyping' in Richard Dyer (ed), *Gays and Film*, London, British Film Institute, 1977, pp 27-39; Sandor L Gilman, *Difference and Pathology*, Ithaca, Cornell University Press, 1985.

[13] cf, Nancy Chodorow, *The Reproduction of Mothering*, Berkeley, University of California Press, 1978.

[14] Michael Banton, *The Idea of Race*, London, Tavistock, 1977; this restrictive definition of racism has been disputed by, inter alia, Stuart Hall, 'Race, Articulation and Societies Structured in Dominance' in UNESCO, *Sociological Theories: Race and Colonialism*, Paris, UNESCO, 1980.

its source to find a white man lying covered in blood on the ground. The black man kneels by his side, apparently about to help him, but then, to the sound of a drum-roll on the soundtrack, draws his machete and plunges it (off screen) into the wounded man. He then walks back to his bike and rides off. Here is encapsulated the fear that ensues if you can't see black men behaving as black men should, the deceptiveness of a black man in Western clothes riding a bike. This theme is then reiterated throughout the film. Which of the servants can be trusted? How can you tell who is Mau-Mau and who not? Why should Alan trust Peter?

This opening sequence is presented in one long take, using panning. As the man rides off, the sound of a plane is heard, the camera pans up and there is the first cut of the film, to a plane flying through the clouds. There follows (with credits over) a series of aerial shots of the African landscape, in one of which a plane's shadow is seen, and ending with shots of white settlement and then the plane coming to land. Here is another aspect of the film's binarism. The credit sequence uses the dynamics of editing following the more settled feel of the pre-credit long take; it uses aerial shots moving through space, rather than pans with their fixed vantage point; it emphasises the view from above, not that from the ground, and the modernity of air travel after the primitivism of the machete. It also brings the hero to Africa (as we realise when we see Bogarde step off in the first post-credit shot), brings the solution to the problems of deceptive, unfixed appearances set up by the pre-credit sequence.

Simba's binarism both establishes the differences between black and white and creates the conditions for the film's narrative pleasures – the disturbance of the equilibrium of clear-cut binarism, the resultant conflict that the hero has to resolve. His ability to resolve it is part of his whiteness, just as whiteness is identified in the dynamism of the credit sequence (which in turn relates to the generic expectations of adventure) and in the narrative of personal growth that any colonial text with pretensions also has. The Empire provided a narrative space for the realisation of manhood, both as action and maturation.[15] The colonial landscape is expansive, enabling the hero to roam and giving us the entertainment of action; it is unexplored, giving him the task of discovery and us the pleasures of mystery; it is uncivilised, needing taming, providing the spectacle of power; it is difficult and dangerous, testing his machismo, providing us with suspense. In other words, the colonial landscape provides the occasion for the realisation of white male virtues, which are not qualities of being but of doing – acting, discovering, taming, conquering. At the same time, colonialism, as a social, political and economic system, even in fictions, also carries with it challenges of responsibility, of the establishment and maintenance of order, of the application of reason and authority to situations. These, too, are qualities of white manhood that are realised in the process of the colonial text, and very explicitly in *Simba*. When Alan arrives at Nairobi, he is met by Mary, a woman to whom he had proposed when she was visiting England; she

[15] cf, Stuart Hall, 'The Whites of their Eyes: Racist Ideologies and the Media' in George Bridges and Rosalind Brunt (eds), *Silver Linings*, London, Lawrence and Wishart, 1981, pp 28-52.

had turned him down, telling him, as he recalls on the drive to his brother's farm, that he had 'no sense of responsibility'. Now he realises that she was right; in the course of the film he will learn to be responsible in the process of dealing with the Mau-Mau, and this display of growth will win him Mary.

But this is a late colonial text, characterised by a recognition that the Empire is at an end, and not unaware of some kinds of liberal critique of colonialism. So *Simba* takes a turn that is far more fully explored by, say, *Black Narcissus* (1947) or the Granada TV adaptation of *The Jewel in the Crown* (1982). Here, maturity involves the melancholy recognition of failure. This is explicitly stated, by Sister Clodagh in *Black Narcissus*, to be built into the geographical conditions in which the nuns seek to establish their civilising mission ('I couldn't stop the wind from blowing'); it is endlessly repeated by the nice whites in *The Jewel in the Crown* ('There's nothing I can do!') and symbolised in the lace shawl with butterflies 'caught in the net' that keeps being brought out by the characters. I have already suggested the ways in which liberalism is marginalised and shown to fail in *Simba*. More than this, the hero also fails to realise the generically promised adventure experiences: he is unable to keep his late brother's farm going, nor does he succeed in fighting off a man stealing guns from his house; he fails to catch the fleeing leader of the Mau-Mau, and is unable to prevent them from destroying his house and shooting Peter. The film ends with his property in flames and – a touch common to British social conscience films – with a shot of a young black boy who symbolises the only possible hope for the future.

The repeated failure of narrative achievement goes along with a sense of white helplessness in the face of the Mau-Mau (the true black threat), most notably in the transition between the two meeting scenes discussed above. Alan has left the meeting in anger because one of the settlers has criticised the way his brother had dealt with the Africans (too soft); Mary joins him, to comfort him. At the end of their conversation, there is a two-shot of them, with Mary saying of the situation, 'it's like a flood, we're caught in it'. This is accompanied by the sound of drums and is immediately followed by a slow dissolve to black people walking through the night towards the Mau-Mau meeting. The drums and the dissolve enact Mary's words, that the whites are helpless in the face of the forces of blackness.

Simba is, then, an endorsement of the moral superiority of white values of reason, order and boundedness, yet suggests a loss of belief in their efficacy. This is a familiar trope of conservatism. At moments, though, there are glimpses of something else, achieved inadvertently perhaps through the casting of Dirk Bogarde. It becomes explicit in the scene between Mary and Alan just mentioned, when Alan says to Mary, 'I was suddenly afraid of what I was feeling', referring to the anger and hatred that the whole situation is bringing out in him and, as Mary says, everyone else. The implication is that the situation evokes in whites the kind of irrational violence supposedly specific to blacks. Of course, being white means being able to repress it and this is what we seem to

16 See Andy Medhurst,
'Dirk Bogarde' in
Charles Barr, *All Our
Yesterdays*, London,
British Film Institute,
1986, pp 346-54.

see in Alan throughout the film. Such repression constitutes the stoic glory of the imperial hero, but there is something about Bogarde in the part that makes it seem less than admirable or desirable. Whether this is suggested by his acting style, still and controlled, yet with fiercely grinding jaws, rigidly clenched hands and very occasional sudden outbursts of shouting, or by the way Rank was grooming him against the grain of his earlier, sexier image (including its gay overtones)[16], it suggests a notion of whiteness as repression that leads us neatly on to *Jezebel*.

'Jezebel'

Like *Simba*, *Jezebel* depicts a white society characterised by order and rigidity, here expressed principally through codes of behaviour and rules of conduct embodied in set-piece receptions, dinner parties and balls. This does contrast with the bare glimpses we get of black life in the film, but *Jezebel* also explores the ways in which whiteness is related to blackness, materially and emotionally dependent on it yet still holding sway over it.

Compositionally, *Jezebel* frequently foregrounds black people – scenes often open with the camera moving from a black person (a woman selling flowers in New Orleans, a servant carrying juleps, a boy pulling on a rope to operate a ceiling fan) across or towards white characters; black people often intrude into the frame while white characters talk. This is particularly noticeable during a dinner-table discussion of the future of slavery; when one of the characters, Pres (Henry Fonda), says that the South will be defeated by machines triumphing over 'unskilled slave labour', the chief black character, Cato (Lou Payton), leans across our field of

A set piece dinner party in *Jezebel*: whiteness dependent on blackness, yet holding sway over it.

A black character intruding in the frame, while white people talk: selling flowers in New Orleans.

vision to pour Pres' wine, literally embodying the fact of slave labour. The film's insistence upon the presence of black people is important in its perception and construction of the white South. As Jim Pines puts it, 'black characters do not occupy a significant dramatic function in the film, but their social role nevertheless plays an explicit and relevant part in the conflict that arises between the principal white characters'[17].

Jezebel is distantly related, through the sympathies of its stars, director and production studio, to progressive ideas on race, making it, as Pines says, 'within the plantation movie tradition . . . undoubtedly the most liberal-inclined'[18]. These ideas have to do with the belief or suspicion that black people have in some sense more 'life' than whites. This idea, and its ambivalences, have a very long history which cannot detain us here. It springs from ideas of the closeness of non-European (and even non-metropolitan) peoples to nature, ideas which were endemic to those processes of European expansion variously termed exploration, nation-building and colonialism.[19] Expansion into other lands placed the humans encountered there as part of the fauna of those lands, to be construed either as the forces of nature that had to be subjugated or, for liberals, the model of sweet natural Man uncontaminated by civilisation. At the same time, ideas of nature have become central to Western thought about being human, such that concepts of human life itself have become inextricable from concepts of nature. Thus the idea that non-whites are more natural than whites also comes to suggest that they have more 'life', a logically meaningless but commonsensically powerful notion.

Jezebel relates to a specific liberal variation on this way of thinking, a tradition in which *Uncle Tom's Cabin* and the Harlem Renaissance are key reference points[20], as is the role of Annie in Sirk's *Imitation of Life.*[21] Ethel Mannin's statement may be taken as emblematic:

[17] Jim Pines, *Blacks in Films*, London, Studio Vista, 1975, p 54.

[18] ibid, p 55. See also Thomas Cripps, *Slow Fade to Black*, New York, Oxford University Press, 1977, pp 299, 304.

[19] See Cedric Robinson, *Black Marxism*, London, Zed Books, 1983.

[20] See George Frederickson, *The Black Image in the White Mind*, New York, Harper and Row, 1972; David Levering Lewis, *When Harlem Was in Vogue*, New York, Knopf, 1981.

[21] I have discussed this in 'Four Films of Lana Turner', *Movie*, no 25, pp 30-52.

[22] Ethel Mannin, *Confessions and Impressions*, New York, Doubleday, Doran, 1930, p 157.

[23] Molly Haskell, *From Reverence to Rape*, New York, Holt, Rinehart and Winston, p 214.

It is of course that feeling for life which is the secret of the Negro people, as surely as it is the lack of it, and slow atrophy of the capacity to live emotionally, which will be the ultimate decadence of the white civilised people.[22]

'Life' here tends to mean the body, the emotions, sensuality and spirituality; it is usually explicitly counterposed to the mind and the intellect, with the implication that white people's over-investment in the cerebral is cutting them off from life and leading them to crush the life out of others and out of nature itself. The implicit counterposition is, of course, 'death', a point to which I shall return in the discussion of *Night of the Living Dead*.

Jezebel is generally, and rightly, understood to be about the taming of a woman who refuses to live by the Old South's restrictive codes of femininity. It is a clear instance of Molly Haskell's characterisation of one of the available models for strong women's roles in classic Hollywood movies, the 'superfemale', who is 'too ambitious and intelligent for the docile role society has decreed she play' but remains 'exceedingly "feminine" and flirtatious' and 'within traditional society', turning her energies on those around her, 'with demonic results'.[23] Davis' character, Julie, is strong, defiant of convention (for example, striding into the bank, a place that women do not enter), refusing to behave in the genteel way her fiancé, Pres, requires of her. The trajectory of the narrative is her punishment and moral growth, in two stages. She learns to conceal her defiance and energy beneath an assumption of femininity, but this is still not enough, since it is still there in the malignant form indicated by Haskell; it is only by literally sacrificing herself (accompanying Pres, who has caught yellow jack fever, to Red Island, where fever victims are isolated) that the film is able to reach a satisfactory, transcendantly punishing climax. All of this is entirely understandable within a gender frame of reference; but the film also relates Julie's energies to blackness, suggesting that her trajectory is a specifically white, as well as female, one.

The most famous scene in the film is the Olympus Ball, at which all the unmarried women wear white. Julie, to embarrass Pres and to cock a snook at out-dated convention ('This is 1852, not the Dark Ages – girls don't have to simper about in white just 'cos they're not married'), decides to wear a red dress. The immediate scandal is not just the refusal to conform and uphold the celebration of virginity that the white dress code represents, but the sexual connotations of the dress itself, satin and red, connotations made explicit in a scene at the dress-maker's ('Saucy, isn't it?', says Julie; 'And vulgar', says her aunt, with which Julie enthusiastically concurs). This is the dress of Julie's that her black maid Zette (Theresa Harris) most covets, and after the ball, Julie gives it to her. It is precisely its *colourfulness* that, stereotyping informs us, draws Zette – the dress is 'marked' as coloured, a definite, bold colour heightened by a flashy fabric, just as black representation is. Thus what appears to be symbolism (white for virginity, colour for sex) within a universally applicable communication circuit becomes ethnically specific. The primary association of white with chastity is inextricably tied to not

Flouting convention: the red dress at the Olympus Ball.

being dark and colourful, not being non-white, and the defiance and vitality narratively associated with Julie's wearing of the dress is associated with the qualities embodied by black women, qualities that Julie as a white woman must not display, or even have. Of course, the red dress looks merely dark in this black and white film.

Wearing the dress causes a rift between Julie and Pres; shortly after, he leaves for the North on business. By the time he returns, Julie has learned to behave as a white woman should. Once again, the specific whiteness of this is revealed through the figure of Zette. There is, for instance, a scene in which Julie is getting ready for the arrival of Pres at a house party at her aunt's plantation. In her room she moves restlessly about, with Zette hanging on to her as she tries to undo Julie's dress at the back; Zette's movements are entirely determined by Julie's but Zette is attending to the basic clothing while Julie is just fussing about. When Julie thinks she hears a carriage coming, she sends Zette to check; Zette runs from the room, and the film cuts to the huge hallway, showing us all of Zette's rapid descent of the stairs and run to the door, before cutting again to show her calling out to the man and boy in livery waiting for carriages at the gate. This apparently unnecessarily elongated sequence not only helps whip up excitement and anticipation at Pres' arrival, but also gives Julie time to take off one dress and put on another, a potentially titillating sight that would not be shown in this kind of film in this period. But using a sequence centred on a black woman is not only a device to heighten suspense and by-pass a taboo image – it works as seamlessly well as it does because it is also appropriate to show a black woman here.

By this stage in the film, Julie has learned the behaviour appropriate to a white woman in her position. Earlier in the film she openly expressed her passion and defiance; now, awaiting Pres, she has learned to behave as she should. She no longer expresses feeling – she 'lives' through Zette. Zette has to express excited anticipation, not in speech, but in physical action, running the length of a long stair and spacious hallway. It is Zette's excited body in action that we see, instead of Julie's body disrobed and enrobed. When Julie hears the servants at the gate call out, 'Carriage is coming!', she sends Zette to the window to see if it is Pres. The excitement mounts as the carriage draws near. There is a rapid montage of black people: Zette shot from below at a dynamic angle looking for the carriage, the servants at the gate no longer still but the man moving about, the boy leaping in anticipation, and crowds of hitherto unseen black children running to the gate, jumping and cavorting. Meanwhile Julie remains perfectly still, only her eyes, in characteristic Davis fashion, darting and dilating with suspense; perfectly, luminously lit, she says nothing, expresses nothing with her body – it is black people who bodily express her desire.

This use of black people to express, to 'live', the physical dimension of Julie's life is found throughout the film, most notably after her manipulations have gone awry to the point that one of her old flames, Buck (George Brent), is now about to duel with Pres' brother. The black plantation workers have gathered at the house to entertain the white guests ('a quaint old custom down here', says Julie to Pres' new, and Northern, wife, Amy). As they arrive they sing a song about marrying, heard over shots of Julie, a bitterly ironic counterpoint. She shushes the chorus and tells them to start singing, 'Gonna Raise a Ruckus To-night', then goes to the edge of the verandah and sits down, beckoning the black children to gather close round her, before joining in with the singing. The song is a jolly one and the shots of the black singers show them in happy-go-lucky Sambo style, but the last shot of the sequence closes on Julie, near to tears against the sound of this cheerful singing. The power of the sequence does not come from this ironic counterpoint alone, but also from the way that Julie, by merging as nearly as possible with the singers and joining in the song, is able to express her pent-up feelings of frustration, anger, jealousy and fear, feelings for which there is no white mode of expression, which can only be lived through blacks.

The point of *Jezebel* is not that whites are different from blacks, but that whites live by different rules. Unlike the two women with whom she is compared, her aunt and Amy, Julie cannot be 'white'. It is her aunt and Amy who confirm that whites are calm, controlled, rational; Julie transgresses, but in the process reveals white calm as an imposition, a form of repression of life. The film's ambivalence lies in its being a vehicle for Davis. She/Julie is a 'Jezebel', a by-word for female wickedness, but nonetheless a star with a huge female following, and who is shot here with the kind of radiance and glow Hollywood reserved for its favoured women stars. There is no doubt that what Julie does is wicked and that her punishment is to be understood as richly deserved; but there is also no doubt that she is to be adored and precisely, as I've tried

Julie with the plantation workers gathered to entertain her guests

to argue, because she does not conform to notions of white womanhood.

'Night of the Living Dead'

If blacks have more 'life' than whites, then it must follow that whites have more 'death' than blacks. This thought has seldom been explored so devastatingly as in the living dead films directed by George Romero - *Night of the Living Dead* (1969), *Dawn of the Dead* (1978) and *Day of the Dead* (1985).

The *Dead* films are unusual among horror films for the explicitness of their political allegory and unique for having as their heroes 'positive' black men. In general, the latter have been applauded merely as an instance of affirmative action, casting colour blind a black man in a part which could equally well have gone to a white actor. As Robin Wood notes, however, 'it is not true that [their] colour is arbitrary and without meaning'; Ben's blackness in *Night* is used 'to signify his difference from the other characters, to set him apart from their norms'[24], while Peter's in *Dawn* again indicates 'his separation from the norms of white-dominated society and his partial exemption from its constraints'[25]. In all three films, it is significant that the hero is a black man, and not just because this makes him 'different', but because it makes it possible to see that whites are the living dead. I shall confine detailed discussion here to the first film of the trilogy.

All the dead in *Night* are whites. In a number of places, the film shows that living whites are like, or can be mistaken for, the dead. The radio states that the zombies are 'ordinary looking people', and the first one we see in the film does look in the distance like some ordinary old white

[24] Robin Wood, *Hollywood from Vietnam to Reagan*, New York, Columbia University Press, 1986, p 116.

[25] ibid, p 120.

Whiteness and death
equated in *Night of
the Living Dead*.

guy wandering about the cemetery, somehow menacing, yet not obviously abnormal. John, the brother in the opening sequence, recalls
pretending to be something scary to frighten Barb when they visited the
graveyard as children; he imitates the famous zombie voice of Boris Kar-
loff to scare her now. Halfway through the film, Barb becomes catatonic,
like a dead person. The other developed white characters emerge from
where they have been hiding, 'buried' in the cellar. Towards the end of
the film, there is an aerial shot from the point of view of a helicopter
involved in the destruction of the zombies; it looks down on a straggling
line of people moving forward uncertainly but inexorably, in exactly the
same formation as earlier shots of the zombies. It is only with a cut to a
ground level shot that we realise this is a line of vigilantes, not zombies.

Living and dead whites are indistinguishable, and the zombies' sole
raison d'être, to attack and eat the living, has resonances with the behaviour of the living whites. The vigilantes shoot and destroy the zombies
with equanimity ('Beat 'em or burn 'em – they go up pretty good', says
their leader, Chief McLelland), finally including the living – the hero,
Ben (Duane Jones) – in their single-minded operations. Brother John
torments Barb while living, and consumes her when he is dead. Helen
and Harry Cooper bicker and snipe constantly, until their dead daughter
Carrie first destroys, then eats them. The young couple, Tom and Judy,
destined generically to settle down at the end of the film, instead go up in
flames through Tom's stupidity and Judy's paralysed response to danger.

If whiteness and death are equated, both are further associated with the
USA. That the film can be taken as a metaphor for the United States is
established right at the start of the film. It opens on a car driving through
apparently unpopulated back roads suggesting the road tradition of 1950s
and '60s US culture – the novel *On the Road* (1957), the film *Easy Rider*

(1969) with its idea of the 'search for America'. When the car reaches the graveyard (the US?), a Stars and Stripes flag flutters in the foreground. The house in which the characters take shelter is archetypally middle, backwoods North American – a white wooden structure, with lace curtains, cut-glass ornaments, chintz armchairs. It, too, is immediately associated with death, in a series of shock cuts from Barb, exploring the house, to stuffed animal heads hung on the walls. Casting further heightens the all-Americanness of these zombie-like living whites. Barb is ultra-blonde and pale, and her name surely suggests the USA's best-selling doll; John is a preppy type, clean cut with straight fair hair, a white shirt with pens in the pocket, straight out of a Brooks Brothers advertisement. Judy too is dazzlingly blonde, though Tom and the Coopers are more nondescript whites.

What finally forces home the specifically white dimension of these zombie-US links are the ways in which the zombies can be destroyed. The first recalls the liberal critique of whites as ruled by their heads; as the radio announcer says, 'Kill the brain and you kill the ghoul' since, it seems, zombies/whites are nothing but their brains. The film diverges from earlier representations of the black/white, life/death opposition by representing Ben's 'life' quality in terms of practical skill, rather than innate qualities of 'being'. Particulary striking is a scene in which Ben talks about what they need to do as he dismantles a table to make boards for the windows, while Barb takes the lace cloth from it, folds and cradles it, hanging on uselessly to this token of gentility while Ben tries to ensure their survival.

The alternative way of destroying the zombies is burning. Some of the imagery, particulary the molotov cocktails going up around empty cars, seems to recall, in its grainy black-and-white texture, newspaper coverage of the ghetto uprisings of the late '60s, and the 'fire', as an image of Black Power's threat to white people, had wide currency (most notably in the title of James Baldwin's 1963 *The Fire Next Time*). The zombies are scared of light as well as fire, and Ben is associated with both, not only because of his skill in warding off the zombies with torches, but in the way he is introduced into the film. Barb wanders out of the house into the glare of a car's headlights, out of which Ben seems to emerge; a shot of the lights glaring into the camera is followed by another with Ben moving into the frame, his white shirt first, then his black face filling the frame in front of the light, in a reversal of the good/bad, white/black, light/darkness antinomies of Western culture.

The film ends with the white vigilantes (indistinguishable from the zombies, remember) killing Ben, the representative of life in the film. Much of the imagery of *Night* carries over into *Dawn*, despite their many differences (most notably the latter's strong vein of humour). The opening sequence has white militia gleefully destroying living blacks and Hispanics who refuse to leave their tenement homes during the zombie emergency; as in *Night*, the black hero, Peter (Ken Foree), emerges from the light (this time from behind a white sheet with strong, bright light flooded unnaturalistically behind it); it is his practical skills that enable him to survive, skills that only the white woman, Fran (Gaylen Ross), is ultimately able to emulate. Zombieness is still linked with whiteness, even though some of the dead are black or Hispanic – a black zombie who attacks a living black man in the tenement is whited up, the colour contrast between the two emphasised in a shot of the whitened black zombie biting the living black man's neck; in the shopping mall, an overt symbol of the US way of life, editing rhymes the zombies with the shop mannequins, all of whom are white.

Day extends the critique of US values to the military-industrial complex, with its underpinnings in masculine supremacy[26]. As Robin Wood argues, the white men and the zombies alike are characterised by 'the conditioned reflex', the application to human affairs of relentless rationality; the scientist, Logan, teaches one of the zombies to be human again, which in practice means killing the military leader, Rhodes, out of atavistic loyalty to Logan. When Logan earlier tells Rhodes that what he is teaching the zombies is 'civility', to make them like the living, there is a sudden cut to a sequence of the men gleefully, sadistically corralling the zombies to be specimens for Logan's crazed experiments. The whiteness of all this is pointed, as before, by the presence of a black character, John (Terry Alexander), who is even more dissociated from both zombies and white male values than were Ben and Peter in the earlier films. He is not only black but West Indian, and he offers the idea of finding an island as the only hope for the two white characters (a WASP woman, Sarah, and an Irish man, Billy) not irrevocably implicated in white male values. He and Billy are not only socially marginal, but also live separately from the soldiers and scientists, having set up a mock home together in the outer reaches of the underground bunker they all share. All the other living characters are redneck males, and although there is a power struggle between them, they are both more like each other and like the zombies than they are like John, Sarah or Billy. At the end of one scene, where Rhodes has established his authority over Logan, there is a final shot of John, who has looked on saying nothing; he rubs the corner of his mouth with his finger ironically, then smiles sweetly at Rhodes, an expression of ineffably insolent refusal of the white boys' games.

The *Dead* films are of course horror movies and there is a danger, as Pete Boss has pointed out, that the kind of political readings that I and others have given them may not be easy 'to integrate . . . with the fantasies of physical degradation and vulnerability' characteristic of the contemporary horror film[27]. However, the use of 'body horror' in the *Dead* films to represent whiteness is not simply symbolism, making use of what happens to the genre's current conventions. On the contrary, body horror is the horror of whiteness and the films' gory pleasures are like an inverted reprise of the images of whiteness that are touched on in *Simba* and *Jezebel*.

The point about Ben, Peter and John is that in their different ways they all have control over their bodies, are able to use them to survive, know how to do things with them. The white characters (with the excep-

[26] Robin Wood, 'The Woman's Nightmare: Masculinity in "The Day of the Dead" ', *CineAction!*, no 6, August 1986, pp 45-49.

[27] Pete Boss, 'Vile Bodies and Bad Medicine', *Screen* January-February 1986, vol 27 no 1, p 18.

tion of Fran, Sarah and Billy) lose that control while alive, and come back in the monstrously uncontrolled form of zombieness. The hysterical boundedness of the white body is grotesquely[28] transgressed as whites/zombies gouge out living white arms, pull out organs, munch at orifices. The spectre of white loss of control is evoked by the way the zombies stumble and dribble in their inexorable quest for blood, often with intestines spilling out or severed limbs dangling. White over-investment in the brain is mercilessly undermined as brains spatter against the wall and zombies flop to the ground. 'The fear of one's own body, of how one controls it and relates to it'[29] and the fear of not being able to control other bodies, those bodies whose exploitation is so fundamental to capitalist economy, are both at the heart of whiteness. Never has this horror been more deliriously evoked than in these films of the *Dead*.

***

Because my aim has been to open up an area of investigation, I shall not even attempt a rounded conclusion. Instead, let me start off again on another tack, suggested by the passing references to light and colour above. I suspect that there is some very interesting work to be done on the invention of photography and the development of lighting codes in relation to the white face, which results in the technicist ideology that one sometimes hears of it being 'more difficult' to photograph black people. Be that as it may, it is the case that the codes of glamour lighting in Hollywood were developed in relation to white women, to endow them with a glow and radiance that has correspondences with the transcendental rhetoric of popular Christianity.

Of no woman star was this more true than Marilyn Monroe, known by the press at the time as 'the Body'. I've argued elsewhere that her image is an inescapably and necessarily white one[30]; in many of her films this combines with the conventions of glamour lighting to make her disappear as flesh and blood even more thoroughly than is the case with other women stars. Her first appearance in *The Seven Year Itch* (1955), for instance, is a classic instance of woman as spectacle caught in a shot from the male protagonist's point of view. It opens on Richard (Tom Ewell), on his hands and knees on the floor looking for something, bottom sticking up, a milk bottle between his legs – the male body shown, as is routine in sex comedies, as ludicrously grotesque; he hears the door-bell and opens the door to his flat; as the door opens light floods in on him; he looks and there is a cut to the hall doorway, where the curvy shape of a woman is visible through the frosted glass. The woman's shape is placed exactly within the frame of the door window, the doorway is at the end of the hall, exactly in the centre of the frame; a set of enclosing rectangles create a strong sense of perspective, and emphasise the direction of Richard's/our gaze. The colouring of the screen is pinky-white and light emanates from behind the doorway where the

[28] cf the discussion of the grotesque carnivalesque body in Mikhail Bakhtin, *Rabelais and His World*, Bloomington, Indiana University Press, 1984.

[29] Philip Brophy, 'Horrality – the Textuality of Contemporary Horror Films', *Screen* January-February 1986, vol 27 no 1, p 8.

[30] Richard Dyer, *Heavenly Bodies*, London, Macmillan, 1986, pp 42-45.

woman is. All we see of her is her silhouette, defining her proportions, but she also looks translucent. The film cuts back to Richard, his jaw open in awe, bathed in stellar light. Later in the film, when the Monroe character's tomato plant crashes onto Richard's patio, we have another shot of her from Richard's point of view. He looks up, and there is a cut to Monroe looking down from her balcony, apparently nude; the wall behind her is dark, as is the vegetation on the balcony, so her face and shoulders stand out as white. Such moments conflate unreal angel-glow with sexual aura.

The Seven Year Itch is a very smart film. Through innumerable gags and cross-references, it lets on that it knows about male fantasy and its remote relation to reality. Yet it is also part of the Monroe industry, peddling an impossible dream, offering another specifically white ideal as if it embodies all heterosexual male yearning, offering another white image that dissolves in the light of its denial of its own specificity.

White women are constructed as the apotheosis of desirability, all that a man could want, yet nothing that can be had, nor anything that a woman can be. But, as I have argued, white representation *in general* has this everything-and-nothing quality.

Representations of Whiteness in the Black Imagination

Although there has never been any official body of black people in the United States who have gathered as anthropologists and/or ethnographers to study whiteness, black folks have, from slavery on, shared in conversations with one another "special" knowledge of whiteness gleaned from close scrutiny of white people. Deemed special because it was not a way of knowing that has been recorded fully in written material, its purpose was to help black folks cope and survive in a white supremacist society. For years, black domestic servants, working in white homes, acting as informants, brought knowledge back to segregated communities—details, facts, observations, and psycho-analytic readings of the white Other.

Sharing the fascination with difference that white people have collectively expressed openly (and at times vulgarly) as they have traveled around the world in pursuit of the Other and Otherness, black people, especially those living during the historical period of racial apartheid and legal segregation, have similarly maintained steadfast and ongoing curiosity about the "ghosts," "the barbarians," these strange apparitions they were forced to serve. In the chapter on "Wild-ness" in *Shamanism, Colonialism, and The Wild Man,* Michael Taussig urges a stretching of our imagination and understanding of the Other to include inscriptions "on the edge of official history." Naming his critical project, identifying the passion he brings to the quest to know more deeply *you who are not ourselves,* Taussig explains:

> I am trying to reproduce a mode of perception—a way of seeing through a way of talking—figuring the world through dialogue that comes alive with sudden transformative force in the crannies of everyday life's pauses and juxtapositions, as in the kitchens of the Putumayo or in the streets around the church in the Niña Maria. It is always a way of representing the world in the roundabout "speech" of the collage of things...It is a mode of perception that catches on the debris of history...

I, too, am in search of the debris of history. I am wiping the dust off past conversations to remember some of what was shared in the old days when black folks had little intimate contact with whites, when we were much more open about the way we connected whiteness with the mysterious, the strange, and the terrible. Of course, everything has changed. Now many black people live in the "bush of ghosts" and do not know themselves separate from whiteness. They do not know this thing we call "difference." Systems of domination, imperialism, colonialism, and racism actively coerce black folks to internalize negative perceptions of blackness, to be self-hating. Many of us succumb to this. Yet, blacks who imitate whites (adopting their values, speech, habits of being, etc.) continue to regard whiteness with suspicion, fear, and even hatred. This contradictory longing to possess the reality of the Other, even though that reality is one that wounds and negates, is expressive of the desire to understand the mystery, to know intimately through imitation, as though such knowing worn like an amulet, a mask, will ward away the evil, the terror.

Searching the critical work of post-colonial critics, I found much writing that bespeaks the continued fascination with the way white minds, particularly the colonial imperialist traveler, perceive blackness, and very little expressed interest in representations of whiteness in the black imagination. Black cultural and social critics allude to such representations in their writing, yet only a few have dared to make explicit those perceptions of whiteness that they think will discomfort or antagonize readers. James Baldwin's collection of essays, *Notes of A Native Son,* explores these issues with a clarity and frankness that is no longer fashionable in a world where evocations of pluralism and diversity act to obscure differences arbitrarily imposed and maintained by white racist domination. Addressing the way in which whiteness exists without knowledge of blackness even as it collectively asserts control, Baldwin links issues of recognition to the practice of imperialist racial domination. Writing about being the first black person to visit a

Swiss village with only white inhabitants in his essay "Stranger in the Village," Baldwin notes his response to the village's yearly ritual of painting individuals black who were then positioned as slaves and bought so that the villagers could celebrate their concern with converting the souls of the "natives":

> I thought of white men arriving for the first time in an African village, strangers there, as I am a stranger here, and tried to imagine the astounded populace touching their hair and mar-veling at the color of their skin. But there is a great difference between being the first white man to be seen by Africans and being the first black man to be seen by whites. The white man takes the astonishment as tribute, for he arrives to conquer and to convert the natives, whose inferiority in relation to himself is not even to be questioned, whereas I, without a thought of conquest, find myself among a people whose culture controls me, has even, in a sense, created me, people who have cost me more in anguish and rage than they will ever know, who yet do not even know of my existence. The astonishment with which I might have greeted them, should they have stumbled into my African village a few hundred years ago, might have rejoiced their hearts. But the astonishment with which they greet me today can only poison mine.

My thinking about representations of whiteness in the black imagination has been stimulated by classroom discussions about the way in which the absence of recognition is a strategy that facilitates making a group the Other. In these classrooms there have been heated debates among students when white students respond with disbelief, shock, and rage, as they listen to black students talk about whiteness, when they are compelled to hear observations, stereotypes, etc., that are offered as "data" gleaned from close scrutiny and study. Usually, white students respond with naive amazement that black people criti-cally assess white people from a standpoint where "whiteness" is the privileged signifier. Their amazement that black people watch white people with a critical "ethnographic" gaze, is itself an expression of racism. Often their rage erupts because they believe that all ways of looking that highlight difference subvert the liberal belief in a universal subjectivity (we are all just people) that they think will make racism disappear. They have a deep emotional investment in the myth of "sameness," even as their actions reflect the primacy of whiteness as a sign informing who they are and how they think. Many of them are shocked that black people think critically about whiteness because

29

racist thinking perpetuates the fantasy that the Other who is subjugated, who is subhuman, lacks the ability to comprehend, to understand, to see the working of the powerful. Even though the majority of these students politically consider themselves liberals and anti-racist, they too unwittingly invest in the sense of whiteness as mystery.

In white supremacist society, white people can "safely" imagine that they are invisible to black people since the power they have historically asserted, and even now collectively assert over black people, accorded them the right to control the black gaze. As fantastic as it may seem, racist white people find it easy to imagine that black people cannot see them if within their desire they do not want to be seen by the dark Other. One mark of oppression was that black folks were compelled to assume the mantle of invisibility, to erase all traces of their subjectivity during slavery and the long years of racial apartheid, so that they could be better, less threatening servants. An effective strategy of white supremacist terror and dehumanization during slavery centered around white control of the black gaze. Black slaves, and later manumitted servants, could be brutally punished for looking, for appearing to observe the whites they were serving, as only a subject can observe, or see. To be fully an object then was to lack the capacity to see or recognize reality. These looking relations were reinforced as whites cultivated the practice of denying the subjectivity of blacks (the better to dehumanize and oppress), of relegating them to the realm of the invisible. Growing up in a Kentucky household where black servants lived in the same dwelling with the white family who employed them, newspaper heiress Sallie Bingham recalls, in her autobiography *Passion and Prejudice,* "Blacks, I realized, were simply invisible to most white people, except as a pair of hands offering a drink on a silver tray." Reduced to the machinery of bodily physical labor, black people learned to appear before whites as though they were zombies, cultivating the habit of casting the gaze downward so as not to appear uppity. To look directly was an assertion of subjectivity, equality. Safety resided in the pretense of invisibility.

Even though legal racial apartheid no longer is a norm in the United States, the habits that uphold and maintain institutionalized white supremacy linger. Since most white people do not have to "see" black people (constantly appearing on billboards, television, movies, in magazines, etc.) and they do not need to be ever on guard nor to observe black people to be safe, they can live as though black people are invisible, and they can imagine that they are also invisible to blacks. Some white people may even imagine there is no representation of whiteness in the black imagination, especially one that is based on concrete observation or mythic conjecture. They think they are seen by black folks only as they want to appear. Ideologically, the rhetoric of white supremacy supplies a fantasy of whiteness. Described in Richard Dyer's essay "White," this fantasy makes whiteness synonymous with goodness:

> Power in contemporary society habitually passes itself off as embodied in the normal as opposed to the superior. This is common to all forms of power, but it works in a peculiarly seductive way with whiteness, because of the way it seems rooted, in common-sense thought, in things other than ethnic difference...Thus it is said (even in liberal textbooks) that there are inevitable associations of white with light and therefore safety, and black with dark and therefore danger, and that this explains racism (whereas one might well argue about the safety of the cover of darkness, and the danger of exposure to the light); again, and with more justice, people point to the Jewish and Christian use of white and black to symbolize good and evil, as carried still in such expressions as "a black mark," "white magic," "to blacken the character" and so on. Socialized to believe the fantasy, that whiteness represents goodness and all that is benign and non-threatening, many white people assume this is the way black people conceptualize whiteness. They do not imagine that the way whiteness makes its presence felt in black life, most often as terrorizing imposition, a power that wounds, hurts, tortures, is a reality that disrupts the fantasy of whiteness as representing goodness.

Collectively black people remain rather silent about representations of whiteness in the black imagination. As in the old days of racial segregation where black folks learned to "wear the mask," many of us pretend to be comfortable in the face of whiteness only to turn our backs and give expression to intense levels of discomfort. Especially talked about is the representation of whiteness as terrorizing. Without evoking a simplistic essentialist "us and them" dichotomy that suggests black folks merely invert stereotypical racist interpretations so that black becomes synonymous with goodness and white with evil, I want to focus on that representation of whiteness that is not formed in reaction to stereotypes but emerges as a response to the traumatic pain and anguish that remains a consequence of white racist domination, a psychic state that informs and shapes the way black folks "see" whiteness. Stereotypes black folks maintain about white folks are not the only representations of whiteness in the black imagination. They emerge primarily as responses to white stereotypes of blackness. Lorraine Hansberry argues that black stereotypes of whites emerge as a trickle-down process of white stereotypes of blackness, where there is the projection onto an Other all that we deny about ourselves. In *Young, Gifted, and Black,* she identifies particular stereotypes about white people that are commonly cited in black communities and urges us not to "celebrate this madness in any direction":

> Is it not "known" in the ghetto that white people, as an entity, are "dirty" (especially white women—who never seem to do their own cleaning); inherently "cruel" (the cold, fierce roots of Europe; who else could put all those people into ovens *scientifically);* "smart" (you really have to hand it to the m.f.'s), and anything *but* cold and passionless (because look who has had to live with little else than their passions in the guise of love and hatred all these centuries)? And so on.

Stereotypes, however inaccurate, are one form of representation. Like fictions, they are created to serve as substitutions, standing in for what is real. They are there not to tell it like it is but to invite and encourage pretense. They are a fantasy, a projection onto the Other that makes them less threatening. Stereotypes abound when there is distance. They are an invention, a pretense that one knows when the steps that would make real knowing possible cannot be taken or are not allowed.

Looking past stereotypes to consider various representations of whiteness in the black imagination, I appeal to memory, to my earliest recollections of ways these issues were raised in black life. Returning to memories of growing up in the social circumstances created by racial apartheid, to all black spaces on the edges of town, I reinhabit a location where black folks associated whiteness with the terrible, the terrifying, the terrorizing. White people were regarded as terrorists, especially those who dared to enter that segregated space of blackness. As a child, I did not know any white people. They were strangers, rarely seen in our neighborhoods. The "official" white men who came across the tracks were there to sell products, Bibles and insurance. They terrorized by economic exploitation. What did I see in the gazes of those white men who crossed our thresholds that made me afraid, that made black children unable to speak? Did they understand at all how strange their whiteness appeared in our living rooms, how threatening? Did they journey across the tracks with the same "adventurous" spirit that other white men carried to Africa, Asia, to those mysterious places they would one day call the "third world?" Did they come to our houses to meet the Other face-to-face and enact the colonizer role, dominating us on our own turf?

Their presence terrified me. Whatever their mission, they looked too much like the unofficial white men who came to enact rituals of terror and torture. As a child, I did not know how to tell them apart, how to ask the "real white people to please stand up." The terror that I felt is one black people have shared. Whites learn about it second-hand. Confessing in *Soul Sister* that she too began to feel this terror after changing her skin to appear "black" and going to live in the south, Grace Halsell described her altered sense of whiteness:

> Caught in this climate of hate, I am totally terror-stricken, and I search my mind to know why I am fearful of my own people. Yet they no longer seem my people, but rather the "enemy" arrayed in large numbers against me in some hostile territory...My wild heartbeat is a secondhand kind of terror. I know that I cannot possibly experience what *they*, the black people, experience...

Black folks raised in the North do not escape this sense of terror. In her autobiography, *Every Good-bye Ain't Gone,* Itabari Njeri begins the narrative of her northern childhood with a memory of southern roots. Traveling south as an adult to investigate the murder of her grandfather by white youth who were drag racing and ran him down in the streets, Njeri recalls that for many years "the distant and accidental violence that took my grandfather's life could not compete with the psychological terror that had begun to engulf my own." Ultimately, she begins to link that terror with the history of black people in the United States, seeing it as an imprint carried from the past to the present:

> As I grew older, my grandfather assumed mythic proportions in my imagination. Even in absence, he filled my room like music and watched over me when I was fearful. His fantasized presence diverted thoughts of my father's drunken rages. With age, my fantasizing ceased, the image of my grandfather faded. What lingered was the memory of his caress, the pain of something missing in my life, wrenched away by reckless white youths. I had a growing sense—the beginning of an inevitable comprehen-sion—that this society deals blacks a disproportionate share of pain and denial.

Njeri's journey takes her through the pain and terror of the past, only the memories do not fade. They linger as does the pain and bitterness:

"Against a backdrop of personal loss, against the evidence of history that fills me with a knowledge of the hateful behavior of whites toward blacks, I see the people of Bainbridge. And I cannot trust them. I cannot absolve them." If it is possible to conquer terror through ritual reenactment, that is what Njeri does. She goes back to the scene of the crime, dares to face the enemy. It is this confrontation that forces the terror of history to loosen its grip.

To name that whiteness in the black imagination is often a representation of terror. One must face written histories that erase and deny, that reinvent the past to make the present vision of racial harmony and pluralism more plausible. To bear the burden of memory one must willingly journey to places long uninhabited, searching the debris of history for traces of the unforgettable, all knowledge of which has been suppressed. Njeri laments that "nobody really knows us." She writes, "So institutionalized is the ignorance of our history, our culture, our everyday existence that, often, we do not even know ourselves." Theorizing black experience, we seek to uncover, restore, as well as to deconstruct, so that new paths, different journeys, are possible. Indeed, Edward Said, in "Traveling Theory," argues that theory can "threaten reification, as well as the entire bourgeois system on which reification depends, with destruction." The call to theorize black experience is constantly challenged and subverted by conservative voices reluctant to move from fixed locations. Said reminds us:

> Theory...is won as the result of a process that begins when consciousness first experiences its own terrible ossification in the general reification of all things under capitalism; then when consciousness generalizes (or classes) itself as something opposed to other objects, and feels itself as contradiction to (or crisis within) objectification, there emerges a consciousness of change in the *status quo;* finally, moving toward freedom and fulfillment, consciousness looks ahead to complete self-realization, which is of course the revolutionary process stretching forward in time, perceivable now only as theory or projection.

Traveling, moving into the past, Njeri pieces together fragments. Who does she see staring into the face of a southern white man who was said to be the murderer? Does the terror in his face mirror the look of the unsuspecting black man whose death history does not name or record? Baldwin wrote that "people are trapped in history and history is trapped in them." There is then only the fantasy of escape, or the promise that what is lost will be found, rediscovered, and returned. For black folks, reconstructing an archaeology of memory makes return possible, the journey to a place we can never call home even as we reinhabit it to make sense of present locations. Such journeying cannot be fully encompassed by conventional notions of travel.

Spinning off from Said's essay, James Clifford, in "Notes on Travel and Theory," celebrates the idea of journeying, asserting:

> This sense of worldly, "mapped" movement is also why it may be worth holding on to the term "travel," despite its connotations of middle class "literary" or recreational journeying, spatial practices long associated with male experiences and virtues. "Travel" suggests, at least, profane activity, following public routes and beaten tracks. How do different populations, classes and genders travel? What kinds of knowledges, stories, and theories do they produce? A crucial research agenda opens up.

Reading this piece and listening to Clifford talk about theory and travel, I appreciated his efforts to expand the travel/theoretical frontier so that it might be more inclusive, even as I considered that to answer the questions he poses is to propose a deconstruction of the conventional sense of travel, and put alongside it, or in its place, a theory of the journey that would expose the extent to which holding on to the concept of "travel" as we know it is also a way to hold on to imperialism.

For some individuals, clinging to the conventional sense of travel allows them to remain fascinated with imperialism, to write about it, seductively evoking what Renato Rosaldo aptly calls, in *Culture and Truth*, "imperialist nostalgia." Significantly, he reminds readers that "even politically progressive North American audiences have enjoyed the elegance of manners governing relations of dominance and subordination between the 'races.' " Theories of travel produced outside conventional borders might want the Journey to become the rubric within which travel, as a starting point for discourse, is associated with different headings—rites of passage, immigration, enforced migration, relocation, enslavement, and homelessness. Travel is not a word that can be easily evoked to talk about the Middle Passage, the Trail of Tears, the landing of Chinese immigrants, the forced relocation of Japanese-Americans, or the plight of the homeless. Theorizing diverse journeying is crucial to our understanding of any politics of location. As Clifford asserts at the end of his essay:

> Theory is always written from some "where," and that "where" is less a place than itineraries: different, concrete histories of dwelling, immigration, exile, migration. These include the migration of

third world intellectuals into the metropolitan universities, to pass
through or to remain, changed by their travel but marked by places
of origin, by peculiar allegiances and alienations.

Listening to Clifford "playfully" evoke a sense of travel, I felt such
an evocation would always make it difficult for there to be recognition
of an experience of travel that is not about play but is an encounter with
terrorism. And it is crucial that we recognize that the hegemony of one
experience of travel can make it impossible to articulate another
experience or for it to be heard. From certain standpoints, to travel is
to encounter the terrorizing force of white supremacy. To tell my
"travel" stories, I must name the movement from racially segregated
southern community, from rural black Baptist origin, to prestigious
white university settings. I must be able to speak about what it is like
to be leaving Italy after I have given a talk on racism and feminism,
hosted by the parliament, only to stand for hours while I am interrogated by white officials who do not have to respond when I enquire as
to why the questions they ask me are different from those asked the
white people in line before me. Thinking only that I must endure this
public questioning, the stares of those around me, because my skin is
black, I am startled when I am asked if I speak Arabic, when I am told
that women like me receive presents from men without knowing what
those presents are. Reminded of another time when I was stripped
searched by French officials, who were stopping black people to make
sure we were not illegal immigrants and/or terrorists, I think that one
fantasy of whiteness is that the threatening Other is always a terrorist.
This projection enables many white people to imagine there is no
representation of whiteness as terror, as terrorizing. Yet it is this representation of whiteness in the black imagination, first learned in the
narrow confines of poor black rural community that is sustained by my
travels to many different locations.

To travel, I must always move through fear, confront terror. It
helps to be able to link this individual experience to the collective
journeying of black people, to the Middle Passage, to the mass migration of southern black folks to northern cities in the early part of the
20th century. Michel Foucault posits memory as a site of resistance. As
Jonathan Arac puts it in his introduction to *Postmodernism and Politics,*
the process of remembering can be a practice which "transforms history
from a judgement on the past in the name of a present truth to a
'counter-memory' that combats our current modes of truth and justice,
helping us to understand and change the present by placing it in a new
relation to the past." It is useful, when theorizing black experience, to

examine the way the concept of "terror" is linked to representations of whiteness.

In the absence of the reality of whiteness, I learned as a child that to be "safe," it was important to recognize the power of whiteness, even to fear it, and to avoid encounter. There was nothing terrifying about the sharing of this knowledge as survival strategy, the terror was made real only when I journeyed from the black side of town to a predominantly white area near my grandmother's house. I had to pass through this area to reach her place. Describing these journeys "across town" in the essay "Homeplace: A Site of Resistance," I remembered:

> It was a movement away from the segregated blackness of our community into a poor white neighborhood. I remember the fear, being scared to walk to Baba's, our grandmother's house, because we would have to pass that terrifying whiteness—those white faces on the porches staring us down with hate. Even when empty or vacant those porches seemed to say *danger,* you do not belong here, you are not safe.

Oh! that feeling of safety, of arrival, of homecoming when we finally reached the edges of her yard, when we could see the soot black face of our grandfather, Daddy Gus, sitting in his chair on the porch, smell his cigar, and rest on his lap. Such a contrast, that feeling of arrival, of homecoming—this sweetness and the bitterness of that journey, that constant reminder of white power and control. Even though it was a long time ago that I made this journey, associations of whiteness with terror and the terrorizing remain. Even though I live and move in spaces where I am surrounded by whiteness, there is no comfort that makes the terrorism disappear. All black people in the United States, irrespective of their class status or politics, live with the possibility that they will be terrorized by whiteness.

This terror is most vividly described by black authors in fiction writing, particularly the recent novel by Toni Morrison, *Beloved*. Baby Suggs, the black prophet, who is most vocal about representations of whiteness, dies because she suffers an absence of color. Surrounded by a lack, an empty space, taken over by whiteness, she remembers: "Those white things have taken all I had or dreamed and broke my heartstrings too. There is no bad luck in the world but white folks." If the mask of whiteness, the pretense, represents it as always benign, benevolent, then what this representation obscures is the representation of danger, the sense of threat. During the period of racial apartheid, still known by many folks as Jim Crow, it was more difficult for black people to internalize this pretense, hard for us not to know that the shapes under white sheets had a mission to threaten, to terrorize. That representation of whiteness, and its association with innocence, which engulfed and murdered Emmett Till was a sign; it was meant to torture with the reminder of possible future terror. In Morrison's *Beloved,* the memory of terror is so deeply inscribed on the body of Sethe and in her consciousness, and the association of terror with whiteness is so intense that she kills her young so that they will never know the terror. Explaining her actions to Paul D., she tells him that it is her job "to keep them away from what I know is terrible." Of course Sethe's attempt to end the historical anguish of black people only reproduces it in a different form. She conquers the terror through perverse reenactment, through resistance, using violence as a means of fleeing from a history that is a burden too great to bear.

It is the telling of our history that enables political self-recovery. In contemporary society, white and black people alike believe that racism no longer exists. This erasure, however mythic, diffuses the representation of whiteness as terror in the black imagination. It allows for assimilation and forgetfulness. The eagerness with which contemporary society does away with racism, replacing this recognition with evocations of pluralism and diversity that further mask reality, is a response to the terror. It has also become a way to perpetuate the terror by providing a cover, a hiding place. Black people still feel the terror, still associate it with whiteness, but are rarely able to articulate the varied ways we are terrorized because it is easy to silence by accusations of reverse racism or by suggesting that black folks who talk about the ways we are terrorized by whites are merely evoking victimization to demand special treatment.

I was reminded of the way in which the discourse of race is increasingly divorced from any recognition of the politics of racism when I attended a recent conference on Cultural Studies. Attending the conference because I was confident that I would be in the company of like-minded, "aware," progressive intellectuals, I was disturbed when the usual arrangements of white supremacist hierarchy were mirrored both in terms of who was speaking, of how bodies were arranged on the stage, of who was in the audience. All of this revealed the underlying assumptions of what voices were deemed worthy to speak and be heard. As the conference progressed, I began to feel afraid. If these progressive people, most of whom were white, could so blindly reproduce a version of the *status quo* and not "see" it, the thought of how racial politics would be played out "outside" this arena was horrifying.

38

That feeling of terror that I had known so intimately in my childhood surfaced. Without even considering whether the audience was able to shift from the prevailing standpoint and hear another perspective, I talked openly about that sense of terror. Later, I heard stories of white women joking about how ludicrous it was for me (in their eyes I suppose I represent the "bad" tough black woman) to say I felt terrorized. Their inability to conceive that my terror, like that of Sethe's, is a response to the legacy of white domination and the contemporary expressions of white supremacy is an indication of how little this culture really understands the profound psychological impact of white racist domination.

At this same conference, I bonded with a progressive black woman and her companion, a white man. Like me, they were troubled by the extent to which folks chose to ignore the way white supremacy was informing the structure of the conference. Talking with the black woman, I asked her: "What do you do, when you are tired of confronting white racism, tired of the day-to-day incidental acts of racial terrorism? I mean, how do you deal with coming home to a white person?" Laughing she said, "Oh, you mean when I am suffering from White People Fatigue Syndrome? He gets that more than I do." After we finish our laughter, we talk about the way white people who shift locations, as her companion has done, begin to see the world differently. Understanding how racism works, he can see the way in which whiteness acts to terrorize without seeing himself as bad, or all white people as bad, and all black people as good. Repudiating us-and-them dichotomies does not mean that we should never speak of the ways observing the world from the standpoint of "whiteness" may indeed distort perception, impede understanding of the way racism works both in the larger world as well as in the world of our intimate interactions.

In *The Post-Colonial Critic*, Gayatri Spivak calls for a shift in locations, clarifying the radical possibilities that surface when positionality is problematized. She explains that "what we are asking for is that the hegemonic discourses, and the holders of hegemonic discourse, should dehegemonize their position and themselves learn how to occupy the subject position of the other." Generally, this process of repositioning has the power to deconstruct practices of racism and make possible the disassociation of whiteness with terror in the black imagination. As critical intervention it allows for the recognition that progressive white people who are anti-racist might be able to understand the way in which their cultural practice reinscribes white supremacy without promoting paralyzing guilt or denial. Without the capacity to

39

inspire terror, whiteness no longer signifies the right to dominate. It truly becomes a benevolent absence. Baldwin ends his essay "Stranger in the Village" with the declaration: "This world is white no longer, and it will never be white again." Critically examining the association of whiteness as terror in the black imagination, deconstructing it, we both name racism's impact and help to break its hold. We decolonize our minds and our imaginations.

OPTIC WHITE: BLACKNESS AND THE PRODUCTION OF WHITENESS

HARRYETTE MULLEN

> *"You know the best selling paint we got, the one that made this here business?"*
> *he asked as I helped him fill a vat with a smelly substance.*
> *"No, I don't."*
> *"Our white, Optic White."*
> *"Why white rather than the others?"*
> *"'Cause we started stressing it from the first. We make the best white paint*
> *in the world, I don't give a damn what nobody says. Our white is so white you*
> *can paint a chunka coal and you'd have to crack it open with a sledge hammer*
> *to prove it wasn't white clear through! . . . Well, you might not believe it, but I*
> *helped the Old Man make up that slogan. 'If It's Optic White, It's the Right*
> *White,'" he quoted with upraised finger, like a preacher quoting holy writ. "I*
> *got me a three-hundred-dollar bonus for helping to think that up."*
> *"'If It's Optic White, It's the Right White,'" I repeated and suddenly had to*
> *repress a laugh as a childhood jingle rang through my mind:*
> *"If you're white, you're right,'" I said.* [Ellison 190]

Two media reports occurring within about a week of each other caught my attention as one seemed to comment on the other: one, a *Time* magazine cover story documenting with a certain unease what it called "The Browning of America"; and the other, a National Public Radio news broadcast in which George Bush, a man whose family includes Mexican-American grandchildren, reassured Soviet leader Gorbachev that the US and the USSR share common interests because "we are Europeans," thus officially marginalizing the growing number of Americans whose heritage is other than European, as well as significant numbers of increasingly militant non-European Soviets. Bush's rhetoric is an apt demonstration of a floating signifier used in an attempt to heal a history of political antagonism through a not-quite-subliminal appeal to racial bonding. That the international appeal to a common racial heritage ignores racial diversity within political borders of the respective nations is not surprising, given the traditional orientation of the US in identifying itself as a white nation allied with other white nations in controlling and policing the globe, as minority populations are routinely controlled and policed within national borders.

The President's insistence that Americans are Europeans, together with the report on America's "browning," suggests to me an interesting connection with the genre of passing literature of which Twain's *Pudd'nhead Wilson* is perhaps the most cynical example. While Bush's statement comments on the contemporary political function of racial identity on a global scale, Twain's problematic and frustrating novel, with all of its shortcomings, is a stinging indictment of a legal tradition that glorifies the freedom of the individual while founding and supporting a race-class-gender system that inexorably

41

reduces individuals to their functions within an economic mode of production. In both cases considerable cultural and political weight is given to the possession of white credentials as a prerequisite for a controlling interest in political and economic transactions. In a nation that has always been at least triracial and that, as *Time* so ruefully reports, is now dazzlingly multicultural and getting browner all the time, Bush presents a vision of a multicolored nation passing as a politically white superpower as it is threatened with diminished influence in a time of global power shifts.

The usual mechanism of passing, which I take as a model for the cultural production of whiteness, requires an active denial of black identity only by the individual who passes from black to white, while the chosen white identity is strengthened in each successive generation by the presumption that white identities are racially pure. Passing on an individual level models the cultural production of whiteness as a means of nation building and as a key to national identity. Just as the white-skinned African-American becomes white through a process of silencing and suppression, by denying, "forgetting," ignoring, or erasing evidence of African ancestry, so does the "pure white" family constitute itself by denying kinship with its nonwhite members, as the racially diverse nation claims a white European identity by marginalizing its non-European heritages.

While some Americans who identify themselves as white will admit to, or even boast of, a Native American ancestor, I have yet to meet a white person who acknowledged African ancestry, unless he or she had made a personal decision to identify racially as black. A few white Southerners will speak openly of sharing a white ancestor with an African-American contemporary (which often goes hand in hand with descent from slaveholders imagined as belonging uniformly to a Southern aristocracy), but the possibility that white Americans may be descended from African-Americans who became white is rarely discussed, except among African-Americans with knowledge of friends or family members who have "passed." Such African-Americans who have used their indistinguishability from white Americans not only become white through the act of severing their relations with black kin and community, but also, historically, through retrospective validation as ancestors of racially secure white descendants. The very decision of a white-skinned American to identify as black is usually dependent on preservation of the memory of African ancestors, which rarely occurs in a family that has identified itself as white, since the very conception of whiteness entails the exclusion of blackness.

The deliberate forgetting of ancestors is what Paula Gunn Allen ponders in a chapter of her book *The Sacred Hoop* that asks "Who Is Your Mother?" There she wonders what has been the cultural effect on American identities of the Indian grandmother or great-grandmother silently assimilated into so many white and African-American genealogies. It may be African-Americans, supposedly those Americans with the most sketchy genealogical records, who have most consistently constructed racial identities for themselves that do not rely on myths of racial purity. African-Americans tend to preserve, at the level of family oral history, an acknowledgment that their genetic heritage is the product of different races and that their traditions are syncretisms of interactive cultures. Our elders often preserve oral memory of ancestors with "white blood" or "Indian blood." Although identified as African-Americans, poets Jayne Cortez and Ai do not deny, forget, or silence their Filipino and Japanese roots. Robbie McCauley's powerful multimedia performance pieces "Indian Blood" and "My Father and the Wars" painfully explore the territory of racial diversity within a family in which African-American men have on the one hand married Native American women; and on the other hand participated, as soldiers in a segregated army, in America's genocidal and imperialist wars against other people of color. America's ethnic minorities have remembered what other Americans have chosen to forget.

The literature of passing, particularly within the African-American tradition, has as its central concern the American mechanism for the cultural and genetic reproduction of whiteness. In its fictive accounting for the decisions of individuals to reproduce either white or black offspring, this literature constructs a startlingly accurate model of assimilation as "passing": assimilation as the production of whiteness. Of course it is impossible to know how many African-Americans actually joined the white race, in over three hundred years of racial interaction, since those individuals carefully erased the traces of their passage. Those who have passed or whose ancestors passed from black to white have produced no literature of passing. The very success of their assimilation is a function of their silence about or ignorance of their African ancestry. Most of the genre of passing literature depicts instances in which an African-American ultimately fails to become categorically white, in order to stress the politics of race espoused by authors who insist on an ethics of racial authenticity as a component of identity, however illogical it may be to conclude that a person acknowledged to be at least "half white" (and frequently more than half) is authentically or properly black and that it would be dishonest or duplicitous for such a person to "pass as" or "pass for" white. Passing is criminalized in *Pudd'nhead Wilson* at the same time that a murderer, a slave mother, and slavery itself are all put on trial. Passing is a kind of theft, a grand larceny compared to the petty thievery of the Driscoll slaves; but since it is individual rather than institutional, passing is a crime that pales compared to the everyday business of slavery.

The look-alike babies in *Pudd'nhead Wilson* are both sons of impeccably white gentlemen. One son is born of a white mother of suitable breeding who dies after fulfilling her function of giving birth to a white heir. The other is born of a woman whose slave status designates her function as a breeder rather than a mother. Both offspring must fulfill, above all else, their structural functions as master and slave. Individuality is important only to the extent that it differentiates the white aristocrat, who may function as master, from the descendant of African captives, who must function as slave. The economic system of slavery put white men in control of black labor, just as it required the reproduction of slaves and masters, ensured by white men's control over the reproductive work of black and white women, who functioned respectively as breeders of slaves and as white race breeders. With the abolition of slavery, the maintenance of a color caste system consigned the mass of black people to the lower rungs of a class hierarchy in which they have functioned historically as surplus labor, thus cushioning white workers, to a certain extent, from the worst shocks that inevitably accompany periods of economic stagnation between periods of expanding markets.

In the United States racial difference has been produced in part as an instrument for dividing and segmenting the workforce, leaving black workers, particularly black women, at the bottom. The black woman remains in last place within the color/economic hierarchy, her disadvantaged status reinforcing the already existing prejudice against her. She is always the fly in the buttermilk, imagined as the least likely candidate for cultural assimilation, just as her dark skin would seem to make it less likely that she could reproduce white children or assure them a secure white identity. It is this woman furthest from whiteness who is therefore imagined as being also furthest from all the advantages that whiteness has to offer in a racist-sexist hierarchy of privilege and oppression, in which the privilege of whites and males is based upon and unattainable without the exploitation and oppression of blacks and females. To be white in melting pot America is to be allowed to operate without a limiting ethnic identity—which is precisely what has never yet been granted to African-Americans as a group, although the mulatto figure is a way of imagining in microcosm what this kind of social mobility might be like, at the level of the individual.

Assimilation relies upon the genetic reproduction of whiteness and the cultural reproduction of the values of Anglo-Saxons within a genetically illogical racial system

43

requiring that racial identity be reduced essentially to a white/not-white binary, allowing the maintenance of a white center with not-white margins. The literature of passing demonstrates the actual fluidity of ostensibly rigid racial boundaries that define the power relations of margin to center. The center exploits the energy of the margin, augmenting and renewing itself as the racially ambiguous are drawn to the self-validating power of the center to define itself as white and therefore pure, authentic, and "naturally" dominant.

That whiteness is produced through the operation of marginalizing blackness is suggested in a significant episode in Ralph Ellison's *Invisible Man*. The Liberty Paint Company's production of "Optic White" offers a remarkably astute parable of the production of whiteness. During his stint as a worker in the paint factory, the narrator must add ten drops of a "dead black" liquid into each bucket of "Optic White" paint, thus producing "the purest white that can be found," a paint "as white as George Washington's Sunday-go-to-meetin' wig and as sound as the all-mighty dollar" according to his white supervisor Kimbro, who adds, "That's paint that'll cover just about anything." According to the ancient toothless black worker Lucius Brockway, who survives by knowing inside out the power dynamics of the factory and its machines, Liberty's paint is "so white you can paint a chunka coal and you'd have to crack it open with a sledge hammer to prove it wasn't white clear through!" While Kimbro stresses the all-American purity of the product, daring the narrator to "express a doubt" about the white chosen to paint national monuments, Brockway seems even more impressed by its superior whitewashing ability. His sly understanding of racism earns him a bonus when he composes a advertising jingle to supplement the company slogan, "Keep America Pure with Liberty Paint." The narrator hears an echo of the black oral tradition's comment on American racial hierachies in Brockway's line: "If It's Optic White It's the Right White." As one of the "machines inside the machine," Brockway has subversive knowledge of the workings of the system, but no political motivation to change it: "These new-fangled advertising folks is been tryin' to work up something about the other colors, talking about rainbows or something, but hell, they caint get nowhere." Although he knows the system exploits him, Brockway continues to keep its machines running. He is grateful to have a job at all, and leery of competitors. Like the mythic black folk hero Shine, whose position in the ship's boiler room allowed him advance notice that the unsinkable Titanic was going down, Brockway is familiar with the fallibility of machines and knows how to save his own skin. He sees through the myth of white America, yet like other Ellisonian tricksters, is not unwilling to accommodate the myth if it can accrue to his advantage.

> *[T]he Old Man ain't goin' to let nobody come down here messing with me. He knows what a lot of them new fellers don't; he knows that the reason our paint is so good is because of the way Lucius Brockway puts the pressure on them oils and resins before they even leaves the tanks. . . . Ain't a continental thing that happens down here that ain't as iffen I done put my black hands into it! . . . Yes sir! Lucius Brockway hit it square on the head! I dips my fingers in and sweets it!"* [Ellison 191]

The American myth may rely for its potency on the interdependent myths of white purity and white superiority, but the invisible ones whose cultural and genetic contributions to the formation of American identity are covered up by Liberty White, those who function as machines inside the machine, know that no pure product of America, including the linguistic, cultural, and genetic heritage of its people, has emerged without being influenced by over three hundred years of multiracial collaboration and conflict.

The cunning accommodation of some African-Americans to the production of whiteness was keenly observed in the nineteenth century by Frances Kemble in an encounter with a slave midwife who seems a prototype of the calculating Brockway, who

74

agrees that Liberty makes "the right white." Knowing nothing of the character of her master's new wife, but certainly hoping to gain any possible influence, the slave woman automatically compliments the master on his recent acquisition, and the mistress on her whiteness.

> *"Oh massa!" shrieked out the old creature, in a paroxysm of admiration, "where you get this lilly alabaster baby!"*
>
> *For a moment I looked round to see if she was speaking of my baby; but no, my dear, this superlative apostrophe was elicited by the fairness of my skin: so much for degrees of comparison. Now I suppose that if I chose to walk arm in arm with the dingiest mulatto through the streets of Philadelphia, nobody could possibly tell by my complexion that I was not his sister, so that the mere quality of mistress must have had a most miraculous effect upon my skin in the eyes of poor Rose.* [Kemble 66]

Roxana, the slave mother in *Pudd'nhead Wilson,* is a similar figure whose subversive potential, like Brockway's, is cancelled by her conditioned acceptance of a race-class-gender hierarchy she hopes to manipulate to benefit herself and her son. Because the economic system in which she is embedded requires both masters and slaves, the most subversive act Twain can imagine for her is to swap one for the other. Her act results ultimately in the death of a slaveholder, and a farcical trial that rehearses the legal grotesqueries of slavery, but otherwise has no impact on the system itself or its requisite racial hierarchies. This is also the case of Johnson's ex-colored man, who reflects with complex irony on his fate as a successful, if ordinary, white businessman and father of two children who may be confident of their white identity; yet the text forgoes the melodramatic denouement of Charles Chesnutt's *The House behind the Cedars* or Nella Larsen's *Passing.* In the last sentence of Johnson's novel, the narrator balances the pros and cons of assimilating into white America. "My love for my children makes me glad that I am what I am and keeps me from desiring to be otherwise; and yet . . . I cannot repress the thought that, after all, I have chosen the lesser part, that I have sold my birthright for a mess of pottage" [Johnson 511]. His calm assessment of his choice avoids the (his)steric conclusion of Twain's novel, when the temporary birthright of a white scion, won by Roxana's exchange, turns out to be far less wholesome than the biblical Esau's "mess of pottage."

The passing genre is reactionary to the extent that such freedom of choice is limited to the individual, who resolves to practice the rules of the system of racist-sexist oppression, and even to reproduce it by reproducing children whose advantage over others is their whiteness. A different, yet still reactionary, approach is that of George Schuyler's 1931 novel *Black No More,* in which a black inventor and entrepreneur team up to become millionaires—and in the process change the complexion of American race relations—with a machine that turns black people white. The result is that everyone in the land of the free is left guessing who among them used to be black. The satire assumes that all African-Americans, if given the chance, would choose to be white, although of course whiteness in this instance cannot be separated from its synonyms: freedom, equality, opportunity, privilege.

Nevertheless this text might be compared usefully with Elijah Mohammed's modern racial myth of Yakub, a black scientist who manufactures "the white man" as a laboratory experiment similar to the brainchild of Dr. Frankenstein. Yakub may be read, perhaps, as a more technologically sophisticated version of Ellison's Lucius Brockway, while Schuyler's Max Disher and Dr. Junius Crookman combine the trickster ethos of Brockway with the technical expertise of Yakub. Schuyler's satire resembles Twain's in its bitter humor, with perhaps a more subversive deployment of irony. At the end of the novel, it is discovered that the former black people are even paler and blonder than the average Anglo-Saxon. The mark of race privilege instantly shifts to a quadroonish tawniness, as the true and pure whites now glory in their high melanin quotient, spend more time than ever working on their tans, and create a huge market for dark cosmetics. Schuyler's shrewd fantasy of an instant assimilation machine was inspired by an advertisement for a hair straightening preparation called Kink-No-More, a purely American product intended to make "the most stubborn Negro hair" conform to the American norm. Yet the idea that black men might control the machines of economic and cultural production, instead of remaining machines within the machine, lies behind such images of technical proficiency as a means of accomplishing the goals of assimilation or of racial self-determination.

The physical fight and literal explosion that end the invisible man's encounter with Brockway may be a convenient resolution of the narrator's anxiety about their analogous positions within the paint factory: the narrator adding the ten drops of "dead black" to each bucket of "Optic White" and Brockway applying "pressure" to the mixture while dipping his black finger into the American melting pot to sweeten it. If dead blacks are an essential ingredient of Liberty's product (corresponding to the "nauseating stench" of the "stinking goo" of which the paint is made, its noxious fumes deadening the narrator's olfactory organs until he "can't smell shit"), then it is with characteristic unease that the narrator's general sense of disgust with the inner workings of the factory focuses on the toothless (castrated) Brockway, whose chief fear is that the narrator will replace him. The narrator hates the old black worker for his pathetic bragging about his influence, his claim to have a finger in the American pie. What can possibly have been gained by Brockway's putative sweetening influence on a system that stinks to heaven? The tree of Liberty is watered with the blood of dead black soldiers who defended a democracy that excludes them, and the 'something rotten' in America's production of whiteness is the lynched and castrated corpse of the black man.

Recall that Johnson's ex-colored man opts out of "the race" for an optically white existence after witnessing the spectacle of a black man's burning body surrounded by a cheering white mob. An unresolved contradiction of the text, of course, is that the passing protagonist's marriage to a white woman would seem to place him in a similar position of jeopardy. His method of avoiding the ultimate punishment is to commit the black man's unpardonable offense as a white man. Thus crime is transformed into marital duty, and the wife conveniently dies after reproducing two children to whom she passes on her white credentials.

Brockway's implied sexual/technical prowess (his upraised finger, preacherly yet sweet, suggests a phallus, if a diminished one) is only a revelation of his castration. The narrator implies that what Brockway does in the factory is beneath the dignity of white laborers. He has attained seniority only because his work must be "something too filthy and dangerous for white men." Brockway himself refers to his job as "cooking." The sweetening gesture to which he alludes in his assertion of influence is that of a cook, a feminized position, despite the penetrating finger. The cunning old worker is a racial relic, like the stereotypical plantation cook or mammy. Although he has kept the machines running with the improvisational skills of an untrained engineer, his position is like that of the black cook behind the scenes in the kitchen of a fancy restaurant in which patrons prefer not to see their meals prepared. Despite his lack of political vision, Brockway has something to teach the narrator. The elder worker correctly points to the unacknowledged contribution of black men and women to the production (and reproduction) of white America. The ostensibly sophisticated equipment of the factory is revealed as an elaborate "nigger rig," just as a significant portion of American culture turns out to be "mammy made."

76

Anxiety about the white man's symbolic phallic power and the black man's symbolic (and occasionally literal) castration may underlie the technological metaphors of production in Ellison, Mohammed, and Schuyler. Women (black and white) are displaced, avoiding biological reproduction and the "problem" of miscegenation. A black partner is most likely to produce assimilably white offspring with a white mate. The technological fantasies feature mechanical production as an asexual reproduction of whiteness, which is not dependent upon the coupling of a black woman with a white man (thus excluding the black male) or upon the coupling of a black man with a white woman (thus risking the castration of the black male). In these technological metaphors/fantasies, miscegenation is effected without sexual reproduction, imagery that continues to be deployed in what I call the production of the media cyborg, which will be discussed later. Assimilation is unimaginable without miscegenation, whether sexual or mechanical-cybernetic: assimilation equals whiteness produced from the resources and raw materials of blackness. Yet the anxiety provoked by the question of the black man's potential assimilation/mastery through technological rather than reproductive power persists in Ellison's narrator, and it is fitting that the machinery's explosion is followed by a scene in the factory hospital: a brutal "rebirth" of the migrant Southerner turned industrial worker, in which the narrator is subjected to yet another traumatizing machine (that he doesn't control) and repeatedly asked, by white doctor-technicians unaware that they are playing the dozens, "Who is your mother?"

The racial romance often focuses on the black woman whose position as the white man's concubine resulted in her reproducing the genetic traits of Anglo-Saxons. Ellison's modernist novel, Schuyler's satire, and Mohammed's modern racial myth all center on the black male in search of technological mastery. In the twentieth century such images of mechanical production increasingly replaced the nineteenth-century romance of the miscegenated family. For if even the whitest Negroes had difficulty passing, how much less likely that the consumers of Kink-No-More might be accepted into the great melting pot as assimilable Americans.

In my reading of the literature of passing, I look at passing as successful assimilation on the terms allowed to Americans of European descent but routinely denied to African-Americans. I read this literature, in part, as an exploration of the mechanics of assimilation as a process of identifying oneself culturally and genetically with white Americans, while severing associations with African-Americans. Passing is not so much a willful deception or duplicity as it is an attempt to move from the margin to the center of American identity. That such movement has been systematically blocked to the mass of black people is perhaps the primary reason that the ability to do so is almost invariably interpreted as inauthenticity when managed by an African-American, but as an exemplary instance of cultural assimilation when accomplished by European immigrants, who shed language, culture, and tradition in order to become, or allow their offspring to become, true (white) Americans. This model of assimilation historically has been open only to those African-Americans who were visually indistinguishable from whites. Rather than "passing for" white, I would say instead that passing individuals actually become white or function as white, which amounts to the same thing when their participation in the normal activities of mainstream Americans is enabled by the perception that they are white. The actual passage from black to white may be self-conscious or unconscious, deliberate or inadvertent, and may operate within spatial or temporal limits. Some individuals maintain a private culturally marginal identity while functioning as white only for privileged access to employment or public facilities. Others may make a decisive break with one identification in order to identify completely with the dominant center, or to allow such complete identification for their offspring.

A person becomes adeptly white when he or she acquires a partner whose white credentials are unquestionable and produces perceptibly white (not "mulatto" or "mixed")

offspring. The mechanism of passing is complete when the individual has "passed on" to his or her offspring both the physical features and the social identity of any other assimilated American who is presumed to be (pure) white. This is the fate of the anonymous fictional protagonist of James Weldon Johnson's *The Autobiography of an Ex-Colored Man;* his children, themselves unaware of their African-American heritage, are the badge of his own successful passing from black to white, since he is white enough to cast no shadow on their white identity and they are white enough to cast no doubt on his. While Francis Harper's Iola Leroy rejects the "opportunity" to enter the white race by successfully reproducing a (legitimate) white child with impeccable social credentials, the morbid anxiety surrounding the possible reproduction of a child too dark to be white pervades the melodrama and repressed sexuality of Nella Larsen's *Passing.* Both novels, along with the biographies of labor activist Lucy Parsons, actress and poet Ada Isaacs Mencken, and stage performer Carrie Highgate Morgan, African-Americans who passed from black to white, also suggest how the institution of marriage, which customarily merged a woman's identity with that of her husband, could serve as a practical vehicle for passing women who married white men.

The implication of the sex-gender system in the mechanism of passing is sometimes a submerged discourse within the genre. Johnson's novel shares, with Kate Chopin's "Desiree's Baby" and Langston Hughes's "Passing," an exploration of phallogocentric anxieties about paternity that intersect with anxieties about racial identity. The presumption of women's impurity that rationalizes patriarchal law is operative in Chopin's short story; but in Johnson's novel, it is displaced by the narrator's preoccupation with his own illicit origins. The narrator's patriarchal authority as a white father is stabilized by the erasure of his own black mother as well as by the death of the white woman he marries. The narrator of Hughes's short story is momentarily disturbed by the complications of passing, and he imagines that if his black family left town, this would make his life as a white man easier. His moment of crisis occurs when he passes his mother on the street. They pretend not to know each other because he is out with his white fiancee. The text of the story is his letter to his mother, his written communication "crossing the color-line" to explain the specific instance of "passing you downtown last night and not speaking to you" along with the more pervasive social disciplines of passing, a racial strategy that paradoxically denies the importance of race. Being a white man means never having to think about race, on the one hand; and on the other hand, having the authority to deny paternity and legitimacy to any of his children who look too dark to be white.

> Since I've begun to pass for white, nobody has ever doubted that I am a white man. . . . But, Ma, I felt mighty bad about last night. The first time we'd met in public that way. That's the kind of thing that makes passing hard, having to deny your own family when you see them. . . . I've made up my mind to live in the white world, and have found my place in it (a good place), why think about race any more? I'm glad I don't have to, I know that much. . . . I'm going to marry white and live white, and if any of my kids are born dark I'll swear they aren't mine. I won't get caught in the mire of color again. Not me. I'm free, Ma, free! I'd be glad, though, if I could get away from Chicago . . . somewhere where what happened last night couldn't ever occur again. . . . Maybe it would have been better if you . . . had stayed in Cincinnati and I'd come away alone when we decided to move after the old man died. Or at least, we should have gone to different towns, shouldn't we? [Hughes 49-52]

In Twain's text the question of legitimacy, the question of who is real and who is imitation, ultimately does not matter as much as the requirement that the positions of master and slave be filled by men who have been bred for each role. The requirement for masters and slaves produces an ideology of racial superiority, with its own philosophers, legal scholars, and pseudoscientists to validate it. At a time when genetic and racial theories were emerging as powerful tools of white domination, Twain exploits the ambiguity in the common use of "breeding" to signify cultural as well as, or instead of, individual or genetic endowments, as well as the conflict between democratic impulses and notions that human virtue and vice are inbred, hereditary, and racial attributes. Twain's preoccupation in *Pudd'nhead Wilson* with the plight of "imitation niggers" is reminiscent of Harriet Beecher Stowe's odd note on reverse passing in her *Key to Uncle Tom's Cabin*. Stowe warns that a system in which white-skinned African-Americans are bought and sold would sooner or later allow some enterprising speculator to profit by selling white orphans to unsuspecting masters as fair-skinned octoroons. Twain's concern with passing, as a metaphor for black assimilation, perhaps registers the dismay with which white Americans during and after Reconstruction viewed the strivings of freedmen and the upward mobility of the black middle class.

The story of an assimilating African-American required to part with kindred in order to establish a new identity could not be more typically American, and as such, it is fitting that the family romance of what Susan Gillman calls "race melodrama" and the literature of passing are present in embryonic form in the slave narrative, where explications of the gendering of race and racialization of gender also have their beginning. The slave narratives themselves are, like Stowe's *Uncle Tom's Cabin,* miscegenated texts that until recently have been disowned by patriarchs of American literature.

Harriet Jacobs's *Incidents in the Life of a Slave Girl* provides one of the earliest representations of racial passing in an African-American text, with the story of Jacobs's uncle, who in the tradition of their family is depicted as a "slave who dared to feel like a man." This uncle, called Benjamin in the text, is close to the narrator in age, but his sex and color give him options unavailable to his olive-skinned kinswoman. He apparently chooses to pass as white, although the narrator only obliquely acknowledges this possibility, in her account of his successive escape attempts following a fight with his master. "He was a bright, handsome lad, nearly white; for he inherited the complexion my grandmother had derived from Anglo-Saxon ancestors" [Jacobs 342]. The fact of his white complexion, mentioned prominently in her initial description of him, is reiterated, along with his dangerous, almost suicidal insistence on acting like a man, which results in his imprisonment and his sale at a reduced price to a speculator. "Long confinement had made his face too pale, his form too thin; moreover, the trader had heard something of his character, and it did not strike him as suitable for a slave. He said he would give any price if the handsome lad was a girl. We thanked God that he was not" [Jacobs 357].

Jacobs underlines the contrast between her own fate and that of her uncle, whose gender allows him mobility and whose white complexion is a chance inheritance the slave receives from white male ancestors. This individual who passes may consider his color as a kind of property or asset, as an inadvertent birthright and a way to freedom requiring only that he separate himself from those who know him as a slave—his family in particular. Racism reifies whiteness to the extent that it is known or presumed to be unmixed with blackness. "Pure" whiteness is imagined as something that is both external and internal, while the white complexion of the mulatto, quadroon, or octoroon is imagined as something superficial, only skin deep, the black blood passing on to the body an inherited impurity. "Pure" whiteness has actual value, like legal tender, while the white-skinned African-American is like a counterfeit bill that is passed into circulation, but may be withdrawn at any point if discovered to be bogus. The inherited whiteness is a kind of capital, which may yield the dividend of freedom. This color capital is as much an asset for the man prepared to use it as it would be a liability to the slave woman who does not wish to be a sexual commodity. The slave woman's color capital may enrich her master, as the white woman's husband controls her inheritance. The white-skinned slave may sell at a higher price for the aesthetic value of her pink or tan complexion, and some women managed to negotiate their own and/or their children's freedom, as Jacobs herself eventually did, but this required the cooperation of a master willing to manumit them. A woman could not pass herself into society, since even a marriageable white debutante had to be formally "introduced" to society and "given" in marriage. Property, including color capital (the only capital available to poor whites), may pass through women (as Benjamin's white complexion, inherited from white ancestors, passes to him through his mother—along with her slave status), but women themselves do not control it or determine its value. Aside from their different positions within the shared role of displaying or embodying the wealth of white men, the function of bourgeois white women is to marry and reproduce heirs, while the function of slave women is to be sexually available to black and white men and reproduce slaves. "If God has bestowed beauty upon her, it will prove her greatest curse. That which commands admiration in the white woman only hastens the degradation of the female slave" [Jacobs 357].

A slave woman as white and attractive-looking as her uncle could be sold for "any price," but the "handsome lad" is sold at a discount because he is a slave who, "no longer a boy," acts like a man. The slave woman may be "broke in" through her role as sexual chattel and as childbearer—an assault upon her body's interiority, in addition to the usual means—while the corporal punishment of the male slave (Douglass comes to mind) is a more exterior means of breaking the spirit of resistance.

> *Benjamin's master had sent for him, and he did not immediately obey the summons. When he did, his master was angry, and began to whip him. He resisted. Master and slave fought, and finally the master was thrown. . . . "I have come," said Benjamin, "to tell you good by. I am going away. . . . To the north." He said he was no longer a boy, and every day made his yoke more galling. He had raised his hand against his master, and was to be publicly whipped for the offence.* [Jacobs 354]

Within the community of "favored" slaves who work as artisans or in domestic service, confinement in jail may replace the public flogging, making her uncle's jail term similar in some respects to her own imprisonment in the master's house, to which "The felon's home in a penitentiary is preferable" [Jacobs 363]. While her own flight only takes her as far as the super-interior of her grandmother's house, where she remains accessible to the adult members of her family in her "loophole of retreat," this uncle "vanished from our sight," in harrowing voyages taking him first toward New York, and later "over the blue billows, bound for Baltimore." Each time, however, he was "pursued, captured, and carried back to his master. . . . I saw him led through the streets in chains, to jail. His face was ghastly pale, yet full of determination" [Jacobs 355].

At the same time that she contrasts his physical mobility with her own confinement (as well as the decision of her other uncle to remain with their mother, her grandmother), she stresses implicitly that her own determination is equal to that of the mobile fugitive. By emphasizing the goal of freedom, which may be approached by various means, she honors all forms of resistance to slavery and also suggests that freedom as well as oppression may be stratified by gender and color. She does not condemn her uncle's decision to "part with all [his] kindred," although the fact that her text resorts to evasively elliptical, metaphorical language in its depiction of his last, successful escape indicates a degree of ambivalence on the narrator's part toward his particular route to freedom.

Almost subliminally, Jacobs prepares the reader for his passing, with images contrasting his paling face and waning body to his fierce determination to be free by any means, which both suggest and evade this resolution. This uncle's eventual decision to fade into the white race, a symbolic death and rebirth that, in its figuration of movement

51

from the confinement of blackness to the freedom of whiteness, anticipates James Weldon Johnson's ex-colored man, who chooses this means of escaping the agonizing dilemma of black manhood. In his second "effort for freedom" when he is "bound for Baltimore," Benjamin uses his color to his advantage. Daring to "act like a man," the slave passes the test of self-confident movement ascribed to the white male traveler, and thus is presumed white and free by those who are unaware of his slave status. He allows himself to betray none of the previous "embarrassment" that had marked him as a suspected fugitive on his earlier passage to New York. "For once his white face did him a kindly service. They had no suspicion that it belonged to a slave; otherwise, the law would have been followed out to the letter, and the thing rendered back to slavery" [Jacobs, *Incidents* 358].

The logic of passing is intrinsic in the logic of slavery, which defines the black as a facsimile or counterfeit of the white in order to deny the rights and privileges of whiteness. The male slave can merely "feel like a man." Only by passing from black to white is he able to be a man in the full sense of the legal entitlement of manhood. Better to be treated as a man than as a thing, and better a free white man than a slave—if he must become white to be treated as the man he is. "Death is better than slavery," a recurring refrain in Jacobs's and other slave narratives, acquires an ironic significance when Benjamin dies as a slave, vanishing into the white race in his third and final escape. Throughout his ordeal of two failed escape attempts and a lengthy jail term, he is described as growing thinner, paler, and ghostlier, yet more fiercely determined to be free, until finally, after an emotional farewell, he fades from their lives altogether. He ceases to exist as a slave—or as a black man—apparently blending into the white population. To his family, who never see him again, it is as if he were dead. "[Phillip] furnished him with clothes, and gave him what money he had. They parted with moistened eyes; and as Benjamin turned away, he said, 'Phil, I part with all my kindred.' And so it proved. We never heard from him again" [Jacobs 360].

Jacobs's grandmother Molly Horniblow is a real Roxana who lost her son as he found a route to freedom. While Jacobs represents her grandmother, a former slave, as an alternative prototype of "true womanhood," contrasting her virtue to the treachery of white mistresses, it could be argued that the image of the black woman as a supermaternal figure in this text is augmented by her dual function as mother to both white and black children. The grandmother (called "Martha" in the text) bears five living children in slavery, breastfeeding her own (when she could) as well as the child of her mistress (when required). Among the generations that follow her is a son whose white complexion enables him to pass from black to white on the way to freedom; as well as a grandson, also very pale, who joins the gold rush in California, and also loses contact with his black kin; and a great-grandson who is presumed to be white until his Northern schoolmates learn of his African-American identity, in an incident similar to an early episode in the fictional life of Johnson's ex-colored man. Like Twain's Roxana, Martha reproduces and mothers "black" and "white" children, although the white children born of their enslaved bodies can function as white only through deformations of white patriarchal law. Even Sojourner Truth relied, for some of her authority with audiences, on her virtue as a supermother who had suckled black and white infants. Roxana carefully separates her mother/breeder functions, which are split in twain by the conflicting requirements of rearing a master and training a disciplined slave. The self-division of Roxana also suggests the child's splitting of the maternal figure into the good and the bad mother, complicated by the shared maternal functions of black and white women in the South. The black woman as a conflicted site of the (re)production of whiteness is figured in Roxana's meticulous distinction, beginning in infancy, between the functions of slave and master; while the dialect-speaking white character Twain invented exemplifies the fears expressed even by such a liberal observer as the English actress Frances Kemble that the speech of white Southerners had been "corrupted" by the influence of black dialect speakers who cared for them as nursemaids and nannies.

> *I am amused, but by no means pleased, at an entirely new mode of pronouncing which S[ally] has adopted. Apparently the Negro jargon has commended itself as euphonious to her infantile ears, and she is now treating me to the most ludicrous and accurate imitations of it every time she opens her mouth. Of course I shall not allow this, comical as it is, to become a habit. This is the way the Southern ladies acquire the thick and inelegant pronunciation which distinguishes their utterances from the Northern snuffle, and I have no desire that S[ally] should adorn her mother tongue with either peculiarity.* [Kemble 280-81]

The legal (white) heir's acquisition of Roxy's black speech, in this case because no white mother is there to prevent it, raises a question about the true mother tongue of Americans nourished on the milk of black mothers, who, like Lucius Brockway inside the machine and umpteen black cooks, have dipped their fingers into the pot to sweeten it. The industrial image of the melting pot, which produces a uniformly white dominant America, has its counterpart in the legislation passed by white males to ensure their jurisdiction over the reproductive work of white and nonwhite women and thus to assert quality control over the production of whiteness and the reproduction of white patriarchy.

The American tradition to which Twain belongs is clearly that of the miscegenated texts of the slave narratives. It is the illicit issue of an oral tradition, often figured as the voice of a maternal slave, mated with a written tradition, figured in Frederick Douglass's narrative as forbidden white texts: "the master's copy-book" as well as dangerous abolitionist pamphlets. In *Pudd'nhead Wilson* the two traditions are at bitter war with each other, and the tools of the master, the legal and scientific discourses of judges and attorneys, are used like an iron bit to mute the resistant slave woman's mother tongue. The young master—or the white author—may acquire Roxana's blackened language, but he may inherit his privileged position only as the legitimate offspring of a white patriarch with a "lilly alabaster" white race breeder.

After the nineteenth century the use of the black image to represent repressed elements of what has been constructed ideologically and semiotically as a "white psyche" becomes more pervasive, as well as more easily subsumed within technical and aesthetic operations. The very means of expression are tied to technologies highly susceptible to regressive and repressive ideological formations, as Jim Pines's analysis of the interlocking racism and increasingly proficient technologies of Hollywood film empires might suggest. Pines argues, for instance, that Al Jolson's groundbreaking "talkie" films *The Jazz Singer* and *The Singing Fool* utilized the sentimental, emotive power of the blackface image in a way that suggests a great deal about the construction of the white male as a (universal) human image. The attenuated humanity of the controlled, repressed, rational, ambitious white male has to be augmented by the animal/child/woman/black who stand in relation to it as dependent/inferior. The white male paternalistically reincorporates the values consigned to the Other, investing the Other with what is repressed and devalued in himself, so that the Other has to exist as reservoir and supplement, expressing for the dominant male the values and emotions that, because of his position of rational authority, he cannot afford to express himself.

> *Jolson's particular use of blackface in both* The Jazz Singer *and* The Singing Fool . . . *shows an interesting deviation from the traditional use of the artifice employed by whites. . . . It is clear from Jolson's play of feature that the primary function of his blackface guise is to inflate the emotional content of the scene, of the (white) character's moral dilemma. His agony, in other words, is*

symbolized and enhanced by the minstrel image, an image that evokes pity. . . . Clearly, the overall effect of the scene is achieved through the emotive visual content of the tragic minstrel image. . . . Jolson's white character (his "normal" role) always conveys tough, self-confident determination, whereas his blackface "alter ego" is most certainly a bundle of tearful sentimentalism. In both The Jazz Singer *and* The Singing Fool *the white Jolson is portrayed as an ambitious type working positively toward some form of quasi-rational solution. At some stage in his development he takes an excursion into simplistic emotionalism via the blackface "alter ego" figure. Exploiting this as a kind of "soulful" reservoir the Jolson character is thus able to exorcise intense and generally repressed feelings—such as sorrow and guilt—without actually having to disrupt the basically white rational world the white "ego" is striving to succeed in. The pathos of the blackface Jolson character is markedly an attempt to inject a sense of spiritual substance into the white character's ambitions and dilemmas; and by so doing facilitate the audience's experience of the white protagonist's development as a popular humanizing figure.* [Pines 17–19]

The black begins to be seen less as the dark body contrasted with the enlightened mind and more as the repressed and emotional soul of a white social-cultural-political-economic body. As DuBois had done in *The Souls of Black Folk*, Martin Luther King, Jr., and other twentieth-century civil rights activists drew upon such imagery in figuring black people as the sign of an incompletely realized ideal, the rumbling conscience of America, guardians of an endangered ethical tradition. As the imagery has become increasingly secularized, its metaphysical implications are both transformed and made graphic via the technological possibilities of electronic media, cropping up in contemporary film and advertising, with black expressivity now encoded in countless images: as black back-up singers in white rock groups (or, for that matter, the miscegenated history of rock and roll itself, with black musical ancestors producing soulful white offspring through the in vitro fertilization of radio and phonograph); as the Motown soundtrack of the film *The Big Chill,* in which black music nostalgically evokes the turbulent youth of the aging cohort of baby boomers—a generation metonymically signified on screen by an all-white clique, as voice-over lyrics sung by unseen black performers on television commercial soundtracks accompany hip white images.

Abolitionist literature—particularly the slave narrative—with its interracial collaborative textual production made possible by the sharing of the technology of writing, despite legal codes prohibiting literacy for slaves with the intent and effect of legislating institutionalized illiteracy, anticipates the technological grafting of white body and black soul through the mechanical synchronization of filmic image and soundtrack. In the narrator-amanuensis dyad, the white hand writes for the black voice, turning speech into text and, in many cases, nonstandard dialects into standard English. (More than anything, the technology of the tape recorder contributes to the desire to transcribe dialects in their nonstandard form, setting the WPA narratives apart from nineteenth-century narratives.) Or the white editor solicits, corrects, tidies, and introduces the black text. The miscegenated text of abolitionist literature constructs the African-American subject as a black body with a white soul (an interiority comprehensible to white readers—with the blushing of white skin as the underlying trope of emotional readability). William Blake's image of the black whose skin is a cloud that obscures a bright soul or a consciousness susceptible to enlightenment, "I am black, but oh, my soul is white," is deployed, with varying degrees of irony or pathos, by African-American writers. Northup, for example, feels compelled to use whiteness as the standard of humanity in order to make white readers understand that he loves his children as much as they love theirs. "Their presence was my delight; and I clasped them to my bosom with as warm and tender love as if their clouded skins

84

had been as white as snow" [Northup, *POM* 233].

Harriet Wilson, in *Our Nig,* has a black character defend his honor by declaring, "I's black outside, I know, but I's got a white heart inside. Which you rather have, a black heart in a white skin, or a white heart in a black one?" Jacobs tropes on the color coding of body and interiority to castigate the hypocritical white Christian, with her angry image of the town constable as a "white-faced, black-hearted brother," a Methodist class leader "who whipped his brethren and sisters of the church at the public whipping post" and who was "ready to perform that Christian office any where for fifty cents." Her inversion of the conventional trope leaves blackness as a negative signifier at the same time that it invalidates whiteness as a positive signifier.

A more complex response than taking up the trope of the black body with a white soul in order to humanize the black, or the simple inversion of the trope, with a white body negated by a black interiority, is the passage below, from Henry Bibb's narrative, in which there is an attempt to problematize and distinguish among the conventional tropes linking African descent, black skin, and darkness as negative signifiers. Bibb signifies, in the African-American tradition, on the privileged position of the white race as well as its conflation of whiteness and "white" skin with goodness and light. Placing himself in the role of actor-trickster whose deceptions are meant to redress the evil of enslavement, Bibb moves deliberately and carefully from literal light and shadow to the symbolic use of light and dark as indicators of moral value to shade of skin, which in his case is not much darker than that of an Anglo-Saxon. Moreover, notwithstanding the social usefulness of a light skin, especially in deceiving slave catchers, he does not negate the value of the "dark complexion" of which he has been "almost entirely robbed" through the white slaveholder's sexual enslavement of black women.

> I crowded myself back from the light among the deck passengers, where it would be difficult to distinguish me from a white man. Every time during the night that the mate came round with a light after the hands, I was afraid he would see I was a colored man, and take me up; hence I kept from the light as much as possible. Some men love darkness rather than light, because their deeds are evil; but this was not the case with myself; it was to avoid detection in doing right. This was one of the instances of my adventures that my affinity with the Anglo-Saxon race, and even slaveholders, worked well for my escape. But no thanks to them for it. While in their midst they have not only robbed me of my labor and liberty, but they have almost entirely robbed me of my dark complexion. Being so near the color of a slaveholder, they could not, or did not find me out that night among the white passengers. [Bibb *POM* 84]

The collaborative literary production re-enacting textually the actual genetic miscegenation embodied by a Frederick Douglass, Henry Bibb, William Wells Brown, or Harriet Jacobs—who were all products of racial mixing—was the nineteenth-century equivalent of today's crossover hit song moving from "black charts" to "mainstream pop," or the latest successful buddy film with the big box office demographic casting coup of a commercially compatible salt-and-pepper team. However, the nineteenth-century textual production of a black body with a white soul gives way in the twentieth century to its inversion, as the soul of black folks is extracted from the black body through textual exteriorizations of black interiority, and rhythmic expressions in traditions of dance, music, and orality in commodified forms of entertainment and media technologies that privilege exteriority over interiority—the body over the soul—draw upon the figure of the black as an icon of expressivity.

The contemporary electronic version of the miscegenated text uses a different model of integration: a media cyborg constructed as a white body with black soul. This production model has become so iconically suggestive and such a pervasive image of racial integration—achieved, if nowhere else, through an audio-visual medium—that its message is almost subliminal. A technology encodes racial ideology so powerfully that it accomplishes an otherwise unachieved racial integration through a synthesized synchronicity of images and voices drawn from disparate sources, the media equivalent of gene splicing. (Gene splicing: a biotechnological metaphor derived from audio and film technology, suggesting the pervasiveness of information models due to the proliferation of information technologies. DNA is regarded as genetic information, while information has long since been transformed into both commodity and capital. The dominance of the information model results in life itself being regarded as simply another form of information storage and retrieval.) Despite the appearance of a merger, a segregated or ghettoized music industry continues to be commercially viable. The split/ merged sound-image has itself been made the content as well as the form of one television commercial that explicitly articulates this figuration of white body/black soul through its depiction of a white teenager alone in her room, with headphones, lip-synching lyrics recorded by Aretha Franklin, illustrating the advertising slogan, "Be the music." This advertisement uses film editing conventions of the music video while parodying the lip-synching common not only to music video (which often goes to great lengths to separate the music and lyric of the song from the visual narrative of the video) but also to early television programs formatted for promotion of recorded rock and roll music, such as *American Bandstand,* and the earlier movie musicals which allowed nonsingers to appear in singing roles with performances dubbed by professional vocalists. This parodic use of a very visible process makes perceptible, rather than subliminal, the technique of grafting or splicing together the sound and image, the white body with a black voice/soul, by cross-cutting the color film image of the white teenager with vintage black-and-white footage of Franklin singing what might be regarded as her personal anthem—"Respect." Here the technical solution for dramatizing the slogan, "Be the music," demonstrates how even the film stock itself may be used ideologically.

The technical resources of film signifying the division and separation of black and white (black-and-white film evokes legalized Jim Crow segregation and the "race records" predating music crossover, Civil Rights, Black Power, and "Black is beautiful") are shown to underlie the merging of black and white in the miscegenated colored image of a media cyborg: the white body with black soul, black-and-white film representing the nostalgic/turbulent past just as the soulful crossover soundtrack of *The Big Chill* evokes yuppie nostalgia. It is as if the visual media of film and television had thoroughly digested the black image, anatomizing and redistributing its energy so that the plasticization of the kinetic visual icon is no longer strictly required, the re-editing of synchronous sound and image (read as the empowerment rather than silencing of the white lip-syncher, whose voice is omitted) producing something like a contemporary whiteface minstrelsy.

This movement has been accompanied by a corresponding shift in the representation of essential blackness from body ("African" skin/hair/features) to (soulful) voice or movement, while the use of a white dancer as body double for the African-American actress Jennifer Beals in the film *Flashdance* suggests that the media cyborg may be constructed paradoxically by splicing in for the dance sequences a soulful white body to provide the rhythm all God's children haven't got. Yet, because she lives alone, works with whites, and dates an affluent white man, the deracinated black character (or generic white American) that Beals plays is probably presumed to be white by movie audiences who don't read *Ebony* or *Jet.* Aside from the surgical strategies, hair weaves, and "commercial voices" of performers like Michael Jackson, Diana Ross, or Whitney Houston, who embody in their public personae a bankable merger of "black" and "white" styles, the racial composition of the media cyborg more typically works by grafting black

86

soul as supplement to a white body, effectively placing the black body offstage, behind the scenes, or in the recording studio as back-up. Whites covering black material: the invention of rock music. Berry Gordy's gold mine: the "sophisticated soul" of Motown and millions of crossover dollars. Who covers? Who crosses over? These are questions anticipated in *The Autobiography of an Ex-Colored Man*, a text that disseminates the ethical problem of passing beyond the individual decision of one man to reproduce black or white offspring, to satirize "passing" as a national mechanism for forgetting a history that links African-Americans with other Americans in kinship, a mechanism for the production of whiteness and suppression of blackness. The unnamed narrator lets his white skin cover his African heritage as he crosses over into the freedom of mainstream USA through a strategy of self-denial; this is a loss of soul, but he finds this preferable to the loss of life of the black man burned alive, whose horrific public execution by a white mob determines the narrator's decision to pass into the white race in order to escape the stigma of blackness. Johnson's musician protagonist is a passable mulatto whose sense of belonging essentially to a black race (acquired rather late in life to begin with) is associated metonymically with the voice of his African-American mother. Her repertoire included black spirituals, those same sorrow songs that inspired the writings of Douglass and DuBois:

> *Sometimes on other evenings, when she was not sewing, she would play simple accompaniments to some old Southern songs which she sang. In these songs she was freer, because she played them by ear. Those evenings on which she opened the little piano were the happiest hours of my childhood. . . . I used to stand by her side and often interrupt and annoy her by chiming in with strange harmonies which I found on either the high keys of the treble or the low keys of the bass. I remember that I had a particular fondness for the black keys. Always on such evenings, when the music was over, my mother would sit with me in her arms, often for a very long time. She would hold me close, softly crooning some old melody without words, all the while gently stroking her face against my head; many and many a night I thus fell asleep. I can see her now, her great dark eyes looking into the fire, to where? No one knew but her. The memory of that picture has more than once kept me from straying too far from the place of purity and safety in which her arms held me. [Johnson 395-96]*

As the sorrow songs provide the content of black soul for DuBois, the voice of the black mother or grandmother figures the transmission of a distinctly African-American culture for Johnson, as well as Brown, Bibb, Jacobs, and others—if not for Douglass, whose mother and grandmother are represented as virtually silent in the 1845 narrative. The soulful singing voice, representative of the repressed or appropriated cultural contribution of the descendants of African slaves, becomes an aural rather than visual conveyor of emotional expressivity, or "soul." The white visual image absorbs the plastic iconicity and emotive content of the black through the expedient of a black soul technologically grafted to a by now thoroughly materialized white body. The inscrutable interiority of the African-American, having by now been pried out of the shell of the body and made comprehensible in its expressiveness, is purveyed in various media representations as a "black" voice which has become the essence of consumable soul.

The commercial potential of black soul to sell everything from raisins ("I heard it through the grapevine") to plastic wrap ("It don't mean a thing if it ain't got that cling") has been proven time and again. It is illustrated spectacularly in a Pepsi Cola advertisement's cyborganic production of Tina Turner as a cross between an 8x10 glossy photo of a conventionally attractive blond white woman and a soft drink accidentally spilled in a high-tech dream machine by mad scientist David Bowie. This absent-minded scientist is himself transformed from klutzy nerd to hip rocker as the plain vanilla erotic appeal of the white woman of his wildest dreams is raised to the tenth power by a racier partner for Bowie's walk on the wild side, to the tune of his hit rock song "Modern Love." Reading the mini-narrative of the commercial alongside Johnson's novel suggests different possibilities, within the twentieth century, for incorporating race into a narrative of (re)production: from the early 1900s when Johnson's novel first appeared anonymously, to the 1980s cola commercial, a shift from repression to expression, from anonymity to celebrity, from blackness as the sign of illicit sexuality to blackness as the sign of sexual freedom. Repression is figured in the novel as a cultural production and racial reproduction of whiteness, a movement from black to white that allows and is reinforced by a corresponding movement from illicit sexuality to marriage. In the advertisement, expression of desire and fulfillment of fantasy lead to a racial integration produced technically with the invention of the cybernetic mulatta as the ideal partner for "modern love"—sex without reproduction. The mechanical production of the sexy cyborg out of the mating of Pepsi and pin-up girl by the scientist taking a cola break replaces the sexual reproduction of the mulatto driven by a puritan work ethic who, once he has become a successful white businessman—concerned with supporting his white offspring, protecting his white identity, and concealing his (black and illegitimate) origins—presumably can no longer afford to waste time or risk recognition by visiting his old haunts, the dives and gambling dens of his youth, marginal sites where blacks and whites met and mingled illicitly.

The "love" without marriage that brought a white Southern aristocrat and his family's colored servant together to produce Johnson's narrator—a musical prodigy who trades his cultural birthright as an African-American for white assimilation, giving up his dream of composing an American classical music based on African-American folksong and ragtime in order to pass as a safe, successfully average white businessman—has been superseded by the "modern love" made possible by technologies that improve on fantasy. The interracial marriage of black rhythm to white melody produces rock and roll, a music that can no longer be seen as a bastard child but has to be acknowledged as big business as well as one of the most successful products the United States exports to other countries. While Johnson's text models itself on the slave narrative and pushes to its logical conclusion its construction as a miscegenated or mulatto text striving to pass the test of humanity measured as whiteness, the Pepsi commercial is a contemporary descendant of Mary Shelley's Frankenstein, with fears of technology, sexual expression, and the irrational or unconscious drives associated with blackness tamed—so that the scientist and his soulful creation make a stylish couple rather than deadly antagonists.

The discursive formation of black soul in the slave narratives, as Douglass sees it, is a textual production somewhat equivalent and parallel to the oral production of spirituals and folksongs, an oral production itself characterized as equivalent to "whole volumes of philosophy." Douglass asserts it is "To those songs I trace my first glimmering conception of the dehumanizing character of slavery." In their exteriorization of the slave's interiority, both have the paradoxical effect of constructing an expressive humanity for African-Americans at the same time that they begin to construct white audiences for cultural productions in which black soul may be a more lucrative commodity than black bodies ever were.

WORKS CITED

Allen, Paula Gunn. *The Sacred Hoop: Recovering the Feminine in American Indian Traditions.* Boston: Beacon, 1986.

The Big Chill. Dir. Lawrence Kasdan. Columbia, 1983.

"The Browning of America." *Time* 142: 3–12+. Special issue Fall 1993.

88

Chesnutt, Charles. *The House behind the Cedars.* Ridgwood, NJ: Gregg, 1968.

Chopin, Kate. "Desiree's Baby." *The Complete Works of Kate Chopin.* 2 vols. Ed. and intro. Per Seyersted. Baton Rouge: Louisiana State UP, 1969. 1: 240–45.

Ellison, Ralph. *Invisible Man.* New York: Modern Library, 1992.

Flashdance. Dir. Adrian Lyne. Paramount, 1983.

Hughes, Langston. "Passing." *The Ways of White Folks.* New York: Knopf, 1979. 49–53.

Jacobs, Harriet. *Incidents in the Life of a Slave Girl. Classic Slave Narratives.* Ed. and intro. Henry Louis Gates, Jr. New York: New American Library, 1987.

Johnson, James Weldon. *The Autobiography of an Ex-Colored Man. Three Negro Classics.* New York: Avon, 1969.

Kemble, Frances Anne. *Journal of a Residence on a Georgian Plantation in 1838–1839.* Ed. and intro. John A. Scott. New York: Knopf, 1961.

Larsen, Nella. *Passing.* New York: Negro UP, 1969.

Pines, Jim. *Blacks in Films: A Survey of Racial Themes and Images in the American Film.* London: Studio Vista, 1975.

Puttin' on Ole Massa: The Slave Narratives of Henry Bibb, William Wells Brown, and Solomon Northup. By Gilbert Osofsky. New York: Harper and Row, 1969. [*POM*]

Schuyler, George. *Black No More.* New York: Collier, 1971.

Stowe, Harriet Beecher. *Uncle Tom's Cabin.* New York: Viking, 1982.

Wilson, Harriet. *Our Nig.* New York: Random House, 1983.

By the Rivers of Babylon: Race in the United States

Part One

Michael Omi and Howard Winant

RESURGENT RACIAL CONFLICT IN THE 1980S

LULLED BY A FALSE SENSE of security, many people in the United States took little notice of race in the 1970s. The wave of urban unrest which had swept many cities from 1964 to 1969 had faded from collective memory. "Burn, baby, burn!," once the militant cry of black frustration, had been transformed by the "me decade" into the snappy chorus of a disco number.[1] Racial oppression had hardly vanished, but it was less likely to be seen as contributing to the national malaise. Perhaps those who suggested that race relations in the United States were moving toward enlightenment, progress, and eventual assimilation were right after all. This faith was shortlived.

The myth of steadily improving race relations is being dramatically exposed by the realities of the 1980s. Both mainstream politics and sensational events have underscored the emergence of a "new racism." On a number of fronts the Reagan administration has attempted to roll back the progressive gains of minorities secured over the last several decades. It has reversed the federal government's already tenuous positions on busing and affirmative

This is the first part of a two-part essay. Part 2 will appear in SR 72. Thanks to the following people for their tireless support, helpful comments, and merciless criticisms: Gary Delgado, Jeff Escoffier, Amber Hollibaugh, Michael Kazin, Robby Meeropol, James O'Connor, David Plotke, Juan Carlos Portantiero, Debbie Rogow, Michael Rosenthal, Pam Rosenthal, Paul Scheifer, Nancy Shaw, Jim Shoch, Ron Takaki, and the SR West collective. —M.O & H.W.

action and exhumed the notorious "states' rights" slogan. In addition, it has made unsuccessful bids to block the renewal of the Voting Rights Act and extend federal tax breaks to schools that discriminate against people of color.

The rightward drift of the country as a whole has fostered a "politics of resentment." The expansion of racial minority rights has been seen as "bending over backward" to appease minority demands. Whites are now seen as a disadvantaged majority. Last year, the Association for White Students at Southern Methodist University in Dallas, Texas, became an official student organization with the expressed goal to "promote equality by ending reverse discrimination."[2]

In minority communities fear abounds as a virtual epidemic of racially motivated violence finds among its victims random children, joggers, and the head of the Urban League. But perhaps the most visible warning that a new period of intensified racial conflict has begun is the presence throughout the nation of various orders of the Ku Klux Klan. From the shooting deaths of Communist Workers Party members in Greensboro, North Carolina, to the violent harassment of Vietnamese shrimpers in Texas, to electoral bids in California, Michigan, and North Carolina, the headlines suggest that the Klan is alive, well, and, unfortunately, growing.

M ORE OMINOUS than these more "visible" expressions of racism is the manner in which political discourse increasingly relies on a *racial understanding* by which to comprehend domestic and international issues.

— The current influx of immigrants and refugees from Mexico, Cambodia, Vietnam, Haiti, and Cuba, among other countries, has been met in a climate of scarcity with "fear and loathing" by many Americans. Rising unemployment, scarce housing, and state cutbacks have contributed to a demand for restriction, if not outright exclusion, of immigration on grounds implicitly shaped by racial criteria. A repressive new immigration law, the Simpson-Mazzoli bill, with bipartisan and administrative support is currently being approved.

— Domestic economic woes are blamed on unfair foreign competition — with Japan receiving an inordinate amount of responsibility. National polls show an increase in unfavorable attitudes toward Japan, and Asian Americans are beginning to feel the brunt of this shift in climate. Last year in Detroit, a Chinese American man was beaten to death by a laid-off auto plant foreman and his stepson who mistook their victim for Japanese and blamed him for the loss of their jobs.[3]

—The decline of the American empire, epitomized by the "losses" of Vietnam, Nicaragua, and Iran, has led to a renaissance of national chauvinism. Revived nationalism in the United States contains important ideological elements which view the geopolitical alignments in racial terms.

—Racial conflict is not confined to the white/nonwhite color line. The battle lines have been redrawn as demographic changes and the impoverishing effects of stagflation have exacerbated tensions among racial minorities. In many regions, whites have remained relatively shielded from conflict as Latinos and Asians collide over housing in Denver and blacks and Southeast Asian immigrants fight over social service benefits in San Francisco.[4]

RACIAL CONFLICT and the very meaning of race itself are becoming central political issues in the 1980s. The many newly emerging patterns of racial conflict will differ significantly from those which the nation has experienced in the past. The confrontations and reforms of the 1950s and 1960s altered the manner in which racism had operated, but these transformations were not far-reaching enough to prevent the subsequent reintroduction of various new forms of racism throughout the social fabric. The nature of this new racism will be one of the major topics of this discussion. Since the early 1970s, a reactive restructuring of the American racial order has been in progress; this process affects all major institutions and interacts with every political issue, even those such as sex/gender, nuclear power, or gun control, which seemingly have no "direct" relationship to patterns of racial oppression.

The reconstitution of racial oppression is not simply a matter of policy-making or social engineering. It can be accomplished only by society-wide political struggle. Ideologically and culturally, in the state institutions and the relationships of domination, and at the level of production relationships, a prolonged reappraisal of ideas and reorganization of social practices has been taking place with regard to race. By no means can such a process be centrally planned or controlled. Its outcome cannot be securely predicted, either by those for whom the consolidation of a new racism would be desirable or by those for whom it would be disastrous.

In many respects the reconstitution of racial oppression in the United States is an ideological process. The contemporary right has demonstrated this. The "new right" has sought to mobilize an alliance, based at least partly on race, between traditionally right-wing sectors of the populace on the one hand, and white workers and middle-class groups threatened by inflation, crime, and high taxes on the other. Right-wing ideologue William Rusher conveys the new alignment of political forces sought:

> A new economic division pits the producers—businessmen, hard-hats, manufacturers, blue-collar workers, and farmers—against a new and powerful class of non-producers comprised of a liberal verbalist elite (the dominant media, the major foundations and re-search institutions, the educational establishment, the federal and state bureaucracies) and a semi-permanent welfare constituency, all coexisting happily in a state of mutually sustaining symbiosis.[5]

Although it is presented as a "new class" alignment, we think Rusher's analysis contains a hidden racist appeal. The "semi-permanent welfare constituency" is implicitly nonwhite; the "pro-ducers" are white.* The right, in grafting together issues of race and issues of class, manages to restructure American racial dis-course (the framework of meaning that makes race comprehen-sible to us) in a way that the left is not presently capable of doing. The political agenda here is the containment and rollback of the democratic and egalitarian achievements of the social movements of the 1980s, particularly the black movement. These gains cannot be flatly opposed or easily reversed, but they can be reinterpreted. The concept of "reverse discrimination" is an excellent case in point. This phrase appropriates the demands for "equal opportu-nity" made by the civil rights movement and rearticulates them in a new conservative discourse which appeals to principles of "indi-vidual merit" in the allocation of scarce jobs and resources. No explicit racial discourse need be employed to accomplish this shift, and no specific racial groups need to be targeted, yet the effect of the concept's use is to justify inequality.

---

*Are "liberal verbalists" Jewish? We note many implicit anti-Semitic ele-ments in new-right discourse.

The Left Response

MUCH OF THE LEFT in the United States has been unable to gauge the depth and appeal of a new "racial discourse" that doesn't need to make explicit reference to race. The left often misreads contemporary currents; it is encumbered with dogmatic understandings of what race and racism are, and it lacks the necessary vision to mount effective anti-racist campaigns. Racism is, in fact, endemic to much of the left itself.

Ironically much of the new left's introduction to politics came from participation in civil rights struggles. Many leftists were originally radicalized in the struggle against segregation and Jim Crow arrangements in the South. The subsequent emergence in the late 1960s of "black power" and the call for self-determination for third-world communities in the United States, however, left white leftists in an ambiguous position. Some viewed racial minorities as the "vanguard" of revolutionary struggle in the heart of the empire, and saw their role as a militant support group for "national liberation" struggles not only abroad but at home. Others castigated the "nationalist" aspirations of racial minorities in the face of the more "fundamental" factor of class struggle. Still others lapsed into uneasy silence about racial oppression and sought to devote their political energies to other causes, often unable to confront the racist dynamics that were present in the organizations with which they worked.

Such problems stemmed, fundamentally, from the inability of Marxist theory to grasp the breadth and depth of racial oppression. Marx and Engels believed, along with the other Eurocentrist social thinkers of their time, that the extension of capitalist social relationships would sweep away such "traditional" social distinctions as race and ethnicity. Racial identity was a remnant of the pre-capitalist order, and was expected to decline in importance as the "final conflict" of the two great capitalist classes loomed up. Its persistence, along with other "traditional" categories, has presented orthodox Marxists with major theoretical problems.

THE MARXIST ANALYSIS of race and racism confronts us with a double distortion. First, race is understood as an epiphenomenon or manifestation of class. Race is explained by reference to class and thus *reduced* to an aspect of class struggle. Second, class itself is seen in an economically determinist way. The "base" (the sphere of production) determines the "superstructure." In classical Marxism, the *objective* nature of class relationships (class "in itself") shapes the consciousness and political organization (class "for itself") required to transform society.

From such a standpoint, racism is explained as "false consciousness"—at odds with the "genuine" interests of the working class to unite against the capitalists. In one version of this approach, capitalists are thought to delude workers, creating and sustaining racial antagonisms as part of a "divide and conquer" strategy to keep wages low and the workers' movement disorganized. In another version, racism is seen as the consciousness appropriate to the economic interests of a privileged stratum of workers—the "aristocracy of labor"—whose immediate interests lie in protection of their better-paid and more secure jobs at the expense of competing, lower-priced minority labor. *

Traditional Marxist analyses which explain racial phenomena by reference to economic interests have limited explanatory power. While class-reductionist accounts are not always wrong, it is not possible to argue a certain political strategy's effectiveness in combating racial oppression from an analytical model of economic interests. Nor is it possible to locate the origins of racial categories and meanings in such a model.

This essay explores the dynamics of race and racism in United States society, from a standpoint both conversant with and critical of existing Marxist viewpoints on race. Its perspective has been shaped by two major developments over the last few decades. The first has been the emergence of "new" social movements in the postwar years: movements largely inspired by and following upon the achievements of the black liberation movement. These movements—racial, sexual, gender-based, environmental, anti-militarist—offer new opportunities for the creation and development of oppositional politics in American society. The second development that has inspired our analysis has been the emergence of new perspectives on the meaning of class rooted in the Italian Marxist

---

*In the case of "white skin privilege" or labor-market segmentation arguments, "false consciousness" consists not in being duped by the bosses, but in failing to recognize long-run interests in working-class unity.[6] While this is a more sophisticated variant of the "false consciousness" approach, it suffers from the same limited conception of racial conflict and its origins.

Antonio Gramsci's conception of *hegemony*. This theoretical tool permits a break with economically determinist viewpoints in Marxist analysis, perspectives that have blocked not only left attempts to grapple with race and racism, but have also limited our understanding of the fluidity of class itself.

"NEW" SOCIAL MOVEMENTS

THE BLACK MOVEMENT of the 1950s and 1960s inspired and galvanized a range of "new" social movements which arose in its wake.* By winning reforms, and by challenging sociocultural relationships as racially oppressive, the movement created new political possibilities and new terrains upon which other subordinated groups could more effectively organize. The upsurge of movements based in other racially defined minority communities (Chicano, Indian, Asian-American, etc.), the emergence of a powerful feminist movement, the appearance of gay liberation and anti-war protest, all owe something to the black liberation struggle of those decades. Bernice Reagon has expressed this point forcefully:

> The exciting thing about the Civil Rights Movement is the extent to which it gave participants a glaring analysis of who and where they were in society. ... People who were Spanish-speaking in the Civil Rights Movement, who had been white, when they got back, turned brown. ... Some of the leaders of the anti-war movement were politicized by their work in the Civil Rights Movement; with the question of U.S. involvement in Vietnam, they

---

*In general, these movements were less "new" than reinvigorated. The black liberation struggle is one of the oldest and perhaps the most central of North American popular movements. Since oppression implies resistance, there is (strictly speaking) no such thing as a "new" social movement. We employ this term with reservations to allow us to distinguish the popular movements of the postwar period both from their earlier predecessors (where these existed) and from movements of "the working class," understood in classical Marxist terms as economically based. Beyond this, the "newness" of these movements, even those which had formidable predecessors, seems to us to consist in their ability to confront oppression simultaneously on the individual and collective levels. Self-determination movements among racial minorities, the feminist movement, or gay liberation, to name the most prominent mobilizations, made a political issue out of the racial, gender-based, or sexual experience their members encountered, adding this politicized identity to the older grievances their predecessors had sought to oppose, such as discrimination and prejudice. This politicization of identity, this "positive" re-articulation of "difference," this "collectivization of subjectivity" is what made these social movements "new."

found themselves in a movement that affected all sorts of citizens. Here was a mass struggle that took another cut across the society, across class and race. The movement for students' rights, the women's movement, the gay movement, all offer the same possibility. Nobody will rest because everybody will check out what their position is.[7]

Perhaps the key factor linking these related and simultaneously very disparate causes was their nature as *social* issues. The black movement served as a powerful catalyst because racial oppression was a society-wide problem which could not be confined within traditional political-economic boundaries. Racism was as much an issue of identity and culture as it was an issue of political rights and access to state institutions, or of discrimination in production—or distribution—relations. The black movement drew its strength, furthermore, from a centuries-long legacy of social struggle, which Bernice Reagon describes as "what black people do to stimulate the salvation of this country."[8]

Although the black movement began its postwar phase as a limited struggle against segregation, it soon called into question the basic legitimacy of the entire social order. By questioning the *meaning* of race, not only for blacks, but for everyone, it made a fundamental element of American culture and identity a political issue. Beyond this, the black movement also adapted and developed an array of strategies and tactics by which to assert political demands. Marches and "riots," sit-ins and civil disobedience, freedom rides and voter registration campaigns were among its repertory.

The mounting of an intensive campaign against the unjust and socially pervasive racial order, the elaboration of a varied arsenal of political strategies and tactics with which to oppose this order, and the generalization of this campaign and these forms beyond the black movement to other minorities of various types signaled a significant shift away from the "fundamental" class contradiction of traditional Marxism. As playwright David Edgar has written, the black movement was "the first to create a vocabulary to describe and counter the oppression of groups not solely defined by class." As such, black struggle could serve "as a central organizational fact or as a defining political metaphor and inspiration."[9]

But the originality of these independently constructed vocabularies, the targeting of arenas of conflict located outside those usually associated with class struggle—culture, community, political rights, issues of "reproduction" rather than production relations— was lost on Marxist analysts and socialist organizations. Following a recipe which viewed racism as a consequence of class exploitation, left strategic thinking has narrowly focused on "working-class unity" as an appropriate response to racial oppression. The development of other "new" social movements did little to alter this strategic outlook. With an almost obsessive single-mindedness, leftists have continued to search for the "class basis" and the "revolutionary potential" of these movements; once these are identified, the conventional wisdom runs, it will be possible to "win them over to socialism." Thus the strangest kinds of theoretical gymnastics are practiced in an effort to reconcile these movements, and the oppression they confront, to the supposedly fundamental contradiction between social production and private appropriation. Indeed, in the United States at least, the much-bemoaned "crisis of Marxism" to a large extent results from the inability of class-reductionist politics to articulate the realities of racial, sexual, and other forms of oppression within the terms of Marxist discourse. Class reductionism thus *both* forces Marxist theory into either silence or error in respect to the actual terms of oppression, inequality, and injustice existing in the United States *and* simultaneously repels many politically active persons whose awareness of racism it cannot address, but only distort and deny. [10]

THE RISE OF THE "new" social movements on the postwar political landscape confronts the left with several crucial questions. How may the variegated forms and dimensions of oppression be understood without resorting to class reductionism? How do the movements that have arisen to confront these antidemocratic and inegalitarian dimensions of society find expression in an oppositional politics? How can these movements be linked in a strategy that both confronts the entrenched social order with some degree of coherent opposition, and at the same time affords very disparate groups the autonomy they require to define their collective identities and organize their potential adherents?

The efforts of the black liberation movement (and the other "new" social movements that followed in its wake) to transform the American racial order in the postwar period make possible an important case study in the dynamics of oppositional politics today. They must be considered in light of the current assault from the right on the gains they achieved. Such an examination can begin the process of linking socialist and anti-racist demands on a basis that avoids class reductionism. It can also contribute to a theory of racial conflict in the United States, and set the stage for further work on the "new" social movements.

In the analysis that follows, we argue that race relations have the capacity to shape class relations in the United States. An important concept advanced is that of *racial formation* —the complex process, at once political, economic, and ideological, by which racial meanings are developed and applied, both to individual identities and to institutions. Racial formation is the counterpart of the *class-formation* process suggested in the Gramscian analysis of hegemony. This approach, combined with an appreciation of the potential of the "new" social movements for oppositional politics today, constitutes the two points of departure for the present analysis. It is to the problem of hegemony that we now turn.

CLASS-FORMATION PROCESSES
AND THE PROBLEM OF HEGEMONY

MARXIST ANALYSIS has sought to understand race in terms of class, but not class in terms of race. Our concern with the depth and significance of race in the United States, and the relationship between race and class, has led us to reappraise both traditional Marxist and "neo-Marxist" approaches to class-formation, and to advance an alternative conception.

The Traditional Marxist Approach to Class-Formation

DESPITE MARX'S occasional suggestions to the contrary, perhaps the most venerable orthodoxy in Marxian thought is the economic determination of classes and class relationships. Classes are portrayed as objective entities, groups united by common relationship with the means of production. Their economic conditions appear as given; these conditions set the stage for political and ideological struggle. Successful organization and "correct" consciousness are judged to exist when these correspond to "objective economic conditions." The "subjective" elements of class struggle are brought to bear because a fundamental transformation of economic conditions cannot be achieved in the economic realm itself.

Collective activity and class consciousness (which makes collective action possible for the members of a class) are essential components of class struggle because revolution is a subjective action. It is a political and ideological intervention into objective economic conditions. Class "in-itself" shapes the subjective possibilities for transforming class relations through class "for-itself."

There are two immediate problems with this approach. First, it defines classes solely in terms of economic relationships, thus reducing them to mere locations or positions in the production process. Such an approach says nothing about the actual occupants of these locations, their capacity for organization, or their ideology.[11]

The second problem that limits the traditional view of class-formation is its misunderstanding of economic relationships themselves. Various "subjective" factors must be present in these relationships before human beings can engage in commodity production at all; they must understand themselves as "workers" for example, and they must come to terms with the organization of the workplace. The traditional view suggests that physical proximity and similar treatment of workers will more or less automatically unify them politically and ideologically. Yet even these minimal conditions permit crucial variations. The exercise of authority in the workplace, for example, may take various forms. It may be harsh or benevolent, paternalistic or impersonal. Authority in the workplace manifests the political power of capital. By the same token, self-organization of workers demonstrates the political power of labor. By setting work-rules or employing "counter-planning," workers develop their own "micro-level" power, which attains collective proportions in strikes and factory occupations.

Ideologically, the very meanings of work, authority, discipline, solidarity are contested in every minute of every working day. What consitutes a "worker" is not obvious. As we shall argue below, the very term was historically applied in the United States, until quite recently, to signify "white man." If non-whites cannot join unions, if women are excluded from various job categories, doesn't the ideological self-recognition and social significance of the term "worker" apply only to some producers and not to others?

The Neo-Marxist Approach to Class Formation

O NE DOES NOT often encounter avowedly economic determinist variants of Marxism. Class-formation is usually understood as a complex phenomenon, involving the "relative autonomy" of the political and ideological from the economic. Economic relationships are seen as crucial to issues of organization or consciousness only "in the last instance," and "contradictory class locations" are recognized. This more contemporary set of approaches to class-formation we designate "neo-Marxist." It incorporates a vast literature to which we cannot do justice here. Yet for all the contributions offered by various neo-Marxist analysts, elements of economic determinism persist in their work and render it incapable of examining contemporary struggles in the United States.

While the traditional view understood class relationships as the *direct* rule by the bourgeoisie (an economically defined class) over society at large and particularly over the proletariat (also economically defined), neo-Marxist currents see this rule as *mediated* in a variety of ways. Economically defined classes are considered still to exist, and through their relationships to structure society, but greater complexity is recognized in these relationships. Mediation may take place:

—Through contradictions in the social psychology of collectivity, which limit the capacity of subordinated classes to confront their oppression and exploitation.[12]

—Through science and technology, which outrun the political, cultural, and perhaps even biological capacities of society to control them.[13]

—Through commodification of culture, which confronts subordinated classes with deformed and manipulative versions of their "true" needs, fostering class compromise and consolidating continuing exploitation.[14]

—Through subaltern groups, or whole new classes, which emerge to take advantage of new production relationships, altering the terms of class struggle and vacillating among the fundamental classes.[15]

While such approaches are more attentive to contemporary realities and more aptly describe class relationships than the classical approach, they are nevertheless insufficient because they begin with the traditional, economically determined class categories, which they augment, but do not fundamentally question. The mediating processes are presented as supplementary new data, which overlap the basic, structured-in conflict.

The "Hegemony" Approach to Class-Formation

VALUABLE INSIGHTS into the relationship between popular struggles and class-formation are emerging from the legacy of Antonio Gramsci, the Italian Communist theorist whose major work was done in Mussolini's prisons. Such analysts as Ernesto Laclau, Christine Buci-Glucksmann, Chantal Mouffe, Adam Prze-worski, and Nicos Poulantzas (particularly in his later works) offer a new perspective on class-formation based on Gramsci's notion of *hegemony*.[16]

Hegemony is the thoroughgoing organization of society on behalf of a class which has gained the adherence of subordinate as well as dominant sectors and groups. Often summarized as rule by means of a combination of coercion and consent, hegemony is better understood as the creation of a collective popular will by what Gramsci calls "intellectual and moral leadership."[17] The exercise of hegemony extends beyond the mere dissemination of "ruling-class" ideas and values. It includes the capacity to define, through a vast array of channels (including the basic structures of economic, political, and cultural life) the terms and meanings by which people understand themselves and their world.

From this perspective class-formation processes continually shape and reshape classes. Classes are not economically determined. Instead they are understood as (1) *multiply determined,* (2) *historical actors,* themselves the (3) *effects of the social struggles* in which they are formed:

1. *Multiple determination:* Political and ideological factors are recognized to constitute classes in combination with economic ones. Once the political and ideological have been released from the iron grip of the economic, the interpenetration of the three types of ·relationships in the concrete can be seen as a complex one. It is not possible to distinguish the economic, political, and ideological "instances" or "moments" of concrete social relationships except analytically. Even production is a fully political and ideological relationship.

2. *Historical actors:* Class relationships are never given, objective, or obvious; rather they are ongoing processes of historical conflict whose participants and outcomes are contingent. Classes are continually being created, transformed, and destroyed—organized and disorganized. Their memberships are not pre-given but to a certain extent self-selected, depending upon the particular social struggles in which the class is engaged, and its ability to link its collective interests with that of potential members.

3. *Effects of struggles:* "Class formation is an effect of the totality of struggles which organize the same people as class members, as members of collectivities defined in other terms, [or] simply as members of 'the society.'"[18] It is *never* correct to attribute an "appropriate" consciousness or political organization to a given group simply on the basis of its economic location in society. The recognition that classes are effects of struggles grasps a reality that traditional and neo-Marxist theories of class-formation usually miss: each social group *interprets its own interest,* and is therefore subject to competing efforts to organize it and define its role in social struggle.

FROM SUCH A PERSPECTIVE, classes may be understood as *political projects.* At any given historical moment, different projects are being implemented by forces seeking to organize particular classes, to interpret their interests, and to (re-)define their role in production relations. The working class Eugene Debs sought to create in 1912 was not the working class Samuel Gompers sought to create. Alternative and competing efforts to identify and organize classes necessarily confront each other, as individuals and groups seek to understand their interests and conditions, and to act upon those understandings.

Beginning with the competing projects of various oppositional groups, the class-formation process continues with the consolidation of such groups into an oppositional or counter-hegemonic bloc. The collective subjectivity of a class can only be attained when an integrative or *articulating principle* is developed to link the various groupings constituting the bloc.*

---

*By way of example, we might say that the principle of *equivalent exchange* played this role in the consolidation of capitalist opposition to feudalism, or that the Marxian value theory articulated the interests of socialist oppositional groups in the nineteenth century. Before the emergence of such an

Hegemony, then, is only the end result of an epochal process in which a class project has been elaborated, consolidated, and finally (as a result of thoroughgoing contest) diffused throughout society. At this point the collective subjectivity or ideology of the hegemonic class appears to the members of the society as "the way things are" or "common sense." This is the point at which a class has not only created itself, but has shaped society in its own image. Such a class must have previously passed through a complex gestation during which various class "projects" were developed in opposition to a pre-existing hegemonic order. These projects—competing modes of organization and strategy, differing conceptions of "we" and "they," experiments in discursive linking of the major national and cultural themes of society in the class's world view—were proposed, fought over, and tested in practice.

The hegemonic perspective on class-formation does not require us to reject economic determination *tout court*. It does not suggest that economic relationships are nonexistent or that locations in the production process cannot be identified. It insists, however, that such locations are occupied by human subjects who are historically produced, live in ideology, and engage in political practice. They are not blank slates upon which the economic position in which they find themselves will simply inscribe a fate. Nor can any organization or leadership presume to dictate, from its understanding of their "objective" role in society, their proper interests or "correct" consciousness.

There is always a concrete historical process by which various social groupings move from isolated opposition, through oppositional bloc to counter-hegemonic class, and finally to hegemony.

"articulating principle," opposition to the hegemonic order of course exists, but in a more diffuse form. It should be stressed that in Gramsci the articulating principle is ideological, even philosophical, in nature: "Critical understanding of self takes place therefore through a struggle of political 'hegemonies' and of opposing directions, first in the ethical field and then in that of politics proper, in order to arrive at the working out at a higher level of one's own conception of reality. Consciousness of being part of a particular hegemonic force (that is to say, political consciousness) is the first stage towards a progressive self-consciousness in which theory and practice will finally be one. Thus the unity of theory and practice is not just a matter of mechanical fact, but a part of the historical process, whose elementary and primitive phase is to be found in the sense of being 'different' and 'apart,' in an instinctive feeling of independence, and which progresses to the level of real possession of a single and coherent conception of the world." [19]

This process is marked by two features that distinguish it radically from classical and neo–Marxist accounts of class-formation. First, every stage of the process is *contingent*. Objective conditions, including the economic situations of various oppositional groups, the political strategies and organizational resources available to them, their ability to identify their interests in sufficiently unified and accessible terms, etc.—combine with subjective and contingent ones, including even luck, audacity, and error, to advance the class-formation project.

Second, there is a great deal of flexibility in the *sources* of opposition. It does not necessarily spring from a core of the most exploited, or from those located nearest to the heart of production processes. Nor from disaffected intellectuals. Sheila Rowbotham has demonstrated the crucial role of women in leading upsurges of social opposition.[20] Herbert Gutman has shown the importance of displaced culturally-rooted and traditional groups, in reacting to the processes of industrialization and modernization.[21] Such forces can be characterized with regard to their participants, programs, or interests at a given historical point, but they are *not fundamentally and irrevocably grouped around an economically defined "class."* The importance of this insight for a study of the role of anti-racist struggle in the modern-day United States cannot be exaggerated.

RACIAL FORMATION

> Until the color of a man's skin
> Is of no more significance
> Than the color of his eyes
> Everywhere is war...
>
> — *Bob Marley*[22]

What Is Race?

S PURRED ON by the classificatory schemes of living organisms devised by Linnaeus, many scholars in the eighteenth and nineteenth centuries were consumed with discerning and ranking the variations in humankind. Race was thought of as a *biological* concept, yet its precise definition was the subject of continual debate. From Dr. Morton's studies of cranial capacity to contemporary efforts to link race with shared gene pools, the concept of race has defied biological definition. Even today the question of *how many* races there are elicits a range of popular responses.[23]

Within the social sciences, race is generally regarded as a *social* as opposed to biological concept. We share this view. Race is a sociohistorical construct which is neither objective nor static. It is a multidimensional complex of social meanings, subjectivities, practices, and institutions organized around the question of human physical characteristics. Race is constantly being reinterpreted and recreated.

Examples of the diversity of racial meanings abound:

—In the United States, the black/white color line has been rigidly defined and enforced. White was considered a pure category— any black parentage made one black. Elizabeth Taylor in *Raintree County* describes the worst of fates to befall whites as "havin' a little Negra blood in ya'—just one little teeny drop and a person's all Negra."[24]

—By contrast, Brazil has had less rigid conceptions and a variety of "intermediate" racial categories exist. Marvin Harris suggests that this difference sprang from the employment of *hypodescent* as a mechanism of racial identity in the United States. Hypodescent means affiliation with the subordinate (in a societal hierarchy) rather than dominant group. No such rigid descent rule characterizes racial identity in many Latin American societies. As Harris notes, "One of the most striking consequences of the Brazilian system of racial identification is that parents and children and even brothers and sisters are frequently accepted as representatives of quite opposite racial types."[25]

—Contradictions abound in what is considered to be the country with the most rigidly defined racial categories, South Africa. The apartheid system considers Chinese as "Asians" while the Japanese are accorded the status of "honorary whites." A race classification agency is employed to adjudicate claims (particularly among the mulatto or "colored" category) for upgrading of official racial identity.[26]

RACIAL CATEGORIES also vary between different societies and historically within a given society. The term "black" in the United States at different times and places has referred variously to non- or semi-human chattels or to the "vanguard of the proletariat" (in certain left-wing analyses). In Britain today, the term "black" is beginning to connote all non-whites, since Asian as well as Afro-Caribbean youth are adopting it as an expression of self-identity.[27]

The various meanings of "black" illustrate that the content of racial categories is shaped politically. The meaning of race is defined and contested throughout society, in both collective and personal practice. In the process, racial categories themselves are formed, destroyed, and re-formed.

An important part of this process is social-scientific. Since the way that race is understood theoretically has great impact on law, policy, and custom, the academic disciplines that have studied the subject might be expected to have been especially sensitive to the complexity and malleability of racial formation processes.

In reality, nearly the opposite is true. Almost every approach neglects to consider racial formation as a continuous process. There is thus a vast failure to consider not only how the meaning of race is formed and transformed, but also how racially defined individuals, collectivities, and institutions encounter racial categories, either accepting or opposing them, and thus act to shape the meaning of race themselves. Race is usually seen as a static entity, a given, even if the theory in question might abstractly recognize the possibility of the transformation of racial categories over time.

This critical error leads to all sorts of interesting but extremely fragmentary approaches, in which race is treated as an objective fact. Economists, for example, look for the quantitative rewards afforded to employers of various racially defined strata of workers as a result of racial segmentation of the labor market.[28] They rarely consider the means by which the system of rewards is politically organized or ideologically articulated.

Political scientists investigate racial issues in a related manner, looking for the power-potentials achieved by various racially defined interests (understood unselfconsciously as so many interest-groups, elites, or even class fractions) explicitly or implicitly seeking to achieve their objectives through state institutions.[29] Infrequently considered are the criteria (often economic determinist) by which interests are imputed to various racial groupings, the effects registered on racial categories and racial-formation process of the various conflicts studied, or the often contradictory patterns of accommodation and resistance adopted by different state institutions in response to racially oriented political demands.[30]

Cultural criticism too has often dealt with race as a fixed category. Analyses have focused in general on the psychological interpretation of aspects of the cultural lives of racially defined minority groups which appeared to deviate from the presumed white norm. Account has not been taken of the ways in which minority cultures have remained flexible and adaptive, both in their capacity to carry on traditions of resistance to subjection along racial lines, and in their responsiveness to shifting demands made upon group members by the majority culture.[31] As we have argued, the very *meaning* of race varies with the relationships in which it is embedded and through which it is perceived.

The Process of Racial Formation

IN THE UNITED STATES, the existence of racial identity and of a racist social order is a historical fact dating from the initiation of European colonization. Every individual and social group, regardless of the contradictions or difficulties involved, and irrespective of the particular historical period in which relationships between that individual or group and the American racial order are examined, has been assigned to and maintained in a racial category: white, red, yellow, brown, and black.[32]

Racial classification is a matter of *identity*. One of the first things we notice about people (along with their sex) is their race. We utilize race to provide clues about *who* a person is and to suggest how we should relate to him or her. This fact is made painfully obvious when we encounter someone whom we cannot conveniently categorize racially. Such an encounter becomes a source of discomfort and momentarily, a crisis of racial meaning. People in our culture need to clarify *who* people are in racial terms. Without a racial identity, one is in danger of having no identity.

"Racial etiquette" encompasses the micro-level rules that govern our perception of race in a comprehensively racial society. This etiquette is quintessentially ideological in that it is fully learned, without obvious teaching, by everybody. It beomes "common sense." Racial beliefs operate as an "amateur biology," a way of explaining the variations in "human nature."[33]

79

Simultaneously, racial classification is *institutionalized*. From the micro-level of individual racial identity to the macro-level of collective racial identity and conflict on the terrain of the state, a seamless continuum of racial meanings pervades society. Every institution in the United States is a *racial* institution. The churches, scientific organizations, the trade unions, etc. — all helped to define and shape, and have been shaped by, racial practices. Since a racial order is a political order, an understanding of the development and character of the racial order of American society requires an approach to the *state* as the focus of racial contradictions over historical time.

Racial categories and racial conflict do not confront the human beings who must live them out as mere blind necessities. Individually and collectively, we struggle to understand (or not to understand), to accept or reject, to strengthen or to undermine, the definitions and social structures within which we discover ourselves.

Racial formation has proceeded in the United States by means of a complex interplay among these elements. It should be understood as a *process*: (1) through which an unstable and contradictory set of social practices and beliefs are articulated in an ideology based fundamentally on race; (2) through which the particular ideology thus generated is enforced by a system of racial subjection having both institutional and individual means of reproduction at its disposal; and (3) through which new instabilities and contradictions emerge at a subsequent historical point and challenge the pre-existing system once more. Racial formation processes have interpenetrated with class-formation processes in ways that have profoundly shaped the nature of political discourse and struggle in the United States.

Racial Discourse

P ERHAPS THE MOST IMPORTANT feature of this approach is its concept of ideology. Racial ideology, as much as that of class or nation, must be constructed from pre-existing ideological elements. This is a task that cannot be carried out all at once, but requires a period of time in which competing discourses, competing projects seeking to articulate similar ideological elements differently, must be struggled with and overcome.

We employ the term "racialization" to signify the extension of racial meaning to a previously racially unclassified relationship, social practice, or group. For the present, we concentrate on the creation of existing American racial *groups* over time.

The racialization process is filled with incongruities and contradictions, and varies enormously. Historically speaking, before the Civil War substantial tendencies existed that sought the classification of Southern Europeans, the Irish, and the Jews among "nonwhite" categories. This brand of nativism was only effectively curbed by the institutionalization of a racial order that drew the color line around, rather than within, Europe. By stopping short of racializing immigrants from Europe after the Civil War, by allowing their assimilation (although not without having "paid some dues" at the bottom of the free labor force first, of course), the American racial order was reconsolidated in the wake of the tremendous challenge placed before it by the abolition of racial slavery. Reconstruction was ended in 1877, and an effective set of tools for limiting the emergent class struggles of the later nineteenth century was forged: the definition of the working class *in racial terms* — as "white." This was not accomplished by any decree but rather by white workers themselves. Many of them were recent immigrants, who organized on racial lines as much as on traditionally defined class lines. In California, for example, 1877 began a period of fierce racial struggle. In that year, white workers in San Francisco rioted and attacked the Chinese quarter of the city, burning laundries, killing any Chinese they could catch, and demanding the exclusion of Asian immigrants from the West Coast.[34]

Racial formation processes are adaptive. Historically, a variety of previously racially undefined groups have required categorization to situate them within the prevailing racial order.

In the United States, the racial category of "black" evolved with the consolidation of racial slavery. By the end of the seventeenth century, Africans, whose specific identity was Ibo, Yoruba, Dahomeyan, etc., were rendered "black" by an ideology of exploitation based on racial logic. Similarly, Native Americans were forged into "Indians" or the "red man" from Cherokee, Seminole, Sioux, etc., people.

Throughout the nineteenth century, state and federal legal arrangements recognized only three racial categories: "white," "Negro," and "Indian." In California, the influx of Chinese and the debates surrounding the legal status of Mexicans provoked a brief juridical crisis of racial definition. California attempted to resolve this dilemma by assigning Mexicans and Chinese to categories within the already existing framework of "legally defined" racial groups. In the wake of the Treaty of Guadalupe Hidalgo (1848), Mexicans were defined as a "white" population and accorded the political-legal status of "free white persons." By contrast, the California Supreme Court ruled in *People v. Hall* (1854) that Chinese should be considered "Indian" and denied the political rights accorded to whites.[35]

A vast range of similar examples could be cited. There is simply no racial order or set of racial categories that comes into being without a complex process of societal struggle, or without the ransacking of pre-existing ideologies and discursive systems for materials which can be invoked to service the "new" racial understanding. Religion, science, nationality, language, art, economics, politics, and the law all contribute to the development of ideology.

R ACIALIZATION CONTINUES today as subtle re-classification procedures operate to adjust the racial "common sense" of society to anomalous or threatening realities. It is often possible to take the racial "blood pressure" of American society by monitoring these events. For example, a new surge of anti-Japanese sentiment is noticeable, spurred on no doubt by economic competition. Iranians have been assigned to the Arab category (itself racially ambiguous but certainly a "non-white" one) in the wake of the hostage affair. This is an irony not lost on Iranians, who, far from being Arabs, have an Arab minority in their native country! Other examples abound. With rising anti-immigrant sentiment abroad in the land, Latin Americans find themselves classified as Latinos (i.e., "brown"), even those who could be considered *Ladino* (i.e., "white") in their home countries. Determinants here include language: Spanish is the language of a racially defined minority; ergo, Spanish-speakers are racialized. Not even Castilians are exempt.

Obviously, racialization is not solely imposed by the state or by dominant social groups. Racial self-definition is an important factor in forging minority collectivity. For example, such categories as "Asian American" and "La Raza" appeared in the sixties proclaiming a new understanding on the part of former "ethnic groups" (e.g., Chinese Americans and Japanese Americans) of their shared *racial* identity.

The Hegemonic Racial Order

WE HAVE SUGGESTED that the racial order simultaneously affects identity and social structure. Every individual is subjected to the particular racial order that obtains during the historical period in which he or she lives, and has a racial identity constructed for him or herself, whether the individual accepts this identity or not.[36] Furthermore, every individual is steeped in the rules governing interpersonal racial relations and recognition of racial characteristics in others. These rules are not codified but are micro-social aspects of the "presentation of self." They are essential elements of racial ideology.

At the level of social structure, race is present in all collective relationships. In each historical period the *shape* of American society has had a distinctly racial pattern, discernible in production relations, laws, political organization, residential patterns, religion, cultural life, and all other aspects of social reproduction. Since the earliest days of the colonial system in North America, a pre-existing racial ideology has served to link the identity of the individual to the racially ordered social structure.

The dominant or hegemonic racial ideology is never objective or natural. It is an adaptation of that which preceded it, an accommodation of knowledge and interest, a grab-bag of ideological elements drawn from a vast variety of different sources, articulated politically and subject to competition from competing sources. Racial ideology, as we have said, is a *political project.*

How is the system of racial subjection secured against challenges? There are several aspects to this answer. Clearly racial subjection has been more monolithic, more absolute, at some historical periods than it has at others. Where political opposition was banned or useless, as it was for slaves in the South and for Native Americans during much of the course of American history, transformation of the racial order, or resistance to it, was perforce military (or perhaps took economic forms such as sabotage). A competing racial discourse requires some space, some available ideological elements, upon which to fasten in order to do its work of constituting alternative institutions and developing new racial subjects.

But even at its most oppressive, the American racial order was unable to arrogate to itself the entire capacity for production of racial ideology, of racial subjects. As scholars such as George Rawick and Herbert Gutman have shown, black slaves developed cultures of resistance based on music, religion, African traditions, and family ties, through which they sustained their own ideological project: the development of a free black identity and a collectivity dedicated to liberation.[37] Roxanne Dunbar Ortiz notes in a recent article in these pages how the examples of Geronimo, Sitting Bull, and other resistance leaders of the Native peoples were passed down to children as examples of resistance, andd how the Native American Church and the Ghost Dance were employed by particular generations of Indian people to maintain a resistance culture.[38] Rodolfo Acuña has pointed out how the same "bandits" against whom Anglo vigilantes mounted expeditions after Guadalupe-Hidalgo—Tiburcio Vasquez, Joaquín Murieta—became heroes in the Mexicano communities of the Southwest, remembered in folktales and celebrated in *corridos*.[39] We do not recite these examples to romanticize brutal repression or to give the air of revolutionary struggle to what were often grim defeats; we simply seek to affirm that even in the most uncontested periods of American racism, oppositional cultures were able, often at very great cost, to maintain themselves.

Without reviewing the vast history of racial conflict in the United States to determine how precisely challenges were deflected or incorporated, it is still possible to make some general statements about the manner in which the racial order is consolidated. Gramsci's distinction between "war of maneuver" and "war of position" will prove useful here. An additional element with which we must reckon, if only briefly, is the enforcement of the racial order by the state.

FOR MUCH OF American history, no political legitimacy was conceded to alternative racial discourses, competing racially defined political projects. The absence of democratic rights, of property, of political *space* within civil society forced racially defined opposition both outward and inward, away from the public sphere. Slaves who ran away, who took part in the subversive operations of the underground railway, who formed communities in woods and swamps; Indians who made war on the United States in defense of their land; Chinese and Filipinos who drew together in Chinatowns and Manilatowns to gain some measure of collective control over their existence—these exemplify the movement of racial opposition outward, away from a political engagement within the hegemonic racial order.

These same slaves, Indians, Asians (and many others), having been driven out of the dominant political framework and relegated to a supposedly permanently inferior sociocultural status, were forced inward upon themselves as individuals, families, and communities. The tremendous cultural resources nurtured among such communities, the enormous labors required under such conditions to survive and still further to develop elements of an alternative society, can best be understood as combining with the continuous violent resistance ("riots," etc.) which characterized these periods to constitute a racial *war of maneuver.*

However democratic the United States may have been in other respects (and it is clear that democracy was in short supply until rather recently), with respect to racial minorities it may be characterized as having been to varying degrees *despotic* for much of its history. War of maneuver, in which the subordinated groups seek to defend their territory from violent assault, as well as to develop their internal society as an alternative to the repressive social system they confront, accurately characterizes the situation of American minority communities during the repressive periods which predominate in American racial history.

More recent history suggests that war of maneuver is being replaced by *war of position* as racially defined minorities achieve political gains within the hegemonic racial order. (The contemporary configuration of racial politics is a major subject later in this essay, so our treatment here will be very brief.) Prepared in large measure by the practices undertaken in conditions of war of maneuver, minority communities were able to make sustained strategic interventions within the mainstream political process beginning with World War II. As we have noted, the black movement for a variety of historical reasons provided leadership in confronting the dominant racial order, mobilizing in the electoral sphere (and demanding the extension of the elementary democratic right of the vote to areas of the country where it was still denied), mounting marches and demonstrations, making use of the judicial system, and harking back to precedents set in those brief historical moments such as Reconstruction when racial despotism had been briefly ameliorated.

A strategy of *war of position* can only be predicated on political struggle—on the existence of institutional and ideological terrain upon which competing projects can be mounted in the face of a hegemonic order. The postwawr black movement, later joined by other racially based minority movements, has sought by a strategy of war of position to transform the dominant racial ideology in the United States, to rearticulate its elements in a more egalitarian and democratic discourse. It has also sought to confront the manner in which state institutions enforce the pre-existing system of racial categories and practices.

The Racial State

R ACE ESTABLISHES the identity of human subjects, it structures social conflict and social cohesion, and it is deeply woven into every aspect of existence. Historically and contemporarily, racial categories have been determined and enforced by the state. The Naturalization Law of 1790, Congress's first attempt to define American citizenship, declared that only free "white" immigrants would be eligible. Japanese could become naturalized citizens only after the passage of the Walter-McCarran act of 1952. *

Whereas the meaning of race has been contested historically through religious and scientific debates, modern disputes occur in the political realm. For example, the question of what is race can become a juridical issue. This past year, Susie Guillory Phipps unsuccessfully sued the Louisiana Bureau of Vital Records to change the racial classification on her birth certificate from black to white. The descendant of an eighteenth-century black slave and white planter, Phipps was subject to the 1970 state law which said that anyone with 1/32 "Negro blood" can be legally classified as black.[40]

Even the census is racially contradictory. Latinos were included in the census as a racial category in 1930 and surfaced as an ethnic

---

*The ideological residue of these restrictions is the popular equation of "American" with "white."

category, "Persons of Spanish Mother Tongue," in 1950 and 1960. In 1970 they appeared as "Persons of Both Spanish Surname and Spanish Mother Tongue," and in 1980 the "Hispanic" category was created.[41] Such attempts betray institutional noncomprehension of the underlying meaning of race. They also reflect the struggles through which particular racially defined groups have pressed their demands for recognition and equality and the state's efforts to manage and manipulate those demands.[42]

The state is indeed the focus of collective demands both for egalitarian and democratic reforms and for the enforcement of existing privileges. The state "intervenes" in racial conflicts, yet it does not do so in a coherent or unified manner. Distinct state institutions often act in a contradictory fashion. Concurrent with the passage of anti-racist legislation and the handing down of judicial decisions prohibiting racial discrimination in the fifties and sixties, other branches of the federal government pursued welfare and urban redevelopment policies that worked to the disadvantage of racial minorities.

It is tempting to see the state as clumsily trying to capture, steer, or organize the realities of racial identity and racial conflict. The notion of a racially interventionist state contains a measure of truth since clearly the state does organize the racial order—it does systematize and operationalize concepts of racial discrimination, for example. Yet this approach implies a state that is not inherently racial, since it is intervening in race relations from *outside* them. Such a state appears open to democratizing demands.

In contrast to this, we suggest that the state *is* inherently racial. Like the society it organizes, the state has been from its foundation penetrated and shaped by racial elements. Every state institution is a racial institution; the United States Constitution (as is well known) is a racial document. Far from *intervening* in racial conflicts, the state is itself increasingly the pre-eminent site of racial conflict. A more accurate model of the racial state, then, would depict a network of state institutions, each linked by history, mandate, internal composition, and constituency to the racial order existing in the United States at the historical point under consideration. ★

★Racial categories, conflicts, and policies may thus be understood as occupying varying degrees of centrality in different state institutions and at different historical moments. The HUD department, for example, forced to deal with

Such a model, we suggest, accounts far better than the "interventionist" one for the variations in the racial character of different state institutions, as well as for the changes in specific institutions' racial policies and activities over historical time. It suggests that state institutions and programs address particular demands as part of an overall political *trajectory*. Conflicts and demands that were previously ignored or asserted to be *outside* the proper realm of state activity are redefined as occurring *within* a given institution's mandate; new politics are developed and some demands are met as a new (temporary) equilibrium is sought; gradually the new equilibrium becomes part of the established order and is revealed to contain new conflicts as new demands are placed upon the state institutions and programs that maintain it.

The racial order has become much more of a terrain of political struggle in the past few decades; there has been a shift toward "war of position." Previously, racial domination was enforced with less recourse to state activity: through terrorism and vigilantism, but also through oppressive custom and by simple, openly discriminatory state policy, such as Jim Crow laws and poll taxes. *

---

questions of residential segregation, urban development processes, housing subsidization programs, and the like, staffed by numerous minority-group members, and subject to constituent pressures from lobbies, community groups, and local and state governments, many of which address racial issues or are organized along racial lines, will presumably be more racially oriented than, say, the National Science Foundation, where staffing along professional/academic lines, a technical mandate, and a politically more limited range of constituents would presumably limit the racial agenda somewhat. Nevertheless, in certain areas (e.g., hiring policies, funding priorities, positions taken in respect to racially oriented scientific disputes — does Shockley get a grant?) the NSF too is a racial institution.

*Increased state activity in the area of race since World War II has not meant the elimination of racially oriented custom, obviously. There remains the vast area of the "micro-politics" of race (which we have discussed in terms of racial "etiquette," subjectivity, etc.), which state activity can affect only in limited and crude fashion. Nevertheless, the autonomy of racial life from the state appears to be decreasing, particularly as policies oriented toward reproduction — such as communications, education, health care, and social programs — are becoming areas of racial contest.

Race and Class

OUR CONCEPTION OF racial formation has stressed the political, ideological, and economic determinants of race which find expression not only in various institutional arrangements, but in the very way we live, love, breathe, and think. Such a conception is drawn from the emerging theoretical literature on class formation processes which has prompted both a re-evaluation of the concept of class and a reassessment of traditional notions of class politics. A re-examination of class and racial dynamics is crucial to fathoming current American political realities. The interpenetration of race and class needs to be considered.

In the modern world, race and class appear nearly synonymous in some societies (e.g., South Africa) while in others they seem to exist as separate axes of stratification as well as cultural and political organization (e.g., the United States). Race and class are complexly structured relationships that are given concrete meaning only by specific political projects. Race and class: (1) exist with some degree of autonomy; (2) are subject to enormous variations over time; and (3) are capable in certain historical moments of encompassing one another.

Central to our conception of race and class as evolving sets of social relationships is the notion that non-economic, non-accumulation-based factors such as ideology, organization, and strategy are crucial to the formation of both races and classes. Such political and ideological factors are not the mere reflections of objectively determined "material" (i.e., economic) interests, but are themselves forces shaping the very definition of interests. In other words, as opposed to viewing these factors as being determined by the economic location of a race or class, we assert that such factors may be crucial to establishing the economic location itself.

In the United States, capitalist development created races as well as classes. African slavery set a racially based understanding of society in motion which resulted in the shaping of a specific *racial* identity not only for the slaves, but for the European settlers as well. Winthrop Jordan has observed:

> From the initially common term *Christian,* at mid-century there was a marked shift toward the terms *English* and *free.* After about 1680, taking the colonies as a whole, a new term of self-identification appeared — *white.*[43]

The consolidation of racial slavery structured the class system as much as the class system determined the racial order.

T HE SELF-CONSCIOUS ORGANIZATION of the working class in the nineteenth century was to a large degree a *racial* as much as a class project. The legacy of racial arrangements and conflicts shaped the definition of interests and in turn led to the consolidation of institutional patterns (e.g., segregated unions, dual labor markets, exclusionary legislation) which perpetuated the color line within the working class. Alexander Saxton has noted that:

> North Americans of European background have experienced three great racial confrontations: with the Indian, with the African, and with the Oriental. Central to each transaction has been a totally one-sided preponderance of power, exerted for the exploitation of nonwhites by the dominant white society. In each case (but especially in the two that began with systems of enforced labor), white workingmen have played a crucial, yet ambivalent, role. They have been both exploited and exploiters. On the one hand, thrown into competition with nonwhites as enslaved or "cheap" labor, they suffered economically; on the other hand, being white, they benefited by that very exploitation which was compelling the nonwhites to work for low wages or for nothing. Ideologically they were drawn in opposite directions. *Racial identification cut at right angles to class consciousness.*[44]

One cannot always objectively determine or disaggregate the class and racial dimensions of a specific conflict. The very *terms* of political struggle are contested by the participants themselves.

Japanese plantation laborers striking against the Hawaiian Sugar Planters Association (HSPA) in 1920 characterized their struggle as a *class conflict* and attempted to forge a class coalition with Filipino workers. Their labor organization, the Japanese Federation, changed its name to the Hawaii Laborers Association and its programs and slogans reflected the class character of its demands. The HSPA characterized the conflict as a *racial* one, emphasizing that the Japanese were seeking the political and economic domination of the islands.[45]

In such a struggle, competing projects seek to organize people along distinct lines by appealing to their interests in racial and/or class terms. Consequently, the strike could simultaneously be portrayed by its participants as labor versus capital or as white versus nonwhite.

R ACIAL CATEGORIES create political subjects. One is not merely
a worker, one is also white; one is not only Chicano, one is
equally a worker. In the history of the United States, race has not
merely been an impediment to the development of working-class
consciousness. It has also shaped it. Sectors of the left historically
and contemporarily have attempted to get racial "false consciousness" out of the way so that the "real" revolutionary project, the
organization of the proletariat and its confrontation with the bourgeoisie, can begin. Such a perspective fails to grasp that the very
nature and composition of the working class has been shaped by
racial projects. In his assessment of the politics of the labor movement Selig Perlman notes that:

> The political issue after 1877 was racial, not financial, and the
> weapon was not merely the ballot, but also 'direct action' — vio-
> lence. The anti-Chinese agitation in California, culminating as it
> did in the Exclusion Law passed by Congress in 1882, was doubt-
> less the most important single factor in the history of American
> labor, for without it the entire country might have been overrun
> by Mongolian [sic] labor and the labor movement might have
> become a conflict of races instead of one of classes.[46]

The conception of race and class as relationships shaped by political projects is crucial to understanding the historical development
of American politics and political discourse. It is just as crucial, we
maintain, for an understanding of contemporary politics. The profound changes brought about by racially based movements in the
post-World War II period are currently being contested forcefully.
The shape of the American racial order and, in important ways,
of capitalism in the United States hangs in the balance as these
struggles are fought out. In Part Two of this article we will spell
out the political implications of our approach to race.

REFERENCES

1 The Trammps, "Disco Inferno," *Saturday Night Fever*, RSO Records, RS-2-
  4001, 1977.
2 *San Francisco Chronicle*, 14 October 1982.
3 The incident further outraged Asian American communities when Wayne
  County Circuit Court Judge Charles Kaufman allowed the two men to
  plead guilty to manslaughter (the original charge had been second-degree
  murder), placed them on three years' probation, and fined them $3,780
  each.
4 Michael Omi, "New Wave Dread: Immigration and Intra-Third-World
  Conflict," *Socialist Review* no. 60 (vol. 11, no. 6; November-December
  1981), pp. 77-87.

5 William Rusher, *The Making of a New Majority Party* (Ottawa, Ill. : Greenhill Publications, 1975), p. 31.

6 See Michael Reich, *Racial Inequality, Economic Theory, and Class Conflict* (Princeton: Princeton University Press, 1980).

7 Interview with Bernice Reagon in Dick Cluster, ed., *They Should Have Served That Cup of Coffee* (Boston: South End Press, 1979), pp. 35-36.

8 Ibid., p. 37.

9 David Edgar, "Reagan's Hidden Agenda: Racism and the New Right," *Race and Class,* vol. 22, no. 3 (Winter 1981), pp. 221-222.

10 Of course many socialists will still be found in the ranks of minority-based groups (and in feminist organizations, gay groups, and others as well). On occasion, they may even be the leading members. But the appropriateness of the class-reductionist perspective is not proved by this fact. How many more minority activists will have nothing to do with Marxism because of its fundamental orientation to class?

11 The "in itself/for itself" distinction is therefore essential to the conception of a "vanguard." Because the mere economic location of class members provides insufficient means for identifying the appropriate strategic, organizational, and ideological orientation for the class, this task falls to the party and to "theory."

12 Jean-Paul Sartre, *Critique of Dialectical Reason* (London: New Left Books, 1976).

13 Herbert Marcuse, *One-Dimensional Man* (Boston: Beacon Press, 1964); Marcuse, *An Essay on Liberation* (Boston: Beacon Press, 1968); E. P. Thompson, "Notes on Exterminism, the Last Stage of Civilization," *New Left Review* no. 121 (May-June 1980).

14 Henri Lefebvre, *Everyday Life in the Modern World* (New York: Harper & Row, 1971); Stanley Aronowitz, *False Promises* (New York: McGraw-Hill, 1973); Werner Sombart, *Why Is There No Socialism in the United States?* (White Plains, N.Y.: M. E. Sharpe, 1976 [1906]).

15 John and Barbara Ehrenreich, "The Professional-Managerial Class," in Pat Walker, ed., *Between Labor and Capital* (Boston: South End Press, 1979); Fred Block, "The Ruling Class Does Not Rule: Notes on the Marxist Theory of the State," *Socialist Revolution* no. 33 (vol. 7, no. 3; May-June 1977); Block, "Beyond Relative Autonomy: State Managers as Historical Subjects," *New Political Science* no. 7 (Winter 1981); Erik Olin Wright, "Class Boundaries in Advanced Capitalist Societies," *New Left Review* no. 98 (July-August 1976).

16 Antonio Gramsci, *Selections from the Prison Notebooks,* ed. Quintin Hoare and Geoffrey Nowell-Smith (New York: International Publishers, 1971); Ernesto Laclau, *Politics and Ideology in Marxist Theory* (London: New Left Books, 1977); Christine Buci-Glucksmann, "Hegemony and Consent," in Anne Showstack Sassoon, ed., *Approaches to Gramsci* (London: Writers and Readers, 1982); Chantal Mouffe, ed., *Gramsci and Marxist Theory* (London: Routledge & Kegan Paul, 1979); Adam Przeworski, "Proletariat Into a Class: The Process of Class Formation from Karl Kautsky's *The Class Struggle* to Recent Controversies," *Politics and Society,* vol. 7, no. 4 (1977); Nicos Poulantzas, *State, Power, Socialism* (London: New Left Books, 1978); Bob Jessop, *The Capitalist State* (New York: New York University Press, 1982).

17 Gramsci, *Prison Notebooks,* p. 57.

18 Przeworski, "Proletariat," pp. 372-373.

19 Gramsci, *Prison Notebooks,* p. 333.

20 Sheila Rowbotham, *Women, Resistance, and Revolution* (New York: Vintage, 1973).
21 Herbert C. Gutman, *Work, Culture, and Society in Industrializing America* (New York: Vintage, 1977).
22 Bob Marley and the Wailers, "War," *Rastaman Vibration*, Island Records 90033-1, 1976.
23 In the fifties and sixties, children in the United States were taught that there were three races: Caucasoid, Negroid, Mongoloid. Anthropologists have devised (in various periods) complex sets of indices (including skin color, anthropometrical data, and cultural elements) to create hundreds of "racial" categories.
24 Quoted in Edward D. C. Campbell, Jr., *The Celluloid South: Hollywood and the Southern Myth* (Knoxville: University of Tennessee Press, 1981), pp. 168-170.
25 Marvin Harris, *Patterns of Race in the Americas* (New York: W. W. Norton, 1964), p. 57.
26 We are grateful to Steve Talbot for consultation on this point.
27 A. Sivanandan, "From Resistance to Rebellion: Asian and Afro-Caribbean Struggles in Britain," *Race and Class*, vol. 23, nos. 2-3 (Autumn-Winter 1981).
28 Reich, *Racial Inequality*, provides the most advanced example of this approach.
29 Robert A. Dahl, *Who Governs?* (New Haven: Yale University Press, 1961) has a sophisticated treatment of the relationship between manifest (i.e., interest-group) power and ethnicity at the local level. As is common in *pluralist* analysis, race is treated as a special case of ethnicity. Peter Bachrach and Morton Baratz, *Power and Poverty* (New York: Oxford University Press, 1961) offer an *elite* theory perspective on race and power in Baltimore. Entrenched elites were able to ward off demands for participation, even from well-organized minority groups (an instance of latent power or "non-decision-making"). Rioting ensued and limited concessions were forthcoming. R. S. Franklin and S. Resnik, *The Political Economy of Racism* (Hinsdale, Ill.: Dryden Press, 1973) see radical realignment of *class* fractions across racial lines, occurring in response to the increasing chaos of the welfare state, as the framework in which an egalitarian impulse may be discovered. The recent highly touted volume by William Julius Wilson, *The Declining Significance of Race* (Chicago: University of Chicago Press, 1978) draws exactly opposite conclusions from the same sort of phenomena, arguing that "class inequalities" have eclipsed "racial inequalities." A permanent split is discerned within minority communities along "class" (i.e., status) lines. See Michael Omi's review in *The Insurgent Sociologist*, vol. 10, no. 2 (Fall 1980), pp. 118-122.
30 Omi has pointed out Wilson's assumption of a unitary state: "Wilson's notion of the 'polity' is vague, and it is often difficult to grasp whether it refers to legal and juridical systems, urban political machines, or simply the electoral arena. . . . The state is portrayed as responding to whomever wields power, with little discussion given to the competing political forces which impel the state to remain aloof or intervene in various periods" (ibid.).
31 The Moynihan and Coleman reports, for example, which challenged the family cohesion and educability of blacks, have been castigated for "blaming the victim." Although this criticism is a worthy attempt to place the burden of cultural domination over racial minorities on the institutions

that enforce racial oppression, it also adopts these same institutions' definitions of cultural viability, by accepting the "victim" status of racial
minorities. See Lee Rainwater and William Yancey, eds., *The Moynihan
Report and the Politics of Controversy* (Cambridge, Mass. : MIT Press, 1967);
James Coleman et al., *Equality of Educational Opportunity* (Washington,
D.C. : Government Printing Office, 1966). The most accessible critique
is William P. Ryan, *Blaming the Victim* (New York : Vintage, 1976), pp.
44-54.

32 Although these "color" categories have been the most basic and recogniz-
able labels, they have not been the only racial categories employed in
United States history. Nor have their meanings held constant. Disagree-
ments over racial categories have been commonplace, and the assignment
of a given group or individual to its racial category is often a matter of
serious conflict. Still, in a comprehensively racial order, the necessity of
racial classification remains.

33 Michael Billig, "Patterns of Racism: Interviews with National Front
Members," *Race and Class,* vol. 20, no. 2 (Autumn 1978), pp. 161-179.

34 Michael Kazin, "Prelude to Kearnyism: The July Days in San Francisco,"
New Labor Review, no. 3 (June 1980), pp. 5-47.

35 For a comprehensive discussion of racial minorities in nineteenth-century
California, see Tomás Almaguer, "Class, Race, and Capitalist Development: The Social Transformation of a Southern California County, 1848-
1903," unpublished doctoral dissertation, University of California, Berkeley, 1979.

36 Obviously a very few individuals may succeed in escaping the racial category assigned them by "passing" or other similar means. This hardly
negates the basic point, which remains true for the vast majority of
people in the United States.

37 George Rawick, *From Sundown to Sunup: The Making of the Black Community* (Westport, Conn. : Greenwood Press, 1972); Herbert C. Gutman,
The Black Family in Slavery and Freedom, 1750-1925 (New York : Vintage,
1976).

38 Roxanne Dunbar Ortiz, "Land and Nationhood: The American Indian
Struggle for Self-Determination and Survival," *Socialist Review* no. 63-64
(vol. 12, nos. 3-4; May-August 1982).

39 Rodolfo Acuña, *Occupied America: The Chicano's Struggle toward Liberation*
(San Francisco: Canfield Press, 1972), pp. 113-118; see also Leonard Pitt,
The Decline of the Californios (Berkeley and Los Angeles: University of
California Press, 1966).

40 *San Francisco Chronicle,* 14 September 1982, 19 May 1983. In 1980 Federal
Judge Gerald Weber blocked the City of Pittsburgh, Pennsylvania, from
preferentially promoting a policeman of Mexican descent as part of a
court-ordered racial quota system because, according to the judge, "Hispanics" are not a race. See David E. Hayes-Bautista, "Identifying 'Hispanic' Populations: The Influence of Research Methodology upon Public
Policy," *American Journal of Public Health,* vol. 70, no. 4 (April 1980).

41 Harry P. Pachon and Joan W. Moore, "Mexican Americans," *Annals of the
American Academy of Political and Social Science,* vol. 454 (March 1981).

42 They also set the stage for tragicomic attempts to manipulate this incomprehension. In 1979, for example, an Anglo named Robert E. Lee changed
his name to Roberto E. Leon in order to qualify for affirmative action
programs available to those with Spanish surnames. See Hayes-Bautista,
"Identifying 'Hispanic' Populations," p. 355.

43 Winthrop D. Jordan, *White Over Black: American Attitudes toward the Negro, 1550–1812* (Baltimore: Penguin Books, 1969), p. 95.

44 Alexander Saxton, *The Indispensable Enemy: Labor and the Anti-Chinese Movement in California* (Berkeley and Los Angeles: University of California Press, 1971), p. 1. Our emphasis.

45 Alan Moriyama, "The 1909 and 1920 Strikes of Japanese Sugar Plantation Workers in Hawaii," in Emma Gee, ed., *Counterpoint: Perspectives on Asian America* (Los Angeles: Asian American Studies Center, 1976), pp. 169–180.

46 Selig Perlman, *The History of Trade Unionism in the United States* (New York: Augustus Kelley, 1950), p. 52.

Slavery, Race & the Languages of Class:
"Wage Slaves" and White "Niggers"

Barry Goldberg

"IT'S SLAVERY, THE MILL, SLAVERY WORSE THAN THE NIGGERS had," lamented Jenkins, a steel worker interviewed by Bertha Saposs in 1919, the year of the Great Steel Strike. According to Saposs, long hours of arduous labor had marked Jenkins' flesh, leaving him "abnormally fat, with white unhealthy looking skin, inflamed eyes with puffy lids, and a way of yawning every minute or so." But while Jenkins' rhetoric impressed her enough to record his exact words, Saposs did not probe its meaning or political significance. Her descriptive notes allow us to visualize the physical toll exacted by the "slavery" of the mills; they do not help us understand Jenkins' "raced" vision of history. This does not mean that Saposs forgot Jenkins' lament. In a tentative analysis of her interviews, Saposs later returned to Jenkins' and other steel workers' condemnations of mill "slavery." But even then, Jenkins' "niggers" fell outside her interpretive framework. Her emphasis was the steel workers' acquiescence to corporate power. As she put it, "When a worker says 'we are not living we are slaves,' he does not have any idea of trying to stop being a slave."[1] Thus, her portrait of Jenkins' body reenforced his emotive comparative history of "slavery"; her analysis of the workers' passivity underscored the weight of corporate "slavery." Together, researcher and informant appropriated the memory of Afro-American slavery in order to dramatize the despair of life and labor in the mills. This allowed the "niggers" who endured bondage to remain invisible, captive black images in the white working class mind.

Efficiently catalogued in an archive, Saposs' typescript field notes are quite probably the only surviving trace of Jenkins' white working class historical consciousness. His words provide no more than a faint outline of his political imagination. Nonetheless, they are worth retrieving. By citing his words we remember his plight in a belated, necessarily ambivalent, but hardly insignificant act of human solidarity. In a culture uncomfortable with the recalcitrant ghosts of, to use Herbert Gutman's phrase, "dependent classes, slave and free," such traces of the past challenge the reigning social amnesia.

BARRY GOLDBERG *teaches American history in the Division of Social Sciences, Fordham University, College at Lincoln Center. Director of the College's Excel Program, an interdisciplinary core curriculum for "non-traditional" students, he has primarily taught working adults.*

If nothing else, Jenkins' words should remind us that American workers did not accept market relations or their consequences as natural; for many, the commodification of their labor marked their unfreedom. Jenkins' usable Afro-American past was not idiosyncratic; it was a common refrain in a long running cultural drama. "Wage slavery" became a standard feature of labor rhetoric in the 1830s and remained a significant term for workers and labor activists into the 20th century. Antebellum workers and labor reformers discovered their voices in the ideological crucible of Jacksonian politics and of the slavery debate. But even after emancipation, in years marked by the corporate restructuring of the economy, labor militancy, and new forms of racial domination, labor activists and workers continued to define their oppression by inserting themselves in America's continuing debate over the meaning of slavery and abolition. His few surviving words were inseparable from, but not reducible to, his or other wage workers' exhaustion and "inflamed eyes."

BUT JENKINS' WORDS ALSO REMIND US HOW MUCH SLAVES and their descendants remained a people without a history, objects of oppression not subjects with their own claims on the future in the eyes of white America — and its working class. Impelled to describe both the exploitation and cultural creativity of workers like Jenkins, we run the risk of sympathetically quoting their language without taking its full measure. To ignore wage slavery's Janus face is to ignore the tragedy of America's working people, black and white. The anomalous creation of a violent racist system of chattel slavery in a liberal capitalist society predicated on individualism and free labor has left its mark on languages of working class protest. Afro-American slavery has haunted and energized the white working class imagination. In order to articulate their own oppression and forge cultures of resistance, working class activists have struggled to narrow the meaning of the difference between slavery and wage labor without necessarily subverting the meaning of racial difference. Even when not explicitly racist, these languages of class — verbal, iconographic, and ritualistic — have been "raced": infused with historical comparisons and metaphors, the data and the tropes of racial discourse and Afro-American experience. Workers and those who claimed to speak for them have often equated their oppression with that of blacks, appropriating the black experience without necessarily surrendering the privilege of their whiteness. The rhetoric of wage slavery voiced class resistance by recasting the familiar language of racial domination.

Undoubtedly the rhetoric of "wage slavery" is of the past. But through our words and silences, our narrative strategies and analytic categories, we continue the (often bloody) "conversation" of a culture marked by the strange hybrid fruits of racial as well as class domination. If anything, as the languages of race and class have become increasingly slippery in recent years, historical accounts of their interrelated meanings enter the current debate. Indeed, the often inchoate white "ethnic backlash" of our time bears a striking resemblance to the fusion of class resentment and race consciousness of the earlier "wage slavery" argument. Confronted with that "backlash," Afro-Americans are advised to wait for the triumph of social democratic policies that have been stymied since the '40s. And having only recently overcome a popular memory which suppressed or legitimated the history of racial oppression, they are told to transcend an allegedly debilitating "enemy memory." What such advice chooses to forget is that white workers and activists, before and after Jenkins, have not simply been racist, but that they have appropriated the "memory" of slavery for their own purposes. Wage slavery was a discursive crossroads where to redeploy Alexander Saxton's geometric metaphor, "class consciousness has cut at right angles to racial identification."[2] It was a congested and confusing place where the meanings of racial and class identity were defined, entangled, and renegotiated, over and over. The result has rarely been a color blind democratic vision. The oppression of Afro-American slavery was acknowledged, but the condition and aspirations of the white working class was privileged. Such a history cannot tell us "what is to be done." But it is a sobering reminder of the hidden (and not so hidden) racism of the American radical tradition. And we must not forget it as we reconstitute the democratic left and its projects.

How has labor's reactive appropriation of Afro-American slavery and abolitionism as tropes of class struggle reconstituted racial as well as class identities over time?

LET US BEGIN IN 1836 IN NEW YORK. The city's master tailors cut their journeymen's pay and agreed not to hire any union men in their shops. During the bitter strike which followed, the masters condemned the union as a coercive anti-republican combination and pressed for a criminal conspiracy indictment against the tailors. A jury agreed and convicted 20 strikers. Shocked by the rejection of their rights to free association and collective action, a local union journal condemned the judge's handling of the case as "an unhallowed attempt to convert the working men of this country into slaves." Union supporters plastered the city with a handbill which read in part:

> The Rich against the Poor! Judge Edwards, the tool of the Aristocracy, against the People! Mechanics and working men! A deadly blow has been struck at your Liberty! The prize for which your fathers fought has been robbed from you! The Freemen of the North are now on a level with the slaves of the South with no other privileges than laboring that drones may fatten on your life blood.

These sentiments were clearly shared by large numbers of artisans and day laborers. A week after sentencing, nearly 30,000 people, one-fifth of the entire adult population of the city attended a protest rally at city hall, the largest protest ever seen in the nation.[3]

As recent studies of antebellum labor have made clear, the journeymen's language of protest was not an aberration, but a striking example of the antebellum labor movement's creative understanding and use of the "key words" of the republican lexicon. Fluent in the language of the revolution, sure of its essential meaning and relevance to the journeymen's plight, the pamphlet framed the immediate labor conflict as an allegory of embattled republican citizenship. By urging the "People," "Mechanics," and "Freemen" to defend their "Liberty" against the "Aristocrats" who would reduce them to the status of "slaves," the leaflet legitimated the journeymen's right to collective action as a defense of an imperiled national heritage, a contemporary enactment of the never ending struggle to protect a fragile republic from the corruptions of privilege. For the tailors and their supporters, not only individuals, but the nation itself had fallen from republican grace. The egalitarian republic of economically and politically independent citizens was in peril. By the 1830s, wage slavery denoted the wage-earner's poverty and servile dependence on employers when labor was a mere commodity. A fusion of the labor theory of value and republican political principles which crossed narrow ideological and temporal boundaries, the critique of "wage slavery" imbued labor protest with a transhistorical moral legitimacy. Wage slavery described and condemned the loss of independence resulting from the expansion of wage labor and capitalist social relations. In the eyes of many workers — journeymen in New York, shoemakers in Lynn, "factory girls" in Lowell, and, in later years, immigrant and native steelworkers in Homestead — the "wages system" undermined the republic's promise of "equal rights."

BUT WAGE SLAVERY WAS MORE THAN A COLOR-BLIND DIALOGUE with the republican past by workers resisting the degradations of wage labor. The critique of wage slavery developed in an ongoing debate with abolitionist, and later Republican, claims that slavery was a sin and violation of republican principles incomparable with the disabilities of wage earners.

Leaving aside, for the moment, the question of race, a huge gulf separated labor activists and abolitionists. While in theory it is possible to imagine an evenhanded struggle against chattel and wage slavery, in practice, the two movements were trapped in a zero sum game of political and ethical mobilization. At a minimum, the rhetoric of wage slavery was unavoidably parasitic: its metaphors and analogies "remoralized" the condition of the working classes by transforming, sharing or devaluing, the special significance of black suffering. Abolitionists believed labor's attempt to relativize bondage robbed chattel slavery of its distinctive immorality, undercutting their attempts to emancipate the slave. Labor reformers and abolitionists, intent on confronting specific injustices, needed to assert the primacy of their distinct demands. But in addition, each had a profoundly different understanding of the sources of human oppression. The labor reformers had developed a working class radicalism which identified the impersonal market forces and social circumstances that distorted human possibilities and restricted freedom. Abolitionists, by and large, remained committed to the celebration of the primacy of the autonomous individual; the crime of slavery was that it robbed slaves of the freedom as responsible moral agents. Indeed antislavery reformers can be seen as "utopian" apostles of a moralistic, individualistic, market oriented modernity. Workers, according to Wendell Phillips were not an oppressed group:

Does legislation bear hard upon them? — their votes can alter it. Does capital wrong them? — economy will make them capitalists . . . [T]o economy, self-denial, temperance, education, and moral and religious character, the laboring class, and every other class in this country, must owe its elevation and improvement.

In essence, Phillips called on the working class to internalize the controls of the emerging industrial order, to become agents of their own labor discipline. For abolitionists, the assertion that chattel slavery was a mere effect of a broader and more significant system of domination, exploitation, and inequality was pernicious. Committed to the sanctity of the individual, abolitionism had rejected the compromise of the revolutionary generation that had robbed blacks of the benefits and responsibilitites of life in a Godly republic. Abolitionism's empathy with the slave exposed the limits of bourgeois radicalism.[4]

As David Brian Davis has argued in a sophisticated analysis of early 19th century British abolitionism, the antislavery appeal had the potential to unleash a critique of domination that could be extended to the new impersonal domination endured by the emerging working class. But, he added, "if contained, the attack might give at least temporary moral insulation to less visible forms of human bondage." And, in perhaps the most noted application of Antonio Gramsci's notion of cultural hegemony by a prominent historian, Davis argues that is precisely what happened (particularly in Britain) in the early 19th century. An "unintended" consequence of the rigid dichotomy between slavery and other systems of labor control was the uncritical veneration of free wage labor: the abolitionists "appeared to look forward to a future when all workers would be citizens, subject to the same laws and forces of the market." Or, as he put it more bluntly, "The antislavery movement, like Smith's political economy reflected the needs and values of the emerging capitalist order."[5]

But did the antislavery critique provide an adequate "trench system," to use Gramsci's battlefield metaphor, securing bourgeois hegemony, particularly in the United States? The rhetoric of "wage slavery" seems to undermine his thesis. Davis acknowledges the labor movement's appropriation of the language and tactics of this allegedly hegemonic reform. Their "metaphors," he observed, "amounted to more than verbal play, since they expanded on the moral vision of the initial abolitionists." Davis concludes, "[I]t is not farfetched to see [Engels'] *The Condition of the Working Class in England* as one of the greatest of antislavery tracts." (466-68) Nonetheless, Davis has recently argued that labor's critique of wage slavery is evidence of middle class hegemony. By successfuly defining slavery as the ultimate social sin, the antislavery movement had forced the working class to wage a struggle on its ideological terrain. Labor activists had to pass a "slavery test." They had to appeal to the governing classes and public opinion with portraits of suffering and analogic arguments proving that wage earners were, in essence, no better off than slaves. Thus, slavery became the master metaphor of languages of social protest as labor activists legitimated their own struggles by equating the evils they combatted with the evil of chattel slavery. Workers may not have accepted middle class ideology, but their oppositional language re-presented the lines of social cleavage only by honoring the power of the dominant classes' representation of social reality. Even in the United States, where emancipation was not a peaceful reform adopted through elite consensus and, therefore, provided a usable past of radical — and violent — challenges to authority, Davis argues that by accepting the legitimacy of the "slavery test," workers failed to develop a more nuanced and appropriate critique of the indirect domination of the market. In sum, workers felt unable to change the world unless they blackened their experience by likening their plight to the unfreedom of slavery.[6]

Davis reminds us that if workers named their world, they did not do it alone, and definitely not under circumstances of their own choosing. The language of class, like class itself, as E.P. Thompson stressed, is a relation. But unlike labor historians influenced by Thompson, he is less taken by the oppositional tone of working class neo-republicanism's critique of wage slavery. Like them, his focus on class formation and legitimation downplays the significance of race. And in the United States you cannot talk about class without talking about race. After all, abolitionism was an attempt to reshape the complexion of the republican community. Beginning in the 1830s and lasting to the end of reconstruction, evangelical abolitionism and antislavery political parties challenged not only the legitimacy of chattel slavery, but the revolution's legacy of racially defined citizenship.

"A LEVEL WITH SLAVES IN THE SOUTH": the phrase reminds us that white workers, like other Americans, knew that a black subaltern class possessing neither property, abstract rights, nor their very persons, had been formally excluded from the promise of republican liberty. "Slavery's" rhetorical efficacy as a "sign" of working class degradation depended upon widespread awareness of millions of black men, women, and children bound in chains, sold on auction blocks, and laboring in fields. The South's "peculiar institution," a specific form of what Orlando Patterson has called the "permanent, violent domination of natally alienated and generally dishonored persons" held as property, was a cultural benchmark of oppression. And on some level, workers knew they did not have to endure the slaves' racially defined "social death." Furthermore, the fear of being reduced to the "level" of black slaves was quite different than the desire to abolish chattel slavery and extend the scope of republican liberty to Afro-Americans. The indignity of wage slavery may have been primarily that the white worker risked losing his racially specific birthright. Black bondage helped define and energize the meaning of white liberty.[7]

Although Wilentz's analytic narrative downplays the significance of race in the making of the New York working class, his own account exposes the "uglier features" of the "republic of the Bowery." In 1834, two years before the tailors' strike, a large segment of New York's laboring people, goaded by Tammany Hall, transformed the city's streets into a brutal defense of slavery and racial privilege. Fearful of rumors that abolitionists were going to encourage blacks to invade and "mullatoize" their neighborhoods, they turned their wrath on the home of Lewis Tappan, leading abolitionist, evangelical reformer, businessmen, and publisher of New York's leading anti-labor journal. These overlapping currents of working class militancy, racism, and Tammany politics came together in the career of Mike Walsh, political voice and hero of Bowery culture. Walsh denounced capitalist wage labor: "[Y]ou are slaves . . . No man devoid of all other means of support but that which his labor affords him can be a freeman, under the present state of society. He must be a humbled slave of capital . . ." But Walsh's condemnation of wage slavery gave a bitter class accent to the Democratic Party's defense of slave owners. By the 1840s he supported Calhoun's proposals for low tariffs and portrayed slaveholders as friends of the working man. Indeed, as a Congressmen during the Kansas-Nebraska debate of 1854, Walsh denounced Republicans as "servants to the barons of wage slavery" to whom workers in the North had "to beg for the privilege of becoming a slave." (326-35) Walsh's mass appeal linked a radical critique of wage labor to white supremacy. And on the Bowery as in the rest of the nation, blackface entertainers helped codify the social imagination of antebellum workers in an imaginary racist resolution of class anxieties. As Alexander Saxton has argued, minstrelry was political theater: the form and content of the minstrel show was tied to the ideological needs of the Democratic Party seeking to maintain a national electoral alliance of urban working men, increasingly Catholic and immigrant, and the slaveholding South. In an era of social dislocation, Saxton argues, minstrelry transformed the slave plantation into a "home": a site of pastoral longing, a place "where simplicity, happiness, and all the things we have left behind, exist outside of time." But this alluring social fantasy depended on creating a subject for whom a lack of self-determination was not degrading, a person who stood outside the standards of republican citizenship: an ahistoric black man without a past or a future, without an authentic desire or a distinct voice. The alternative life of the plantation could be "ahistorical because its germinating inspiration was to fix the black slave as an everlasting part of nature rather than a figure in history." If blacks were real "men" this idyllic place without a history would be a tyranny no one would want to call home.[8]

WHILE IT IS IMPORTANT TO KEEP IN MIND abolitionism's valorization of free labor and labor's often explicitly racist critique of the "wages system," we must avoid static ahistorical ideological dichotomies. The Democratic Party and the minstrel theater may have forged a political and psychosocial alliance between members of the urban working class and Southerners against the modernizing, nationalizing, and antislavery Protestantism which coalesced in the Republican Party in the 1850s. But not all workers linked the critique of wage slavery to a defense of chattel slavery. There were political and cultural alternatives to Jacksonian Democracy's particular version of "white egalitarianism." In most Northern communities, anti-abolitionist mobs were made up primarily of "gentlemen of property and standing" who resisted abolitionists' religiously inspired challenge to secular order. And in New York as well as other cities, studies of abolitionist petitions reveal a plurality of artisan signatures.

Working-class grievances and attacks on wage slavery did not necessarily translate into proslavery Jacksonian racism. While hardly evidence of fundamental concern for freedmen or a commitment to racial equality, "labor abolitionism," however muted and inchoate, did exist. Despite the race of the victim and a belief in white superiority, a significant strand of labor republicanism kept faith with Paineite antislavery sentiments, and German "forty- eighters" eventually added a European-based republicanism to working class ideology. For such workers, the plantation was a house of anti-republican horrors unfit for any human being, a perverse exercise of power that sons and daughters of the age of revolution should not tolerate.

In addition, the crisis of the Union and the debate over Reconstruction policy created an opening for renewed debate over the relationship between wage labor and equal rights. The Republicans constructed a unifying consensual ideology of labor celebrating the unlimited possibilities of free labor in a land purged of the slave power. While not the peaceful reform from above characteristic of British abolition, the antislavery struggle and Civil War bound workers to their employers in an interclass crusade against slavery, inhibiting the rise of independent labor politics.

But there is little evidence to suggest that either loyalty to the Union or Republican ideology eradicated working-class racism or the critique of wage slavery. The New York city Draft Riots of 1863 are only the most glaring evidence of the persistence of racist anti-Republicanism among Northern workers unwilling to sacrifice their lives, material well-being, and racial superiority for the slave's freedom or the Republicans' vision of the Union. On the other hand, and more important, the aftermath of the war included a revitalized labor movement that sought to extend the meaning of "equal rights" and that saw itself as a continuation of the abolitionists' democratic ideology. Ira Steward, machinist, organizer, and intellectual founder of the eight-hour movement filled his speeches and writings with references to the antislavery struggle and often quoted their words.

Labor did not, however, abandon its criticism of the abolitionist definition of freedom. Rather, the Civil War and Emancipation made it easier for labor reformers to celebrate abolitionism's liberatory thrust while rejecting its acceptence of the Northern labor system. Labor reformers like Steward could now employ the language and example of the antislavery movement while repudiating the restrictive theoretical postulates of antebellum abolitionism. As Steward, put it in 1873, "There is a closer relation between poverty and slavery, than the average abolitionist ever recognized." Steward explained,

> The laborer instinctively feels that something of slavery still remains, or that something of freedom is yet to come, and he is not much interested in the antislavery theory of liberty. He wants a fact, which the labor movement undertakes to supply.

We should not take Steward's postbellum "labor abolitionism" lightly: it reveals how difficult it was to contain the challenge to authority embedded in evangelical abolitionism and an antislavery struggle that required a mass political party and bloody war. Rather than closing off discussion or necessitating a new political vocabulary, Emancipation and the Civil War, like the Revolution, became contested terrain.[9]

But it is crucial to recognize labor abolitionism's racially defined limits. After Emancipation, the litmus test of labor abolitionism was not an ex post facto identification with the abolitionist legacy but, rather, the labor movement's response to the "fact" of four million freedmen living in the shadow of slavery. Labor's neo-republican definition of equal rights did not "supply" the answer to their needs. The labor movement remained overwhelmingly the preserve of white men. Only three national unions admitted blacks to membership. While Steward developed an "antislavery" defense of the eight-hour day, white caulkers in Baltimore battled for eight hours and tried to eliminate blacks from their craft. William Sylvis, perhaps the first modern national union leader, exemplified the limits of the postwar labor revival. Against strong opposition in the National Labor Union, he advocated organizing black workers. But Sylvis oppposed the Freedmen's Bureau, denounced Reconstruction governments, and expressed dismay at the social contact between the races. Echoing Walsh, Sylvis dismissed the party of Lincoln as an arm of the "money power" "which under the cloak of philanthropy for the Negro" had begun to fashion a new — and worse — slavery for all labor. His rhetoric betrayed the Democratic Party's populist racism, animosity to abolitionism, and tendency to downplay the suffering of the chattel slave. Like most white Americans, including Republicans, he never understood that the ex-slaves, caught between slavery and "free" labor, a racist counterrevolution and national citizenship rights, had their own vision of "equal rights." Labor abolitionism grafted the antislavery legacy to its critique of wage slavery, but the labor movement did not make room for the ex-slaves or their aspirations.[10]

FOUR YEARS AFTER STEWART'S CALL TO EXPAND THE ABOLITIONIST definition of freedom, federal troops, recently removed from the South, were deployed to suppress the railroad strike of 1877. It was one of the most dramatic conjunctures in American history: the military power of the state no longer protected the freedmen's citizenship rights; it protected capital from white labor. If the Civil War was the "Second American Revolution," its "thermidor" had begun. Black and white labor, in different ways, faced what W.E.B. DuBois had called "the counter revolution of property."

The political compromise of 1877 and the suppression of the railroad strike were the beginning of a multifaceted attempt to redefine the meaning of slavery and freedom in an era of escalating labor conflict. As in other nation states in the late 19th century, political order involved "the invention of tradition," selective readings of the past, often institutionalized in rituals and monuments, wedding diverse citizens to a shared national identity. Undoubtedly, patriotic rituals were meant to assimilate a militant and increasingly foreign born working class. But we cannot forget that the Civil War was the central event of 19th century America and national unity required more than military victory; peace required finding common patriotic ground for "the blue and the gray." This more broadly defined "road to reunion" was not smooth or ever complete, but by the turn of the century the dominant culture had forged an interpretation of the past legitimating sectional peace, white supremacy, and class harmony.

The Civil War's massive carnage provided the common symbol for spiritual reunification. By the 1880s, Memorial Day had come to embody the shared sacrifice of North and South in defense of what Oliver Wendell Holmes called opposing "sacred principles." The nation was recast as a blood brotherhood sanctified on the battlefield. Yet we should not be misled by Holmes' words. The celebration of martial heroism took place in the context of a broader renegotiation of sectional, class, and racial identities. The end result was a new set of "sacred principles" transcending sectional loyalties. Southerners accepted the destruction of slavery, acknowledging its economic backwardness, but not its exploitive moral depravity. Rather, they portrayed slavery as a costly but necessary structure of racial control — and civilization. For their part, with the superiority of the national government and free labor established, Northerners acknowledged that Reconstruction's attempt to empower ex-slaves had been dangerous and accepted the growing institutionalization of racial control. They accepted the South's contention that black slaves had been a childlike — innocent yet violent — people who needed control. The conflict between slave and free labor over, the nation forged a united definition of white civilization and citizenship. This new nation celebrated its "birth" in D.W. Griffith's "screen memory" of reconstruction.

Labor's characteristic response to the dominant culture's vision of the past and present was a hybrid discourse through which labor activists likened their fate to that of the slave while disassociating white working-class character from the naturalized representations of black savagery and docility. Undoubtedly, after 50 years, wage slavery had a formulaic quality, but it would be misleading to discount it as a stale metaphor. Wage slavery had become an historical discourse challenging smug middle class visions of technological and material progress. According to many labor activists, the Civil War and Emancipation had not heralded a reign of freedom but an expansion of the new impersonal bondage of the marketplace. Not suprisingly, some labor activists attacked the conservative nationalism embodied in the rituals of patriotic remembrance. Benjamin Perry, the machinists union Denver business agent, was struck by the "pathetic" parade of "bent, white haired old men (gray and blue) who march[ed] side by side" on Memorial Day. He

> could not help but think of the great cause for which old heroes battled, namely the abolition of chattel slavery, and how much of it still exists through poverty, and how much better off the negroes were before the war than the white slaves of today are.[11]

Perry questioned the bourgeois vision of progress and national unity, but he did

105

not have to reject all aspects of the official culture's interpretation of the Civil War and slavery. His comparison of antebellum slaves to the "white slaves of today," added a militant class accent to an already compromised narrative of freedom's progress.

Like Perry, other labor activists recast the Civil War into a working-class narrative of America's unfinished democratic revolution. But it was not unfinished because of the fate of freedmen, as Frederick Douglass had struggled to convince Americans in the decades after the war. Just as labor activists appropriated the meaning of slavery, they now appropriated the meaning of Emancipation, dismissing the freedmen as bystanders to their own history. Their didactic histories from the bottom up legitimated class resistance but reproduced the ideology of white supremacy. Let us examine two such versions of this usable past.

IN JULY, 1899, LUKE McHENNY, A LEADER OF CLEVELAND'S striking street railway workers complained that blacks failed to honor the strikers' request for a boycott of the cars. At a minimum, he charged "the colored race remained passive." On one route he complained, "none ride but coons." He then complained that "the negro, who owes his freedom and rights of suffrage to the white working class" betrayed his saviors:

> I have been pondering to myself the past few days on what would have been the result had the position of black and white been reversed in '61. Would the negro take the same stand to abolish white slavery that the white men of the North did to free blacks? . . . Well, in view of the attitude of the Cleveland colored people in this emergency. I am rather inclined to think that white slavery would exist forever.

Nowhere does McHenny note that Southern blacks had been recently disfranchised. Nor does he reflect on labor's own tarnished record of discrimination. Indeed, in Cleveland, union membership policies "effectively kept most eligible negroes out of the trade union movement." These omissions are central to his rhetorical construction of white working-class identity. Through his selective portrayal, blacks become secure and privileged citizens of Cleveland, white workers the vulnerable victims of oppression. McHenney's counterfactual invention of "white slavery" adds force to his argument by appropriating and subverting the meaning of the Civil War. But most important. McHenny's fictitious invention of "white slavery," his fantasy that white men could have been slaves in need of black emancipators recasts history as a record of white oppression and courage, black privilege and cowardice. His political fiction enchains white workers to demonstrate the fundamental difference between the races: whites are the courageous liberators, blacks are passive victims undeserving of their freedom — and a threat to white labor. The Civil War and the strike exemplify white working class "manliness" and the servility of black Americans.[12]

THE SECOND EXAMPLE IS THE ANALYSIS OF ABOLITION and Reconstruction developed by the socialist theorist and historian Algie M.Simons. An apostle of a crude economic determinism, Simons criticized working-class activists who celebrated the abolitionists and Lincoln. Slavery would still exist, he argued, "if it had not happened that the owners of wage-slaves wanted the government which the chattel slave owners possessed." For Simons, the inexorable march of History propelled by the evolving logic of material accumulation generated beliefs, struggle and historical change. Garrison's passion was immaterial to emancipation; John Brown's raid "recklishly foolish." And like McHenney, he denied Afro-American slaves any role in their own emancipation since, as he put it, "there were no slave insurrections during the war." The slave's alleged "failure to play any part in the struggle that broke his shackles, told the world that he was not one of those who to free himself would strike a blow." In a portrait of Reconstruction that would have pleased D.W.Griffith, Simons argued that the freedmen became the pawns of "a horde of mercenary Goths and vandals." The vote was an instrument of their new masters' power. He concluded, "I do not raise the question of the rightness or wrongness of universal negro suffrage, but I am only discussing the forces which led to its being conferred at this time and the results which flowed from it."[13]

Simons' "objective" analysis of the franchise was disingenuous. He was more than a scientific student of the forces of history. A decade earlier, Simons had led the battle at the Socialist Party convention opposing a resolution condemning lynching and disfranchisement for fear that it would hurt organizing efforts in the South. And his totalizing theory expressed a race-conscious vision of working class empowerment. Although his analytic narrative is quite different from McHenney's deliberate fiction, Simons' theoretical voice presents a similar racial allegory: don't trust the black voter since he is a docile tool of greedy and corrupt capitalists. Simons' teleological narrative of history does not ask workers to identify with slaves. As the passive victims of power the slaves and freedmen were a people without a history and therefore hardly a people with whom to identify. Simons' History was a racist narrative of power. Blacks had no place in his economistic "lily white" geneology of class rule.

THAT NEITHER THE SLAVES NOR FREEDMEN were or should have been puppets of whites is unquestioned among contemporary historians of slavery and Reconstruction. But when the black scholar-activist W.E.B. DuBois published his pathbreaking *Black Reconstruction in America* in 1935, the racist "Propaganda of History" still dominated the academy and popular culture. DuBois' impassioned portrait of the role of Afro-American slaves in their own emancipation attacked more than Southernist racist historiography; he challenged white labor's insurgent usable past, a vision of history voiced by theorists, labor activists, and workers like Jenkins, the steelworker interviewed in 1919 by Bertha Saposs.

Writing in the midst of the Depression, as a "socialist of the path," DuBois was far from insensitive to the hardships of wage earners like Jenkins. But as an

107

Afro-American radical he was impatient with attacks on "wage slavery" that slighted the distinctive degradation Afro-American chattel slavery. When Americans heard the word slavery, he explained, they might "think of the ordinary worker . . . without enough to eat, compelled by his physical necessities to do this or do that, curtailed in his movements and possibilities; and [they] may say here . . . is a slave called a 'free worker' and slavery is merely a matter of name." But, DuBois argued, that would be a dreadful mistake. As he put it, "[T]here was in 1863 a real meaning to slavery different from that we may apply to the laborer today." The root of that difference, epitomized by "the defenselessness of family life," rested in the slave's personalized subjection to "the arbitrary will of any sort of individual." DuBois reminded his readers that the wage-earner is never the object of "direct barter in human flesh . . . No matter how degraded the factory hand, he is not real estate."[14]

Equally important, DuBois' affirmation of the freedmen's participation in their own liberation undermined a crucial assumption of Eurocentric radicalism and labor's popular memory: the primacy of the white working-class experience. Redeploying Marxian categories while subverting the popular memory of white labor and the left, he challenged Simons' interpretation of Emancipation. DuBois depicted the slaves' "Great Strike" against their masters during the Civil War and their search for power during Reconstruction as the central drama of democratic struggle in America, a struggle in which the white working class fell woefully short. The freedmen's tragic defeat and its erasure from popular memory insured the future exploitation of white and, especially, black labor. He directed his most detailed attacks against the "counter-revolution of property" but he could not excuse the white working class. As he explained, "The resulting color caste founded and retained by capitalism was adopted, forwarded and approved by white labor, and resulted in the subordination of colored labor to white profits the world over."[15]

As an Afro-American radical, all too aware of his "twoness," Dubois questioned the existence of the singular revolutionary subject at the heart of Western radical theory and white American labor's interpretation of the national heritage. From DuBois' perspective, a truly emancipatory politics had to recognize — in order to overcome — the pernicious language and history of racial domination. Black men and women, prisoners of white men's colonial and commercial dreams, did not experience the alienation of free wage labor. Africans had been swept into America as racial outsiders subjected to racially defined bondage and, after two centuries, their descendants endured an incomplete freedom. The working class rhetoric of "slavery" as a figure of speech for class exploitation whitewashed this history. For DuBois, it was not simply poetic radical hyperbole; it was a chapter in the popular memory of a racist society.

That chapter is now over — more or less. DuBois' reputation has never been higher among historians. In spite of the continuing romantic pull of the ever popular "Gone With the Wind," "Roots" and "Glory" have provided significant alternatives to the pervasive disparagement of slaves and freedmen. In addition to the decline in racist historiography, New Deal reforms and the Cold War consensus which pitted the "Free World" against the "slavery" of totalitariansim stifled the impassioned critique of the compulsions and unfreedom of "wage slavery." But, in recent years, a new chapter of white working class memory has been written in response to the racial and class tensions of the post-war welfare state.

CRITICS OF "WAGE SLAVERY" DID NOT FALL MUTE OVERNIGHT. Initially, confronting the hardships of the Depression and mobilizing resistance, the metaphor of slavery continued to animate labor's critique of Depression America and to legitimate unionism. The year DuBois published his revisionist account of Reconstruction, a twenty-year old rag sorter wrote "a letter of hope" to Secretary of Labor Frances Perkins. He complained, "We work, ten hours a day for six days. In the grime and dirt of a nation. We go home tired and sick — dirty — disgusted with the world in general . . . We handle disease rags all day. Tuberculosis roaming loose, unsanitary conditions — slaves — slaves of the depression!" The language of slavery continued to remoralize the plight of wage-earners in a collapsed market economy. And union activists kept alive the "antislavery" critique of tyranny on the shop floor.[16]

But by the late '40s, their very triumphs — the industrial unions of the CIO, the Wagner Act, and a general increase in the "social wage" — as well as the growing ties between "labor statesmen," the state, and the Democratic Party eroded wage slavery's cultural salience and political efficacy. Union power in conjunction with the passage of the Social Security Act, the GI Bill, and housing loans for veterans, enabled a large segment of the white working class to escape not only the insecurity of working-class life — the "whip of starvation" condemned by critics of wage slavery — but to enjoy the benefits of a middle class standard of living. Even before the fruits of this "victory" had been fully realized, labor's rhetoric of slavery conflicted with the staid language of modern labor relations. Labor had won its place at the state-sanctioned bargaining table by abandoning the original neo-republican and Marxist premises of the wage slavery argument and adopting a legalist corporatist terminology. In 1947, facing the Taft-Hartley Act's conservative challenge to union power, labor leaders like George Meany invoked the specter of a return to an era when workers could be compelled to toil against their will. Meany had no difficulty labelling the Taft-Hartley Act's limitations on the right to strike and secondary boycotts as a "slave labor law." But except for this momentary rhetorical flourish, Meany's grievance was as dry as a labor economics text. Labor's rhetoric of slavery lost persuasiveness since it was overwhelmed by the dominant institutional language to which it was now grafted. While labor reforms (and the Cold War) shifted labor discourse, the contradictions of the liberal welfare state set the context for the emergence of the languages of class, race, and slavery associated with white ethnic blue collar workers and their leaders in the late 1960s and 70s. The distribution of New Deal social benefits

109

proved to be highly uneven. The social wage was built upon industry by industry contracts, not universal entitlements. Most important, this new era of labor relations did not unify the working class, but replaced old ethnic and occupational hierarchies with a firmer racial divide. Blacks remained distant second cousins in the new political economy. The New Deal had not set the groundwork for the universal entitlements of European social democracy, nor had it overthrown the political economy of racism; its "Broker State" established a highly politicized — and therefore visible — opportunity structure. The state set the parameters of labor relations and distributed benefits to specific groups with political clout or ethical capital to legitimate their claims on the commonweal.

THE AFRO-AMERICAN STRUGGLE FOR EQUALITY CONFRONTED — in rapid succession — both the burden of America's racist past and the contradictions of this more recently constructed semi-welfare state. In an era when groups struggled over the regulatory and distributive uses of state power, blacks first had to struggle for the fundamental citizenship rights that would let them enter the fray. They faced fierce racist resistance and at times deadly political lethargy and compromises. Nonetheless, demands for equal political and civil rights could draw upon a relatively uncomplicated American political vocabulary. Indeed, the ideological mobilization against totalitarianism undermined racist definitions of citizenship. But when activists and policy planners sought to use state power to secure a more egalitarian distribution of social opportunities and rewards they confronted formidable and widespread resistance. While the entire panoply of recently won union benefits and non means-tested middle-class entitlements had been granted to native and immigrant labor, black demands to redistribute opportunities and rewards were often seen as an un-American politicization of opportunity, as demands for preferential treatment which amounted to "reverse racism."

Legitimating "race conscious" but antiracist extensions of state action required an end to black historical invisibility: a usable and publicized past which emphasized the historical specificity — duration, extent, and severity — of racial oppression. In his opinion in the 1974 Bakke case, for example, Justice Thurgood Marshall argued, "It is unnecessary in 20th century America to have individual Negroes demonstrate that they have been victims of racial discrimination; the racism of our society had been so pervasive. that none. regardless of wealth or position, has managed to escape its impact." A decade earlier, Malcolm X, looking at "America through the eyes of a victim" had been blunter. Parroting the terms of nativist and interethnic bigotry while denying the significance of nativism and ethnic prejudice, he proclaimed:

> Those Hunkies that just got off the boat, they're already Americans: the Italian refugees are already Americans. Everything that came out of Europe. every blue-eyed thing. is already an American. And as long as you and I have been over here, we aren't Americans yet. . . . They don't have to pass civil-rights legislation to make a Polack an American.

A masterful street orator who captured both the anger of much of urban black America and the distinctive reality of the color line, Malcolm X's rhetoric foreshadowed the tone and substance of the escalating conflict between conflicting memories of injustice.[17]

By the late '60s, ethnics — or those who claimed to speak for them — fashioned competing memories of victimization. Facing economic and political demands of the black community and its liberal allies, working class ethnics or their representatives forged a distinctive if inchoate ideology which bore a striking resemblance to labor's critique of abolitionism. White liberals, like abolitionists, were accused of selective humanitarian zeal, all the worse since they were relatively insulated from the costs of reallocating opportunity and fiscal resources. In addition, citing affirmative action programs and welfare benefits received by the black poor, an increasingly popular ideology defined Afro-Americans as the pampered wards of liberals oblivious to the harsh reality of the overworked and overtaxed white working class. The lazy welfare recipient and the unqualified but "first hired" black job applicant became the stock characters of the new idyllic welfare "plantation" wrought by liberalism.

Interpreting and amplifying white ethnic anger, ethnic advocates stressed the continuing injuries of class and questioned the distinctiveness of racial oppression. Csand Toth, campaigning for Robert Kennedy in 1968, discovered that America "was not a haven for refugees and immigrants, but a hell of smog, squalor, industrial accidents, low wages, poverty for the old and dreariness for children." He believed the ethnic working class, "liv[ed] no better off than the blacks in the inner cities about whom we liberals have recurring pangs of conscience." Even the term "nigger" lost its racial specificity and became a voluntarily appropriated badge of ethnic working class powerlessness and vulnerability. Steven Abudato, a Newark city councilman, put the matter bluntly: "We're the niggers, now that's what happened. It's just who's on top. The group that's second gonna catch shit — they're gonna be niggers. That's what this country is really all about." According to journalist Peter Shrag, "In the world of social planners everyone tends to become a nigger."[18]

Working class ethnics did not necessarily ignore the historical reality of slavery, but confronted by politicized intrusions of black history in their present, they either denied the political relevance of the past, or hoped to bury it. Alice McGoff, a working class Irish-American, acknowledged the great injustice of slavery, but, according to J. Anthony Lukacs, "she didn't see why whites who weren't even alive during slave times should be penalized for it." Similarly a Canarsie cab driver explained, "I didn't have anything to do with slavery. What's past is past. Nobody can give them what they owe them." Another white Canarsian, responding to the showing of "Roots," dreaded the consequences of bringing the past alive in the present. As one woman put it, "What upset me was that they rehashed history, but history is dead!" [Emphasis added.] She realized the atrocity and violence of slavery but feared black retribution: "The blacks were treated worse than animals, they were taken from their own happy soil . . . They don't need to be reminded of that." And we might add, neither did she.[19]

While some sought to forget and suppress the past in order to restore black invisibility, other white ethnics developed alternative narratives of suffering. An atypically class conscious young construction worker asked sociologist Jonathan Reider, "Do you call it a living when your grandfather had to dig a tunnel from morning until night? They made us dig the tunnels. When the earth caved in, it was always one of the Italians who died, nobody of any consequence! We were slaves." According to one ethnic cleric, blacks and ethnics "were equally exploited and suppressed. The ethnics worked as hard and died as frequently as any slave ever did." When not referring to class exploitation, ethnic leaders could cite the legacy of nativist discrimination. Or, they would look back even further. Slavic Americans argued that their ancestors experienced serfdom under Russian, Prussian, and Hungarian rule: this "was far more cruel an experience than was slavery for blacks in America." Ethnic intellectuals tempered such claims. Still, the legitimacy of white ethnic grievances remained tied to a polemical rediscovery of roughly equivalent historical victimization. Eventually this rhetoric entered the offical language of legal discourse. Justice Powell's opinion in the Bakke case argued that since white America contained minorities "most of which can lay claim to a history of prior discrimination," there was no basis for according one group " 'heightened judicial solicitude.' "[20]

The ostensible aim of establishing an equivalence of suffering was to forge a multi-ethnic biracial coalition. According to Monsignor Gino Baroni, blacks and white working people were natural allies capable of mutual understanding and joint action since they "shared a common oppression." Of course, such a judgment required downplaying the history, power, and relative autonomy of white racism, particularly within the working class. In a revealing selective account of the past, Michael Novak reduced the New York Draft Riots to a "labor uprising" and cited its Irish-American casualties without so much as acknowledging the politics, culture, and economics of race in the Civil War era. Tacitly accepting the ethnic claim that racial hierarchy was simply a legacy of slavery, ethnic advocates ignored the evidence that the white immigrant and ethnic working people were agents in creating and maintaining segregated occupations and neighborhoods before the "Second Reconstruction" of the '60s. Ethnics' racism, they argued, was simply a reaction to the excesses of a juridical and bureaucratic liberalism deaf to the pleas of overworked workers of immigrant roots. Novak claimed racial stereotypes embodied "the cries of people who are desperate and do not know how to get anyone to listen." If their concerns were addressed, their racism would supposedly vanish.[21]

Advocates of multiracial urban working class populism not only shared a highly skewed popular memory of injustice; they also underestimated the extent to which ethnic workers' identities were tied to racially defined visions of work and sacrifice. While no longer described as "slavish," blacks remained a negative reference defining white working class virtues. If whites had been "slaves" and "niggers" as ethnics suggested, it was because of their objective conditions, not their inner qualities. Their "blackness" was only skin deep, a marker of an exploitive nativist society. Ethnics took great pains to extol their embodiment of the work ethic, describing themselves as deserving Americans who played by the rules, accepting gradual and limited mobility. They did not complain and did not ask for welfare. Unlike angry blacks and their guilty liberal supporters, their oppression had not caused them to question the system that had brought many the trappings of "middle class" life. The white ethnic became the quintessential American — Horatio Alger in steerage — who struggled to improve his lot without the assistance of a beneficent state. As one ethnic cleric expressed the dominant ethnic wisdom: "[The white ethnic] worked hard to provide himself and his children without aid or assistance from government. Now a paternalistic government showers generous favors on the Blacks and continues to ignore him." A Slavic American steelworker asked rhetorically, "What are the Niggers, the government's chosen people? They are getting everything, what about us? Hell, those lazy bastards don't work, why cater to them." In simplified stories of immigrant poverty and ethnic prejudice, ethnics invoked an alternative history of white immigrant suffering and mobility. Ignoring the role of the liberal state as a foundation of their own individual mobility, they argued that blacks had no distinctive history of oppression or claims on the state. Ethnics had to wait in line and work hard, like their idealized ancestors. While turn of the century labor activists condemned blacks for their failure to resist the boss, they now stood condemned for failure to work hard. If they shared a common oppression, they did not share a common character.[22]

IN THE 1960S AND '70S, THE ANGRY, ANTI-ELITIST, ethnicized language of class pitted race against race, protecting limited pride and turf in the stultifying political discourse of an embattled semi-welfare state. In a sense, the competitive suffering of the critique of wage slavery had reached a tragic culmination. By the 1970s, white working class toil had become a badge of sacrifice. The ethnic cry of pain served as a resentful legitimation of the existing class and racial order.

This does not mean we should downplay class and ethnic grievances. It does not mean we should uncritically privilege every policy aimed at redressing racial injustice and every African-American voice that invokes the memory of racial injustice. Nor should our appreciation of the cultural creativity of slaves and their descendants lead to a romantic portrait of "teflon" coated African-Americans immune to the ravages of white supremacy. The tragedy of American history is that "dependent workers, free and slave" have been scarred by the injuries of class and race, their languages imbued with overlapping, alternative, and competing memories of injustice.

THE HISTORY OF ''WAGE SLAVERY'' TELLS US THAT NO UNILINEAR, inspirational narrative of domination and resistance is possible. As James Baldwin once reminded us, class and race are not the discrete analytic categories often studied by social scientists; they are mutually defining, publicly and privately negotiated American identities. White Americans, Baldwin observed, need blacks. Without them they would not know who they are. In a society where you can fall down as well as climb up the slippery ladder of success, the American Dream can easily become a nightmare of failed hopes, status, unemployment, foreclosed mortgages, bitter resentment, and shattered identities. "When one slips," Baldwin wrote, "one slips back not a rung but back into chaos and one no longer knows who one is." Standing before this psychosocial abyss, white Americans can look to the Negro to remind themselves of who they are. "In a way, the Negro tells us where the bottom is: because he is there, and where he is, beneath us, we know where the limits are and how far we must not fall."[23]

But in spite of its rich evocation of the internal relations of the injuries of class and race, even Baldwin's powerful insight cannot do justice to America's tragic history. Without denying the persistent reconstruction of symbolic and institutionalized racial boundaries, the working class rhetoric of slavery is historical and its meaning has been double edged. Through metaphors of slavery, white workers and labor activists fashioned their own highly politicized word play of racial difference. By comparing their past and current plight to that of Afro-Americans, slave and free, they have "made history" in rhetorical "blackface," momentarily and symbolically joining slaves on the bottom rung in order to advance their own interests. Disempowered by the impersonal forces of the free market or the planners of the corporate state, they have cried, "We are 'slaves.' " "We are 'niggers' too," but *we* deserve better.

Undoubtedly, such rhetoric called attention to the hidden and not so hidden injuries of class. By challenging the moral certitude of capitalist individualism in the 19th and early 20th centuries, wage slavery portrayed a system of domination masked by the bourgeoisie's restrictive definition of freedom. Later, by calling into question the classlessness of post-New Deal America it exposed some of the limits of centralized bureaucratic liberalism. And in each period, some labor activists tried to transcend the established limits of a racially defined workers' republic. But these metaphoric bonds between slave and "wage slave," between nigger and white "nigger" have been temporary, partial, instrumental, and above all, self-serving. In its most extreme articulation blacks were not even victims, but the lazy undeserving beneficiaries of paternalistic slavemasters, abolitionists, Union soldiers, and welfare bureaucrats: the pampered wards and instruments of white elites, or the ignorant foes of their white working-class saviors. As DuBois emphasized, Afro-Americans have been the victims of a selective memory of injustice and have been marginalized — if not always excluded — in the white working class vision of emancipation. "Wage slavery's" challenge to the moral economy of capitalism did not break the bonds of white egalitarianism. Glib equations between the white working class and black experience reconstituted the discourse of white supremacy.

NOTES

In writing this essay, I have benefitted from the criticism and encouragement of friends and colleagues. In addition to thanking the editors who helped me cut a much longer manuscript down to manageable size, I would like to thank Nicole Ferman, Eric Foner, Colin Greer, Peter Schneider, and Stephen Steinberg. Needless to say, I did not always follow their advice, but the essay is the better for their time and effort.

1. Jenkins Interview, David J. Saposs Papers, Box 26, Folder 11, Wisconsin Historical Society, Madison, Wisconsin; Bertha T. Saposs, untitled manuscript, ibid., Folder 11.

2. Alexander Saxton, "Race and the House of Labor," in Gary B. Nash and Richard Weiss, eds., *The Great Fear: Race in the Mind of America* (New York, 1970), 98.

3. Sean Wilentz, *Chants Democratic: New York City and the Rise of the American Working Class, 1788-1850* (New York 1984) 291-92.

4. Aileen Kraditor, *Means and Ends in American Abolitionism: Garrison and His Critics on Strategy and Tactics, 1834-1850*, (New York, 1969), 248-50.

5. David Brian Davis, *The Problem of Slavery in the Age of Revolution* (Ithaca, 1975), 348-349, 13, 252-54, 258-62, 381-82, 350.

6. David Brian Davis "Reflections on Abolitionism and Ideological Hegemony," *American Historical Review* 92 (October 1987). 807-9.

7. Orlando Patterson *Slavery and Social Death: A Comparative Study* (Cambridge, 1982), 33-34.

8. Alexander Saxton "Blackface Minstrelry and Jacksonian Ideology" *American Quarterly* 36 (1984) 211-235.

9. Ira Steward *Poverty* (Boston, 1873), 4.

10. David Montgomery, "William H. Sylvis and the Search for Working-Class Citizenship," in Melvyn Dubofsky and Warren Van Tine, eds., *Labor Leaders in America* (Urbana, 1987), 3-29.

11. Benjamin F. Perry, Denver, Colorado, *Machinists Monthly Journal*, (July 1911), 692.

12. Luke McHenny to editor, *Cleveland Artisam* (July 29, 1899); Kenneth L. Kusmer, *A Ghetto Takes Shape: Black Cleveland, 1870-1930* (Urbana, 1976), 67-75.

13. Algie M. Simons, *Social Forces in American History* (New York, 1912), 266, 274, 288, 292-94.

14. W.E.B. DuBois, *Black Reconstruction in America, 1860-1880*, (New York, 1935), 8-11.

15. Ibid., 55-83, 580-636, 711-730, 30, 16.

16. Gerald Markowitz and David Rosner, eds., *"Slaves of the Depression": Workers Letters About Life On the Job* (Ithaca, 1987)., 35.

17. Richard Polenberg, *One Nation Divisible: Class, Race, Ethnicity in the United States Since 1938* (New York, 1980), 273-74; *Malcolm Speaks*, ed., George Brietman, (New York, 1965), 26.

18. Csand Toth, "The Media and the Ethnics," in Michael Wenk, S.M. Tomasi, Geno Baroni, eds., *Pieces of a Dream: The Ethnic Workers Crisis With America* (New York, 1972), 16; Richard Gambino *Blood of My Blood: The Dilemma of Italian Americans* (Garden City, 1974), 327; Peter Shrag *The Decline of the WASP* (New York, 1971), 144, 250.

19. J. Anthony Lukas, *Common Ground: A Turbulent Decade in the Lives of Three American Families* (New York 1985), 27; Jonathan Rieder *Canarsie: The Jews and Italians of Brooklyn Against Liberalism* (Cambridge 1985), 120, 71.

20. Ibid., 35; Howard F. Stein and Robert F. Hill *The Ethnic Imperative: Examining the New White Ethnic Movement* (University Park, 1977), 157, 141; Michael Novack "New Ethnic Politics vs. Old Ethnic Politics," in Wenk, et. al., 127; Gambino, 75; Polenberg, 272-73.

21. Geno Baroni, "Ethnicity and Public Policy," in Wenk et. al., 59-60; Novak, "New Ethnic Politics," 126; idem., *The Rise of the Unmeltable Ethnics,* 16; Richard Krikus *Pursuing the American Dream: White Ethnics and the New Populism* (Garden City 1976), provides the most thorough history and justification of ethnic "populism."

22. Stein and Hill, 141.

23. James Baldwin, *Nobody Knows My Name* (New York, 1960), 111.

Colette Guillaumin

Race and Nature: The System of Marks

The Idea of a Natural Group and Social Relationships

The Idea of Race and of a "Natural" Group

The idea of race

The idea of race. What is this self-evident notion, this "fact of nature"? It is an ordinary historical fact—a social fact. I deliberately say *idea* of race: the belief that this category is a material phenomenon. For it is a heterogeneous intellectual formulation, with one foot in the natural sciences and one foot in the social sciences. On the one hand it is an aggregate of somatic and physiological characteristics—in short, race as conceived by the physical anthropologists and the biologists. On the other hand it is an aggregate of social characteristics that express a group—but a social group of a special type, a group *perceived as natural,* a group of people considered as materially specific in their bodies. This naturalness may be regarded by some people as fundamental (a natural group whose nature is expressed in social characteristics). Or it may be regarded by others as a secondary fact (a social group that "furthermore" is natural). In any case, in the current state of opinion, this naturalness is always present in the approach which the social sciences

Originally published in *Pluriel* no. 11, 1977.

take, and which the social system has crystallized and expressed under the name of "race."

So apparently it's all very simple. A purely "material" approach to observed characteristics on the one hand; and on the other hand, a mixed approach, more interested in sociosymbolic traits than in somatic traits, all the while keeping the latter present in the mind, in the background in some way or another. But with no profound clash between the two approaches; it's indeed a matter of the same thing in both cases. And equilibrium seems assured with the natural sciences referring to physical forms and the classical social sciences referring to social forms. Nevertheless, one might expect from the latter that their classifications and commentaries, even if they render discreet homage to the natural sciences, would still declare their specificity, first by defining with precision their concerns, and then by questioning the meaning in social terms of the fact that certain social categories are reputed to be natural. In fact, the social sciences are fascinated by the natural sciences, in which they hope to find a methodological model (which at the very least is debatable), but in which also (and this is the most serious matter) they believe they find an ultimate justification.[1] This attitude is not unrelated to the social reasons which lead to the usage of the idea of nature in the classification of social groups.

But, to proceed, let us accept for the moment that the division is effective and that equilibrium is realized between the disciplines, and let us take for established fact a separation between them, at least in their explicit concerns. So we have, on the one hand, a *supposedly natural* taxonomy, that of physical anthropology, population genetics, etc., declaring the existence of "natural" groups of humans, finite and specific (whites, blacks, brachycephalics, dolichocephalics, etc.); and on the other hand, a *social* taxonomy, that of history and sociology, taking into account the relational and historical characteristics of groups (slaves, the nobility, the bourgeoisie, etc.). The two types of classification can overlap or not, can have common areas or have no meeting point.[2] An example of *nonoverlap*: The blacks of the American social (read racial) system obviously have nothing (or very little) to do with the blacks and whites of physical anthropology in the anthropological meaning of the term. An example of *overlap*: The whites and blacks of the apartheid system are indeed what anthropology designates them as. But let us note that this is only at the price of another category, which is, if you wish, nonexistent, or out of consideration—the "coloreds"— bringing together both an aggregate of socioeconomic criteria (an aggregate without which and outside of which this group would literally not be *seen*) and an ideological *denial*—the denial of the nonexistence of naturally finite groups. The denial is constructed as follows:

First step: The fantasizing initial position postulates that an unbreachable barrier separates human groups, that races are radically dissimilar from each other.

Second step: The reality nevertheless is that this barrier does not exist, since the continuity between groups is proven in action by individuals who, belonging to two (or several) "races," show that there is only one.

Third step: Then comes the denial: "I do not want to know that there is no barrier, because I assert that there is one, and I consider null and void any contradiction of that barrier. I don't see it, it doesn't exist." In other words, the constitution of a "colored" group says that *it is not true that there is no* unbreachable barrier between "blacks" and "whites." By the creation of this "nongroup" no evidence exists of the continuity between groups, for the evidence of it is turned into a particular and independent entity. That class formed by people belonging in fact to one *and* the other group is declared to belong to neither the one nor the other, but to itself.[3] And thus the system proclaims that human groups are natural, and that in one's natural materiality one can belong to one *or* the other of these groups (or to some other *group*) but in no case to both one *and* the other. But the reality meanwhile is that people do belong to one *and* the other (or to some other groups).

A first questioning can already begin: The two preceding statements—that certain (social) blacks are whites (in the United States) and that a group belongs to both one *and* the other group (in South Africa)—are exactly the opposite of what is implied by the idea of race itself, which is supposed to be a *natural closed category*, and which thereby certifies the status of a group that is first of all fixed and secondly hereditary. In the impassioned proclamations of the social system there is the fantastic and *legalized* affirmation (we will return to this) that the boundaries between the groups are beyond the reach of, and anterior to, human beings—thus immutable. And, in addition, these boundaries are considered as obvious, as the very avowal of common sense ("You are not going to tell me that there are no races, no!" and "That is plain to see!").[4] And on the other hand, one cannot but charge such affirmations with lack of reality when one looks at what actually goes on and when one tries to apply the most ordinary rules of logic to it. For what goes on is the opposite of the impossibility that they affirm to us—no barrier nor separation, but a close association, a deep social and material imbrication which far outstrips the simple somatic continuity between the groups so violently denied.

The idea of a "natural" group

Material "imbrication"? Social "imbrication"? Yes, for supposedly "natural" groups only exist by virtue of the fact that they are so interrelated that effectively each of the groups is a function of the other. In short, it's a matter of social relations within the same social formation. One doesn't care to assert naturalness when there is economic, spatial, and other independence among groups. Only certain specific relations (of dependence, exploitation) lead to the postulation of the existence of "natural heterogeneous entities." Colonization by the appropriation of people (traffic in slaves, later in laborers) and of territories (that of the last two centuries) and the appropriation of the bodies of women (and not solely of their labor power) have led to the proclamation of the specific nature of the groups that endured or still endure these relations.

In fact, the groups concerned are *one and the same natural group* if one accepts this classification in terms of nature. The social idea of natural group rests on the ideological postulation that there is a closed unit, endo-determined [determined from within], hereditary, and dissimilar to other social units. This unit, always empirically social, is supposed to reproduce itself and within itself. All this rests on the clever finding that whites bear whites and blacks bear blacks, that the former are the masters and the latter the slaves, that the masters bear masters and the slaves slaves, etc., and that nothing can happen, and that nothing does happen, to trouble this impeccable logic. The children of slaves are slaves, as we know, while the children of slaves can also be—and often are—the children of the master. What "natural" group do they belong to? That of their mother? That of their father? That of their slave mother or that of their master father? In the United States in the eighteenth century the person who was on either side (the mother or the father) the child of a slave was a slave. The child of a slave man and a free woman was a slave (in Maryland as far back as the seventeenth century); the child of a slave woman and a free man was also a slave (in all the slave states). What "natural" group did they belong to? It was said (this line of argument developed in the United States) that the child of a slave woman was a slave "because it is difficult to dissociate a child from its mother," but what becomes of this argument when the slave child is the child of a free woman? If it is "difficult to dissociate a child from its mother," shouldn't it be free? In Maryland a free woman who married a slave saw her children born slaves.

We can move one step further if we take into consideration the social relationships of sex in this matter. They clarify the relationships of "race" (theoretically involved in slavery) better than considerations about "maternity." The child and the wife are the property of the husband-father, which is forgotten. A woman slave is the property of the master as a slave; her child is therefore the property of the master; a free woman is the property of her husband as a wife and—her husband being the property of the master as a slave—her children are the property of the master, thus slaves. She herself, moreover, was obliged to serve the master as long as her husband was living.

In addition, the sexed division of humanity is regarded as leading to and constituting two heterogeneous groups. The fantasy implies that men make men and women make women. In the case of the sexes, emphasis is more and more placed on intragroup homogeneity: men with men, women with women, in their quasi-speciation. This can be seen in the scientized expressions used in discussing parthenogenesis and in the half-reproving, half-condescending attitude which surrounds fathers who father "only" girls. But, for the time being, men are the children of women (a fact which is well known, perhaps too well known). What is less known seems to be that women are the children of men. To what "natural" group do they belong? Being a man or being a woman, being white or being black means to belong to a social group regarded as natural, but certainly not to a "natural" group.

And moreover the American system—first a slave system, later transformed into a racial system in the nineteenth century with the abolition of slavery—has well and truly defined belonging to a "race" according to class criteria, since the whites who had (or might have had) a supposed slave ancestor were (and still are) "blacks." Thus, a great-grandparent—that is, one out of eight direct genitors (since we have eight grandparents)—or even one grandparent out of sixteen makes you belong to a determined social group, under the mask of naturalness—the most adulterated naturalness in this case. For logically if one takes the suggestions of natural realism literally (and not figuratively), having seven white grandparents, certainly means being white. But it is not so! You are not white, you are "black," for it is the social system that decides. The social situation is that you are black because that is the way the (social) definitions have decided it. Why then speak of presocial, outside-of-society, "scientific" classification—in a word, of "natural" classification? It is this which makes us ask ourselves about this "natural" that claims to be natural while being something else than what it claims to be, a Natural that defines a class by something other than that which is effectively at work in constituting a class. In short, beneath this single notion there stretches a network of relationships covered with a justifying mask— that of Nature, of our Mother Nature.

The denial of reality in the apartheid system illustrates this extraordinary operation of masking. This system claims—having found another, more subtle means of defining membership in a group—that there is no material mixing between groups. There are supposed to be two races, one white, the other black, each exhibiting its own characteristics and its own nature, *and* another race, completely different, without any relation to the preceding ones, a pure product in and of itself. Institutionally separate, the "coloreds" constitute the "other" race, the third element that renders any questioning of the system irrelevant.

These two examples of naturalist false consciousness have been taken from Western industrial society and refer to two historical extreme points: the sequels of the period of capital accumulation (plantation slavery) and the contemporary technological society of South Africa. This is not by chance, for the development of the idea of race is coextensive with that spatial and temporal zone. But it is more than doubtful that this idea still has spatial limits today.

The Systems of "Marks"

The conventional mark

During the two preceding centuries, the geographical localization of productive forces has been the determining factor in the *form* taken by the imputation of naturalness to social groups. The European labor force, in Europe itself, produced a certain number of products (metal ingots, cloth, weapons, etc.) which served as the means of exchange in Africa, especially in the Gulf of Guinea, for a labor force directly transported to the Americas (the South, the Caribbean, and the North) to cultivate the land by "industrial" (or intensive) exploitation. This agriculture, which at first had been extensive and devoted to luxury products (tobacco, indigo, etc.), rapidly became intensive, with the growing first of sugarcane and then of cotton to be exported to Europe. This triangular traffic, as it is called, maintained the European labor force in Europe for mining and manufacturing and exported the African labor force to America for the industrial-agricultural production of tropical products. But the recruitment of the labor force was not immediately so neatly divided. During the seventeenth century, the American agricultural slavery system recruited in both Europe and Africa; the indentured slaves of that period came from the two old continents.[6] It is then as a byproduct of, and in a manner dependent on, geographical origin that skin color acquired a role, insofar as the occasion presented by the search for a labor force and the extension of the triangular traffic offered the possibility for "marking." For if the idea of naturalness is modern, written into the industrial-scientific society, it is not the same, on the other hand, for the sociosymbolic system of marks put on social groups. This latter system concerns a large number of historical and contemporary societies. It is not linked, as the race system will be, to the position of the dominated as such. It comes into play at all levels of the relationship, dominating and dominated, although the mark has specific characteristics according to the level, as we shall see.

Distinct from the idea of nature,[7] and even in a sense contrary to it, since it bears witness to the conventional and artificial inscription of social practices, the system of marks has been present for a very long time as the accompaniment of social cleavages. It still exists, although it is not always noticed, and in its most constant form it is too familiar to be seen. The fact that men and women dress differently, with clothes that are not cut in the same way (draping persists to some extent in women's clothes, while it has disappeared from men's) is an example of marking that continues to be generally unrecognized.

Nevertheless people recognized the dress differentiation between the bourgeoisie and the nobility during the feudal period of the eighteenth century, which gave the nobility the right to furs, jewels, bright colors, and metallic cloth, and gave the bourgeoisie almost a monopoly on the wearing of black.[8] This distinction disappeared when the noble class melted into the bourgeoisie during the nineteenth century, after the bourgeois revolutions. These latter, by abolishing clothing prohibitions, are the source of so-called peasant "regional" costumes, in which color, lace, and embroidery express a newly acquired right. It is well known that during the Middle Ages the members of nondominant religions wore a clothing mark such as the yellow pointed hat or the yarmulke (varying according to regions and period) of the Jews, the yellow cross for the Cathars, etc. The nobles marked their various family groups (groups that, from the fifteenth to the eighteenth century, were called "races") with "coats of arms" on movable objects such as harnesses, shields, armor, vehicles, paintings, servants (objects like the others), or on their buildings, on the porticos, gates, etc. In the sixteenth and seventeenth centuries the galley slaves, the deported prostitutes, and then the slaves until the nineteenth century, were marked by an *immovable* sign, directly inscribed on the body (physical marking of slaves was abolished in 1833 for France), as in the twentieth century deportees were marked by the Nazi state; this same state imposed a cloth badge on Jews before it started to exterminate them. We know that today military personnel and street cleaners (among others) wear a uniform, but we have forgotten that only a short while ago (in the nineteenth century) a man's shaving his beard was a sign of being in domestic service; the tonsure of Catholic priests, ringlets of very orthodox Jews, and long hair for women and short for men were (or still are) some of the many signs and marks, either external or inscribed on the body, that expressed (and imprinted) the fact of belonging to a definite social group. And there is a very long list of such signs and marks.

The characteristics of the mark vary, and its indelibility, as well as its more or less close proximity to/association with the body, is a function of: 1) the assumed permanence of the position that it is a sign of; and 2) the degree of subjection that it symbolizes. The convict under the *ancien regime*, the contemporary concentration camp victim, and the American slave bore the mark on their body (tatooed number or brand), a sign of the *permanence* of the power relationship. The dominating group imposes its fixed inscription on those who are materially subject to them. The mark of status is inscribed in a reversible fashion when it signifies *contractual* subordination: transitory bodily adaptations, such as shaving the beard or not (domestic service), the wearing of a wig (marriage), the tonsure (religious vows), the length of hair, etc. Marking by clothing, much more subject to change in one sense, is without doubt the zero expression of belonging to a *social station*,[9] or, if you prefer, the expression of place in social relations. It is only in the division between the sexes that the clothing mark persists in a permanent fashion today. For although a person puts on a uniform (professional, military, or other) for work—that is, for a specified time and in a limited area—a person is, on the contrary, at every moment when dressed, and in all circumstances, in the uniform of sex. In short, the idea of visually making known the groups in a society is neither recent nor exceptional.

Naturalization of the system of marking and development of the idea of a natural group

However, the idea of classifying *according to* somatic/morphological criteria is recent and its date can be fixed: the eighteenth century. From a circumstantial association between economic relations and physical traits was born a new type of mark ("color"), which had great success. Later developments turned it from the traditional status of a *symbol* to that of a *sign of a specific nature* of social actors. Then began the fabrication of taxonomies that were to be progressively qualified as "natural." This naturalness was not obvious at the beginning, when the concern for form unquestionably overshadowed it.[10] The taxonomies were transformed into classification systems based on a morphological mark, in which the latter is *presumed to precede* the classification, while social relationships created the group on which the mark—because of the social relationship—is going to be "seen" and attached. The taxonomies thus served as anchoring for the development of the idea of race, but the idea of endo-determinism spread little by little onto the schema of marking, which was completely classical at its beginning.

However that may be, the morphological "mark" doesn't precede the social relationship, any more than branding or the tatooing of a number do. I alluded above to the triangular traffic and to the role played by the spatial/temporal extension of this process. At the end of the seventeenth century and at the beginning of the eighteenth, the capture of a labor force for the Americas from just one region of the world—the Gulf of Guinea and East Africa—to the exclusion of Europe, played the role of catalyst in the formation of the idea of race, which was done through the means of the classic "mark." The accidents of economic history furnished in this case a *ready-made* form. But in fact the process of the appropriation of slaves had *already* been going on for around a century when the first taxonomies that included somatic characteristics appeared: the mark *followed* slavery and in no way preceded the slave grouping. The slave system was *already* constituted when the inventing of the races was thought up.

This system developed from something completely different than the somatic appearance of its actors. It is heart-rending to hear so many well-intentioned people (then as now) question themselves about the reasons that could exist for "reducing the blacks to slavery" (contempt, they think; visibility; who knows what else?). But no "blacks" per se were reduced to slavery; slaves were made—which is very different. All these strange reasons are sought and advanced as if "being black" existed in itself, outside of any social reason to construct such a form, as if the symbolic fact asserted itself and could be a cause. But the idea of "reducing 'the blacks' to slavery" is a modern idea which only came about at a specific historical juncture when the recruitment of slaves (who at the beginning were blacks *and* whites) was focalized. People were enslaved wherever they could be and as need dictated. Then at a certain historical moment, from the end of the seventeenth century on, slaves ceased to be recruited in Europe because their labor power from then on was needed there, with the development of industrialization. Consequently they were taken only from a specific and relatively limited region of the world, constituting one of the poles of the triangular traffic. During the period of European/African recruitment, there was not (not yet) a system of marking other than that used for this purpose (branding). So, *a fortiori*, neither was there any reflection about the somatic/physiological "*nature*" of slaves. This reflection, moreover, only appeared after the marking by the somatic sign itself. The taxonomies preceded the racist theories.

The "Nature" of the Exploited

During the nineteenth and twentieth centuries there have been (and moreover still are) many scholars looking for a "naturalness" in classes and exploited groups. For example, the presumption and affirmation of a genetic and biological particularity of the working class, expressed in the form of a lesser intelligence, was—and still remains—one of the strong points of the naturalist discourse. It must also be said that this approach is strongly opposed; it may even be censured. Nevertheless the censure only occurs when it is a matter of the white, male, urban part of the exploited class. All censure or hesitation disappears at the moment that it is a question of the female part, or the immigrant part, or the neocolonized part in the relations of exploitation. Nature is nature, isn't it?

The obsession with the natural mark (proclaimed as the "origin" of social relationships) operates today with great effectiveness. It doesn't do so with the same facility in all circumstances. But whatever the twists and turns of the line of argument, the natural mark is presumed to be the intrinsic *cause* of the place that a group occupies in social relationships. As such this "natural" mark differs from the dress mark or the mark inscribed on the body known by premodern societies. For the old mark was recognized as *imposed* by social relationships, known as one of their consequences, while the natural mark is not presumed to be a mark but the very *origin of* these relationships. It is supposed to be the internal (therefore natural) "capacities" that determine social facts. This is a throwback to the idea of endogenous determinism in human relationships, an idea characteristic of mechanistic scientific thought.

In short, the modern idea of a natural group is the fluid synthesis of two systems: 1) the traditional system of the mark, purely *functional*, in which there is no endogenous implication and which is no different than the marking of livestock; and 2) the archaeo-scientific deterministic system which sees in any object whatever a substance which secretes its own causes, which is *in itself its own cause*. What interests us here is the social group, and its practices are supposed to be the product of its specific nature.

For example: "It is the nature of women to clean up the shit," a statement that (practically throughout the world) means: "Women are women; it's a natural fact; women clean up the shit; it's their nature that makes them do it; and besides, since this is a specialization of genetic origin, it doesn't disgust them, which is itself proof that for them it's natural." In the same way (in the United States), "It's the nature of blacks not to work" means: "It's a natural fact; blacks are unemployed; that's the way their nature makes them; and moreover they are lazy and don't want to do a stroke of work, which shows very well that for them it's natural to be out of work." Notwithstanding that women don't "like" shit more than men do (which is to say, not at all) and that blacks don't "like" to do less work than whites do (which is to say, not any more), what we have here is an intentionally purely subjective critique of their states of mind. On the other hand, that which refers to the effective experiences of the groups of "women" and "blacks" (cleaning up, unemployment), that which refers to the facts is correct: women do clean up the shit, and being black condemns one to unemployment—but *the relationship between the facts is false.*

The spontaneous idea of nature[11] introduces an erroneous relationship between the facts; it changes the very character of these facts. And it does this in a particular way: Nature proclaims the permanence of the effects of certain social relations on dominated groups. Not the perpetuation of these relations themselves (on which no one cares to fix their eyes, and that is understandable; they are like the sun, they burn), but the permanence of their effects—the permanence of shit and of unemployment. The crux of the question really is: A *social relationship*, here a relationship of domination, of power, of exploitation, which secretes the idea of nature, is regarded as the product of traits internal to the object which endures the relationship, traits which are expressed and revealed in specific practices. To speak of a specificity of races or of sexes, to speak of a natural specificity of social groups is to say in a sophistical way that a particular "nature" is *directly productive* of a social practice and to bypass the *social relationship* that this practice brings into being. In short, it is a pseudo-materialism.

The idea of the nature of the groups concerned precludes recognition of the real relationship by concentrating attention first (with the explanation to follow) on isolated, fragmented traits, presumed to be intrinsic and permanent, which are supposed to be the direct causes of a practice which is itself purely mechanical. It is thus that slavery becomes an attribute of skin color, that nonpayment for domestic work becomes an attribute of the shape of sexual organs. Or more exactly, *each* of the numerous obligations imposed by the precise relationships of race and sex are supposed to be a natural trait, with the multiplicity of these natural traits becoming merged to indicate the specific nature of the social group that suffers the relationship of domination. At this precise point the idea of a natural group is invented—of "race," of "sex"—which inverts the reasoning.

Current Form of the Idea of Nature in Social Relationships

Some ideas of race and sex can be said to be imaginary formulations, legally sanctioned and materially effective. Let us look at these three points one after the other.

Natural groups: imaginary formulations

It is certainly not an accident that the classic arguments abut the non-pertinence of the idea of race (I would say, moreover, more aptly, of the idea of a natural group) have been made about natural categories that are not very "distinguishable," and have been made in the case of those where the quality of the mark is rather ambiguous and even wholly evanescent. Both Jean-Paul Sartre in the past in his *Réflexions sur la question juive* and Jacques Ruffié today in his *De la biologie à la culture* use the same subject to support in an immediately convincing fashion the fact that races don't exist. Although their perspectives are different, both of them refer to a group, the Jews, who, whatever the time and place, are not physically distinguished from the dominant group.[12] Showing that belief in the natural characteristics of sociality is illusory, that this belief has been built up by a coercive history, is certainly much easier in the case where no fallacious distraction in terms of physical evidence or visibility is possible. The absence of visual criteria, which might support a counterattack by supporters of the natural inscription of social characteristics, helps considerably in arguing a case that is in itself extremely difficult.

But, all things considered, is it such a good tactic? I don't believe that one can overcome preconceived ideas and commonplace beliefs—which go hand in hand with a unanimous and naive belief in "races" and other natural groups—by a rational argument making appeal to the suspension of judgment and to waiting for an examination of the facts. It seems to me that, on the contrary, it would be more logical to treat the problem by what is most "evident" about it to the eyes of the believers in naturalness, and not by what seems at first view to support the argument of the ideological character of naturalness. What is "least visible" is a trap in this field. For one is not operating within a classical framework of discussion where the terms of the debate are common and the definitions approximately shared. One is well and truly in a situation of conflict. The idea of the endo-determined nature of groups is precisely *the* form taken by the antagonism between the very social groups which are concerned. First let us try to start from scratch and take another approach that calls into question, at their level of highest visibility, the ideas of visual evidence themselves.

No, it is not a matter of fact that the idea of race, since its historical appearance, is found both in common sense and in the sciences.[13] Although physical traits, elsewhere and in the past, have certainly drawn attention, this was done without making distinctions and with a nonclassifying attitude that has become difficult for us to understand. In short, such traits were noticed little more than baldness, eye color, or size are today—interesting certainly, but not the basis for discrimination.[14] Today we are confronted with fierce realities, which it is not enough to say don't exist. We see them, we draw conclusions—1) classifying conclusions, and 2) conclusions about *nature*—stages which are historically and analytically distinct, as we have seen by following the passage from the conventional mark to the natural mark, but which today are mingled, almost syncretically. Moreover, these classifying conclusions are not false, since people do belong to a group, a social group which is defined by its practices within one relationship (among many).[15] It is not by virtue of its (constructed) membership that the group is defined, despite the perception imposed on us by a naturalist apprehension that places the somatic nature of social actors as the origin of classifications and practices.

So there is both truth and falsehood in these classifications—truth (a group), falsehood (the "somatic nature" of the group)—and the falsehood lives on the truth. Appearance (color, sex) furnishes very good information about work (and even about the jobs within a line of work), about pay (or nonpay), and even, if there is one, about the wage level. In 1977 (and still today) in France, for example, if one encounters a woman, one surely encounters someone who does domestic work gratis and probably someone also who without pay, or sometimes for pay, physically cleans the youngest and oldest people in a family or in public or private establishments. And there is a very good chance one will encounter one of those workers at the minimum wage or below who are women. This is not nature; it is a social relationship. In France, if one encounters a Mediterranean man—and it is by design that I don't use a word indicating nationality, because nationality has nothing to do with it, while the region of the world is the determining factor—there is a very good chance that one will encounter one of those workers with a specific type of contract or even one who risks having none at all, and maybe not even a residence permit, someone who works longer hours than other workers, and does this in a construction trade, the mines, or heavy industry. In short, he is one piece of the very structural "labor cushion," which also includes the 46 percent of women who have access to a paid job. If one encounters in France a Caribbean or West Indian man or woman, it is very likely that one encounters someone employed in the service sector—in hospitals, transportation, communications—and precisely someone employed in the public sector. In France, if one encounters a Mediterranean woman, one will very likely encounter someone who also works in the service industries, but not in the public sector; she will be working in the private sector, for an individual employer or a collective employer (a company)—a cleaning woman, a *concierge*, a kitchen employee, etc. One will encounter someone who, for less than the minimum wage (as a woman) does domestic work (as a Mediterranean person), and who does family domestic work (as a woman) gratis.

So here we have these obvious "natural" groups, whose activities, presumed to be "natural" like those who do them, are only the actualization of a very social relationship. It is important to find out how these groups are reputed to be "natural," and natural *first and foremost*. To find out how that is the "logical consequence" of that nature to some people, who consider that one is born with a precise place and task in life, or how it is an "abominable injustice" to others, who think it is cruel and unjustifiable to confine to the "lower strata" or quasi-castes the members of these groups, who, poor things, can do nothing about where they naturally belong. Although the conception of what is wished for varies, the perception of reality is the same—there are natural groups. It is indisputable that nature, which serves us today as portable household god, is the ideological form of a certain type of social relationships. But, stratum or caste ("nature," no less!), it is also true that attention is focused on the subject in order to refuse to see the relationship that constituted it.

The idea of the somatic-physiological internal specificity of the social groups concerned is an imaginary formulation (in the sense that naturalness exists in the mind) associated to a social relationship. This relationship is identifiable through the criteria we have noted, which are completely material, historical, technological, and economic. These traits are connected to a naturalist affirmation whose contradictions, logical silences, and affirmations (all the more confident because based on unclarified implications) demonstrate ambiguity and dubiousness. And the imaginary character of a term of the connection is invisible—thanks to Nature.

Imaginary formulation, legally sanctioned

Legally, and not, as has been claimed for a century, scientifically sanctioned. And the two terms—*legal* and *scientific*—form a pair in the social system. In the case of the natural, the legal plays the role of guarantee theoretically ascribed to scientific fact.

The *institutionalization*, the transformation of the idea of a natural group into a category sanctioned at the level of the state, was not done by the scientific community, despite all its efforts in that direction, but was in fact done by the legal system. Race became an effective legal category *as a category of nature* (that is, a category of non-divine, non-sociohuman origin) at the end of the nineteenth century in the United States (the Jim Crow laws), in 1935 in Nazi Germany (the Nuremberg laws), and in 1948 in South Africa (the apartheid laws). These discriminatory, interdictory, segregating laws, which touch practically all areas of life (marriage, work, domicile, moving about, education, etc.), stipulate the interdictions as a function of racial criteria *by name*. It is not the fact of their being interdictions that is new—interdictions were not created yesterday—but the fact that they write into the law the "natural" membership of citizens in a group. The failure to devise logical naturalist categories by scientific means was only a superficial episode in a process that could do without them. The law came to furnish the sociogovernmental, institutional sanction which had not been produced by the channel from which it had at first been expected, even though the scientific field itself had not given up pursuing it.

The gigantic and grotesque enterprise of physical anthropology that Nazism launched in order to enunciate "scientifically" its racial-legal "truth" was not an enigmatic dysfunction, but the result of a logic of previous social relationships. This scientific justification, unceasingly proclaimed and actively researched in all possible directions, proved to be as elusive as it was forseeable. And particularly elusive, since, aiming at a *functionality* of the idea of race, they tried, looking for a legitimation of a natural order, to create indicators that could coincide with a previous definition of "Aryans" and Jews" according to the Nazi system. Frenzy by the dominant group about the racial or sexual "nature" of the groups concerned bursts out in periods of open conflict or explicit antagonism. Witness the works on the various human "races" in the post-slavery United States,[16] or the Jews in Nazi Germany, on the particularities of sexual chromosomes in the whole industrial world since the 1960s, and on the chemophysiological or genetic nature of deviance in the contemporary USSR. Whether it be in the United States, in colonizing France, in Nazi Germany, or in the transnational patriarchal system, it remains impossible to claim—despite the efforts in which considerable means and great energy were (and are) invested—that human heterogeneity is demonstrated or demonstrable.

So then it is a legal category and a *natural* category of the law. For it is not at all true that when one leaves the domain of the natural sciences in order to enter the realm of the law, one renounces the idea of nature. Quite the contrary. What is involved is the same nature and a guarantee directed at the *same* objective. The law more than science came to serve as witness of and assurance for the strong usable belief in the endo-determined character of groups in a given society. This transference shows that race is a category peculiar to social relationships, springing from them and in turn orienting them. The actual relationships come to be expressed in one of the two possible superstructural forms: legal institutions or science.

Imaginary formulation, legally sanctioned, materially effective

The social sciences themselves have a strangely ambiguous relationship, both reluctant and submissive, with the idea of a natural group. They are reluctant in that they don't accept the thesis that races are, insofar as they are a natural category, an effective, nonmediated cause of social relationships (the proponents of the naturalist thesis are found mostly among physicists, physical anthropologists, or psychologists). They are submissive in that they nevertheless accept the idea of a natural category, but as something dissociated from social relationships and somehow able to have a pure existence. This results in an untenable position. A total abstention from the idea of naturalness would be an easier position to maintain. But the ideological implications of the idea of nature and of natural groups *cannot be passed over*, and therefore it occupies—even if one is loath to see it—a central place in almost all social relations. Ideologically hidden (if the ideology is hidden beneath the "obviousness" of it, as I think), the "natural" form, whether it be common knowledge or already institutionalized, is at the center of the *technical means* used by the relationships of domination and power to impose themselves on dominated groups, and to go on using them.

As a technical/legal category, the proclamation of the existence of natural groups enters the order of material facts. The law is the expression of the ideological/*practical* techniques of the system of *domination*. One finds there the privileged guarantee of what is ideologically supposed to not need guarantee in social rules, since it is a fact of nature. Who can go against Nature, the law of the world, the writing down of which can only be a nullity or a tautology? In affirming the specificity of groups, nature passes through legal inscription; it is affirmed as a social fact at the same time that it claims to be the origin of and the reason for human society. It is a sinister game of "one is supposed to act as if . . ." and then, in fact, one does "act as if."

In fact, a natural characteristic (race, sex), being a legal category, intervenes in social relationships as a constraining and impelling trait. It inscribes the system of domination on the body of the individual, assigning to the individual his/her place as a dominated person: but it does not assign any place to the dominator.[17] Membership in the dominant group, on the contrary, is legally marked by a convenient lack of interdiction, by unlimited possibilities. Let me explain: Legally nothing prevents a member of the dominant group (which, moreover, is only a "natural" group by negation; it is "neither" this, "nor" that) from taking up the activities of the dominated categories. Such a person can become a migrant farm worker, do home sewing, do the laundry gratis for a whole domestic group, be paid to do typing, not be paid to care for, wash, and feed children. Outside of a low wage or none at all, this person wouldn't encounter anything but sarcasm, contempt, or indifference. In any case, there would be no barrier to doing it, but this person wouldn't do it—it's just a theoretical possibility. For 1) while no one would prevent someone from doing it, 2) no one would require it. The two propositions are only meaningful in combination; *each* is important in itself *and when taken together*.

However, everything keeps the members of the dominated groups from: 1) getting paid for jobs that are socially defined as being jobs performed without pay; and 2) becoming part of certain state or religious establishments. They are forbidden to them. And I am not even speaking here of the usual barriers so effective in barring access to high salaries, to personal independence, to freedom of movement. The dominated persons are in the symmetrical and inverse situation of the dominators, for 1) everything prohibits certain activities to them, and 2) on the contrary, everything requires them to do domestic work gratis, to be laborers, to work at (or below) the minimum wage level, etc. And this is done with an array of resources, including legal resources.

Conclusion

The invention of the idea of nature cannot be separated from domination and the appropriation of human beings. It unfolded within this precise type of relationships. But appropriation which treats human beings as things and from that draws diverse ideological variations, is not enough in itself to lead to the modern idea of natural groups. Aristotle after all talked about the nature of slaves, but it was not with the meaning that we give today to this word. The word *nature*, applied to any object, fixed its purpose in the world order, an order which at that time was regulated by theology. In order for the modern meaning of the word to come into being there had to be another element, a factor internal to the object. Endogenous determinism, which ushers in scientific development, will come, by attaching itself to the "purpose," to form this new idea of the "natural group." For beginning with the eighteenth century, rather than appealing to God to explain material phenomena, people turned to analyzing mechanical causes in the study of phenomena, first physical phenomena, and then living phenomena. The stake, moreover, was the conception of Man, and the first materialism was to be mechanistic during this same century (see *L'Homme machine* by Julien Offray de La Mettrie).

If what is expressed by the term *natural* is the pure materiality of the implicated objects, then there is nothing less natural than the groups in question, which precisely are constituted *by* a precise type of relationship: the relationship of power, a relationship which makes them into things (both destined to be things and mechanically oriented to be such), but which *makes* them, since they *only* exist as things within this relationship. This is the social relations in which they are involved (slavery, marriage, migrant labor) and which makes them such at every moment. Outside of these relations they don't exist; *they cannot even be imagined.* They are not givens of nature, but naturalized givens of social relationships.

Translated by Mary Jo Lakeland

Notes

1. For a critical presentation of this position, see the collective work, *Discours biologique et ordre social*, ed. Pierre Achard et al. (Paris: Seuil, 1977), which endeavors to demonstrate this fascination and constant reference at work.
2. In fact, the same problem arises in classical physical anthropology, for the "natural" position is practically untenable. But it is with the social sciences that the present discussion is concerned.
3. At the time that the present arrticle was written, an evening newspaper, in a review of recent books in French on South Africa, used the term *métis* (half-breed) to refer to the "colored" group. Correct in the logical sense, this is false in the social sense, the South African particularly. The word *colored* exists precisely in order to censor the word *half-breed*. Everybody knows that half-breed is what is referred to—that is not the question—but *nobody wants to know it.*
4. But it would be pointless to keep resorting (as is the case) to reaffirmations of morphosomatic evidence if—as is often said (even among social scientists)—the somatic traits were "striking" and "obvious" and were, becaue of that, the cause of racial prejudice, conflicts, and power relations between groups.
5. *Colored* and not *uncolored*, an appellation that would logically be just as pertinent. This shows what the referent of the system is.
6. On the process that separated the two strands of the recruitment of forced labor, the European and the African, see Eric Williams, *Capitalism and Slavery* (Chapel Hill: University of North Carolina Press, 1944).

7. I mean here the idea of "nature" in the present scientific sense. The theological societies gave to this word the meaning of "internal order," a meaning always present within the contemporary idea, but until the nineteenth century it *did not include* an endogenous determinism, which is a fundamental characteristic today.

8. An allusion to this practice can be found in Tallement des Réaux (a leading member of a bourgeois banking family) in the seventeenth century: "She called him over to a corner of the room to ask him if he didn't find that black suited me well. At that time young people didn't wear black so early in the day as one does now."

9. I distinguish here between dependence and belonging. Belonging—"being" in a social station, in a religion—is supposed to be both permanent *and* subject to change. One could be ennobled or change one's religion in certain circumstances. Dependence implies a direct relationship, either contractual or coercive: The "indentured" servant, the cleric bound by his vows, and the appropriated slave were considered to be in an irreversible situation for a specific term of time (which could be limited but which also could be for an entire lifetime).

10. Carl von Linné, the first great taxonomist of the human species, had, as in his vegetable classifications (which it may be noted in passing were, all the same, his essential preoccupation), a conception of method that did not place him at all within an empiricist perspective. His system is a set of statements of principle. He would probably have been very surprised if one had connected him to some endo-determinism, which today necessarily accompanies the idea of nature.

11. "Spontaneous idea": that is, an idea which is tightly associated with—or indissociable from—a specific historical relationship, and which is always present at the heart of this relationship.

12. Even supposing that one accepts this kind of argument, one can also point out that the "obvious distinction" between a Tunisian and a Dutch person is completely invisible to someone who is neither North African nor European, as I have been able to note on numerous occasions. In any case these distinctions are less than those that distinguish between social classes or the sexes, where weight, height, etc. are differentiated.

13. I take the liberty of referring to some of my own previous works: Colette Guillaumin, *L'idéologie raciste. Genèse et langage actuel* (Paris: Mouton, 1972); Colette Guillaumin, "Les caractères specifiques de l'idéologie raciste," *Cahiers Internationaux de Sociologie*, vol. 53 (1972); and Colette Guillaumin, "The Idea of Race and Its Elevation to Autonomous, Scientific and Legal Status," in *Sociological Theories: Race and Colonialism* (Paris: UNESCO, 1980).

14. One can only ask oneself why it is so frequently argued (and by important scholars) that the somatic—so-called racial—mark (in fact, skin color) is supposed to be so much more relevant than eye color or hair color and that it is supposed to have so much more value as a discriminating factor than the latter, which (I quote) "can differ from parent to child." It is forgotten curiously quickly that, as a matter of fact, racial characteristics such as skin color can be *different between parents and children* (in the United States and the West Indies a white parent can have a black child). And this difference is more important than the shade of eye color or hair color not because it is more visible, but because it is socially proclaimed to be racial and assumes the characteristic of constraining violence. Here we have again an example of the lack of reality in the propositions that are presented as evidence of simple common sense.

15. For—let me repeat it—if there was not a *social* group, the physical trait (whatever it might be) would not be discriminating.

16. See, for example: John S. Haller, *Outcasts from Evolution. Scientific Attitudes of Racial Inferiority 1859-1900* (Urbana: University of Illinois Press, 1971); and Marvin Harris, *The Rise of Anthropological Theory* (New York: Crowell, 1968).

17. And it is at this precise point where we find the break with the traditional system of marks, which conventionally applied to all opposing groups. The groups of slaves, of deported prostitutes, of condemned criminals are in an intermediate classification, between those based on the conventional mark and the natural mark, in which the mark on the body was imposed only on the dominated persons.

The No-Drop Rule

Walter Benn Michaels

In the final section of my essay "Race into Culture: A Critical Genealogy of Cultural Identity" (*Critical Inquiry* 18 [Summer 1992]: 655–85), I criticize the idea of antiessentialist accounts of identity, which is to say that I criticize in particular the idea of cultural identity as a replacement for racial identity. My central point is that for the idea of cultural identity to do any work beyond describing the beliefs people actually hold and the things they actually do, it must resort to some version of the essentialism it begins by repudiating. Thus, for example, the idea that people can lose their culture depends upon there being a connection between people and their culture that runs deeper than their actual beliefs and practices, which is why, when they stop doing one thing and start doing another, they can be described as having lost rather than changed their culture. This commitment to the idea that certain beliefs and practices constitute your real culture, whether or not you actually believe or practice them, marks the invention of culture as a project (you can now *recover* your culture, you can *struggle to preserve* your culture, you can *betray* your culture, and so on), and it marks also the return to the essentialism that antiessentialists mean to oppose. For insofar as your culture no longer consists in the things you actually do and believe, it requires some link between you and your culture that transcends practice. That link, I argue, has, in the United States, characteristically been provided by race. Thus, I conclude, cultural identity is actually a form of racial identity.

Critical Inquiry 20 (Summer 1994)

136

Daniel Boyarin and Jonathan Boyarin in their essay "Diaspora: Generation and the Ground of Jewish Identity" (*Critical Inquiry* 19 [Summer 1993]: 693–725; hereafter abbreviated "D") and Avery Gordon and Christopher Newfield in their essay "White Philosophy" (pp. 737–57), criticize this argument. They offer counterexamples to my notion that in order to make possible the kinds of projects mentioned above (preserving your culture, and so on) identity claims must be essentialist, and they deny that the only coherent alternative to essentialism is pure description. They also offer, respectively, a socioreligious reading of my argument (the Boyarins identify it as a form of the "radical individualism" that can be described as a "characteristically Protestant theme" ["D," p. 704])[1] and a sociopolitical reading of it (according to Gordon and Newfield, my argument is an example of "liberal racism" in its "postpluralist" phase [pp. 737, 753]).[2] Finally, Gordon and Newfield identify my argu-

1. Gordon and Newfield repeat this criticism and link it to my supposed refusal to acknowledge that "what we do or who we are is always imposed and chosen within determinate social relations" (p. 743 n. 9). But my argument that only what people actually do and believe determines their identity is indifferent to the question of how many people share certain beliefs or practices and to the question of how they acquired those beliefs and practices. My point is only that their cultural identity cannot be determined by anything other than those beliefs and practices, however widely they are shared and however they were acquired.

2. Their idea here is that the question "'But why does it matter who we are?'" is a Rodney King-style plea for all of us to just "get along," to "ignore the conflicts and coercions, the innumerable interdependent historical circumstances that make us who we are" (p. 742). A critique of Gordon and Newfield's piety about "history" (it "make[s] us who we are") is beyond the scope of the current essay, but the idea that criticizing antiessentialist racism is a way of ignoring conflict and coercion merits some notice. How, exactly, does the refusal to deploy cultural identity as an explanation of the difference between someone living on welfare and, say, a middle-class English professor count as a way of *ignoring* conflict? The truth is just the opposite; it is the redescription of economic differences as racial that makes them tolerable. The current university commitment to curing middle-class white students of racial prejudice is exemplary in this regard since as long as we preach respect for the culture of others as the cardinal virtue, we will be able to regard economic inequality with our customary equanimity. Which is only to say that it's the pluralist discourse of race, not its critique, that makes getting along the great desideratum. (And which is also why Gordon and Newfield's complaint about pluralism—that it's a "milder, more sophisticated" form of "white supremacism" [p. 742]—is just that it isn't pluralist enough.)

Walter Benn Michaels is professor of English and the humanities at The Johns Hopkins University. He is the author of *The Gold Standard and the Logic of Naturalism* (1987) and of a monograph on American literature in the Progressive period, forthcoming in the *Cambridge History of American Literature*. His previous contributions to *Critical Inquiry* include "Against Theory" and "Against Theory 2," both written in collaboration with Steven Knapp.

ment with a form of thinking that they call "white philosophy" and that they associate (pejoratively) with "reason" and "logic." This is what they call "reproducing the existence of a 'color line'" (p. 744)—although they think that I'm the one who has done the reproducing. In any event, what their responses make clear is that the commitment to antiessentialist identitarianism is undiminished and that the question of whether and where to draw the color line remains crucial.

The Boyarins believe that Jewish identity constitutes a counterexample to my argument, and they instance male Jewish circumcision as "a particularly sharp disruption" of my effort to define identity in terms of "'one's actual practices and experiences,'" remarking that the fact of being circumcised "can reassert itself, and often enough does, as a demand (almost a compulsion) to reconnect, relearn, reabsorb, and reinvent the doing of Jewish things" ("D," p. 705). But, setting aside the bizarre use of "re" (if, because you've been circumcised, you go to Hebrew school and learn "Jewish things," in what sense are you *re*learning them?) and setting aside also the even more bizarre idea that it's *circumcision* that compels you toward "Jewish things" (think of the millions of circumcised men not so compelled, that is, not Jewish), what's truly remarkable here is the idea that being circumcised should be presented as the mark of identity that transcends "'one's actual practices and experiences.'" Indeed, the Boyarins themselves appear to realize that circumcision obviously doesn't do this; they describe it as "a mark that transcends one's actual practices and (at least remembered) experiences" ("D," p. 705). But while I do argue (in "Race into Culture" and elsewhere) that you can't remember or forget experiences you didn't have, I don't, of course, argue that you can't remember or forget experiences you *did* have. Indeed, insofar as Jewish identity is crucially dependent upon circumcision, it is crucially dependent precisely upon one's actual experience.

This is why the Boyarins' suggestion that it is "not quite as obvious" as I claim that "a New York Jew cannot become a Mashpee Indian" and their insistence that "a Mashpee Indian can become a Jew" makes my point rather than theirs ("D," p. 705). The Mashpee Indian who became a Jew would do so by altering his or her actual practices and experiences, by getting circumcised, by observing the Jewish holidays, by learning (not relearning or remembering) "Jewish things." His or her Jewish identity would depend *entirely* on his or her actual practices and beliefs, and the minute the Mashpee stopped practicing and believing Jewish things he or she would cease to be a Jew. But insofar as being a Mashpee is different, under U.S. law, from being a Jew, it's because being a Mashpee does *not* depend simply on believing and doing Mashpee things. Tribal status cannot, in other words, be earned by conversion, and in describing the convert as "the ideal type of the Jew" the Boyarins commit themselves to a model of identity that reiterates rather than refutes the primacy of actual practices and experiences ("D," p. 705).[3] Indeed, insofar as conversion is equivalent to assimilation (they both involve exchanging one set of beliefs and practices for another), the Boyarins' hymn to the former simply repeats my paean to the latter.[4]

For Gordon and Newfield, it is not the Jew but the Mashpee Indians, as discussed by James Clifford, who provide a counterexample to my analysis. In a footnote, I criticized Clifford's claim to be offering an ac-

3. My point here is not, however, that the Boyarins simply give the same account of identity that I do and just fail to realize it. For their discussion of cultural and linguistic transmission does suggest the possibility in their view of a certain discrepancy between at least the language children actually speak and the language that will count as theirs. "What about a thirteen-year-old child whom we have allowed until now to concentrate on learning the language/culture of the dominant group?" they ask. "Is it racist to send him or her to a school to learn 'our' language?" ("D," p. 704). Obviously, it isn't wrong to want one's child to learn a new language, but, of course, teaching a child a new language is not the issue. The issue is whether "our" language should count as the child's, whether a culture in which the child has not (according to the terms of the example) been instructed should count as his or hers. If my parents can speak Hebrew as well as English, but I am raised (until thirteen) speaking only English, in what sense is the Hebrew language mine? It will, of course, *become* mine if I learn it, but to say that the motive for learning a language is to make the language mine is obviously different from saying that the motive for learning it is that it already is mine.

The point of my criticism of cultural identity was that the concept of culture could not coherently provide us with such motives, could not, that is, provide a link that would enable us to describe languages we don't speak as in some sense ours. If I grow up speaking Hebrew and always regard it as my native language and my children grow up speaking English and always regard it as their native language, they will no more have lost their cultural identity than I will have lost mine; our identities will just be different. Indeed, if I myself eventually stop speaking Hebrew altogether and speak only English, I will still not have lost my cultural identity, for why should what I used to do (speak Hebrew) determine my identity in a way that what I now do (speak English) does not? The point here is not that nothing has been lost or even that nothing of value has been lost; my ability to speak Hebrew has been lost, and insofar as that ability was valuable, I have lost something of value. But I have not lost my culture; I have not lost my identity. Indeed, if everyone who spoke Hebrew stopped doing so and everyone who practiced "Jewish things" also stopped doing so, *no one* would lose his or her cultural identity. Cultural identity can't be lost.

4. This bears also on their reminder—with respect to my criticism of "compulsory assimilation"—that "power operates in many ways other than the exercise of actual compulsion" ("D," p. 705). Insofar as this is true, it is true for conversion as well, but I leave it to others to decide when conviction becomes compulsion and note here only that "the ideal type of the Jew" has presumably been convinced rather than compelled and thus that, at least according to the Boyarins, the difference between the two survives. It may be worth noting, however, that if we were to accept the idea that *all* cultural practices were the results of something like compulsion, then the projects of cultural survival defended by the Boyarins and Gordon and Newfield would become utterly incomprehensible. These projects depend upon the idea that some beliefs and practices are linked to our identity in such a way as to make them ours even if we don't believe and practice them. But if *all* our beliefs and practices are the products of compulsion, why should some seem more ours than others? Why wouldn't the compulsory replacement of one set by another simply count as the replacement of an old tyranny by a new tyranny?

count of Mashpee identity that did not rely on what he calls the "organicist" criterion of cultural "continuity." Pointing out that participation in "traditional" Mashpee practices had been "intermittent," Clifford denied that Mashpee culture had, in the usual sense, "survived" but insisted that, nevertheless, Mashpee identity had not been "lost," since "any part of a tradition" that can be "remembered, even generations later," cannot be understood as "lost."[5] What's wrong with this account, I argued, is that in recasting the historical past as the remembered past and so redescribing the person who does Mashpee things for the first time (the Boyarins' convert) as a person who remembers the Mashpee things he used to do, it restores the "continuity" Clifford claims to repudiate and restores it at a level deeper than culture. For the invocation of memory makes the person who now does Mashpee things, "even generations later," the same as the person who used to do them, generations before. According to Gordon and Newfield, however, "Mashpee memory" (as Clifford describes it) "is not deeper than culture but is culture, the historical narrative of a society" (p. 750). My effort to link Clifford's account of Mashpee identity to what Gordon and Newfield call "interior identity" rather than *"knowledge of history"* is rejected by them with the assertion that the Mashpee are "indifferen[t] to this kind of depth" (pp. 749, 750 n. 16). When "asked in court about the source of their Mashpee identity," Gordon and Newfield write, the Mashpee "say they are Mashpee because other people have always thought they were, because they think they are, because they say they are." When asked, "How do you know you're an Indian?" the Mashpee makes no appeal to "interior identity" (which is to say, to the essentialist categories I describe); instead she replies, "My mother told me" (p. 750 n. 16).

But why should we understand this question—"How do you know you're an Indian?"—as a question about the "source" of Indian identity? For, after all, the epistemological question of how you know you're a Mashpee is not the same as the ontological question of what it takes to make you a Mashpee, which is only to say that there's a difference between the source of your identity and the source of your knowledge of your identity.[6] And, although Gordon and Newfield may be confused on

5. James Clifford, *The Predicament of Culture: Twentieth-Century Ethnography, Literature, and Art* (Cambridge, Mass., 1986), pp. 341, 342; hereafter abbreviated *PC*.

6. It's interesting that Gordon and Newfield continually double their cultural geneticism with an epistemological geneticism, insisting that what they call "reasons of philosophy" be subordinated to the "interests" those reasons are judged to "reflect," and suggesting that my reasons in particular "reflect the perspective of historically [a nice touch] white interests" (p. 751). If there were any merit to this geneticism, it would, in my view, work against the defense of racial identity since racial identity was, in the U.S., invented by whites and enforced upon blacks. But, of course, there isn't any merit to it. The commitment to disinterestedness—which is to say, the commitment to the idea that the validity of our beliefs depends upon the conditions in which we come to hold them—is simply reproduced here as the commitment to interest—which is to say that Gordon and Newfield have missed the point of

this point, the Mashpee clearly aren't: when asked the ontological question, "What does it take to be a member of the Mashpee tribe?" their medicine man replies, "Tracing ancestry back to your great-grandfather or great-grandmother" (*PC*, p. 292). You may *know* you're a Mashpee because your mother tells you you are, but you *are* a Mashpee because you have Mashpee ancestors. So if converted Jews cannot exemplify an antiessentialism that goes beyond the description of actual beliefs and practices because their identity as Jews is *entirely determined* by their actual beliefs and practices, then the Mashpee cannot exemplify an antiessentialism that goes beyond the description of actual beliefs and practices because there is *nothing antiessentialist* about the way they determine their identity. My original point in discussing Clifford was to show that his account of a Mashpee identity that stayed the same despite numerous changes in Mashpee beliefs and practices could only be defended by the appeal to what another interested anthropologist called "a traceable heritage to aboriginal ancestors" (*PC*, p. 321). And while almost everyone involved in the trial agreed that insistence on "'some fairly high degree of blood quantum'" (*PC*, p. 326) would be unfair, the history of race in the United States has conclusively proven that—for the purposes of racial classification—only one drop is needed.

Gordon and Newfield acknowledge that there are some "inconsistencies" in Clifford's discussion of Mashpee identity, but they insist nevertheless that everything he says "does in fact lead away from both racial and narrowly cultural identity toward some conjuncture like historical socioculture" (p. 750). And it is, of course, perfectly true that everything Clifford says is *meant* to lead away from race and toward "some conjuncture like historical socioculture," which seems to be enough for Gordon and Newfield. Making good on their suggestion that, with respect to identity, "remembering a grievance" counts more than exposing a "logical inconsistency" (p. 755), they reject the idea that people could be mistaken about the direction of their own thought; indeed, they seem unhappy with the idea of mistakes altogether, associating my claim that the defenders of antiessentialist accounts of racial identity are mistaken about their antiessentialism with "white philosophy"'s valorization of "contemporary standards of valid reasoning" (p. 755) and with "liberal racism"'s interest in "conceptual errors" (p. 737).[7] Thus the fact that "many commentators

---

the critique of objectivity and that they continue to think that the truth of people's views should be determined by reference to a causal account of how they came to hold them.

7. Gordon and Newfield assert that the Mashpee are somehow indifferent to "conceptual errors," but the closest they come to demonstrating this claim is with quotations like the one reproduced above in which a young woman says she knows she's an Indian because her mother told her, and as we've already seen, the only conceptual error here is Gordon and Newfield's. In any event, it's hard to see why the defense of identity claims should involve any less logic than the critique of them, and harder still to accept the kind of primitivism implied by Gordon and Newfield's racialization of "logic."

on identity politics" have repudiated racial essentialism but "have retained the use of *social* identities" is itself a liability for my argument because, presumably, one can say of these commentators what, as it turns out, one cannot say of the Mashpee, that they really have given up on essentialism (p. 744). At least according to Gordon and Newfield, these "scholars of color," if asked what it takes to be a scholar of color, would not reply, "Tracing ancestry back to your great-grandfather or great-grandmother." So what does it take to make a scholar a scholar of color? How does race without biology work in the United States today?

That the commitment to race without biology, to what Michael Omi and Howard Winant call "race as a social concept,"[8] is widespread cannot be questioned. Writers like Omi and Winant are hostile to the explanation of behavior by appeal to a biology of race and criticize more generally efforts to give the concept of race a "scientific meaning" (*RF*, p. 68), but they decline to abandon the concept of race as such. On the contrary, regarding race as "a pre-eminently *social* phenomenon" (*RF*, p. 90), they celebrate what they call "the forging of new collective racial identities during the 1950s and 1960s," arguing that "the racial subjectivity and self-awareness which [were] developed" have taken "permanent hold" in American society (*RF*, p. 91). And this commitment to racial identity without biology certainly does extend beyond the writings of social scientists like Omi and Winant or Gordon and Newfield and clearly has become what Gordon and Newfield say it is, "one of the most important principles by which U.S. social relations are organized" (p. 740). In a widely noticed racial identity case in Louisiana, for example, the Fourth Circuit Court of Appeals, remarking (like Gordon, Newfield, and others) that "the very concept of the racial classification of individuals . . . is scientifically insupportable,"[9] ruled that Susie Phipps, "who had always thought she was white, had lived as white, and had twice married as white,"[10] was not in fact white because her parents, who had provided the racial information on her birth certificate, had thought of themselves and of her as "colored." "Individual racial designations are purely social and cultural perceptions" (*JD*, p. 372), the court said; the relevant question, then, was not whether those perceptions correctly registered some scientific fact (since the court denied there was any relevant scientific fact) but whether they had been "correctly recorded" at the time the birth certificate was issued. Since in the court's judgment they had been, Phipps and her fellow appellants remained "colored."

8. Michael Omi and Howard Winant, *Racial Formation in the United States* (New York, 1986), p. 60; hereafter abbreviated *RF.*

9. *Jane Doe v. State of Louisiana, through the Department of Health and Human Resources, Office of Vital Statistics and Registrar of Vital Statistics,* 479 So. 2d 372 (1985); hereafter abbreviated *JD.*

10. F. James Davis, *Who Is Black?* (University Park, Pa., 1991), p. 10; hereafter abbreviated *W.*

Because Phipps was by credible evidence at least one-thirty-second black, commentators like Omi and Winant cite this case as an example of racial biologism and F. James Davis in his important book *Who Is Black?* describes the Phipps case as confirming the legality of the one-drop rule.[11] This rule had, of course, a biological meaning. In older racist texts like Robert Lee Durham's *The Call of the South* (1908), the justification for counting as black anyone with a traceable amount of black blood is the conviction that this trace will at some point manifest itself, as when the savagery of his African grandfather emerges in the quadroon Hayward Graham and he rapes his white wife: "With a shriek of terror she wildly tries to push him from her: but the demon of the blood of Guinea Gumbo is pitiless, and against the fury of it, as of the storm, she fights and cries— in vain."[12] The idea, then, is that black blood makes a difference to the intrinsic identity of the person, and even if this difference is ordinarily invisible (even if the person characteristically looks and acts even more white than Hayward Graham who is "unobtrusively but unmistakably a negro"),[13] at some point his blackness will show itself. The reasoning, in other words, depends on a commitment to the biology of race. But it turns out that the designation of people who neither look nor act black as nonetheless black does not necessarily depend on the idea that their blackness might actually show itself or might even be the sort of thing that could in principle show itself, which is to say that it's a mistake to see that biological account of race confirmed in the Phipps decision. On the contrary, the court, as I have noted, firmly insists that "racial designations are purely social and cultural perceptions." Phipps is "colored" not because of her traceable amount of black blood but because her parents said she was.[14]

The rule the court enforces here is the rule that Gordon and Newfield imagine for the young Mashpee woman, Vicky Costa: "Q.: How do you know you're an Indian? A.: My mother told me" (*PC*, p. 301). "The witness," Gordon and Newfield remark, "knows she is an Indian because

11. Noting that both the Louisiana Supreme Court and the United States Supreme Court refused to review the decision of the court of appeals, Davis argues that "the highest court in the United States saw no reason to disturb the application of the one-drop rule" (*W*, p. 11). Although, as will become clear below, I do not entirely agree with Davis's interpretation of *Jane Doe* v. *State of Louisiana* (which is how the Phipps case was filed), I have learned a great deal from his history of the one-drop rule and from his comparison of racial practices in the United States to racial practices elsewhere.

12. Robert Lee Durham, *The Call of the South* (Boston, 1908), p. 290.

13. Ibid., p. 7.

14. When the Phipps case went to trial, a 1970 statute declaring that anyone with "one thirty-second or less Negro blood" could not be counted as black was still in effect. But by the time the case reached the court of appeal, that statute had been repealed and the court, since it based its own decision on "social and cultural perceptions," declared that it was, in any event, "not relevant." The statute that replaced it, according to Davis, explicitly gives "parents the right to designate the race of newborns" (*W*, p. 10).

she trusts her mother" (p. 750 n. 16). The court requires that Phipps, like Costa, trust her mother. And, in the spirit of Gordon and Newfield, what this produces is not a one-drop rule but a no-drop rule, the legal equivalent of the social scientist's *"social* phenomenon." It solves the problem of the scientific establishment of racial identity by denying that racial identity is anything more than a question of "social perception." But, of course, this solution is accompanied by a problem. If racial identity is no longer understood to have anything to do with "blood," what are we to imagine that Phipps's parents were thinking when they thought of themselves and of her as black? If their criteria for racial identity were the same as the state's criteria, they weren't thinking that she had some proportion of black blood; according to the court, "purely social and cultural perceptions," not blood, determine racial identity. But they could not be thinking of her as someone who was *perceived* by them as being black; that is, they could not think that their perception of her as black was what made her black because to think that would be to beg the question why they perceived her as black in the first place. The perception of blackness, in other words, may be enough to make someone black in the eyes of the state, but it isn't enough to explain what blackness is. (And, of course, her behavior couldn't do this either since, as a newborn, she presumably didn't talk in an imaginably black dialect or exhibit any of the forms of behavior that might conceivably be associated with the cultural behavior of blacks.) What, then, is the perception of blackness a perception of?

The standard interpretation of this case is, as we have seen, that it restored the one-drop rule; since everybody agreed that Phipps did have *some* black ancestry, she counted as black. But, despite this ancestry, if her parents had perceived themselves and her as white, she would—even acknowledging this very small proportion of black blood—have counted as white. Louisiana law, in other words, as articulated by the majority in this decision, insists on the "subjective nature of racial perceptions" and takes no account of the ancestry. Perhaps one could argue that Louisiana doesn't go far enough in discounting ancestry; after all, why should her *parents'* perception of her racial identity be determining? Gordon and Newfield point out that "the Indian Reorganization Act of 1972 appeared to abandon the 'blood quantum' standard of Indian identity in favor of 'self-identification,' only to be evaded by the Reagan Administration's attempt to 'enforce degree-of-blood requirements'" (p. 746 n. 12). Maybe the injustice in the Phipps case is that the wrong social perceptions were enforced; Phipps should be white because even though her parents perceived themselves and her as black, she perceived herself as white. It is, as Omi and Winant say, her "racial self-awareness" that should be respected. But, of course, this doesn't solve the problem posed by the parental perception of her as black; it just relocates it: what's her perception of whiteness a perception of?[15] When Phipps looks back on the little baby that her parents perceived as black, what makes her perceive it as white?

The truth is that Louisiana law, acknowledging no biological basis for the determination of racial identity and therefore refusing to establish a biological standard for the law, has decided instead to establish not biology but people's mistaken accounts of biology as the legal standard. In other words, the fact that Phipps had at least one black ancestor could not make her black under the law, but the fact that her one black ancestor made her parents perceive her as black *did* make her black under the law. The biological determination that the state itself regards as "scientifically unsupportable" nonetheless counts as determining as long as the determination isn't made by the state. Refusing itself to apply the one-drop rule, the state chose instead to enforce Phipps's parents' application of the one-drop rule. What it means, then, to accept the idea of racial identity as a function of "purely social and cultural perceptions" instead of as biology is to accept the idea of racial identity as the codification of people's mistakes *about* biology. In a way, then, Davis is right to assert that some version of the one-drop rule is being enforced under current Louisiana law, but what is being enforced is not the claim that one drop of black blood makes a person black; what's being enforced is the claim that the *perception* that one drop of black blood makes a person black makes a person black. Everything the court says, as Gordon and Newfield might put it, leads away from race and "toward some conjuncture like historical socioculture." And everything in "historical socioculture" leads right back to race.

According to Louisiana law, Phipps was passing, pretending to be white when she was, in fact, black. Both the law and the very idea of passing require that there be some fact of racial identity, a requirement that was easily met as long as there could be some appeal to science but that the repudiation of scientific racism has made more difficult. The requisite fact must now be social or cultural rather than biological. Thus, in a recent and powerfully written essay called "Passing for White, Passing for Black," Adrian Piper denies that there is any "set of shared physical characteristics" that "joins" her "to other blacks" because, she says, "there is none that all blacks share."[16] What makes blacks black is rather "the shared experience of being visually or cognitively *identified* as black by a white racist society, and the punitive and damaging effects of that identification" ("PW," pp. 30–31). This is the Louisiana standard: if you're per-

---

15. The problem with self-identification from the standpoint of racial essentialism is that you can't trust people to tell the truth; the problem with self-identification from the standpoint of racial *anti*essentialism is that you have no idea what criteria might help you to determine the truth and so no reason to believe that there is any truth.

16. Adrian Piper, "Passing for White, Passing for Black," *Transition*, no. 58 (1992):30; hereafter abbreviated "PW."

ceived as black, you are black. But Piper's account of her own experience makes the incoherence of this standard even more obvious than it is in the Phipps case. For Piper describes herself as so light skinned that she is constantly (both by people whom she identifies as black and by people whom she identifies as white) being treated as if she were white. She is thus made to feel that she is passing for white, and since passing for white seems to her "a really, authentically shameful thing to do" ("PW," p. 10), she is led into strenuous efforts to identify herself as black. (The irony that produces her title is that these efforts lead her to be accused—again by both whites and blacks—of passing for black.) But what consequences must these efforts have for her nonbiological definition of racial identity? The point of that definition is that being black means being identified by a white racist society as black. On what grounds, then, can someone who is *not* identified by that society as black be said to be black?

Piper makes this dilemma even clearer by going on to remark that she has "white friends who fit the prevailing stereotype of a black person" and thus have "experiences" "similar" to the ones that make blacks black ("PW," p. 31). If they really do have such experiences, what can she mean by calling these friends "white"? That they can be white even if they are treated as black; that she can be black even if she is treated as white— these facts are tributes to, not critiques of, racial essentialism. The very idea of passing—whether it takes the form of looking like you belong to a different race or of acting like you belong to a different race—requires an understanding of race as something separate from the way you look and the way you act. If race really were nothing but culture, that is, if race really were nothing but a distinctive array of beliefs and practices, then, of course, there could be no passing, since to believe and practice what the members of any race believed and practiced would, by definition, make you a member of that race. If race really were culture, people could change their racial identity, siblings could belong to different races, people who were as genetically unlike each other as it's possible for two humans to be could nonetheless belong to the same race. None of these things is possible in the U.S. today. And, were they to become possible, we would think not that we had finally succeeded in developing an antiessentialist account of race but that we had given up the idea of race altogether.

On rehearing, the Louisiana court took the opportunity to remind the appellants that we can't afford to give up the idea of race, that the accumulation of "racial data" is "essential" for "planning and monitoring public health programs, affirmative action and other anti-discrimination measures" (*JD*, p. 374). Or, as Gordon and Newfield put it, race "is one of the most important principles by which U.S. social relations are organized" (p. 740). My point in this response has not been simply to argue that these claims are wrong for, at least in one sense, they are obviously right: U.S. social relations have been and continue to be organized in part by race. My point has been to assert that this organization is the consequence of a mistake, and that antiessentialist defenses of race amount to nothing more than new ways of making the mistake. As absurd as the one-drop rule of Jim Crow is, the no-drop rule of antiessentialism is even more absurd. Omi and Winant cite two "temptations" that they believe must be resisted in thinking about race: the first is the temptation "to think of race as an *essence,* as something fixed, concrete and objective"; the second is "to see it as a mere illusion" (*RF,* p. 68).[17] Their point, of course, is that in seeing race as a social construction we can avoid both temptations. But if, as I have argued, to see race as a social construction is inevitably (even if unwillingly and unknowingly) to essentialize it, then race really is either an essence or an illusion. The two "temptations" are the only choices we have.

17. From the standpoint of antiessentialism, in other words, what's wrong with the idea of race is that it's essentially essentialist or, to put the point a little more precisely, what's wrong with it is that there can be no coherent antiessentialist account of race. It may be worth wondering, however, why this should count as a problem. Those who believe that individual racial identity is a biological reality don't need an antiessential account of race; those who don't believe individual racial identity is a biological reality don't need one either, unless, of course, their commitment to the category of race is so complete that they understand themselves to be required to maintain it at all costs. And this does seem to be the point of the whole debate over racial essentialism, the point, that is, of insisting that the problem with the biology of individual racial identity is that it's *essentialist* rather than *false.* Transforming the question of whether or not there is such a thing as individual racial identity into the question of whether or not race is an "essence" and thus deploying race as the grounds of the question rather than as its object, this debate reinvigorates and relegitimates race as a category of analysis. If, then, racial antiessentialism is a mistake, it is, at least, a mistake with a purpose, and if race is, as Gordon and Newfield say, "one of the most important principles by which U.S. social relations are organized," then racial antiessentialism turns out to be one of the ways in which U.S. intellectuals can make their own modest contributions to the maintenance of that most important principle.

147

White Philosophy

Avery Gordon and Christopher Newfield

> The court acted like a philosopher who wanted to know positively
> whether a cat was on the mat in Mashpee.
> —JAMES CLIFFORD, *The Predicament of Culture*

1. Racism and the "Appeal to Race"

Liberal racism has recently been attracting the attention it deserves. Its
defining feature is an antiracist attitude that coexists with support for
racist outcomes. Liberal racism rejects discrimination on the basis of race
or color and abhors the subjection of groups or individuals on racial
grounds. But it upholds and defends systems that produce racializing
effects, often in the name of some matter more "urgent" than redressing
racial subordination, such as rewarding "merit" or enhancing economic
competitiveness.

A particularly powerful form of liberal racism displays two additional
features that will be especially important here. First, rather than explicitly
rationalizing racism, it treats the categories through which racism operates, is felt, and is addressed as conceptual errors. It thus directs less
attention to the histories, current forms, and social effects of racism
(though it agrees racism is a problem) than to the problems of race and
racial identity, categories it considers politically troubling and intellectually flawed. Liberal racial thinking seeks to go "beyond race" and does

Critical Inquiry 20 (Summer 1994)

not support racialized perspectives on racism on the grounds that they are a kind of reverse racism. Second, it seeks to describe its own move beyond race as part of reason rather than of history; the move is not, in other words, a racial ideology in its own right, with a genealogy that links the gesture to the social positions and racial interests of white progressives, but an expression of the rational truth about race.

It is one of the virtues of Walter Benn Michaels's essay "Race into Culture: A Critical Genealogy of Cultural Identity" (*Critical Inquiry* 18 [Summer 1992]:655–85) that it focuses attention on liberal racism, particularly the kind that appears in cultural pluralism. We have learned a great deal from his insistence that racism is not an accidental by-product of the liberal reforms that replaced the appeal to race with the appeal to culture but is part of the structure of such reforms. We have benefitted from his unveiling of racialization where it is most often invisible and his outline of racism's historical persistence through major intellectual watersheds. It is one of the symptoms of the times, however, that Michaels's essay locates the racism of cultural pluralism in its use of racial and cultural identity rather than in the liberal racism with which pluralism coexists. Writing in a period when a post–civil rights liberalism has been accumulating increasing political and intellectual influence, Michaels's call for an America "without race" does not get beyond the white moderate position on race but furnishes it with a philosophical rationale.

This ascendent race liberalism thrives on a contemporary debate about whether racism or race consciousness is the greater social problem. Where race consciousness involves a sense of links between one's social position and historical patterns of racialization, is it racist to be conscious of one's "racial" identity?[1] Or is racial identity (including its deployment) the result of racism? These questions—starkly polarized here—have become especially confusing at the present time, when signs of racial progress and racial regression exist side by side and can be difficult to tell

1. Gary Peller offers an analysis of the "racial compromise" by which "the price of the national commitment to suppress white supremacists would be the rejection of race consciousness among African Americans" (Garry Peller, "Race Consciousness," *Duke Law Journal* [Sept. 1990]: 760).

Avery Gordon is assistant professor of sociology at the University of California, Santa Barbara. She is editor, with Christopher Newfield, of *Multiculturalism?* and author of *Ghostly Matters* (both forthcoming). **Christopher Newfield** is assistant professor of English at the University of California, Santa Barbara. He is currently completing one book entitled *The Submissive Center: Ralph Waldo Emerson and the Problem of Democratic Authority* and another on the corporate culture of post-1950s literary study.

apart. Biologically defined racism appears very much on the wane, and color-blind hiring practices are a presumed norm; at the same time, racially patterned inequality has not only persisted but has gotten worse. The idea that we are "post" civil rights suggests the period of civil rights protest to have been a success but also a failure. It has produced indications that the genuine progress represented by civil rights has not been enough to withstand embedded institutional and psychological resistances like the white backlash against affirmative action programs or unabating white anxiety about the presence of social and political actors who insist on the continuing significance of racism. The changing U.S. economy has intensified the attention paid to the multiracial composition of the workforce, but this has encouraged an ambiguous stress on higher productivity through cultural sensitivity *and* the rejection of race politics. Many experience all this as a dilemma: should racism—as a mode of hierarchical social differentiation—be granted ongoing social significance, or is racial identity itself an obstacle to progress?

The latter response has been especially influential in the political realm, for it locates the solution to racism in color blindness and the end of race consciousness.[2] The New Democrats, for example, have argued that too much emphasis on minority (especially African American) concerns for equity has itself been responsible for the racial setbacks of the Reagan-Bush era. In analyses made most prominent by liberals like Thomas Byrne Edsall, Mary Edsall, and E. J. Dionne, and put into practice by Bill Clinton, the persistence of racial inequality gets blamed not on white racism but on the invocation of race.[3] They regard the *explicit* appeal to race as separable from the racist past and present in which the appeal has most often been made.[4] Once the appeal to race is seen analytically, free of the context of racism, the usual causality becomes reversed: racism does not make people talk about race; talk about race sustains racism. One overriding characteristic of post–civil rights is a spurious equalizing effect: uses of race are the same regardless of the

2. See, for example, Kimberlé Williams Crenshaw, "Race, Reform, and Retrenchment: Transformation and Legitimation in Antidiscrimination Law," *Harvard Law Review* 101, no. 7 (1988): 1331–87, and Neil Gotanda, "A Critique of 'Our Constitution is Color-Blind,'" *Stanford Law Review* 44 (Nov. 1991): 1–68.

3. See Thomas Byrne Edsall and Mary D. Edsall, *Chain Reaction: The Impact of Race, Rights, and Taxes on American Politics* (New York, 1991), and E. J. Dionne, Jr., *Why Americans Hate Politics* (New York, 1991).

4. Such writers are themselves making an appeal to race in their address to the middle class as a supposedly inclusive and populist political category in the United States, but this appeal, though racially encoded as white, is not explicit. In this context, the concept of white supremacy is preferable to that of racism, which remains popularly conceived as intentional, psychological, and attitudinal, as a problem that minorities—those who are overtly racialized—create for those who are not, that is, whites. White supremacy, by contrast, views whiteness as a constitutive dimension of complex relations of governance in continual negotiation with other (and overlapping) governance systems.

race of the user; discrimination is no worse than reverse discrimination. In short, these analyses replace the race *problem* with the *"race"*
problem.

This of course undoes civil rights era common sense, in which the
more basic problem was considered to be racism itself. That sensibility
promotes discussion of racism in all of its forms, particularly in its friend-
lier modern ones, like institutional racism. It asks for increased use of the
category of race not because race is a biological fact or even because it
defines one's intrinsic personal or cultural identity but because it is one
of the most important principles by which U.S. social relations are organized. This is something like the way scholars who are interested in gender relations can speak about the impact of the American sex/gender
system without believing that this system produces its effects biologically.
These writers, while expressing a considerable range of views, generally
regard race *"as an unstable and 'decentered' complex of social meanings constantly transformed by political struggle,"* a changing complex that nonetheless has decisive racializing effects.[5] They hold that it is racism and
racialization that keep race alive.[6]

How has this idea gotten completely turned around? How has the
turnaround endowed white racial moderates with a political influence
they have not enjoyed in years? Part of the answer is of course that many
have become persuaded that it was too upsetting to talk about America
as an apartheid state; it was too offensive to talk about who continues to
benefit; it was too disruptive to talk about pointed remedies. So they have
offered an effective pragmatic argument that good coalition politics requires working around the racial resentments of white voters offended
by the old Democrat social agenda; lessened race consciousness would
lessen racism. But for this position to succeed, it requires a more complete reengineering of the terrain of racial common sense; nothing less
will keep this river flowing upstream. Too much in the American world
says that race consciousness largely issues from racism to make it easy to
show the reverse. The reversal, racism from race, requires bigger upheavals in the old terrain. Ideally, such an upheaval would dwarf empirical and sociological conditions like white racial backlash, where racism is
too inextricably mixed in with appeals to race to allow the elimination of
racism as a major social cause. It would be better to be able to show that
the appeal to race is the prior problem on grounds that *it is itself intrinsi-*

5. Michael Omi and Howard Winant, *Racial Formation in the United States: From the 1960s
to the 1980s* (New York, 1986), p. 68.

6. Racialization and racism operate autonomously but rarely alone. Understanding the
intersections among race, class, and gender dynamics—three of the most important modern social determinants—has been a major preoccupation of scholars for decades. It is unfortunately beyond the scope of this paper to pursue this, but it may suffice to note that
pluralist racism evades consideration of gender altogether and tends to use a specifically
American-style understanding of class to chart the declining significance of race.

cally racist, solid gold racism, too much the fountainhead of racism to have received racism from any lesser source.

Such a demonstration appears in "Race into Culture." Our next section considers the construction of this demonstration—the reasons Michaels offers for shifting from criticizing a history of veiled white racism to criticizing the appeal to race. This shift hinges on Michaels's categorical association of race consciousness with essentialist identity practices. The final section describes three undesirable outcomes of the type of racial management that Michaels's work implies (irrespective of his undoubtedly antiracist personal intentions), and sketches an alternative.

2. Making Racial Ontology

> Q.: If you were telling them about it, it would be because they didn't know about it, isn't that right?
> A.: Not at all times, no.
> —RAMONA PETERS under cross-examination from James St. Clair, *Mashpee Tribe* v. *New Seabury et al.* (1977)

Michaels's genealogy of U.S. cultural identity offers an extremely important general conclusion: "Our current notion of cultural identity both descends from and extends the earlier notion of racial identity" (p. 658). Cultural identity is "the project of lining up [one's] practices with [one's] genealogy" (p. 679). Lest one doubt the ongoing relevance of this description of certain cultural critics, *Time*'s recent special issue on America as the "world's first multicultural society" pictures multi*culturalism* as technologized color blending of the facial characteristics of seven ethnic types of both genders.[7] Michaels concludes that "the modern concept of culture is not . . . a critique of racism; it is a form of racism" (p. 683). To the extent that they have rested on the category of "cultural" identity, even liberal, progressive positions like cultural pluralism, positions that formally repudiate racism, have done little more than "rescue . . . racism from racists" (p. 684 n. 40).

But what is it about cultural identity that is racist? Is it that a certain group, like the white-acculturated corporate media professionals at *Time*, deploys cultural identity for its own interests or from its own exclusionary perspective? Or is something wrong with cultural identity itself, an inherent flaw that renders irrelevant historical or political distinctions among different uses? To polarize the issue again, does the problem lie in racist uses or in the appeal to race itself?

The former belief would lead to answers like this: the architects of

---

7. *The New Face of America: How Immigrants Are Shaping the World's First Multicultural Society,* special issue of *Time* (Fall 1993).

pluralist identity held milder, more sophisticated, more culturalized but nonetheless deep-rooted views about white superiority. Pluralism would then be racist because it articulates a complex white supremacism. But Michaels's essay does not trace racist pluralism to the history of progressive white racial thought. It traces it to the presence of racial ontology in all uses of culture. His conclusion expands the source of the race problem from racial identity to cultural identity but retains the causal claim of the post–civil rights liberalism noted earlier: "It is only the appeal to race that makes culture an object of affect and that gives notions like losing our culture, preserving it, stealing someone else's culture, restoring people's culture to them, and so on, their pathos. . . . Without race, losing our culture can mean no more than doing things differently from the way we now do them and preserving our culture can mean no more than doing things the same" (pp. 684–85). Michaels is suggesting that, without race, the deprivations and dominations linked to racism would disappear.[8] Free of cultural identity, we will be able to treat people as people rather than as races. This ideal has strong appeal in a variety of racialized communities—if we could all stop talking race, then we would have a chance to get along. When Michaels exclaims, "But why does it matter who we are?" the question harbors an insistent entreaty: our dealings with one another can ignore the conflicts and coercions, the innumerable interdependent historical circumstances that make us who we are in the first place (p. 682).

We agree with Michaels that replacing racial with cultural identity fudges the central questions about what the invocation of identity means. But the tangled relations between cultural and racial identity do not necessarily point to their union in racial ontology, as Michaels suggests. How does he demonstrate that "accounts of cultural identity that do any cultural work require a racial component" (p. 682)? How does he show that liberal racism consists of the appeal to race rather than, for example, to an investment in a (gentler) regime of racial inequality?

The answer lies in his argument that any invocation of identity is a form of racial ontology.

But why does it matter who we are? The answer can't just be the epistemological truism that our account of the past may be partially determined by our own identity, for, of course, this description of the conditions under which we know the past makes no logical difference to the truth or falsity of what we know. It must be instead the onto-

8. Michaels appends a disclaimer to his text: "Needless to say, the situation is entirely different with respect to compulsory assimilation; what puts the pathos back is precisely the element of compulsion" (p. 685 n. 41). This suggests that he regards cultural relations and compulsion as usually separable things, that he thinks that appeals to race are not generally produced or even coexistent with the compulsions of racism. In spite of his conclusion, this merely brackets rather than resolves the causal connection between them.

logical claim that we need to know who we are in order to know which past is ours. The real question, however, is not *which* past should count as ours but why *any* past should count as ours. . . .The history we study is never our own; it is always the history of people who were in some respects like us and in other respects different. When, however, we claim it as ours, we commit ourselves to the ontology of "the Negro," to the identity of "we" and "they," and the primacy of race. [P. 682]

Michaels distinguishes between studying history and studying "our" history. The introduction of a connection between history and identity makes even a social or historical question about one's placement, one's power, and so on a question about one's essence—about biology, ancestry, or similarly determinate and constitutive cultural traditions. Michaels rejects the possibility that identity questions are about one's historical and social relations to others who "were in some respects like us and in other respects different." Nonessentialist history, for Michaels, avoids identity questions because it knows that "the conditions under which we know the past," our social position, can "mak[e] no logical difference" to historical knowledge. Identity questions and historical questions are essentially different, and the former are always ontological. *All* identity questions are about this because, logically, none are embedded in collective history: "The real question" is "why *any* past should count as ours." Cultural identity is ontological, the ontology refers to a prehistorical essence, and this essence is the idea of race.

What does it mean for Michaels to reduce group histories to racial identity? Taking this citation by itself, it appears that Michaels achieves his reduction of identity questions to racial ontology by proposing an essentialist definition of genuine knowledge of the past—such knowledge has no "logical" connection to the position of the person creating the knowledge. "What we know" is independent of who we are and what made us this way.[9] Another factor may be his apparent indifference to a major development in cultural theory in the past decade, the attempt to

9. At the essay's pivotal junctures, Michaels imputes essentialism to identity as used by others: all uses (that do cultural work), and particularly pluralist uses, require "us to be able to say who we are independent" of what we do; "instead of who we are being constituted by what we do, what we do is justified by who we are" (pp. 683–84 n. 39, 683). In general, Michaels's antiessentialism works through a supplementary cultural *individualism*. Antiessentialism says only that we should not derive what we do from who we are in the sense in which "who we are" is logically prior to and undetermined by what we do. We agree with this sociological commonplace. It is *individualism* that allows us to ignore that what we do or who we are is always imposed and chosen within determinate social relations. Cultural studies must be antiessentialist to be *social* studies in the first place. We hope to be lending an air of gratuity—even of conformity—to the project that makes antiessentialism the vanguard of individualism. Daniel Boyarin and Jonathan Boyarin link Michaels's view of cultural identity to his individualism in "Diaspora: Generation and the Ground of Jewish Identity," *Critical Inquiry* 19 (Summer 1993): 702, 704.

render the use of individual and group identity fully antiessentialist *and* social. Antiessentialist uses of identity have been pioneered by feminist thought, race and postcolonial studies, and lesbian and gay studies, to name some of the most active fields. Writers such as Norma Alarcón, Gloria Anzaldúa, Homi Bhabha, Ed Cohen, Diana Fuss, Giles Gunn, Stuart Hall, Donna Haraway, June Jordan, Duncan Kennedy, Ernesto Laclau, Lisa Lowe, Wahneema Lubiano, Kobena Mercer, Chantal Mouffe, Gayatri Chakravorty Spivak, and Patricia J. Williams have emphasized the variable, indeterminate, shifting boundaries of any group identity. Many commentators on identity politics have lived through the abundant political failures of essentialism and have retained the use of *social* identities even as they have repudiated—with a passion born of disappointed hopes—a dream of sharing essences. Much of this work, though of course not all, has been associated with scholars of color. When Michaels proceeds without engaging the work that challenges his claim that identity is always essentialist, he is reproducing a "color line" in cultural studies.

These are some odd liabilities for Michaels's demonstration that racism is the appeal to race, but we do not think they mean that Michaels "really" possesses essentialist or racist intentions; we presume he harbors neither of these. We see these features as signs of a broader discourse in play—a liberal racial common sense that transcends the present effects of racism by minimizing history. We will spend some time on Michaels's attempt to bring a nonliberal description of cultural identity into his orbit. We do this to suggest that the apparently plausible color-blind outcome depends heavily on an implausible dehistoricization of culture. This dehistoricization wreaks havoc on descriptions of commonplace U.S. racial divisions and does so through a philosophy that, historically speaking, is white.

Michaels makes his most sustained argument against identities in his discussion of James Clifford, who, in a two-page footnote, is joined to a cultural theorist that Michaels shows to harbor racialist thoughts.[10] Clifford's account of a federal trial, *Mashpee Tribe* v. *New Seabury et al.*, argues for the kind of strongly historical contextualization of the uses of culture that Michaels denies. The Mashpee, as Clifford tells it, went to trial in order to determine whether they were legally a tribe under federal statute. Were they able to prove tribal status, the Mashpee would have been

10. This writer is Melville Herskovits. Andrew Apter offers a critique of Herskovits's antiessentialism that leads to a different outcome from Michaels's. Trying to avoid the "double bind" in which "either we essentialize Africa or renounce it" (the latter being Michaels's solution to any "cultural identity"), Apter suggests a focus on cultural practices "as strategies of appropriation and empowerment" within "relations of domination." His use of phrases like "inner logic of syncretic practices," however, would be grist for Michaels's mill, and the confusions in our vocabularies about culture suggests the heuristic value of Michaels's criticisms (Andrew Apter, "Herskovits's Heritage: Rethinking Syncretism in the African Diaspora," *Diaspora* 1 [Winter 1991]: 251).

able to use the Non-Intercourse Act of 1790 to recover some land that had been sold to non-Indians, since the act prohibited such "alienation" of Indian land without the approval of the federal government. For Clifford, "Identity in Mashpee" makes sense only in relation to "'complex historical processes of appropriation, compromise, subversion, masking, invention, and revival'" (p. 680 n. 36). He explicitly criticizes the court's incomprehension of these processes and traces the Mashpee's defeat to the court's demand for an essential group identity, which effectively erased the contingencies of the group's actual history. Clifford also sees the court's position as reflecting a highly politicized Euro-American view of identity whose emergence cannot be separated from the history of in-terracial relations in the colonization of the New World. For Clifford, the appeals to identity on both sides of this case emerge from the history of colonization and of race as a mode of social organization. Given all this, Michaels will need to work hard to show that Clifford's use of cultural identity as a historical dynamic is actually an appeal to racial identity.

Michaels makes an argument that, as we read it, consists of four sepa-rate claims: (1) For Clifford, Mashpee tribal status turns on the existence of Mashpee identity. (2) Mashpee identity is expressed by the possession or recovery of a Mashpee cultural practice like drumming. (3) Any cul-tural identity that involves "'remembering'" as well as "'reinvention'" must rest on an appeal to a continuous, inherent, precultural identity, one that exists prior to the cultural practice (p. 680 n. 36). (4) This non-cultural identity is racial identity. Taking these claims in turn, it becomes apparent that they reflect and defend current liberal racial common sense rather than describe Clifford's actual deployment of cultural identity.

1. *Tribal status, which involves cultural practices, is about cultural identity rather than social relations.* To the contrary, Clifford describes the Mashpee as attempting to establish a valid *tribal* rather than cultural identity; cul-ture comes up as the demand of the court. The tribe is a political entity; the reason there is a question about Mashpee identity in the first place has nothing to do with anyone's confusion over whether drumming makes you an Indian or being an Indian makes you drum but over the way to retain some control over land use around the town of Mashpee. The Mashpee had political independence until the 1960s, "when local government passed out of Indian control, perhaps for good, and . . . the scale of [white land] development increased."[11] The recovery of legal sta-tus as a tribe would restore to the Mashpee a town government that they felt had been seized by absentee developers; the Mashpee do not seek to affirm the racial or cultural integrity of this government so much as to make the government again responsive to the political wishes of the ma-

11. James Clifford, *The Predicament of Culture: Twentieth-Century Ethnography, Literature, and Art* (Cambridge, Mass., 1988), p. 280; hereafter abbreviated *PC.*

jority of the town's historical inhabitants. Clifford makes his endorsement of Mashpee identity talk contingent on the legal and historical context of their petition for tribal status: "I concluded that since the ability to act collectively as Indians is currently bound up with tribal status, the Indians living in Mashpee and those who return regularly should be recognized as a 'tribe'" (*PC*, p. 336). Clifford's use of phrases like "act collectively as Indians" refers to relations both chosen and imposed within the history of power relations between different social groups. The most obvious sign of the Mashpee's identity as Mashpee is that they are on trial to see whether they are tribe enough to go on trial. *Culture* is one word for group agency; rather than express established identity, it is part of the process that creates it. In its complicated relation to tribal status, culture does not show that one is now or already was or can now become a Mashpee but that one has the right to petition a state apparatus for political sovereignty.[12]

In separating cultural identity from the history of intergroup conflict, Michaels approximates the epistemology of the federal court. It was the court that demanded cultural continuity as proof of valid tribal exis-

12. The Mashpee case was one chapter of the long and unfinished story of U.S. efforts to supersede the sovereignty of American Indian nations. The United States possesses title to its own land mass entirely because of land it acquired through treaties with Indians; American identity depends on this history of expropriation, and, for Americans, "Indian" identity existed and exists only within this history. The essentializing identity claims come most powerfully from the state's laws governing Indian identity. One native organization, Native American Consultants, Inc., summarizes the effect of the statutes this way:

1. An Indian is a member of any federally recognized Indian Tribe. To be federally recognized, an Indian Tribe must be comprised of Indians.
2. To gain federal recognition, an Indian Tribe must have a land base. To secure a land base, an Indian Tribe must be federally recognized. [Quoted in M. Annette Jaimes, "Federal Indian Identification Policy: A Usurpation of Indigenous Sovereignty in North America," *The State of Native America: Genocide, Colonization, and Resistance*, ed. Jaimes (Boston, 1992), p. 133]

The Mashpee trial took place within federal identity designations that, on top of the catch-22 quality Jaimes observes, determine whether any Indian or group of Indians can hold land independently of the white property system that has been swallowing their land for centuries. The question of Indian identity has a long and violent political history. It ranges from the 1887 General Allotment Act, which established Indian identification according to the "blood quantum" or "degree of Indian blood"; the aim here was to transform collective land holdings into individual private property. The Indian Citizenship Act of 1924 endowed Indians or groups of Indians with American identity (as U.S. citizens) regardless of their wishes. The 1934 Indian Reorganization Act overrode existing Indian governing councils in favor of more pliable councils modelled on corporate boards. The Indian Reorganization Act of 1972 appeared to abandon the "blood quantum" standard of Indian identity in favor of "self-identification," only to be evaded by the Reagan Administration's attempt to "enforce degree-of-blood requirements for federal services, such as those of the Indian Health Service." Most recently, the Indian Arts and Crafts Law (1990) restricted "definition of Indian artists to those possessing a federally issued 'Certificate of Degree of Indian Blood'" (pp. 130–31). At no point can Indian identity be distinguished from struggles over Indians' right to collective self-governance.

tence (see *PC*, pp. 320–25, 333–35). Clifford insists that identity is social and historical, discontinuous and changing; he holds that a proper historical awareness of cultural practices around Mashpee would show that "often the 'tribe' in Mashpee was simply people deciding things by consensus, in kitchens or at larger ad hoc gatherings where no records were kept. . . . The 'tribe' in Mashpee was simply shared Indian kinship, place, history, and a long struggle for integrity without isolation" (*PC*, p. 310). The court eclipses Mashpee history with Mashpee culture and in so doing successfully ignores Mashpee sovereignty while *also* evading the federal role in regulating it for two hundred years. The problem of cultural identity comes up in the context of domination. The Mashpee are trying to *avoid* American-style cultural identity: "Identity as an American meant giving up a strong claim to tribal political integrity in favor of ethnic status within a national whole. Life as an American meant death as an Indian" (*PC*, p. 341).[13] Tribal status would allow the Mashpee to avoid pregiven, ethnic identity in favor of the ongoing group agency made possible by national sovereignty (see *PC*, p. 280).

2. *Cultural identity is constituted by the possession or repossession of cultural practices.* Michaels writes that Clifford's "appeal to memory makes it clear that the resumption of a discontinued Indian practice cannot in itself count as a marker of Indian identity; going to powwows, taking up drumming, and starting to wear 'regalia' wouldn't turn a New York Jew into a Mashpee Indian" (p. 680 n. 36). "If, then," he concludes, "the criteria of Mashpee identity are drumming, dressing in 'regalia,' and so on, it should be the case that anyone who meets these criteria counts as a Mashpee" (p. 681 n. 36). In fact, however, drumming and dressing are not the criteria of Mashpee identity, which is only as mysterious as there being more to an engineer than wearing a pocket protector.

Michaels offers no evidence that Clifford reduces group identity to the pursuit of stereotypical activities. Mashpee cultural practices include whatever engages the ordinary and extraordinary historical convergences of coercive force and attempted self-direction. What makes the Mashpee different are the different details of these convergences: the Mashpee are subject to the racial, cultural, political, and economic forms of subordination American Indians experience generally, yet they are not governed by the Indian Reorganization Acts of 1934 and 1972 as admin-

13. Clifford is by no means entirely consistent on this and other points. Elsewhere he says, "The individuals of Indian ancestry from Mashpee who filed suit in 1976 were American citizens similar to Irish- or Italian-Americans with strong ethnic attachments." They were taking "advantage of the latest wave of pan-Indian revivalism" (*PC*, p. 301). Such an inconsistency might be explained through the many differences among the Mashpee involved in the suit, as one might expect of the individuals of any group. In any case, the point of reading Clifford, for us, is to continue to explore the complexities of radically discontinuous American sociocultural life by working through his contradictions and ambiguities rather than to use them to deny the major issue he addresses.

istered by the federal Bureau of Indian Affairs; they had controlled local politics in Mashpee until the mid-1960s; they are more assimilated into Euro-American society than many Native groups; and they retain a certain ideological and political solidarity in spite of this relatively greater assimilation. These five of the most obvious and outsider influences on their experience could reasonably be supplemented by dozens of others, and they can only arbitrarily be reduced to the simplistic culturalism of "drumming, dressing in 'regalia,' and so on."

The Mashpee themselves attempt to evade this drumming standard of culture when the court tries to apply it to them.[14] They display no anxiety about the markings of continuous cultural identity. They regard regalia as something you use, that you invoke "as long as needed" and for contingent reasons ("when my hair was long enough"). The meaning of bandannas and drums must be sought in the framework of multiple, varying, and conflicting social determinations.

3. *All forms of cultural identity that "do any cultural work" rest on a personal identity that "runs much deeper than culture"* (pp. 682, 681 n. 36). Having claimed that culture is about identity and that attitudes toward identity can be evaluated by the drumming standard, Michaels says that Clifford grounds cultural identity in an appeal to a continuous, inherent, precultural identity:

> Clifford rejects culture as a mark of identity because culture tolerates no discontinuities. But he himself can tolerate discontinuity only if it is grounded in a continuity that runs much deeper than culture: drumming will make you a Mashpee not because anyone who drums gets to be a Mashpee but because, insofar as your drumming counts as remembering a lost tradition, it shows that you already *are* a Mashpee. [P. 681 n. 36]

Michaels's second and third claims set up this binary choice for a member of a group: either you perform stereotyped activities associated with a group and this makes you a member *or* you are a member ontologically.

14.

Q. (St. Clair): I notice you have a headband and some regalia?
A.: Yes.
Q.: How long have you been wearing such clothing?
A.: Oh, I have been wearing a headband as long as needed, when my hair was long enough.
Q.: How long has that been?
Judge: That which you have on there, is that an Indian headband?
A.: It is a headband.
Judge: It has some resemblance to an ordinary red bandanna?
A.: Right, that's what the material is, yes.
Judge: A bandanna you buy in the store and fold up in that manner?
A.: Yes. ["Chiefy" Mills under cross-examination from James St. Clair, *Mashpee Tribe* v. *New Seabury et al.*, quoted in *PC*, p. 346]

If you are Chicano, this is either because you wear a T-shirt and khakis while driving a lowered Chevy *or* because you think *Chicano* describes your identity at birth. If you are not already doing Chicano things but think you "are" Chicano, then you must be assuming a biological identity with Chicano traditions. Either your connection to the status of Chicano consists of a set of existing behaviors or it is an essentialist and hence racial tie.

Why are these the two choices for the basis of group identity? The sentence that Michaels invokes in support of this reading says, "But is any part of a tradition 'lost' if it can be remembered, even generations later, caught up in a present dynamism and made to symbolize a possible future?" (*PC*, pp. 341–42). Clifford has just rejected the "either-or" choice posed by the face-off between plaintiffs and defendants—either continuous or wholesale assimilation. Both narratives are wrong for him, and "identity," both "real yet essentially contested," re-created yet potentially authentic, is precisely that which the "either-or" logic of the court is unable to capture (*PC*, pp. 341, 340). Identity involves culture and "tribal institutions," the history of events, conflicts, defeats, and resistances that are put together, dismantled, and reassembled by the ongoing process of collaborative narrativization. The tradition once lost and now and again, here and there remembered is *knowledge of history* rather than interior identity, and it is used in the present, continually changing situation and redefined by the living in relation to a "possible future."[15] Clifford sees "Identity in Mashpee" as "relational and political" and, rather than posit its continuity, argues that it can be discontinuous with its previous forms and *unbaffled by this changeability*. In fact, he suggests that identity is always discontinuous since change constitutes the social and political dimension of collective life. Remembering consists of all of the stories, social relations, personal ties, "changing federal and state policies and the surrounding ideological climate" that make up what you could and could not do, what you have and have not done, and what you can and cannot

15. Michaels offers similar arguments for racial essentialism at various points in the essay. His other contemporary example concerns Arthur Schlesinger, Jr., and this statement in particular: "We don't have to believe that our values are absolutely better than the next fellow's or the next country's, but we have no doubt that they are better *for us*, reared as we are—and are worth living by and worth dying for" (quoted p. 683). Michaels notes that if these values "are not just better but are just better 'for us,' then our reason for holding them can only be that they are ours." Schlesinger's use of the word *ours*, Michaels argues, rests on "something stronger than the claim that . . . they are the beliefs we actually hold"; to be "ours," these beliefs must be connected to an "essentialist assertion of identity," of "who we are" (p. 683). But it may be that Schlesinger means to say that our beliefs are better for us for a whole host of historical and cultural reasons. For example, we may think they are better for us because we read our sociocultural experience as saying that we are better off because of our beliefs, or because we have read a lot of books like Schlesinger's. Again, this separation of questions of identity from questions about history and society has more to do with individualism than with antiessentialism.

161

do now. Remembering, in Clifford's account, describes past social possibilities and is often invoked to imagine a different future through the collaborative destruction and invention of cultural processes. Mashpee memory is not deeper than culture but is culture, the historical narrative of a society.[16]

4. *The noncultural continuity that Clifford purportedly invokes is racial identity.* Having affirmed that Clifford's notion of cultural identity is rooted in something "beyond" culture, Michaels's next sentence defines what that beyond must be. Clifford winds up believing, as Michaels sees it, that since "your drumming counts as remembering a lost tradition, it shows that you already *are* a Mashpee"; thus "his rejection of cultural identity gets him no further away from racial identity than does the more usual insistence on cultural identity." This is true but only because, for Michaels, no amount of historical and social relations gets any discussion of culture away from racial identity. He offers no evidence to support his claim, and since everything Clifford says, inconsistencies and all, does in fact lead away from both racial and narrowly cultural identity toward some conjuncture like historical socioculture, Michaels backs away: "The point here is not that Clifford is secretly depending on some notion of racial identity" (p. 681 n. 36). This too is true: Michaels's point is less to detect proof of biological racial meaning than to discredit claims that a differential identity is also historical and political. Once again, Mashpee

---

16. Reflecting an indifference to this kind of depth, Mashpee witnesses, when asked in court about the source of their Mashpee identity, say they are Mashpee because other people have always thought they were, because they think they are, because they say they are.

> Q.: How do you know you're an Indian?
> A.: My mother told me. [quoted in *PC,* p. 301]

> Q.: How do you know your ancestors?
> A.: My mother, grandparents, word of mouth. [quoted in *PC,* p. 287]

The witness knows she is an Indian because she trusts her mother. The verification of identity is an interpretive decision made within a group. Identity emerges from the history of stories that members of a group tell to each other. The witness knows her ancestors not because they are already "hers" or are culturally "her" but because of stories told about them. Some come from family, some come from no specific source, and none lay claim to legal or ontological authority. None establish an identity of the kind a contractual, property-owning society would recognize.

> Q.: How was your youth different from that of any small-town youth?
> A.: We were different. We knew we were different. We were told we were different. [quoted in *PC,* p. 281]

The identity is in the experiencing and the hearing, the accepting and the telling. Mashpee on the stand, and against their best interests, do not claim to be Mashpee prior to the stories told to them. They reverse Michaels's dictum: "who we are" turns out to come from "what we do," most of us together, and in conjunction with what has been done to us.

identity in Clifford's texts leads a very different life, a life involving the dynamic of the Mashpee's relations to those that had long lived among them without racial or ethnic connection.[17]

Michaels's assimilation of cultural identity to racial essentialism lends an air of credibility to an analysis that would otherwise be more readily seen to reflect the perspective of historically white interests. This perspective denies its own historical presence in the creation of cultural relations and diverts attention from an ongoing struggle for power under conditions of inequality. It further avoids a reckoning with the fact that the moments of nearest approach between culture and race are, in U.S. history, those most likely to be utterly inseparable from power struggles. The Mashpee trial, where the state demands identification, is an example of the inappropriateness of this separation.

But we do not regard Michaels's reading as an individual mistake. When an analyst of his acuity draws such conclusions, some larger forces are affecting the instruments. We think these forces, to repeat, consist of post–civil rights race moderation, which makes certain arguments seem implausible and impractical. It is to these forces, their content and aims, that we now turn.

17.

Q.: And now, before you went away to school—Incidentally, is that a private institution, if you know?
A.: Private?
Q.: Is it owned and operated by the state or federal government or is it owned and operated on a private basis, if you know?
A.: Private.
Q.: Do you know or are you guessing?
A.: I am not sure what they call themselves, Daughters of American Revolution and some Christian organizations involved in it.
Q.: Let's see, the Daughters of the American Revolution is not an organization that you would associate with Indians, is it?
A.: In our history, yes.
Q.: Pardon?
A.: I said in our history, yes. Wampanoag history—Mashpee Wampanoag history.
Q.: Daughters of the American Revolution, in your understanding of what you say is your history, have an Indian origin?
A.: It is not our history, but we were involved with that revolution and 149 of our Mashpee people died in that fighting for your independence.
Q.: Fighting for what?
A.: Independence.
Q.: But is it your understanding that the Daughters of the American Revolution have an Indian origin or are in some way related to persons of Indian descent?
A.: They embrace me as a member.
Q.: Pardon?
A.: I said the women that I met that were involved with the Daughters of American Revolution felt a kinship with me because of the Mashpee Wampanoags that had died in the war. [Ramona Peters under cross-examination from St. Clair, quoted in *PC*, pp. 316–17]

3. Postpluralism and the New Supremacism

> The question of my "identity" often comes up. I think I must be a mixed-blood. I claim to be male, although only one of my parents was male.
>
> —JIMMIE DURHAM, a Cherokee, quoted in *The State of Native America*

Race moderation remains largely in the hands of cultural pluralism. Though pluralism takes a variety of forms, a diffusely evangelical type has recently become influential through high-profile works like Arthur Schlesinger, Jr.'s, *The Disuniting of America*. Michaels explicitly rejects Schlesinger's pluralism by suggesting that it rests on the same racial essentialism it attacks in Afrocentrism. This distinction between essentialist and antiessentialist views, even assuming its validity here, should not obscure the extent to which Schlesinger and Michaels are pressed in a similar direction by the same general structure of liberal racial thought. Michaels's position repudiates Schlesinger's cultural pluralism while preserving important aspects of its project. We will briefly survey what we regard as the negative aspects of this "beyond race" liberalism and, in closing, suggest some features of a more desirable white racial outlook.

Cultural pluralism may frequently reflect democratic expectations, but it harbors other features that become especially prominent in times of perceived threat. First, it regards race as consciousness rather than as a mode of social power and as *false* consciousness at that. Race refers to *identity* rather than to cultural or social relations, and this view, which prevails in most officially color-blind institutions, builds on the longstanding ethnicity paradigm which, since the 1920s, has assumed that "racial and ethnic groups are neither central nor persistent elements of modern societies. . . . Racism and racial oppression are not independent dynamic forces but are ultimately reducible to other causal determinants, usually economic or psychological."[18] Second, cultural pluralism sees racial or cultural differences as properly subordinate to common culture and shared social institutions. Schlesinger, for example, calls for a return to George Washington's ideal of a "'new race'" forming "'*one people*'" in the

18. Robert Blauner, *Racial Oppression in America* (New York, 1972), p. 2. Nathan Glazer and Daniel Patrick Moynihan offered such an influential version of this thesis because they acknowledged the persistence of "the ethnic group" even as they declined to allot race, as distinct from white ethnicity, any reality apart from—and any superior importance to—a whole range of factors like "history, family and feeling, [political] interest, formal organization life" (Nathan Glazer and Daniel Patrick Moynihan, *Beyond the Melting Pot: The Negroes, Puerto Ricans, Jews, Italians, and Irish of New York City* [Cambridge, Mass., 1963], p. 19).

New World.[19] Third, this cultural pluralism does not mean cultural equality but a putatively nonracial Western supremacism. As Schlesinger puts it, "Whatever the particular crimes of Europe, that continent is also the source—the *unique* source—of those liberating ideas of individual liberty, political democracy, the rule of law. . . . There is surely no reason for Western civilization to have guilt trips laid on it by champions of cultures based on despotism, superstition, tribalism, and fanaticism" (*DA,* pp. 127–28). Schlesinger's pluralist sense that there are indeed other systems of values that might be (or might seem to be) better for other people easily coexists with his general belief that ours really is better. The payoff of this strain of cultural pluralism is that it combines tolerance and hierarchy, difference and inferiority, into pluralist, democratic supremacism.

These features of pluralism form the influential background for Michaels's efforts to reject pluralism, whose gravitational field is difficult to escape. For our present purposes we will call this postpluralism, without meaning by this term to designate various nonpluralisms in existence and under development. We mean instead a position that opposes pluralism's use of identities, particularly group identity, while retaining other features of a pluralist project.

On the first issue, Michaels separates race from its social dynamics by defining it as a concept of biological identity; he pulls the ostensibly more social category of culture into the same biologistic system. Rather than traditional pluralism's empirical or sociological arguments against the significance of race, Michaels sidesteps the social environments in which racism and race get deployed. His position excludes social relations not only from the analysis of racialized culture but also from any methodological discussion of the legitimacy of this exclusion. One need not make a historical or sociological case for the exclusion of history and society in this or that particular cultural system, a process that of course involves precisely those elements. One can offer instead reasons of philosophy, which perform clean separations of domains. The distinction between essentialist and antiessentialist uses of identity is itself a *historical* question, but Michaels uses the distinction to render history and politics irrelevant to the evaluation of cultural identity.

In this way, a controversial subject like race can be protected from the realm of politics and power without this protection being itself a political issue. The "truth" of race will then not vary depending on where the analyst stands in a network of racializing systems. With conventional cultural pluralism, these different political positions and interests are

<hr>

19. Quoted in Arthur M. Schlesinger, Jr., *The Disuniting of America* (New York, 1992), pp. 24–25; hereafter abbreviated *DA*. Horace Kallen's pluralism offered a far more tolerant celebration of the commerce in difference, but it too looks toward "unity . . . [as] a future formation we desirably steer our present imaginations toward" (Horace Kallen, *Cultural Pluralism and the American Idea: An Essay in Social Philosophy* [Philadelphia, 1956], pp. 47–48).

bound up with any discussion about overcoming them. A cultural pluralist usually starts by conceding that racial reality looks different to Asian
Americans and Chicanos and must then make some kind of ethical,
historical, or social case for conceiving of race as an identity that should
be set aside. Within the domain of philosophy, the question of power and
society need not even arise.

Equally important, ahistorical antiessentialism allows the analyst to
disavow his or her own social position. The analyst exists in a field of
reason rather than a discontinuous terrain of social antagonisms. It is not
surprising, then, that philosophy would come to the fore in the analysis
of race issues at a time when pluralism itself is under more scrutiny as
the racial ideology of a minority white culture than at any time since the
zenith of black nationalism twenty years ago. For unlike pluralism, which
has a racial history into which it drags its adherents, philosophy is, to
itself, never white.

Second, while Schlesinger's nationalist "'American Creed'" (*DA*,
p. 27) visibly demands compliance with some substantive principles, the
postpluralist produces a common culture through constitutive rules.[20]
While pluralists like Schlesinger write as though there is a common culture—whose core beliefs form a creed by which any group can be judged
according to its adherence or rejection of these beliefs—the postpluralist
establishes boundaries between legitimate and illegitimate uses of social
identity. The mode here is not to suggest that a person or group's practices and beliefs place them on the margins of Western values but that a
person's individual or group identity corrupts reason. The postpluralist
need not contest the Afrocentric's interpretation of the race record of
U.S. democracy but only say that the Afrocentric's constitutive sense of
racial difference prevents his or her views from counting as genuine
knowledge. "Common culture" is translated into the zone of rational discourse or public reason; it excludes certain factors not because they differ
from white or Western beliefs but because their belief in difference vio-
lates a criterion of reason.

In Michaels's essay, that criterion is antiessentialism. While pluralists
might have judged a group according to its espousal of a unifying value
like representative democracy, Michaels writes as though a group can be
judged by its relation to an antiessentialism that remains unaffected by
cultural, ideological, or historical differences. Individuals and groups as
otherwise dissimilar as Oliver La Farge, James Clifford, Melville Herskovits, the Mashpee, and a scrivener for the Klan can be tested for essentialism and assimilated via the presence of that quality. If they are found
to be essentialist, they can be excluded not from Americanness but from

20. Michael Hardt has described how contemporary liberalism, as represented by John
Rawls, defines the boundaries of political communities by constituting the rules of public
rationality in "Les Raisonnables et les différents: Le Libéralisme politique de Rawls," *Futur
antérieur* (forthcoming 1994).

the sphere of reason itself. Those who consider racial or cultural identity an asset, a liability, a source of social knowledge, or any combination of these, can, under postpluralism, be shown *not* violating nationalistic ideals like a unified "'new race'" but violating contemporary standards of valid reasoning. Racialized experience becomes irrelevant to and indeed obstructive of authentic knowledge, knowledge of the kind that can legitimately be applied to social and political disputes. A common culture stripped down to what are presented as the minimum requirements of knowledge avoids Schlesinger's philistine assimilationism while excluding the identity talk that allows what opposes assimilation to enter into negotiation.

But is the postpluralist also a supremacist? Although reason seems to be an equal opportunity operation, and though it avoids oafish chauvinism and unprofessional derogations of others' beliefs, the kind of race philosophy we have been discussing assumes the power of epistemology to make the rules for political or ethnographic arguments. This superiority of the epistemological is not directly argued in Michaels's text, but it presumes its ability to settle the rules of discourse and judgment. Such a tacit supremacism easily coexists with political liberalism, flexibility, inclusion, and generosity; it consists of the quiet expectation that its procedures and standards will be taken as a dispute's rules of arbitration—that its concerns count the most.[21] This supremacism need never appear as an obviously rude insistence. When distinctively white philosophy criticizes someone for essentialism, it can work simply by taking for granted that people will care; it can proceed by assuming that the confusing intricacies of historical cases will have less weight. It knows that a Mashpee's indefiniteness about the status of a bandanna will not seem brilliant, not compared to, say, the claim that a position secretly rests on its apparent opposite. The taste culture addressed by such assumptions is also white in a sociocultural sense, and postpluralism can assume that this fact about its audience's group identity will seem less important within this group than the exposure of logical inconsistency. Schlesinger, still an old-fashioned pluralist, thinks he must openly state his belief that the West is the best and then marshall evidence for this belief. The postpluralist works with more pervasive and invisible presumptions that are not explicitly defended: the difference between essentialism and antiessentialism is independent of historical context; analysis of identity as a logic "knows" more than remembering a grievance, and so on. Postpluralist supremacism appears delicately, coasting on the historical prestige, the

21. Cheryl I. Harris importantly describes socially defined "whiteness" as the power to make rules *and* as the "settled expectation" that whites will face no "undue" obstacles. Of particular importance here is her claim that "whiteness as property is also constituted through the reification of expectations in the continued right of white-dominated institutions to control the legal meaning of group identity" (Cheryl I. Harris, "Whiteness as Property," *Harvard Law Review* 106, no. 8 [1993]: 1761).

institutional investments, and the economic and social superiority of the generally white powers with which it shares its modes. Lately, color blindness has been on the economic rise, and epistemology's assumption of the irrelevance of its social connections to the interests and history of this ideology, its irrelevance in creating the superiority of epistemological over political or identity claims, is itself a symptom of its assumed supremacy.

The pluralist's carefully relativized claims to his or her culture's superiority give way to the postpluralist's (perfectly liberal) discrediting of the modes by which a group's superiority might be overcome. Regardless of the postpluralist use of antiessentialism, many racialized groups know that their identity is bound up with their subordination and their pursuit of sovereignty; the Mashpee trial exemplifies this common phenomenon. Supremacism is maintained not by affirming the supremacy of one's own values but by defining contestations of the existing rules as irrational.

Postpluralism defines the most basic racism as the appeal to race. It says, in effect, that if you believe in a society beyond racism (meaning, it believes, beyond race), you must expose cultural difference as racialist pathos. This rejection would not appear to reflect your racialized political agenda but simply your enlightened, postessentialist philosophy. Postpluralism, shorn of pluralism's more obvious supremacist outbursts, would take over its role as racial management. It would never need to say, It doesn't matter who you are, I don't care who you are, or I don't like who you are. It would only ask, whenever racial hierarchy comes up, "But why does it matter who we are?" (p. 682). Around race, the artificial separation of cultural processes from politics enables such containment, intended or not.

We have been trying to make more explicit the reasons why evangelical pluralism *and* postpluralism can be regarded as liberal racism—not because their advocates hold racist attitudes but because they support the dehistoricization, the monopolized rule making, and the subtle supremacism that allow democratic institutions to produce nuanced but still racially discriminatory effects. Indirect, contemporary forms of racial subordination receive (often unintended) support from the opposition to race.

Rather than go down Michaels's particular path of postpluralism, we would suggest taking his important insights into pluralist racism in a different direction. For white Americans, particularly professionals, this starts with avoiding postpluralism's "'bad'. . . utopianism," which "grabs instantly for a future, projecting itself by an act of will or imagination beyond the compromised political structures of the present."[22] It involves

22. Terry Eagleton, "Nationalism: Irony and Commitment," in *Nationalism, Colonialism, and Literature,* ed. Eagleton, Fredric Jameson, and Edward Said (Minneapolis, 1990), p. 25.

reconceiving postpluralism through the rejection of the three prominent features we have discussed.

First, this redefined white nonpluralism must refuse to associate the advent of reason with the white version of cultural separatism—the belief that culture can be cleansed of political history. It is especially important to evade the pull of cultural separatism around the study of race by acknowledging that the appeal to race cannot be separated from the endurance of racism. If we do not grant the presence of conflict and contestation, of politics and history, of context and determinations in the study of culture, we are not avoiding politicization, but we are avoiding cultural knowledge itself. Second, the common culture formed by portable antiessentialism should be replaced with negotiation across perceived boundaries. This will require granting the existence of such boundaries when one party declares them and avoiding the impulse to simply assert a principle of reason to rule all domains in the same way. It will involve white Americans in repudiating the protective and legislative power of both the "'American Creed'" *and* its color-blind philosophies. Finally, it means that white Americans must reject the forms of pluralism discussed here as liberal racism—as cultural racism, in Michaels's useful concept— not because cultural pluralism rests on an essentialist notion of racial identity, Michaels's problematic, but because it is white/West supremacist and remains so in ever more objectivist and managerially abstract guises. A better future for race relations will require supporting ongoing race consciousness as the basis of negotiated group identities, intergroup equality, separatism, and autonomy. The democratic solution entails more careful and complex race consciousness rather than less. And this will require cultural studies to respond more fully to its history of using pluralism as racial management.

BEYOND ESSENTIALISM: RETHINKING AFRO-AMERICAN CULTURAL THEORY

Elliott Butler-Evans

The recent emergence of Afro-American cultural theory and practice as a legitimate area of intellectual inquiry is arguably one of the most significant events in the area of literary and cultural theory within the past decades. Nearly all major universities offer, quite often within traditional literature and English programs, upper division and graduate level course in Afro-American literature and theory, have on their faculties at least one member who claims Afro-American literature as an area of specialization, and incorporate into their genre and period courses works by Afro-American writers. The Modern Language Association's recent meeting in New Orleans featured numerous papers on Afro-American literature; and major academic presses, among them Harvard, Oxford, and Chicago, have published the works of young black scholars whose works are characterized by rigorous scholarship and theoretical sophistication. Moreover, scholars such as Harold Bloom and Barbara Johnson have, through their institutional bases and exciting interventions, inserted minority discourse into the broader academic community. The euphoria surrounding these developments was perhaps most succinctly stated recently by Jonathan Culler:

The introduction of Afro-American writing to literature courses owes much to the civil rights movement of the 1960s, when James Baldwin, Ralph Ellison, and Richard Wright became canonical authors, but at the same time the Black Power movement energized the Black Arts movement, with its quest to identify a Black Aesthetic. . . . In the 1980s, however, two factors combined to change the situation: on the one hand, the remarkable efflorescence of black women's writing, which had been neglected by the men promoting the Black Aesthetic, reopened the question of the black tradition; on the other hand, the efforts of critics such as Houston Baker and Henry Louis Gates, Jr. to bring contemporary theoretical concerns to the reading of black literature effected an intervention of black writing in contemporary theoretical debates. Even though large numbers of blacks and members of minority groups have not been hired by literature factulties, the role of Afro-American and Third World writing in literary studies has been transformed.[1]

One might very well quarrel with Culler's reading of the interventions of black writers. The argument that women had been excluded from the Afro-American literary "tradition," while largely true is somewhat reductionist. Some women, among them Gwendolyn Brooks, Lucille Clifton, Toni Cade Bambara, and Sonia Sanchez, not only wrote within that tradition but also were among its major spokespersons. Nor is there evidence that the theoretical projects launched by Gates and Baker "effected an intervention of black writing in contemporary theoretical debates." The Gates-Baker interventions might be more clearly understood as incorporated alternative practices, to use Raymond Williams's felicitous phrase.[2] The truth of the matter is that the study of Afro-American culture and theory, while receiving belated recognition, is still largely a marginal intellectual pursuit in most academic departments. Culler's claim that it has somehow transformed literary studies is somewhat hyperbolic.

It is not my objective, however, to launch a captious attack on Professor Culler's reading of the current state of Afro-American letters. Nor is it my intention to engage in still another of those acrimonious exchanges that have focused on what might be loosely called the politics of Afro-American cultural theory. Rather, I wish to interrogate some of the ideological and philosophical assumptions underpinning recent theoretical discourse on Afro-American texts. I would argue that it largely rewrites the nationalist essentialism from which it apparently distances itself. In doing so, it would seem, that discourse is not only silent about

---

[1] Jonathan Culler, *Framing the Sign: Criticism and Its Institutions* (Norman and London: University of Oklahoma Press, 1988), pp. 32-33.

[2] See Raymond Williams, *Marxism and Literature* (Oxford: Oxford University Press, 1977).

its own political agenda but also wholly inadequate as an effective tool for the interpretation of contemporary Afro-American literature.

Perhaps one of the most significant achievements of current practices in minority critical discourse is its impressive success in rescuing that discourse from the seemingly inexorable banality into which it would readily descend. A critical enterprise that would focus on the repetition and reinscription of certain binary oppositions—white/black, dominant/marginal, oppressor/oppressed—would in due time exhaust itself. The current experiments conducted by theorists with the numerous post-structuralisms, therefore, provide innovative and exciting modes of deconstructing hegemonic narratives and exploring marginal discourses.

Central to these critical enterprises, however, in spite of the rather deft appropriation, modification, and deployment of post-structuralist frames of reference, is the predication of a black essence and its necessary corollaries: the creation of a tradition and the formation of a canon. It is as if two projects—one committed to the deployment of recent developments in theory, the other to a politics of strategic essentializing—stand in a relationship of tensions. Minority critics can quite brilliantly read dominant narratives as structured by a desire for power, exploring the manner in which the semiotic strategies of hegemonic texts suppress difference and support hegemony. They convincingly show that dominant narratives are intertextually implicated in other discourses of domination and involved in the reproduction of the late capitalist mode of production.

The same rigorous reading of "minority" discourse, however, is largely nonexistent. Overdetermined by ideological agendas, critics who focus on nondominant texts generally address the manner in which these texts valorize, validate, and express some true essence of the existential modalities of the group. Within a broader social and political context, Barbara Harlow cites Maxime Rodinson's analysis of this phenomenon:

> Ideology always goes for the simplest solution. It does not argue that an oppressed people is to be defended because it is oppressed and to the exact extent to which it is oppressed. On the contrary, the oppressed are sanctified and every aspect of their actions, their culture, their past, present, and future

behavior is presented as admirable. Direct or indirect narcissism takes over and the fact that the oppressed are oppressed becomes less important that the admirable way they are themselves. The slightest criticism is seen as criminal sacrilege. *In particular, it becomes quite inconceivable that the oppressed might be oppressing others.* In an ideological conception, such an admission would imply that the object of admiration was flawed and hence in some sense deserving of past or present oppression.[3]

Perhaps the starting point for Afro-American critics, or any other marginal critics, should be some awareness of the real situation which generates their scholarship. The rhetoric and mythologies of oppositionality that characterize discussion of Afro-American cultural production and critical discourse greatly obscure the material context in which that discourse is produced. The problem with this perception of the role of the Afro-American critic was recently very ably addressed by Cornel West. West argues that the empowerment of a specific class of critic and the implications of their discourse in dominant ideology are central to recent critical developments.

[Afro-American literary critics] become the academic superintendents of a segment of an expanded canon or a separate canon. Such supervisory power over Afro-American literary culture—including its significant consulting activities and sometimes patronage relations to powerful white academic critics and publishers—not only ensures slots for black literary scholars in highly competitive English departments. More important, these slots are themselves held up as evidence for the success of prevailing ideologies of pluralism. Such talk of success masks the ever growing power of universities over American literary culture, and more specifically, the increasing

---

[3] Cited in Barbara Harlow, *Resistance Literature* (New York and London: Methuen, 1987), p. 29. Original source: Maxime Rodinson, Introduction to *People Without a Country: the Kurds and Kurdistan* ed. Gerard Chaliland (London: Zed Press, 1980), p. 5. (Emphasis mine).

authority of black literary professional managers over Afro-American literary practices and products.[4]

Perhaps one might begin by heeding Raymond Williams's caution of the need to arrive at "a non-metaphysical and non-subjectivist explanation of emergent cultural practice."[5] A significant starting point for such an enterprise would be an investigation of the semiotic infrastructure upon which a race or ethnic specific discourse is constructed. Ideologies of difference, underpinned by specific strategies of representation, structure form and content of narrative. Irene Portis Winner, employing a model drawn from Lotman's paradigms of textual modalities, has argued that the semiotic construction of ethnicity is dependent upon the inscription of certain patterns in binary oppositions, e.g., we/they, our world/their world, inner world/outer world.[6] This practice is significantly marked in Afro-American fictive and theoretical discourse by the discursive construction of an opposition between "blackness" and "whiteness" as epistemological categories. Within both theoretical and fictive discourse, this has taken the form of the appropriation of the forms of everyday life of ordinary black people and the representation of them as authentic. This might take the form of representation of rituals, attempted reproductions of "black speech," and a somewhat broad ethnographic picture of black culture. From this textual strategy is generated an ideology of authenticity, in which "real black life" is seen as contained within the existential modalities of peasant and working-class black life as it is mediated by writers largely of the middle class.

The construction of "whiteness" is even more complex. Teresa de Laruetis has commented on the problematic Afrocentric/Eurocentric opposition that generally characterizes nonhegemonic discourse in the United States and the manner in which such a reductionist opposition ignores "the histories of internal colonization, not to mention various forms of class, sexual, and religious oppression, within Europe and

---

[4] Cornel West, "Minority Discourse and the Pitfalls of Canon Formation," *The Yale Journal of Criticism* 1 no. 1 (Fall 1987).

[5] Raymond Williams, *Problems in Materialism and Culture* (London: Verso, 1980), p. 42.

[6] Irene Portis Winner, "Ethnicity, Modernity, and the Theory of Culture Texts," in *The Semiotics of Culture*, Irene Portis Winner and Jean Umiker Sebeok ed. (The Hague: Mouton Publishers, 1979), pp. 103-147.

within each country of Europe."[7] Yet in the programmatic texts and theoretical treatises of the past sixty years, such has been the major approach in Afro-American cultural practice. What Hazel Carby called the "romanticization of the fold" and I have referred to as an ideology of authenticity is parasitic on such an opposition. "Whiteness" is inscribed as a sign of difference, or as hostile threatening force. It may take the form of caricature, as in the works of Richard Wright or much of the writings of the Black Aesthetic period, or the embodiment of deficiency, as in Toni Morrison's works, in which deracination, false consciousness, and spiritual imperfection are invariably associated with fair skin.

What needs to be explored more thoroughly is the manner in which such fictive and theoretical projects obviously structure any critical discourse on Afro-American fiction and elide complex ideological issues. One might start, for example, by interrogating and problematizing the very concept of an Afro-American literature as a unified, ideologically coherent homogeneous body of discourses. While individual Afro-American writers have been engaged in their arts for more than three hundred years, the concept of an Afro-American literature is a recent historical invention. Even Wright's "Blueprint for Negro Literature," a text often mistakenly read as the master narrative of the Black Aesthetic, actually focuses on the writings of blacks rather than black writing and argues for a need to transcend such writing.[8] Moreover, there needs to be a more rigorous examination of early narratives outside of the totalizing concept of race and within the admittedly uncomfortable problematics of caste and class. It seems that many of the slave narratives, particularly those of Equiano and Douglas, for example, might be reread in the context of the appropriation of racial discourse to promote certain caste and class interests. In the same light, vernacular theories, the construction of blues matrices, and the insistence on expressive aspects of an "always already" black culture are in need of radical deconstruction. Vernacular theories implicitly argue for the

---

[7] Teresa de Lauretis, "Displacing Hegemonic Discourses: Reflections on Feminist Theory in the 1980s," *Inscriptions*, nos. 3/4 (1988, p. 127.

[8] See Richard Wright, "Blueprint for Negro Literature," in *Richard Wright Reader*, Ellen Wright and Michel Fabre ed. (New York: Harper & Row, 1978).

interchangeability of the oral and the written. But this is, in fact, problematic.[9]

Allow me, however, to address for a moment an equally serious problem with some current critical practices. What I am most concerned with is the methodological inadequacy of these practices as critical tools for the interpretation of contemporary literature. While I would not wholly embrace Ishmael Reed's assertion that Afro-American literary criticism is fifty years behind Afro-American cultural practice, I would agree that the two are moving in entirely different directions. Before addressing these issues, however, I would like to briefly discuss two developments in "black situations" outside the United States and their implications for similar situations in this country and the issues I am raising here.

In a paper recently presented to the English Department at the University of Minnesota, Manthia Diawara presented a critique of Chinweizu, Jemie, and Madubuike's attempts to formulate a theory of African literature in which "family resemblances are pragmatically employed to decide which of any doubtful or borderline cases should be included within the indisputable canon of African literature." Chinweizu, Jemie, and Madubuike argued that only works done by and for Africans and written in African languages can constitute the canon of African literature. The end result is the discursive construction of an African essence and the exclusion from the canon of the works of writers who do not reflect that essence. Diawara challenges that notion of an "authentic

---

[9] Houston Baker claims a semiotic basis for his argument about the blues matrix. But his formulation glosses over a basic premise of the semiotic discourse it purports to embrace. Addressing the problem of the interchangeability of semiotic systems, Emile Benveniste argues:

> The first principle [of semiotics] can be stated as the principle of nonredundancy between systems. Semiotic systems are not "synonymous." We are not able to "say the same thing" with words that we can say with music, as they are systems with different bases. In other words, two semiotic systems of different types cannot be mutually interchangeable. In the example cited, speech and music have as a common trait the production of sounds and the fact that they appeal to hearing; but this relationship does not prevail in view of the difference in nature between their respective units and their types of operation. . . .

See Emile Benveniste, "The Semiology of Language," in *Semiotics: An Introductory Anthology*, Robert E. Innis (Bloomington: Indiana University, 1985), p. 235.

literary canon" by deconstructing the ideological premises upon which it
is predicated. He argues:

> One must not always assume that there is a homogeneity of
> culture and literature in Africa which one can. . .oppose to
> European literature. Such categories as African literature,
> "family resemblance," African tradition, African ethos, etc. by
> assuming the cultural unity of Africans, leave unsaid the
> diversity of desires and the desire for diversity. . . .[10]

Stuart Hall, addressing the production and reception of black film in
Britain, recently advanced an analogous argument. In England, where the
signifier "black" was generally used to designate a non-European
immigrant population, "black" in Hall's view became "hegemonic over
other ethnic/racial identities." Calling for "a new cultural politics that
engages rather than suppresses difference," Hall posits the end of the
"innocent notion of the essential black subject." He argues:

> What is at issue here is the recognition of the extraordinary
> diversity of subjective positions, social experiences, and cultural
> identities which compose the category "black"; that is that "black
> is essentially a politically and socially constructed category,
> which cannot be grounded in a set of fixed, trans-cultural or
> transcendental categories and which therefore has no guarantees
> in Nature. What this brings into play is the recognition of the
> immense diversity and differentation of the historical and
> cultural experience of black subjects. This inevitably entails a
> weakening or fading of the notion of "race" or some composite
> notion of race around the term black will either guarantee the
> effectivity of any cultural practice or determine in any sense its
> final value.[11]

I would argue that the positions entertained by Diawara and Hall
present a framework through which we might rethink Afro-American
cultural production. While I have indicated elsewhere that the ideological

---

[10] Manthia Diawara, "Canon Formation in African Literature," a paper presented to the
English Department, University of Minnesota, Minneapolis, January 19, 1989.

[11] Stuart Hall, "New Ethnicities," *ICA Documents 7,* "Black Film, British Cinema," p.
28.

environment surrounding the Black Aesthetic was conducive to the production within literature of a unified black subject,[12] the material context for the development of such a discourse no longer exists. The eruption of feminine desire has generated a new politics that must embrace both race and gender; black sociologists speak of the declining significance of race and the emergence of more rigid class distinctions; the Jackson campaign was characterized by the foregrounding of a multiethnic or Rainbow coalition; and the recent debate over naming—that might very well replace "black" with African American—signifies a not too subtle shift from an emphasis on race to a mythology of ethnicity. All of these factors may very well force us to rethink both the politics of everyday life and the politics of cultural criticism and production.

It is the latter, however, with which I am immediately concerned here. When one encounters the narratives of Charles Johnson, Gayl Jones, Ishmael Reed, Toni Cade Bambara, and others, one is confronted with texts that reject the linear marratives that have generally characterized writings by Afro-Americans. These writers problematize the concept of a monologic, homogeneous Afro-American literature, and their novels often become the site of the playing out of a multiplicity of diverse and heterogeneous body of desires. What occurs in their narratives is what Hal Foster, in his appropriation of Roland Barthes, sees as the passage from "work" to "text." In distinguishing between the two, Foster writes:

> I use those terms heuristically: [the modernist] work to suggest an aesthetic, symbolic whole sealed by an origin (i.e., the author) and an end (i.e., a represented reality or transcendent meaning) and [the postmodernist] text to suggest an a-aesthetic, "multidimensional space in which a variety of writings, none of them original, blend and clash." The difference between the two rests finally on this: for the work the sign is a stable unit of signifier and signified (with the referent assured, or in abstraction, bracketed), whereas the text reflects on the

---

[12] See Elliott Butler-Evans, "Narrativizing the Black Zone: Semiotic Strategies in Black Aesthetic Discourse," *The American Journal of Semiotics* 6, no. 1 (1988-89), pp. 19-35.

contemporary dissolution of the sign and the released play of signifiers.[13]

It is this movement from "work" to "text" that essentialist critical theories are incapable of addressing. The "text" refuses coherence, is not primarily engaged in reflecting an extratextual black culture, and is not generally focused on situating itself within a blues matrix or yielding itself to vernacular theories. Reproducing its historical moment, it is irrational and idiosyncratic, signalling a break with traditional notions of Afro-American cultural expression.

A text that extensively deploys postmodern narrative strategies, Alice Walker's "Advancing Luna—and Ida B. Wells," a short story in the collection *You Can't Keep a Good Woman Down*, received only limited critical treatment, largely because of the sensationalism surrounding the publication of *The Color Purple*. Yet it is a paradigmatic black feminist text. It blurs the lines between autobiography, fiction, and the essay; reifies specific historical moments as metaphorical constructs; employs metafictional strategies that call attention to its textuality; and resists ideological closure, presenting instead an interrogative textual modality that invites the reader to resolve the argument it presents.[14]

The story focuses on the impact of an apparent rape on the friendship of two women: an "I," the nameless narrator whose personal history—a black Georgia native, an engaged writer, civil rights activist, and general advocate for liberal causes—generally parallels Walker's political involvements and commitments, and Luna, a young white woman. Luna reveals to the narrator that while engaged in the civil rights work in the South during the 1960s she was raped by Freddie Pye, a black fellow civil rights worker. Several years later, upon awakening in an apartment that she shared with Luna, the black woman observes Freddie Pye

---

[13] Hal Foster, *Recodings: Art, Spectacle, Cultural Politics* (Seattle: Bay Press, 1985), p. 129.

[14] My reference to an "interrogative textual modality" is taken from Catherine Belsey, who discusses three textual modalities in terms of how the reader is situated in relationship to the text. In the declarative mode, associated with classic realism, the reader is a passive consumer of the text's ideology; the imperative mode, generally identified with propaganda, invites the reader to engage in a given action; and in the interrogative mode, the text refuses closure by "[inviting] an answer or answers to the questions it poses." See Catherine Belsey, (London and New York: Methuen, 1980), pp. 91-93.

leaving Luna's bedroom. These two incidents constitute the textual dominant, determining the focus of the narrative and the ideological issues it foregrounds, tensions and fragmentations experienced by black women attempting to reconcile the politics of race and that of gender.

The racial memory that informs the black woman's psychic character allows her to be anchored in the world. Through it she achieves a personal and collective identity that is in conflict with her friendship with Luna. In narrating her fieldwork in the South with Luna, she reveals the strong race-identified aspect of her character:

> This month with Luna of approaching new black people every day taught me something about myself I had always suspected: I thought black people superior to white people, because even without thinking about it much, I assumed almost everyone was superior to them. . . .Only white people, after all, would blow up a Sunday-school class and grin for television over their "victory," i.e., the death of four small black girls. Any atrocity, any time, was expected from them. On the other hand, it never occurred to me that black people could treat Luna and me with anything but warmth and concern.[15]

The race-gender tension is intensified as the "I" of the narrative identifies her situation with that of black women in general, breaking the fictional frame and directly inviting the reader to enter a dialogic relationship with the narrative. The realist frame of the narrative is broken so as to allow the reader to confront the ideological issues being mapped out in the text:

> Who knows what the black woman thinks of rape? Who has asked her? Who cares? Who has even properly acknowledged that she and not the white woman in this story is the most likely victim of rape? Whenever interracial rape is mentioned, a black woman's first thought is to protect the lives of her brothers, her

---

[15] Alice Walker, "Advancing Luna—and Ida B. Wells," in *You Can't Keep a Good Woman Down* (New York: Harcourt Brace Jovanovich, 1981), p. 88.

father, her sons, her lover. A history of lynching has bred this reflex in her.[16]

In this passage we see the fundamental tension between subject positions based on gender and race. The text's strong identification with women's experience is relentlessly complicated by an insistent racial problematic. Racial ideology is reinforced by the narrator's metonymic reconstruction of the violence directed against blacks during the 1960s. Evocations of the assassinations of King, Malcolm X, and the Kennedys represent the suppression of black hopes during that period. Overall, the story foregrounds the conflict inherent in a politics that would merge race and gender.

Moving from the general issue of race and gender to a focus on the particular Freddie-Luna incident, the narrator again explores history as a metonymic construct that might be useful in exploring the text's ideology. Two historical moments are evoked and "read" within the context of their ideological implications: the moment of the Black Power movement and the anti-lynching efforts of Ida B. Wells.

Upon being informed by Luna of the alleged assault, the narrator responds with anger and repulsion. The immediate context in which she views the act is that of some of the extremist statements that characterized black nationalist rhetoric of the 1960s.

> This was the time before Eldridge Cleaver wrote of being a rapist/revolutionary; "practicing" on black women before moving on to whites. It was also . . . before LeRoi Jones wrote the advice to young black insurrectionaries. . . . "Rape the white girls. Rape their fathers. . . ." It was clear that he meant this literally and also as: to rape a white girl is to rape her father. It was the misogynous cruelty of this latter meaning that was habitually lost on black men (on men in general, actually) but nearly always perceived and rejected by women of any color.[17]

This representation of Jones and Cleaver as signs of a political movement hostile to women enables the narrator to identify with women as an

---

[16] *Ibid.*, (p. 93).
[17] *Ibid.* (p. 91).

oppressed group. The concluding sentence of the passage is particularly significant, for it goes beyond commentary and argues that essentially different ethical and moral perspectives determined the respective male and female responses.

The issue, however, is not brought to closure. Turning to the autobiography of Ida B. Wells, the narrator invokes a second historical moment and personage that enters a dialogic yet contestatory relationship with her first citation. It is Wells, the late nineteenth and early twentieth century crusader against the lynching of black men, who appears in a "vision" to the narrator and warns:

"Write Nothing. Nothing at all. It will be used against black men and therefore against all of us. Eldridge Cleaver and LeRoi Jones don't know who they're dealing with. But you remember. You are dealing with people who brought their children to witness the murder of black human beings, falsely accused of rape. . . ."[18]

Through these inscriptions of two different historical moments, the text foregrounds its dominant ideological problematic: the need to resolve tensions generated by competing loyalties, one focused on racial solidarity, the other addressing the oppression of women. Yet the resolution of this conflict is left to the reader. The tension remains unresolved as the narrator presents her argument but refuses to state an ideological position. This interrogative mode is further reinforced by the manner in which the narrative unfolds. Identifying herself as a writer, the narrator foregrounds the story's textuality and constructs it as a dialogue between her and the reader. The ideological issues, then, are simultaneously represented in two contexts: one that is "fictional" and one a commentary that situates the fictional in the context of the real. This is particularly evident when mediations of the narrator, historical references, and the "story" intersect.

In a final moment of metafictionality, the narrator moves outside the text and focuses on it as written discourse. In doing so, she poses three possible readings of the events represented: (1) a reflection on the possible handling of of the rape incident in a society in which racism was

---

[18] *Ibid.* (p. 94).

not a factor, (2) the imaginary construction of a scenario in which Freddie's second visit to Luna did not involve a sexual encounter, and (3) a conversation with a male friend who suggests that Freddie may have been an agent provocateur, hired by the Central Intelligence Agency to discredit the civil rights movement.

All of these possibilities are left for the reader to explore. The story simply maps out within a fictional space ideological issues confronted by black women who must embrace a politics of both race and gender. What the text addresses and leaves largely unresolved is the manner in which the multiple positions black women occupy result in irresolution. This issue is at the core of black women's political emergence, and "Advancing Luna—and Ida B. Wells," through its brilliant deployment of post-modernist narrative strategies, invites the reader to enter debate on the question.

Narratives such as "Advancing Luna. . ." present contemporary critical practices with their most demanding challenges. Overdetermined by the political issues of their moments, they cannot be contained by interpretive strategies that privilege blues matrices, vernacular theories, and expressive concepts of culture, all of which are implicated in ahistorical and essentialist notions of a transcendent black culture. Fictional narratives such as "Advancing Luna. . ." become sites in which differences are theorized and foregrounded and the very nature of narrative is problematized.

Race under Representation

David Lloyd

This racism that aspires to be rational, individual, genotypically and phenotypically determined, becomes transformed into cultural racism. The object of racism is no longer the individual man but a certain form of existing.

Frantz Fanon, 'Racism and Culture'

Far from having to ask whether culture is or is not a function of race, we are discovering that race—or what is generally meant by the term—is one function among others of culture.

Claude Lévi-Strauss, 'Race and Culture'[1]

In the main, the experience and the analysis of racism or race relations have been and continue to be cast in *spatial* terms. On the one hand, the concept of race has throughout its history been articulated in terms of the geographical distribution of peoples or, as the discreteness of geographical location gradually dissolves, as if there were a spectrum of races in contiguity with one another. On the other hand, in the politics of racism it is the *confrontation* of races in opposition to one another and the literally and figuratively spatial disposition of inequitable power relations between them that is most striking. Unquestionably, neither the history nor the theory of racism can be thought without reference to spatial categories, whether we attend to the global geographies of imperial expansion and international capital or to the more intimate geographies of the inner city, ghettoization or the displacement of peoples. The human experiences recorded in these terms are the material substrate of other, equally spatial terms in which the anti-racist cultural politics of the last decade has been expressed: euro- or ethnocentrism, marginalization, exclusion, not to mention those now critical categories, orientalism and the West.

It is not my intention here to critique those categories, without which neither the analysis of nor the political struggle against racism could have been articulated, but rather to argue that these spatial terms need to be supplemented by an analysis of the temporal axis which is equally

186

constitutive of racist discourse. Recent critiques of development and modernization theories have drawn attention to the manner in which racist and ethnocentric discourses in economic and political spheres deploy a normative temporality of human development which is applied at once to the individual, to individual nations or cultures, and to the human race in general.[2] But beyond even such critiques, the discourse on culture that emerges in the 'modern era' of the West is itself structured at every level by this normative developmental schema: the racism of culture is not a question of certain contingent racist observations by its major theoreticians nor of the still incomplete dissemination of its goods, but an ineradicable effect of its fundamental structures. These structures, indeed, determine the forms, casual and institutional, that racism has taken in the post-enlightenment era and account for the generally racist disposition of the 'West', understood not as a bounded geographical domain but as a global complex of economic, political and cultural institutions which represent, in a universal *temporal* schema, the locus of the modern in any society. The discourse of culture is not merely descriptive but crucially productive, in that it directs the formation of the modern subject both in the geographical west and wherever the West has imposed its institutions.

In their recent study, *Racial Formation in the United States*, Michael Omi and Howard Winant discuss the manner in which racial formations operate on both micro- and macro-levels of society:

> The racial order is organized and enforced by the continuity and reciprocity between these two 'levels' of social relations. The micro- and macro-levels, however, are only analytically distinct. In our lived experience, in politics, in culture, in economic life, they are continuous and reciprocal.[3]

Part of the intention of this essay is to indicate how the meshing of racial formations can take place between various levels and spheres of social practice, as, for example, between political and cultural spheres or between the individual and the national level. In doing so, I will be restoring to the concept of 'formation', properly used here in its current socio-cultural sense, the equally important sense that it has traditionally had in aesthetic pedagogy, the sense of self-formation or *Bildung*. Culture will have here not, in the first place, its generalized sense of the totality of life-forms of a particular society or group, but quite strictly the sense of *aesthetic culture*.[4] It will be my contention that the terms developed for aesthetic culture in the late eighteenth century, as constituting the definition of human identity, continue to regulate racial formations through the various sites of contemporary practice.[5] Crucial to this function of aesthetic culture is its formulation and development of a *narrative of representation*, by which is meant not only the representative narratives of canonical culture, but also the narrative form taken by the concept of representation itself. As we shall see, within this narrative the same processes of formalization occur at every level, allowing a series of transferred identifications to take place from individual to nation, and from the nation to the idea of a universal humanity. By the same token, the fissures and contradictions that trouble this narrative are replicated equally at every level or in every site which it informs.[6]

What I will attempt here, then, is to sketch a phenomenology of racism as it is embedded in the 'disposition of the subject' produced and maintained by Western culture. Though I will use the term 'culture' throughout to imply first of all 'aesthetic culture', it will become clear that the idea of aesthetic culture governs not only what is loosely referred to as 'high culture' but also, if less evidently, most other subsequent usages of the term. For the theoretical construction of a domain of aesthetic judgement in late eighteenth and early nineteenth century cultural theory provides the constitutive forms of the 'public sphere' itself. Grounding the idea of a common or public sense, the subject of aesthetic judgement supplies the very possibility of a disinterested domain of culture and prescribes the development of that domain through history as the ethical end of humanity itself.

For this reason, I wish to start with a moment from one of the founding texts of cultural theory, namely Immanuel Kant's third critique, *The Critique of Judgement*. As is well known, Kant's deduction of the universality of the aesthetic judgement relies on the disinterest of the subject of judgement, on what I shall call the 'Subject without properties'. This abstract Subject is merely regulative in the case of pure aesthetic judgements: it is the measure of the disinterest of the judge by which he conforms ideally to the condition of universality. In the case of the *social* faculty of taste, however, to judge as if one were the Subject without properties is constitutive of the possibility of such a universal validity, actualizing that common sense which is otherwise assumed only as a latent condition of disinterested judgement in all humans.

Kant makes this positive or constitutive function of taste clear in #40 of the *Third Critique*, 'Taste as a kind of *sensus communis*'. Here, a movement within the judgement itself, from the material particularity of the object to its formal universality as a disposition of the subject, doubles an identical movement from the peculiarity of a singular judgement to its representative universality. What is universal, and therefore constitutive of the domain of common or public sense, is the *form* of the judgement rather than its object or matter:

> However, by the name *sensus communis* is to be understood the idea of a *public* sense, i.e. a critical faculty which in its reflective act takes account (*a priori*) of the mode of representation of every one else, in order, *as it were*, to weigh its judgements with the collective reason of mankind, and thereby avoid the illusion arising from subjective and personal conditions which could readily be taken for objective, an illusion that would exert a prejudicial influence upon its judgement. This is accomplished by weighing the judgement, not so much with actual, as rather with the merely possible, judgements of others, and by putting ourselves in the position of every one else, as the result of a mere abstraction from the limitations which contingently affect our own estimate. This, in turn, is effected by so far as possible letting go of the element of matter, i.e. sensation, in our general state of representative activity, and confining attention to the formal peculiarities of our representation or general state of representative activity.[7]

In this prescription for the aesthetic judgement, the movement from matter to form in the representation of the object corresponds to a less immediately evident formalization internal to the subject, a formalization that becomes the condition for the existence of a public sense. Only a subject formalized, if momentarily, into identity with 'every one else', that is, with the Subject in general, can provide the conditions for the universal accord of a common or public sense. In turn, it is the idea, not necessarily always actualized but nonetheless operative, of this common sense that underlies the concept of a public sphere. As we shall see, what is at first the merely logical temporality of the aesthetic judgement becomes prescriptive for the narrative of representation through which this actualization of common sense in the modern public sphere is to be realized.

That process can be summarized in the following propositions:

    1) the ordering of 'our general state of representative activity' is such as to imply a narrative organization of the senses which moves from sensation to form;

    2) this narrative of the senses within the individual human subject finds a correspondent form in the development of the human race;

    3) this narrative can be expressed as, or, alternatively, depends upon a movement from contiguity to identity, or from metonymy to metaphor.

Each of these formally correspondent narratives gives in its way the condition for the emergence of the public sphere.

    1) As the simultaneously literal and metaphoric usages of both the terms 'common sense' and 'taste' might suggest, what these concepts describe is the very movement they require from the immediate particularity of sensation to the formal generality of the social. For 'sense' to become 'common', its conditions must be formalized as a disposition of the Subject in each of us; for 'taste' to emerge as a social phenomenon, the cultivation of the senses must proceed from the pleasure derived from the existence of the object that is characteristic of literal 'taste' to the contemplative relation to the object which is the capacity of sight. This narrative of the organization of the senses towards an increasing distance from the object and an increasing formalization of its representation is parallel for Kant to the movement from the merely agreeable, which is private and entirely singular, to the beautiful, which is to be universally communicable. In the discourse of aesthetic culture, which itself emerges in the increasing abstraction of *aesthetics* itself from the science of pain and pleasure to that of fine art, this narrative organization of the senses in a crucially *developmental* hierarchy is fundamental. Indeed, in the most minimal moment of perception, such a development is already present within any judgement as the move from *Darstellung* [presentation], in which the senses are merely passive recipients, to *Vorstellung* [representation], in which the object is constituted as a possible object for the reflective or the logical judgement. A process of formalization, the initial abstraction of a form from a manifold of sensations as an object assimilable to other such objects, is inseparable from any completed act of perception.

As Friedrich Schiller puts it with characteristic clarity:

It is nature herself which raises man from reality to semblance, by furnishing him with two senses which lead him to knowledge of the real world though semblance alone. In the case of the eye and the ear, she herself has driven importunate matter back from the organs of sense, and the object, with which in the case of our more animal senses we have direct contact, is set at a distance from us. What we actually see with the eye is something different from the sensation we receive; for the mind leaps out across light to objects. The object of touch is a force to which we are subjected; the object of eye and ear a form that we engender. As long as man is still a savage he enjoys by means of these tactile senses alone, and at this stage the senses of semblance are merely the servants of these. Either he does not rise to the level of seeing at all, or he is at all events not satisfied with it. Once he does begin to enjoy through the eye, and seeing acquires for him a value of its own, he is already aesthetically free and the play-drive has started to develop.[8]

2) As Schiller's remarks suggest, the developmental narrative of sensual organization is required by the developmental history of the race of which, at every stage of that development, it is the index. In a version of the thesis that 'ontogeny recapitulates phylogeny', the movement, as Kant puts it, from 'the charm of sense to habitual moral interest' that taste makes possible (CJ 225; cf. also 65) is at once an affair of the individual and of the human 'race'. The same development that produces in each individual a capacity for subjectively universal judgements of taste produces in human societies the civilized form of the public sphere. Kant thus describes the movement from a primitive interest in the 'charms of sense' to 'universal communicability':

Further, a regard to universal communicability is a thing which every one expects and requires from every one else, just as if it were part of an original compact dictated by humanity itself. And thus, no doubt, at first only charms, e.g. colours for painting oneself (roucou among the Caribs and cinnabar among the Iroquois), or flowers, sea-shells, beautifully coloured feathers, then, in the course of time, also beautiful forms (as in canoes, wearing-apparel, &c.) which convey no gratification, i.e. delight of enjoyment, become of moment in society and attract a

considerable interest. Eventually, when civilization has reached
its height it makes this work of communication almost the main
business of refined inclination, and the entire value of sensations
is placed in the degree to which they permit of universal
communication. (CJ 155-6)

The narrative of sensual development is thus directed towards the
emergence of the public sphere and depends clearly on an ever-
increasing degree of formalization. On the face of it then the relegation
of the Iroquois or the 'Carib' to a correspondingly low stage of
development could be taken as merely incidentally 'racist'
(parenthetically, to be precise), especially given that the interest in
universal communicability is already conceived as 'an original compact
dictated by humanity itself'. It would indeed be incidental in the case
that the interest in immediate gratification or in universal
communication were seen as merely among the accidental cultural characteristics of the Native American and the European respectively. On the
contrary, however, it is in a very real sense the capacity for 'universal
communicability' that *defines* civilization, with the Europeanness of that
civilization being strictly speaking merely incidental.   Despite   its
articulation through the ascription to particular races of 'essential'
characteristics, racism is structured in the first place by the cultural
determination of a public sphere and of the subject formation that is its
condition of existence.   Though this proposition finds some empirical
corroboration in the constant appeal of white racism to ethical
categories, its justification is to be found rather in the (albeit
contradictory) logic of racist thought and culture, the fuller analysis of
which follows. Suffice it to say at this point that it is not the claim of
an ethical disposition as a racial characteristic but the establishment of
a peculiar and historically specific social form, the public sphere as
defined in aesthetic theory, as the end of humanity that defines the
logical structure of racist discourses. For this reason, it is possible for
an interchangeably ethical, political and aesthetic judgement as to the
inferiority of the 'savage races' to saturate post-enlightenment
discourses on race from liberals such as John Stuart Mill or Matthew
Arnold to extreme conservatives such as Gobineau, Klemm, Nott or
Hunt.[9]   The inadequacy of the native to self-government is
demonstrated by 'his' lack of aesthetic productions or by 'his'
subordination to immediate sensual gratification: the capacity for

autonomy is either as yet undeveloped or absent in the savage and requires to be developed or supplied by external force.

Though both arguments continue even now to be presented, it is the developmental model rather than that of irredeemable lack that tends eventually to dominate. Sound material grounds for this gradual transition can be traced. As Colette Guillaumin has argued, the discourse on race (as on other categories of heterogeneity) undergoes a crucial shift in the late eighteenth century from a system of arbitrary marks to the ascription of natural signs. We can, as Fanon does, attribute such a shift to the necessity to legitimate, within the context of appeals to universal humanity, the intensified and systematic domination of subordinated peoples: in this case, any discourse on difference must cease to be contingent and casual and establish instead a regular scheme of discriminations which at once preserves and legitimates domination. Initially there may be no absolute correlation between racist and imperialist discourses, since fear of contamination and environmental derivations of racial variation can offer strong arguments for not encouraging interracial encounters or even the colonization of alien climes. Gradually, however, through the intersection of liberal humanism with the necessities of imperial polity, the developmental discourse on race comes to dominate, precisely because it allows for the assimilation of a fraction of the colonized population to the imperial culture in order that they may function as administrators and professionals.[10]

To this last point we will return. It is important here, however, to note that Guillaumin's formulation allows us to grasp how racist discourse maintains its capacity to replicate and circulate in several spheres. For what she indicates, in describing the transition from *allegorical* marks, which retain the arbitrariness of their social constitution, to *symbolic* 'natural signs', which represent externally the inner, organic constitution of the object, is the regulatory force of the narrative of representation across the social field. For even where a representation is at first a representation of difference, it conforms formally to the general demand for any representation to maintain the structure of identity within which the part can stand for the whole. Across differences, identity is formally preserved; across cultures, human nature is essentially the same and can therefore be developed along identical lines.[11]

As Guillaumin points out, to the 'natural mark' (colour, gender, facial appearance) that inscribes the dominated correspond the absence of marks attributed to the dominator:

> It inscribes the system of domination on the body of the individual, assigning to the individual his/her place as a dominated person: but it does not assign any place to the dominator. Membership in the dominant group, on the contrary, is legally marked by a convenient lack of interdiction, by unlimited possibilities.[12]

We can reformulate this as indicating that the position occupied by the dominant individual is that of the Subject without properties. This Subject with 'unlimited possibilities' is precisely the undetermined subject, Schiller's Person as yet abstracted from Condition, whose infinite potential is a function of a purely formal identity with humanity in general.[13]   Its universality is attained by virtue of literal indifference: this Subject becomes representative in consequence of being able to take anyone's place, of occupying any place, of a pure exchangeability. Universal where all others are particular, partial, this Subject is the perfect, disinterested judge formed for and by the public sphere.

The Subject without properties is the philosophical figure for what becomes, with increasing literalness through the nineteenth century, the global ubiquity of the white European. His domination is virtually self-legitimating since the capacity to be everywhere present becomes an historical manifestation of the white man's gradual approximation to the universality he everywhere represents. It is still not uncommon to hear it remarked that the human race (as opposed, implicitly, to the Eskimo or Nuer, for example) is singular in its capacity to occupy any habitat. By the same token, in the post-colonial era, immigration from former colonies is a source of especial ideological scandal not least because it upsets the asymmetrical distribution of humanity into the local (native) and the universal. What governs this distribution, as, perhaps until quite recently, it governed the discipline of anthropology, is the regulative idea of Culture against which the multiplicity of local cultures is defined. Like Kant's Saussure, the anthropologist and the colonial administrator occupy the place of disinterest as representatives of that Culture, with the critical consequence that every racial judgement is simultaneously an aesthetic, an ethical and a political one.[14]

3) To reformulate the foregoing, it is not in the first instance the antagonistic recognition of difference which constitutes the discourse of racism but the subordination of difference to the demand for identity. This identity principle governs racism in both its exclusive and its assimilative modes, the former narrowing the domain of identity, the other apparently expanding it but, as we shall see, only at the cost of a dissimulated but logically necessary exclusion. As the very expression 'assimilation' might suggest, racism elevates a principle of likening above that of differentiation such that its rhetorical structure is that of metaphorization.

Paul Ricoeur observes that the tension between likeness and difference constitutes the metaphoric process:

> The insight into likeness is the perception of the conflict between the previous incompatibility and the new compatibility. 'Remoteness' is preserved within 'proximity'. To see *the like* is to see the same in spite of, and through, the different. This tension between sameness and difference characterizes the logical structure of likeness.[15]

Such a description accounts quite adequately for the pleasurable shock of novel metaphors. What it is unable to do, however, is to grasp the finally normative function of metaphor that makes it so central a figure both for an organic poetics and for post-romantic literary pedagogy. The point can be made most succinctly by remarking that Ricoeur's description would allow no distinction between metaphor and those poetic figures which a pre-Romantic poetics terms conceit or wit. Unlike metaphor, which Condillac more succinctly and classically describes as 'thinking of the properties in which things agree', wit and conceit derive their effects from the salience of difference.[16]

Accordingly both Ricoeur's definition and, among others, Paul de Man's even more radical reading, which sees metaphor as rhetorically subversive of the identity principle of philosophy by virtue of its catachrestic foundations, require supplementation. What both arguments omit is the narrative subordination within metaphor of difference by identity, a narrative entirely coherent with the philosophical as with the literary critical tradition. Metaphor is not merely the oscillation between sameness and difference, but the process of subordinating difference to identity, and it is precisely that narrative that makes metaphor ultimately compatible with philosophical projects in general and with aesthetic projects in particular.

Ricoeur virtually acknowledges the narrative aspect of metaphor in another essay when he remarks on the conjunction in Aristotle's *Poetics* of metaphor and plot. Metaphor functions structurally and mimetically at a minimal stylistic level as does plot at the largest organizational level. Both are directed towards the uncovering of concealed identities, to moments of *anagnorisis*.[17] In the last instance, even the most jarring of metaphors, if it is to be accepted as tasteful, must allow the *recognition* of an identity which was already there. It is recreative, not transformative. The question with regard to metaphor becomes, not what it signifies, but how it signifies within the larger matrix of cultural elements. What this allows us to perceive is the function of metaphoric processes, as minimal narratives of identity, within the larger plot of self-formation: both are directed towards the gradual overcoming of difference by identity. But, as Ricoeur's own argument implies, it is not merely that a happy analogy exists between metaphor and the plot of self-formation. More pertinently, metaphor operates at the most fundamental levels of feeling to produce effects of identification or 'assimilation' in the subject:

> If the process [of metaphor] can be called, as I have called it, predicative *assimilation*, it is true that *we* are assimilated, that is, made similar, to what is seen as similar. This self-assimilation is a part of the commitment proper to the 'illocutionary' force of the metaphor as speech act. We feel *like* what we see *like*.[18]

This being the case, we can locate in metaphor a minimal element of the processes of cultural formation which is replicated at larger and larger levels of identity and identification. Culture can, so to speak, be understood as a learning to be like what we should like to like.[19] That is, as assimilation.

Like the expressions 'taste' and 'common sense', 'assimilation' is a concept which is at once a metaphor and structured like a metaphor. But unlike taste and common sense, which embody the narrative of a movement from immediate sensation to universality, the very logic of assimilation betrays an inverse movement equally intrinsic to the process of metaphorization in general but accentuated by its status as a material practice. The constitution of any metaphor involves the bringing together of two elements into identity in such a manner that their differences are suppressed. Just so, the process of assimilation, whether in bringing two distinct but equivalent elements into identity or in absorbing a lower into a higher element as by metastasis, requires that which defines the difference between the elements to remain over as a residue. Hence, although it is possible to conceive formally of an equable process of assimilation in which the original elements are entirely equivalent, the product of assimilation will always necessarily be in an hierarchical relation to the residual, whether this be defined as, variously, the primitive, the local or the merely contingent.[20] The process of identification, therefore, whether instanced in metaphorization, assimilation or subject formation, not only produces difference but simultaneously gives that difference a determinate sense which is to be resistant to sense. Differences that in the first instance have no meaning and no law come to signify negatively under the law of identity that produces them. Racial discriminations, accordingly, 'make sense' and achieve their self-evidence only in relation to the law of identity which governs equally assimilation and exclusion.

A contradictory logic thus structures equally the abstract, identical Subject and the public sphere which it subtends. Since the production of difference as negative identity is inherent to that logic, the Subject which results may be conceived as obsessionally anxious, since its very formation produces what might undo that formation. It would be proper in this, if not all, instances to speak of the insistence rather than the return of the repressed, since the repressed is here produced in every moment of the Subject's formation. What is true for the Subject is, on account of the logic of doubling analyzed above, true on other levels for the public sphere and for aesthetic culture. In the following section, the consequences of the insistence of the repressed will be examined in terms of the resistance it poses to the assimilative drive and developmental claims of a universalizing culture. Since the emphasis here will be on the logic of individual self-formation, and since I have been stressing till now rather how cultural formation *works* than how it breaks down, it is worth making the remark that it is racism itself, as a social phenomenon, that brings to light the contradictory nature of the powerful and remarkably effective institutional logic of culture. At a later point, we will return to this issue through the work of two third world writers.

II

It is a frequent characteristic of racism that where the apparently neutral ascriptions of difference depend on relations of contiguity and therefore on metonymic usages (for example, skin colour for race—black, yellow, white), the racist epithet which asserts relations of superiority is generally metaphoric: black boy, savage, baboon. The metaphoric structure of the epithet here legitimates a violent assertion of superiority by way of the appeal to developmental categories: against the achieved identity of the white man, the black appears as being in greater proximity to childhood or animality. Yet at the same time, racism constantly makes appeal to the *immediacy* of its discriminations, to their self-evidence: 'you only have to look at them...'.

The argument of the foregoing section establishes, however, that the appeal to visual immediacy is always illusory, not insofar as there is no difference to be seen but insofar as the significant difference that is registered depends already on the transfer from metonymy to metaphor or on the acculturation of the subject that sees. These processes transform the recognition of differences into a positing of lack of identity in the object. Indeed, the very emergence of the subject that sees, or, more properly, the Subject that *judges*, is already predicated on a prior development of the senses that is ethically structured. What is seen by the racist vision is an underdeveloped human animal whose underdevelopment becomes the index of the judging subject's own superior stage of development.

The visual structure of racism can, accordingly, better be compared with what psychoanalysis supposes to take place in the castration complex than, as some have argued, with the processes of fetishism.[21] For, while fetishism is produced out of a *disavowal* of anatomical difference, the fetishist refusing 'to take cognizance of the fact of his having perceived that a woman does not possess a penis' (OS 352), the castration complex emerges in the recognition of difference and its interpretation as a mutilation of identity.[22] On the one hand, the castration complex is the primary agency of the formation of the little boy as at once male and ethical, initiating the internalization of the father in the form of the super-ego. In a phrase highly significant for the meaning of identity formation, Freud remarks that this process constitutes 'the victory of the race over the individual' (ADS 341). On the other hand, it achieves this only at the cost of producing an ineradicable anxiety in the subject as to the possibility of itself undergoing a mutilation which would undo that identity. In an associated move, woman is seen, by virtue of her mutilated identity, as incapable of ethical development: the impossibility of a castration complex prevents the internalization of the father as superego and the identity formation of the woman remains incomplete (ADS 342). Freud's interpretation at this juncture nicely recapitulates the little boy's. Where the little boy reinterprets the girl's or woman's 'lack of a penis' at first as the sign of an underdeveloped organ and then as a mutilation, Freud reads the 'lack of a penis' as the grounds of an underdeveloped ethical sense only then to confront female sexuality as something gapped and interrupted.

That Freud's interpretation should thus appear to recapitulate that of the little boy whom it seeks to interpret is not surprising once we reflect that the boy's judgement is in any case not as immediate as the phrase 'first catches sight of' implies, but is predicated on a prior development of the organs and of the ethical sense of which the castration complex is only the final stage. In the first instance, Freud is quite clear that the castration complex depends on what he had long before identified as 'The Phases of Development of the Sexual Organization'.[23] It depends on the movement of the organization of sexual pleasure away from the 'polymorphous perversity' of infancy towards the 'phallic stage'. Once again, the narrative of development moves from a moment of contiguity and substitution to one organized around a single term which, like a metaphor, comes to effect the distribution of phenomena into identity and difference. (For this reason, regression to the point prior to the castration complex in psychosis produces the effects of verbal non-sense and physical disintegration.) The development of the organs, like that of the senses in Schiller, is already directed towards an ethical end. Accordingly, in the second instance, the apparent visual immediacy of the little boy's judgement is in fact prepared for by an ethical formation of however rudimentary a kind. Freud's revision of his understanding of the process between 'The Dissolution of the Oedipus Complex' (1924) and 'Some Psychical Consequences of the Anatomical Sex Distinction' (1925) makes this clearer. Where in the first essay, it is the 'first sight' of the female genitals that induces the castration complex, in the second essay, the first sight may be attended by

disavowal and 'irresolution' and it is only 'later, when some threat of
castration has obtained a hold upon him, that the observation becomes
important to him' (ADS 336). The visual index, in other words, only
gains sense in relation to moral development.[24] In turn, it is the sense
given to the visual as a mark of identity and of difference reinterpreted
as the mutilation of identity that structures the Subject in its very
identity as always subject to the ineradicable threat of a difference upon
which it depends. The identity of the Subject is not only structured
against difference, its own possibility depends on producing the
possibility of precisely the internal difference which threatens it.

In the field of racism as of sexuality, the appeal to visual immediacy
in any judgement of difference may be seen as a disavowal of the
contradictory logic of the Subject's identity formation.[25] The anxiety
of the racist is that what is constantly represented as an immediately
visible, self-evident difference is in fact internal to the Subject. The
racist shares with the obsessional neurotic the anxiety of being found
out. But while it is doubtless the case that the psychic structure of
racism depends, as some have argued, in large degree on projection, the
critical point that needs to be stressed is that it is the *insistence* of a
difference internal to the constitution of identity which underlies the
cultural logic of racism rather than either the return or the projection of
repressed material.[26] Instances of racism where the visual index of
difference is by any measure minimal if not absent throw the cultural
logic of racism into relief with peculiar force. In such instances of
white on white racism, the fantasmatic projection of differences appears
as a wishful resolution of a disturbance in the visual field. In what has
become a celebrated passage, Charles Kingsley wrote to his wife of the
poor Irish in 1860:

> But I am haunted by the human chimpanzees I saw along that
> hundred miles of horrible country. I don't believe they are our
> fault. I believe there are not only many more of them than of
> old, but that they are happier, better, more comfortably fed and
> lodged under our rule than they ever were. But to see white
> chimpanzees is dreadful; if they were black, one would not feel
> it so much, but their skins, except where tanned by exposure, are
> as white as ours.

In such perceptions, what is disturbed is the law of verisimilitude which
governs the metaphorical system of racism. For this law, the identity

between ape and black is self-evident and it is scandalized by the possibility of a conjunction between whiteness, as the outward sign of human identity, and the simian, which, as a metaphor, becomes a metaphor of non-identity in the very structure of the human. The same scandal to the order of identity is registered in Thomas Carlyle's phrase for the Irish, 'the white negroes', an impossible, catachrestic conjunction that persists as an anomaly in English racist discourse: 'if only they were black...'.[27]

The point here is not to underestimate the importance of external marks of difference to racist practices, but rather to emphasize how the apparent visual anomaly of white on white racism is the index of a prior constitution of the racist Subject-who-judges by which alone the appeal to visual immediacy of discrimination is legitimated. Whiteness is the metaphor for the metaphorical production of the Subject as one devoid of properties rather than the natural sign of difference to which the attributes of civilization and culture are in turn attached. Where whiteness is suddenly, forcibly conjoined with the metaphors of difference, the order of development is radically disrupted. And insofar, as we have seen, the metaphoric logic of culture works always through the production of a residual order of difference, what Kingsley or Carlyle discover in the form of an anomaly constantly troubles the discursive and institutional practices of assimilation.[28]

III

As is well known, different colonial regimes have had quite various policies with regard to the assimilation or exclusion of dominated populations. It is often remarked, for example, that French colonialism differs from British in that French policy tended to emphasize the process of acculturation while British policy instituted virtual apartheid, especially in its African domains. Though such distinctions may be accurate with regard to the regulatory tendencies of each imperial state, it is nonetheless the case that any imperial apparatus, once the initial period of conquest and domination by force is over, requires a greater or lesser number of native administrators and professionals to mediate its hegemony. Even if, as in many British colonies, this caste is relatively small numerically, its political function is crucial both for the colonial administration and for the development of national resistance movements.[29]

Many writers have noted and analyzed the regularity with which nationalist movements are formed among the most assimilated elements of the colonized population.[30]   One constant and critical factor in this process is the confrontation with racism precisely as a contradiction in the logic of assimilation itself. Unlike the 'subaltern' population, whose oppression and resistance alike remain largely outside the domain of state institutions for which the subaltern has no subjective existence at all, the colonial intellectual confronts racism as a limit to the line of development that cultural assimilation appears to propose to him *as Subject*. Racism exposes the residual elements required by the logic of assimilation in constituting the colonial subject as a divided self, one part constituted by acculturation as 'modern', the other identified by the racist judgement as permanently lodged in a primitive moment incapable of development. Nationalism offers to suture this division by relocating the institutions of the modern state on the very terrain that the colonizer regards as primitive. It restores continuity to the interrupted narrative of representation by reterritorializing it within the newly conceived nation. Nationalism, in other words, accepts the *verisimilitude* of imperial culture while redefining its purview.

In an essay on the Sudanese writer Tayeb Salih's *Season of Migration to the North*, Samir Seikaly expresses the predicament of colonialism's 'divided man' succinctly:

> For whatever else it may be on the economic plane, colonialism, for every man, or society, who feel its full force, is essentially and permanently deformative, serving to bisect native society.... Of the two antithetical halves, the first, because of imperialism itself, is no longer traditional, while the other, because of its longing for a primordial identity, can never become fully modern. This is the origin of the divided man....[31]

But in grasping the extent to which one of the cultural and psychological consequences of the assimilative drive of colonialism is the production of divided subjects, we need equally to perceive the extent to which that process can contribute to a transformation of the colonizing as of the colonized culture. The force of novels such as *Season of Migration*, which indeed dramatizes the predicament of the divided subject of colonialism across two generations, lies less in their representation of the damage inflicted than in the radical critique of Western cultural forms that they draw from it. What comes into question in Salih's novel is that order of verisimilitude that I have termed the narrative of representation.

Both the narrator of *Season of Migration* and its other principal character, Mustafa Sa'eed, are British educated Sudanese, the latter of the generation immediately following the consolidation of British rule in the late nineteenth century, the former of the period of independence. The narrator, returning to his village after a long absence in England, is devoted at every level to the concept of identity. His return seems to be a reassumption of identity, 'continuous and integral', making him 'happy ... like a child that sees its face in the mirror for the first time'. To the villagers' questions as to the nature of the Europeans, he replies repeatedly that 'with minor differences' they are 'just like us'.[32] But virtually from the moment of his arrival, the narrator is confronted by the alien presence of the stranger Mustafa Sa'eed, who is an insistent reminder of their mutual alienation: by the end of the novel, the child's narcissistic content will be displaced by the narrator's mistaking his face in a mirror for the portrait of Mustafa Sa'eed (SMN 135).

The novel becomes a forensic quest as the narrator seeks obsessively to establish Sa'eed's identity, to reconstruct his past in the Sudan and in England. But the novel refuses to deliver the generic denouement of the classic detective story. Sa'eed's narrative, rendered in fragments of flashback, is a narrative of multiple dislocations, literal and figural, and insistently raises the question of identity rather than resolving it. As the narrator, in the final scenes of the novel, enters the dead or disappeared Sa'eed's library, he finds not a single portrait or identity paper, but a proliferation of portraits of Mustafa Sa'eed in various guises and poses together with a blank book that was to have contained his autobiography (SMN 138-9; 150). Rather than a narrative of self-formation, or a narrative of identification, we are confronted with a proliferation of types unable to cohere into a single form. Just as Mustafa Sa'eed in England manipulates stereotypes of the African man as a means to seducing English women, Salih parodies each of the genres with which the novel seems momentarily to align: detective fiction, racial romance, tragedy, even farce.[33] Above all, however, it is the novel of self-formation which is seen to fracture, as even this most successful of colonial intellectuals fails to integrate with the English culture that summons and even idolizes him.

Sa'eed's trajectory, from the streets of Khartoum to the lecture rooms and salons of England, has all the elements of a narrative of self-making. Most significantly, it involves a reorganization of his desire such that at the social level it is directed towards English culture (the narrator eventually finds only European works in the deceased man's library) just as at the sexual level it is directed at English women. In the typical *Bildungsroman*, from *Wilhelm Meister* through *A Portrait of the Artist as a Young Man*, erotic and cultural or economic desires are mapped on one another so as to produce a certain coherence in the subject. For Mustafa Sa'eed, on the contrary, both modes of desire become ultimately sites of frustration and of dislocation for all his apparent success. And in both modes, the logic of the racial stereotype becomes inescapable. For as Sa'eed manipulates time and again the stereotype of the sexual African man as a means to seduce, he projects as the truth what he admits to be entirely inauthentic. Yet he does so, with a certain dogged literalness, as a means to penetrate the culture which is finally closed to him precisely because he represents to it the very stereotypes that he thinks he can control and manipulate.

So much becomes apparent at his trial for the murder of his English wife, Jean Morris. Here, the prosecution represents him as a beast, 'a werewolf who had been the reason for two girls committing suicide, had wrecked the life of a married woman and killed his own wife', while the defence, more liberally, represents him as 'a noble person whose mind was able to absorb Western civilization but it broke his heart' (SMN 32-3). The stereotypes are logically interdependent: on the one hand, the representation of the colonized as bestial or savage generally requires the at least hypothetical possibility of mistaking them for human—hence the werewolf; on the other hand, for the more common, liberal appeal to cultivation and assimilation to seem legitimate, it must also represent the native, prior to the civilizing process, as a passionate savage, endowed that is with a desire which can be and requires to be 'broken'. The first version accordingly arouses the anxiety of a Kingsley at the spectacle of human simulacra; the second holds out the promise of self-formation but only at the expense of a detachment from the native's 'authentic' being. The claim of culture to harmonize the self at each and every level devolves, in the colonial relation, into the repetitive production of inauthentic images, like the multiple mirrors of Sa'eed's bedroom (cf. SMN 31).

We are forcibly reminded, accordingly, that if English culture negates and dislocates Mustafa Sa'eed, its own confrontation with him brings its own laws of verisimilitude face to face with their founding incoherence. The either/or of racism—the native as savage or as object of cultivation—reveals itself as a contradictory both/and. The law of verisimilitude that governs cultural racism depends on the normative temporality of what I have termed the narrative of representation, that is, the regulative or ideal passage within the individual as within races or cultures from absolute specificity (which, as preexisting *form*, is indistinguishable from absolute indifference) and subordination to the pure formality of representative man. But the functioning of that narrative, which regulates the form of western institutions, requires the continual production of a constitutive difference. Mustafa Sa'eed will always be perceived as that problematic category the 'black Englishman', as the Sudanese *Mamur* puts it, not because of his failure to assimilate to English culture but precisely in time with his success (SMN 53). The closer his identification, the more forcefully his difference insists. Perceived by others as a catachrestic anomaly, Mustafa Sa'eed affirms rather that he is a lie, the figure of non-identity itself. Rejecting the defence lawyer's attempt to represent him as the victim of 'a conflict between two worlds', Sa'eed recognizes that the complexity of his situation lies rather in the manner in which the process of assimilation itself transforms him successively, vertiginously, into subject *and* object.[34] It is in acting as if a Subject that he runs against his status as the object of racist discourse. Hence the final proliferation of photographs in which he seems to seek to represent himself as subject for the gaze of others. Hence also two phrases which recur through his monologue take on the status of metaphors of radical ambivalence, doubling at this minimal level what the novel narrates at length, the simultaneity of assimilation and dislocation undergone by the colonial subject in racist culture: 'My mind was like a sharp knife. The train carried me to Victoria Station and to the world of Jean Morris' (SMN 31). The rhythms of dislocation, from the body, from other worlds, punctuate at every level the normative temporality of assimilation within which the Subject emerges. Racism imposes the limit to the assimilative process, but not simply as an external force antagonistic to that process: the developmental logic of culture depends upon the continuous reproduction of a stereotypical otherness which is, in every sense, the expelled origin of its identity.

IV

Tayeb Salih's work, formed under the pressure of British colonialism, shows remarkable affinities with the theoretical work of Frantz Fanon as he reacts primarily to the racist culture of French colonialism. Salih commented, indeed, that he read Fanon after finishing *Season of Migration*, and 'discovered that [he] was in total agreement with him'.[35] The work to which he is almost certainly referring, Fanon's *Black Skin, White Masks*, is deeply informed by the experience of assimilation as a cultural practice with a dense and contradictory history both at the level of colonial institutions and for each particular subject of colonialism. It is also a work deeply informed by the realization that not only is race a cultural construct but that racism is the structure of culture. From the very opening pages, Fanon is quite clear that the analysis of racism can only proceed in relation to the discourse on man and on 'his' development to which culture itself gives the structure:

> What does a man want?
> What does the black man want?
> At the risk of arousing the resentment of my coloured
>   brothers, I will say that the black is not a man....
> The black man wants to be white. The white man slaves to
>   reach a human level. (BSWM 10-11)

The identity of the black man is to be a difference always suspended in the developmental trajectory of a humanity figured in terms of whiteness. Only in terms of this trajectory can what Fanon names in the title of one chapter of the work 'The Fact of Blackness' be understood in the full network of the social relations that constitute that 'fact'. If, in the course of this chapter, Fanon makes clear that the appeal to 'negritude' has, for him, no longer any sense, it is because the larger trajectory of *Black Skin, White Masks* shows in detail that the appeal to essences is of no account where racist social relations constitute the black in a merely negative relation to an other defined as human. The enormous task that this work proposes is the transformation of the non-identity of the black into the means to a dismantling of the discourse of racism on several axes: that of the formation of the individual subject, that of the metaphoric structure of culture, and that of the social institutions in which the former are sedimented.

This task involves what at the outset Fanon describes as the attempt 'to penetrate to a level where the categories of sense and non-sense are not yet invoked' (BSWM 11). That is to say, it entails a decomposition of the subject akin to what would be required to break with the effects of the 'castration complex' and a collapsing of the metaphoric organization of identity and non-identity which structures the Subject as such. Fanon is constantly aware how closely his analysis must skirt psychosis, yet it is only in the light of this task that we can grasp the process of transfiguration involved in the remark, late in the work, that 'The Negro is comparison' (BSWM 211). This remark is, in the first place, an analytic description of the neurotic condition of Antillean society:

> We have just seen that the feeling of inferiority is an Antillean characteristic. It is not just this or that Antillean who embodies the neurotic formation, but all Antilleans. Antillean society is a neurotic society, a society of 'comparison'. (BSWM 213)

But these remarks make quite clear that 'we are driven from the individual back to the social structure' (213). This suspension in perpetual comparison of self and other is not an individual aberration but to be seen as the very social condition of being black in racist culture. This recognition transforms an analytic description of a malformation of the black subject into a culturally critical concept which opens up the inherently contradictory metaphoric logic of identity. For if the 'Adlerian comparison' of the *individual* neurotic consists only of two terms 'polarized by the ego', and is expressed as 'Ego greater than The Other', the social neurosis of 'Antillean comparison' is 'surmounted by a third term: Its governing fiction is not personal but social' (BSWM 215). The comparison is expressed thus:

White

Ego different from The Other

The formula is of exceptional analytical force. The surmounting term consists of one, self-identical word, the metaphor of metaphorical identity: white. As the citation from Fanon which opens this section indicates, the possibility of placing 'White' in this position derives from positing the white man as standing closer to the identity of the human which is the telos of history. The white occupies the position of universally representative man within a narrative which we can describe as the narrative of representation itself. But what its elevation produces, in relation to the 'Adlerian comparison', is a dissolution of the previous axis of superiority (Ego greater than The Other) into a relation of pure difference. What this implies, finally, is that there can be no therapeutic adjustment of the neurotic *individual*, not only because racist society continually reproduces the conditions of the neurosis but also because that adjustment would necessitate the impossible, a total crossing of the line that demarcates superior from inferior, identity from difference.

This is, nonetheless, the demand imposed by imperial culture on its colonized subjects, and of which *Black Skin, White Masks* is an extended analysis.[36] Its larger narrative, schematized in the formula above, is that of a process of *Bildung* which falters in the workings of its own logic. Imperial culture, in Fanon's case, French culture, holds out the promise of citizenship to all its subjects, but at the cost of the abandonment of 'local cultural originality':

> Every colonized people—in other words, every people in whose soul an inferiority complex has been created by the death and burial of its local cultural originality—finds itself face to face with the language of the civilizing nation; that is, with the culture of the mother country. The colonized is elevated above his jungle status in proportion to his adoption of the mother country's cultural standards. He becomes whiter as he renounces his blackness, his jungle. (BSWM 18)

It is perhaps worth stressing again that the question of race and colour is secondary to and produced by the question of culture, and to culture seen as a process of development. This developmental narrative absorbs the geographical narrative which is that of the move to and return from the metropolis, allowing the trajectory of displacement to be conceived as a cycle of completion, a *Bildungsroman*:

By that I mean that Negroes who return to their original environments convey the impression that they have completed a cycle, that they have added to themselves something that was lacking. They return literally full of themselves. (BSWM 19n)

But *Black Skin, White Masks* is a *Bildungsroman* against itself and demonstrates over and again that the taking on of the imperial culture, whose first embodiment is the language, 'is evidence of a dislocation, a separation' (25) rather than a fulfillment. If greater mastery of the language is the index of a greater approximation to whiteness (38), it is always precisely as approximation that development takes place, producing in the assimilative process of 'likening' the one who can never be more than 'just like a white man', 'l'homme pareil aux autres': a 'black Englishman'. The process of assimilation for the colonized is one which discovers within the identity which is to be formed the difference on which assimilation's very logic depends. The process of likening produces a residue of difference which insists as the ineradicable blackness of the culturally racialized subject. For this reason, for the colonized, who had never conceived of themselves as black while 'at home', the trajectory of *Bildung* must be inverted:

More especially, they should become aware that the line of self-esteem that they have chosen should be inverted. We have seen that in fact the Antillean who goes to France pictures this journey as the final stage of his personality. Quite literally I can say without any risk of error that the Antillean who goes to France in order to convince himself that he is white will find his real face there. (BSWM 153n)

The end of *Bildung* is not identity but the discovery of the culturally *constitutive* function of racism; it reveals the insistence of a splitting rather than the fulfillment of a developed Subject. Racism appears at once as the product and the disabling limit of the cultural formation of that Subject which subtends and gives the possibility of the 'public sphere'. At that limit, the racialized individual splits between what assimilation absorbs and what it necessarily produces as its residue. That impossible predicament issues perforce in madness or resistance as the subjective correlative of the process by which the colonizer's attempt to assimilate produces the national consciousness that revolts. Fanon's subsequent writings accordingly become increasingly concerned with the necessity of violence as the only means to the overthrow of imperial domination.

I have argued throughout this essay that culture itself constitutes the formal principles of racist discourse, that the indices of difference on which racism relies gain their meaning from a distribution of values determined by that culture which founds the idea of common sense and its space of articulation, the public sphere. This implies that there can be no simply cultural solution to the problem of racism and that all the measures taken by liberal cultural institutions in the name of assimilation are at best half measures, at worst misrecognized means to the reproduction of a singular cultural form which will continue to produce racialized residues. For the demand for representation within existent institutions will be self-defeating so long as it is not accompanied by the demand for the transformation of those institutions, since every partial instance of representation of difference succumbs to the larger narrative of representation which absorbs it.

Current debates on cultural education have helped to highlight the pivotal role played by educational institutions in the interpellation of individuals as subjects for the state. Fanon's work, in highlighting the cultural and, more importantly, hegemonic dimensions of racism, brings out the necessity to conduct the analysis of racist discourse and practices in relation to the *form* of the state. The persistence of racism is then to be understood, in keeping with the foregoing arguments, as an effect of ideological interpellation: approximation to the position of the Subject, theoretically available to all regardless of 'race or creed', in fact requires the impossible negation of racial or cultural differences. To Fanon's diagram we can add the formula of 'race under representation':

Representation

———————————

Race

Just as it is impossible for the colonized individual to escape the social neurosis of colonialism by passing over into identity or 'whiteness', so it is impossible for the racialized individual to enter the domain of representation except as that Subject which negates difference.

One consequence of this argument is that the concept of the 'racial state' developed by Omi and Winant stands in need of supplementation by the *idea* of the state which regulates the formation of citizen-Subjects fit to participate in what is effectively state culture. For the state is not merely a contingent ensemble of institutions but is ultimately determined by the desire to unify the public sphere. What the Subject is to individuals, the state represents for civil society, the site of its formal identity. Obscured as the idea of the state generally is by the contradictions that in practice seem to frustrate it, its unifying ends become quite apparent at moments of pressure. Such has been one effect of recent educational debates in the United States where appeal is made explicitly to the need to adhere to a common, central culture as a means to preserving loyalty to the state's institutions. At the same time, 'ethnic' cultures are relegated increasingly to the recreationary and pre-aesthetic domain of private cultural consumption. If race is, as Omi and Winant argue, 'a *central axis* of social relations', this is because it is continually, and necessarily, constructed and reproduced as the constitutive negation of the identity which the state represents.[37] No more than are class or gender, race is no ontological or essential quality but is constructed in differential relation to the normative culture of the state.

These remarks indicate how the elements of that vexed triad—race, gender, class—can be articulated with one another without collapsing them into false identity or allowing one or other to 'be subsumed under or reduced to some broader category or conception'.[38] Indeed, the analysis of the formation of these categories in relation to the Subject of ideology ultimately *requires* an unrelenting specificity which we have scarcely even begun to produce here. Both moments are indispensable: on the one hand, the formal analysis of the ideological Subject, precisely because its effectiveness is inseparable from its very formality; on the other, material histories of the specific transformations that take place through the dialectic between the state and what it perforce negates as a condition of its existence. This implies, of course, that the theoretical model of the ideological Subject to which I have been alluding, Althusser's 'Ideology and Ideological State Apparatuses', stands in need of correction insofar as it claims a transhistorical existence for ideology and the impossibility of standing outside it. The analysis of racist discourse is instructive in this respect, precisely because one can show the history of its transformation in relation to specific political or economic demands and, more importantly, because many of its contradictions derive from the capacity for any individual to be at once inside and outside, subject and object of the discourse.

The insistence of contradiction in racial formations, their inability to totalize the domain of the Subject, is politically as well as historically instructive. It suggests at once a theoretical agenda and a practical purpose for that agenda. For if the public sphere or culture furnishes a crucial ideological, and racist, regulative site, its critique is guided by what Benjamin designated as the task of the materialist historian—'to brush history against the grain'. This entails, in Gramscian terms, the reconstruction of histories of subaltern classes, of those social groups, that is, whose practices fall outside the terms of official culture.[39] To do so is, in effect, to decipher the history of the possible and to trace the contours of numerous alternatives to dominant modes of social formation. Without such a history, not only is the universal history of cultural development—the narrative of representation—all the more difficult to displace, but radical politics becomes all the more confined to issues of civil rights, that is, to the extension of representation and the implicit affirmation of assimilation.

Notes

1. Frantz Fanon, 'Racism and Culture', in *Toward the African Revolution. Political Essays*, trans. Haakon Chevalier (New York: Grove Press, 1988), 32; Claude Lévi-Strauss, 'Race and Culture', in *The View From Afar*, trans. Joachim Neugroschel and Phoebe Hoss (New York: Basic Books, 1985), 15. It seems appropriate to say here that this essay has benefitted to a more than usual extent from others' criticisms and comments. It originated as a paper given at the conferences on 'The Formation of Culture' at the University of Ljubljana, June 1989, and on 'Colonialism Now' at the University of Southampton, June 1989. Subsequent versions were delivered to the Conference on Race and Difference, Centro Interdisciplinar por Estudos Contemporaneos, Rio de Janeiro in October 1989 and to the seminar on 'The Function of Cultural Criticism' at the UC Humanities Research Institute, December 1989. I am grateful to the organizers of these sessions for the opportunity to present this work and to the participants for their comments. I am especially indebted to Rastko Mocnik, John Higgins, Robert Young, Homi Bhabha, Carlos Alberto Pereira, Abdul JanMohammed, Paul Rabinow, Martin Jay and Dipesh Chakrabarty for their attentive criticisms. I am also greatly indebted to Michel Chaouli for his detailed critical reading of the essay and for his invaluable research assistance. Most of all, however, I have benefitted from Zita Nunes's careful criticism and, more generally, from her work on anthropology, race and culture. The specific citations from her work are an insufficient indication of the degree to which I have learnt and borrowed from

her thinking in the course of writing this essay, particularly in discussing the question of assimilation.

2. Among many such critiques, see Johannes Fabian, *Time and the Other: How Anthropology Makes its Object* (New York: Columbia University Press, 1983); André Gunder Frank, *On Capitalist Underdevelopment* (Bombay: Oxford University Press, 1975); Arturo Escobar, 'Discourse and Power in Development: Michel Foucault and the Relevance of his Work to the Third World', *Alternatives* 10 (1984-5), 377-400; Majid Rahnema, 'Under the Banner of Development', *Seeds of Change* 1-2 (1986), 37-46.

3. See Michael Omi and Howard Winant, *Racial Formation in the United States. From the 1960s to the 1980s* (1986; repr. New York: Routledge, 1989), 67.

4. For an elaboration of the concept of 'aesthetic culture', see the introduction to David Lloyd, *Nationalism and Minor Literature: James Clarence Mangan and the Emergence of Irish Cultural Nationalism* (Berkeley: University of California Press, 1987), 6, 14-19.

5. I follow Omi and Winant in deriving this concept of sites from Herbert Gintis and Samuel Bowles: 'A site is defined not by what is *done* there, but by what imparts *regularity* to what is done there, its characteristic "rules of the game" ', cited from 'Structure and Practice in the Labor Theory of Value', *Review of Radical Political Economics*, 12:4 (1981), 4, in *Racial Formation*, 166. As may be apparent from what follows, I would annex the notion of a *regularity* within sites to a quite Kantian concept of the 'regulative idea' in order to indicate that it is the implicit teleology, and not merely the contingent practices, of social institutions that structures those institutions as reproducible at all levels including that of the subjects formed by them.

6. I have developed the concept of a narrative of representation further in 'The Narrative of Representation: Culture, the State and the Canon', to appear in *Rethinking Germanistik* (Peter Lang-Verlag, 1990).

7. See Immanuel Kant, *Critique of Judgement*, trans. James Creed Meredith (Oxford: Clarendon Press, 1982), 151. I discuss this passage and the process of Subject-formation further in 'Analogies of the Aesthetic: the Politics of Culture and the Limits of Materialist Aesthetics', forthcoming in *New Formations*, 1990.

8. Friedrich Schiller, *On the Aesthetic Education of Man, in a Series of Letters*, ed. and trans. Elizabeth M. Wilkinson and L.A. Willoughby (Oxford: Clarendon Press, 1967), 195. In an interesting extension of this narrative of the senses, the German philosopher and racial theorist, Lorenz Oken would divide the races of man according to whichever of the five senses dominated a race. Cited in Michael Banton, *Racial Theories* (Cambridge: Cambridge University Press, 1987), 18-19.

9. Cf. Frantz Fanon's remarks on this aspect of colonial self-legitimation in 'Concerning Violence', *The Wretched of the Earth*, preface by Jean-Paul Sartre, trans. Constance Farrington (New York: Grove Press, 1968), 41: 'The native is declared insensible to ethics; he represents not only the absence of values, but also the negation of values'. I have discussed the cases of Arnold and Mill more extensively in *Nationalism and Minor Literature*, 6-13, and in 'Genet's Genealogy: European Minorities and the Ends of the Canon', *Cultural Critique*, 6 (1987), 162-170. On the conservative figures mentioned here, and others, see Michael Banton, *Racial Theories*, 19-60.

10. See Colette Guillaumin, 'Race and Nature: the System of Marks. The Idea of a Natural Group and Social Relationships', in *Feminist Issues*, 8:2 (1988), 25-43; Fanon, 'Concerning

Violence', 41. On the misfit between racism and imperialism, see Banton, *Racial Theories*, 62.

11. Guillaumin, 'Race and Nature', 32-3. Guillaumin uses the expression 'symbol' to describe arbitrary marks. We would prefer to keep the term 'symbol' for those signs which, in principle, 'participate in what they represent', which have, that is, 'an organic relationship' to the signified. It is a commonplace of literary critical history that the devaluation of allegory in favour of the symbol takes place in the late eighteenth century and early nineteenth century. A shift in aesthetics accordingly corresponds to a shift in racist discourse, confirming one's sense of a certain congruence between relatively discrete spheres of cultural practice.

12. Guillaumin, 'Race and Nature', 41.

13. On Person and Condition, see Schiller, *Aesthetic Education of Man*, 73-77. I discuss these concepts further in *Nationalism and Minor Literature*, Chapter 1.

14. On the botanist Saussure, see Kant, *Critique of Judgement*, 115-6. Jacques Derrida discusses the complicity between a moral discourse and an empirical culturalism in relation to the Third Critique in 'Le Parergon', *La vérité en peinture* (Paris: Flammarion, 1978), 42. The anthropological subject is, as Gregory Schrempp has put it in a very valuable article, 'boundless'. See Schrempp, 'Aristotle's Other Self: On the Boundless Subject of Anthropological Discourse', in George W. Stocking, ed. *Romantic Motives: Essays on Anthropological Sensibility* (Madison: University of Wisconsin Press, 1989), 10-43. In tracing anthropology's founding terms to Aristotle and, more immediately, Kant, Schrempp most valuably demonstrates its indebtedness to the 'principle of identity', a point which has interesting implications for the present essay. For an eloquent defence of the value of anthropology's encounter with other cultures, though still ultimately oriented towards the understanding of modern society, see Louis Dumont, *Homo Hierarchicus: an Essay on the Caste System*, trans. Mark Sainsbury (Chicago: University of Chicago Press, 1970), 2:

> Anthropology, by the understanding it *gradually* affords of the most widely differing societies and cultures, gives proof of the unity of mankind. In doing so, it obviously reflects at least some light on our own sort of society. But this is not quite enough, and anthropology has the inherent and occasionally avowed aim of achieving this in a more systematic and radical way, that is, of putting modern society in perspective in relation to the societies which have preceded it or which co-exist with it, and of making in this way a direct and central contribution to our general education.

It is perhaps unnecessary to remark that the tendency of this remark is to place the achievement of that unity finally in modern societies, that is, in the West. On the relation between scientific rationality, Western cultural hegemony and anthropology, see Partha Chatterjee, *Nationalist Thought and the Colonial World. A Derivative Discourse?* (London: Zed Books, 1986), 14-17. Zita Nunes's work on modernism and anthropology in Brazil shows powerfully how the unity of the national culture is constructed through a racializing discourse and how anthropology contributes to this process: see her essay 'Os Males do Brasil: Antropofagia e a Questao da Raca', Papeis Avulsos do CIEC, 22. For a valuable study of the formation of the white colonial self as 'ubiquitous', as 'abstract, unspecifiable in its contents', see S. Mohanty, 'Kipling's Children and the Colour Line', *Race and Class* 31:1 (1989), 36.

15. Paul Ricoeur, 'The Metaphorical Process as Cognition, Imagination, and Feeling', in Sheldon Sacks, ed., *On Metaphor* (Chicago: University of Chicago Press, 1979), 146.

16. Condillac quoted by Paul de Man, 'The Epistemology of Metaphor', On Metaphor, 20.

17. See Paul Ricoeur, 'Metaphor and the Main Problem of Hermeneutics', *NLH*, 6:1 (1974), 108-110. Cyrus Hamlin draws attention to this moment in Ricoeur's essay in order to develop his argument concerning the place of metaphor in the Romantic construction of selfhood. See 'The Temporality of Selfhood: Metaphor and Romantic Poetry, *NLH*, 6:1 (1974), 172. His argument has been very valuable for some of the contentions of the present essay. See also, on the relation between metaphor and implicit narrative. de Man, 'Epistemology of Metaphor', 21-2: 'From the recognition of language as trope, one is led to the telling of a tale, to the narrative sequence I have just described. The temporal deployment of an initial complication, of a structural knot, indicates the close, though not necessarily complementary, relationship between trope and narrative, knot and plot'.
18. Ricoeur, 'Metaphorical Process', 154. Original emphasis.
19. If a little playful, this formulation is close, for example, to the insistent terminology of Matthew Arnold's *Culture and Anarchy*. In light of Ricoeur's argument as developed here, Donald Davidson is perhaps saying more than he means concerning the intimate relation between aesthetic culture and metaphor when he remarks that 'there is no test for metaphor that does not call for taste', 'What Metaphors Mean', in *On Metaphor*, 29. Rastko Mocnik has remarked very cogently on the crucial ideological function of a certain teleology in the reception and interpretation of metaphorical utterances. See Mocnik, 'A Theory of Metaphor', TS, 17: 'We may call it a teleological trope—or, as Lacan conceptualizes it, as a subjectifying trope: a metaphor does autonomize a signifier in its meaninglessness, but only in view of producing a sense-effect'.
20. Banton notes how the term 'assimilation' transforms in meaning from 'any process by which peoples became more similar' to a process by which one people 'was expected to absorb another ... without itself undergoing any significant change', *Racial Theories*, ix. Fanon's comment ('Racism and Culture' 38) is a fittingly acerbic comment on the ideological bent of *both* understandings: 'This event, which is commonly designated as alienation, is naturally very important. It is found in the official texts under the name of assimilation'.
21. I think here especially of Homi K. Bhabha's 'The Other Question', *Screen* 24 (1983), 18-36. I might remark here that the 'four-term strategy' of colonial discourse which Bhabha posits (circulating between metaphor and metonymy, narcissism and aggression) seems to restore to the stereotype the fixity which his analysis critiques, only in the form of an anxious oscillation between lack and the masking function of the fetish. I would contend that the transfer from metonymy to metaphor in the process of assimilation is both irreversible and determinant for the forms which resistance to assimilation takes—a dialectic succinctly analyzed by Fanon in 'Racism and Culture'.
22. Sigmund Freud, 'On Fetishism', in *On Sexuality: Three Essays on the Theory of Sexuality* (Harmondsworth: Penguin, 1977), 352. For the theory of castration, see the essays 'The Dissolution of the Oedipus Complex' (1924) and 'Some Psychic Consequences of the Anatomical Distinction between the Sexes' (1925), in *On Sexuality*, 313-22 and 323-344 respectively. Cited hereafter as DOS and ADS in the text.
23. In Freud, 'Infantile Sexuality' (1905), *On Sexuality*, 116-119.
24. The subject of psychoanalysis, which is produced, as Lacan's Schema L illustrates, in suspension between the ego and the superego, that is, between the I formed in the mirror stage and the Other or 'Name-of-the-Father', is not identical to the Kantian aesthetic Subject, but is similarly structured in a process of formalization. For Schema L, see Jacques Lacan, 'D'une question preliminaire a tout traitement possible de la psychose', *Ecrits* 2 (Paris: Seuil, 1971),

63. Louis Althusser begins to sketch the relation between this subject, the ethical subject and the ideological subject in 'Ideology and Ideological State Apparatuses (Notes Towards an Investigation)', *Lenin and Philosophy and Other Essays*, trans. Ben Brewster (New York: Monthly Review Press, 1971), 127-186.

25. The considerable anxiety aroused in many racist societies by miscegenation is a mark of the loss of verisimilitude in appeals to immediate visual discrimination. Miscegenation, as a metaphor for different possible cultural formations, is in turn troublesome precisely insofar as it raises the question of the verisimilitude or canonicity of dominant cultural narratives and suggests the possibility of a limitless transformation of cultures. Unlike assimilation, it cannot be organized in terms of a developmental hierarchy and in relation to the formation of national culture must always be recast in the form of an *embranqueamento* which restores both the developmental narrative and, at a quite literal level, its 'residual' logic. I am indebted for these observations, and for much of the thinking on assimilation in this essay, to Zita Nunes' work on Brazilian modernism and anthropology in relation to the formation of national culture. See her 'Os Males do Brasil', especially 1-2. See also Jean Bernabé, Patrick Chamoiseau, Raphael Confiant, *Eloge de la creolité* (Paris: Gallimard, 1989), 27-8: 'Du fait de sa mosaïque constitutive, la Creolité est une spécificité ouverte....L'exprimer c'est exprimer non une synthèse, pas simplement un métissage, ou n'importe qu'elle autre unicité. C'est exprimer une totalité kaleidoscopique, c'est à dire la conscience non totalitaire d'une diversité preservée'.

26. Though in most respects this essay is profoundly indebted to Frantz Fanon's analysis of racism in *Black Skin, White Masks*, trans. Charles Lam Markmann, foreword by Homi K. Bhabha (London: Pluto Press, 1986), at this point I would depart somewhat from the emphasis he places on projection as the psychic mechanism of racism. See Chapter 6, 'The Negro and Psychopathology', especially 190-194. As I shall argue below, Fanon very rapidly moves beyond and complicates the notion of projection, not least by invoking what he terms 'cultural imposition' (193). Cited in the text hereafter as BSWM.

27. Kingsley cited in L. Curtis, *Anglo-Saxons and Celts: A Study of Anti-Irish Prejudice in Victorian England* (Bridgeport, Ct.: University of Bridgeport, 1968), 84. Thomas Carlyle's oxymoron is to be found in *Sartor Resartus*; I discuss its implications for understanding the ascription of inauthenticity to the colonized in *Nationalism and Minor Literature*, 206-7. For further discussion of Kingsley's remarks, see the essay by Luke Gibbons in this volume. The omphalic nature of this passage is signalled by its independent citation by three of the speakers in the 'Colonialism Now' conference.

28. On the relation between 'whiteness', as a metaphor, and the identitarian structure of metaphor, for which it is a metaphor, see Jacques Derrida's 'White Mythology: Metaphor in the Text of Philosophy', *NLH* 6:1 (1974), 5-74. In a longer paper, it would be necessary to supply here some account of the history and contradictory logic of imperial practices of assimilation. Suffice it to say here that racism is at once the structure and limit to assimilation insofar as it is predicated on a hierarchy of cultural differences yet universal in its claims and aims. Nunes's work, cited above, is very suggestive in this respect.

29. For some comments on the differences between British and French colonialism, see Renate Zahar, *Colonialism and Alienation: Concerning Frantz Fanon's Political Theory* (Benin: Ethiope Publishing, 1974), xxi-xxii. Though differences of intensity may appear, the structure of assimilation remains largely the same where applied by either regime.

30. See, for example, Benedict Anderson, *Imagined Communities: Reflections on the Origin and Spread of Nationalism* (London: Verso, 1983), especially 106-7. This phenomenon is crucial to the dialectic of decolonization outlined throughout Fanon's writings, and especially in 'Concerning Violence' and 'The Pitfalls of National Consciousness' in *The Wretched of the Earth*.

31. Samir Seikaly, '*Season of Migration to the North*: History in the Novel', in Mona Takieddine Amyune, ed., *Tayeb Salih's Season of Migration to the North: A Casebook* (Beirut: American University of Beirut, 1985), 137-8. It should be remarked that the implication here that the 'primordial identity' sought by the colonized is an essential category stands in need of correction by Fanon's dialectical grasp of the turn of the colonized to a revalorization of cultures termed primitive or primordial by the colonizer. See especially 'Racism and Culture', 41-3.

32. Tayeb Salih, *Season of Migration to the North*, trans. Denys Johnson-Davies (London: Heinemann, 1976), 1-4.

33. Salih himself remarked on how he first intended to write a straightforward thriller but became gradually more interested in figures 'who showed a strange attraction to the Arab world, the type of romanticism which I started to challenge in the novel.' Lecture to American University of Beirut, quoted by Amyune, 'Introduction' to *A Casebook*, 15. The critique of romantic orientalism entails a critique also of its formal vehicles.

34. Carmen Torres has pointed out that the destructive, and often disturbing, relations between Mustafa Sa'eed and English women could be attributable to the contradictory relation between gender and colonialism: white women are, as white, dominant subjects, but as women, dominated objects. The reverse is true for the African man. See her 'Colonialism and Gender in *Season of Migration to the North*' (M.A. Thesis, University of California, Berkeley, May 1990), 11-23. But I am also indebted to Kadiatu Kanneh's reminder of the *hilariousness* with which these relations can be perceived: both colonial history and interracial sexual relations can be perceived alternately as tragedy or farce. In the latter case, what is perhaps emphasized is the element of performative masquerade and the ease with which characters can take one another's places. See Kanneh's essay in this volume.

35. From an interview with Salih, cited in Ali Abdallah Abbas, 'The Father of Lies: the Role of Mustafa Sa'eed as Second Self in *Season of Migration to the North*', *A Casebook*, 30. Since Abbas argues that Sa'eed is not a 'representative' character but 'a fragment of the human psyche' and that the novel is a confrontation between two halves of the human psyche rather than between East and West, I would comment that such readings, though failing to give sufficient due to the novel's exploration of colonialism, do draw attention properly to the impossibility of integration which it dramatizes. The tantalizing 'incompleteness' of the novel itself is matched by a certain incompleteness within its characters.

36. Zahar comments: 'There can be no doubt that by the very fact of idealizing assimilation, while at the same time brutally preventing its realization, the officially proclaimed policy of French colonialism contributed in no small measure to the specific phenomena of alienation and frustration analyzed [in her study]' (*Colonialism and Alienation*, xxii).

37. See Omi and Winant, *Racial Formation*, 61; on the 'racial state', see 76-7.

38. Omi and Winant, *Racial Formations*, 62.

39. Walter Benjamin, 'Theses on the Philosophy of History', *Illuminations*, ed. Hannah Arendt, trans. Harry Zohn (London: Fontana, 1973), 259; Antonio Gramsci, *Selections from the Prison Notebooks*, ed. and trans. Quintin Hoare and Geoffrey Nowell Smith (New York:

International Publishers, 1971), 52-55. The concept of 'Subaltern Studies' has been most consciously put into practice by the Indian Subaltern scholars. See, for a selection of their work, *Selected Subaltern Studies*, ed. Ranajit Guha and Gayatri Chakravorty Spivak, foreword by Edward Said (Oxford: Oxford University Press, 1988).

romancing the shadow

*A*t the end of *The Narrative of Arthur Gordon Pym,* Edgar Allan Poe describes the last two days of an extraordinary journey:

> "*March 21st.*—A sullen darkness now hovered above us—but from out the milky depths of the ocean a luminous glare arose, and stole up along the bulwarks of the boat. We were nearly overwhelmed by the white ashy shower which settled upon us and upon the canoe, but melted into the water as it fell . . .
>
> "*March 22d.*—The darkness had materially increased, relieved only by the glare of the water thrown back from the white curtain before us. Many gigantic and pallidly white birds flew continuously now from beyond the veil, and their scream was the eternal *Tekeli-li!* as they retreated from our vision. Hereupon Nu-Nu stirred in the bottom of the boat; but upon touching him, we found his spirit departed. And now we rushed into the embraces of the cataract, where a chasm threw itself open to receive us. But there arose

in our pathway a shrouded human figure, very far larger in its proportions than any dweller among men. And the hue of the skin of the figure was of the perfect whiteness of the snow."

They have been floating, Pym and Peters and the native, Nu-Nu, on a warm, milk-white sea under a "white ashy shower." The black man dies, and the boat rushes on through the white curtain behind which a white giant rises up. After that, there is nothing. There is no more narrative. Instead there is a scholarly note, explanation, and an anxious, piled-up "conclusion." The latter states that it was *whiteness* that terrified the natives and killed Nu-Nu. The following inscription was carved into the walls of the chasms the travelers passed through: "I have graven it in within the hills, and my vengeance upon the dust within the rock."

No early American writer is more important to the concept of American Africanism than Poe. And no image is more telling than the one just described: the visualized but somehow closed and unknowable white form that rises from the mists at the end of the journey—or, at any rate, at the end of the narration proper. The images of the white curtain and the "shrouded human figure" with skin "the perfect whiteness of the snow" both occur after the narrative has encountered blackness. The first white image seems related to the expiration and erasure of the serviceable and serving black figure, Nu-Nu. Both are figurations of impenetrable whiteness that surface in American literature whenever an

Africanist presence is engaged. These closed white images are found frequently, but not always, at the end of the narrative. They appear so often and in such particular circumstances that they give pause. They clamor, it seems, for an attention that would yield the meaning that lies in their positioning, their repetition, and their strong suggestion of paralysis and incoherence; of impasse and non-sequitur.

These images of impenetrable whiteness need contextualizing to explain their extraordinary power, pattern, and consistency. Because they appear almost always in conjunction with representations of black or Africanist people who are dead, impotent, or under complete control, these images of blinding whiteness seem to function as both antidote for and meditation on the shadow that is companion to this whiteness—a dark and abiding presence that moves the hearts and texts of American literature with fear and longing. This haunting, a darkness from which our early literature seemed unable to extricate itself, suggests the complex and contradictory situation in which American writers found themselves during the formative years of the nation's literature.

Young America distinguished itself by, and understood itself to be, pressing toward a future of freedom, a kind of human dignity believed unprecedented in the world. A whole tradition of "universal" yearnings collapsed into that well-fondled phrase, "the American Dream." Although this immigrant dream deserves the exhaustive scrutiny it has received in the scholarly disciplines and the arts, it is just as important to know what these people were rushing from as it is to know what they were hastening to. If the New World fed dreams, what was the Old World reality that whetted the appetite for them? And how did that reality caress and grip the shaping of a new one?

The flight from the Old World to the New is generally seen to be a flight from oppression and limitation to freedom and possibility. Although, in fact, the escape was sometimes an escape from license—from a society perceived to be unacceptably permissive, ungodly, and undisciplined—for those fleeing for reasons other than religious ones, constraint and limitation impelled the journey. All the Old World offered these immigrants was poverty, prison, social ostracism, and, not infrequently, death. There was of course a clerical, scholarly group of immigrants who came seeking the adventure possible in founding a colony for, rather than against, one or another mother country or fatherland. And of course there were the merchants, who came for the cash.

Whatever the reasons, the attraction was of the "clean slate" variety, a once-in-a-lifetime opportunity not only to be born again but to be born again in new clothes, as it were. The new setting would provide new raiments of self. This second chance could even benefit from the mistakes of the first. In the New World there was the vision of a limitless future, made more gleaming by the constraint, dissatisfaction, and turmoil left behind. It was a promise genuinely promising. With luck and endurance one could discover freedom; find a way to make God's law manifest; or end up rich as a prince. The desire for freedom is preceded by oppression;

a yearning for God's law is born of the detestation of human license and corruption; the glamor of riches is in thrall to poverty, hunger, and debt.

There was very much more in the late seventeenth and eighteenth centuries to make the trip worth the risk. The habit of genuflection would be replaced by the thrill of command. Power—control of one's own destiny—would replace the powerlessness felt before the gates of class, caste, and cunning persecution. One could move from discipline and punishment to disciplining and punishing; from social ostracism to social rank. One could be released from a useless, binding, repulsive past into a kind of history-lessness, a blank page waiting to be inscribed. Much was to be written there: noble impulses were made into law and appropriated for a national tradition; base ones, learned and elaborated in the rejected and rejecting homeland, were also made into law and appropriated for tradition.

The body of literature produced by the young nation is one way it inscribed its transactions with these fears, forces, and hopes. And it is difficult to read the literature of young America without being struck by how antithetical it is to our modern rendition of the American Dream. How pronounced in it is the absence of that term's elusive mixture of hope, realism, materialism, and promise. For a people who made much of their "newness"—their potential, freedom, and innocence—it is striking how dour, how troubled, how frightened and haunted our early and founding literature truly is.

romancing the shadow 35

223

We have words and labels for this haunting—"gothic," "romantic," "sermonic," "Puritan"—whose sources are to be found in the literature of the world these immigrants left. But the strong affinity between the nineteenth-century American psyche and gothic romance has rightly been much remarked. Why should a young country repelled by Europe's moral and social disorder, swooning in a fit of desire and rejection, devote its talents to reproducing in its own literature the typology of diabolism it wanted to leave behind? An answer to that seems fairly obvious: one way to benefit from the lessons of earlier mistakes and past misfortune is to record them so as to prevent their repetition through exposure and inoculation.

Romance was the form in which this uniquely American prophylaxis could be played out. Long after the movement in Europe, romance remained the cherished expression of young America. What was there in American romanticism that made it so attractive to Americans as a battle plain on which to fight, engage, and imagine their demons?

It has been suggested that romance is an evasion of history (and thus perhaps attractive to a people trying to evade the recent past). But I am more persuaded by arguments that find in it the head-on encounter with very real, pressing historical forces and the contradictions inherent in them as they came to be experienced by writers. Romance, an exploration of anxiety imported from the shadows of European culture, made possible the sometimes safe and other times risky embrace of quite specific, understandably human, fears:

Americans' fear of being outcast, of failing, of powerlessness; their fear of boundarylessness, of Nature unbridled and crouched for attack; their fear of the absence of so-called civilization; their fear of loneliness, of aggression both external and internal. In short, the terror of human freedom—the thing they coveted most of all. Romance offered writers not less but more; not a narrow a-historical canvas but a wide historical one; not escape but entanglement. For young America it had everything: nature as subject matter, a system of symbolism, a thematics of the search for self-valorization and validation—above all, the opportunity to conquer fear imaginatively and to quiet deep insecurities. It offered platforms for moralizing and fabulation, and for the imaginative entertainment of violence, sublime incredibility, and terror—and terror's most significant, overweening ingredient: darkness, with all the connotative value it awakened.

There is no romance free of what Herman Melville called "the power of blackness," especially not in a country in which there was a resident population, already black, upon which the imagination could play; through which historical, moral, metaphysical, and social fears, problems, and dichotomies could be articulated. The slave population, it could be and was assumed, offered itself up as surrogate selves for meditation on problems of human freedom, its lure and its elusiveness. This black population was available for meditations on terror—the terror of European outcasts, their dread of failure, powerlessness, Nature without limits, natal loneliness, internal aggression, evil, sin, greed. In other words, this slave population was understood to have offered itself up for reflections on human freedom in terms other than the abstractions of human potential and the rights of man.

The ways in which artists—and the society that bred them—transferred internal conflicts to a "blank darkness," to conveniently bound and violently silenced black bodies, is a major theme in American literature. The rights of man, for example, an organizing principle upon which the nation was founded, was inevitably yoked to Africanism. Its history, its origin is permanently allied with another seductive concept: the hierarchy of race. As the sociologist Orlando Patterson has noted, we should not be surprised that the Enlightenment could accommodate slavery; we should be surprised if it had not. The concept of freedom did not emerge in a vacuum. Nothing highlighted freedom—if it did not in fact create it—like slavery.

Black slavery enriched the country's creative possibilities. For in that construction of blackness *and* enslavement could be found not only the not-free but also, with the dramatic polarity created by skin color, the projection of the not-me. The result was a playground for the imagination. What rose up out of collective needs to allay internal fears and to rationalize external exploitation was an American Africanism—a fabricated brew of darkness, otherness, alarm, and desire that is uniquely American. (There also exists, of course, a European Africanism with a counterpart in colonial literature.)

What I wish to examine is how the image of reined-in,

bound, suppressed, and repressed darkness became objectified in American literature as an Africanist persona. I want to show how the duties of that persona—duties of exorcism and reification and mirroring—are on demand and on display throughout much of the literature of the country and helped to form the distinguishing characteristics of a proto-American literature.

Earlier I said that cultural identities are formed and informed by a nation's literature, and that what seemed to be on the "mind" of the literature of the United States was the self-conscious but highly problematic construction of the American as a new white man. Emerson's call for that new man in "The American Scholar" indicates the deliberateness of the construction, the conscious necessity for establishing difference. But the writers who responded to this call, accepting or rejecting it, did not look solely to Europe to establish a reference for difference. There was a very theatrical difference underfoot. Writers were able to celebrate or deplore an identity already existing or rapidly taking a form that was elaborated through racial difference. That difference provided a huge payout of sign, symbol, and agency in the process of organizing, separating, and consolidating identity along culturally valuable lines of interest.

Bernard Bailyn has provided us with an extraordinary investigation of European settlers in the act of becoming Americans. I want to quote a rather long passage from his *Voyagers to the West* because it underscores the salient aspects of the American character I have been describing:

"William Dunbar, seen through his letters and diary, appears to be more fictional than real—a creature of William Faulkner's imagination, a more cultivated Colonel Sutpen but no less mysterious. He too, like that strange character in *Absalom! Absalom!,* was a man in his early twenties who appeared suddenly in the Mississippi wilderness to stake out a claim to a large parcel of land, then disappeared to the Caribbean, to return leading a battalion of 'wild' slaves with whose labor alone he built an estate where before there had been nothing but trees and uncultivated soil. But he was more complex than Sutpen, if no less driving in his early ambitions, no less a progenitor of a notable southern family, and no less a part of a violent biracial world whose tensions could lead in strange directions. For this wilderness planter was a scientist, who would later correspond with Jefferson on science and exploration, a Mississippi planter whose contributions to the American Philosophical Society (to which Jefferson proposed him for membership) included linguistics, archaeology, hydrostatics, astronomy, and climatology, and whose geographical explorations were reported in widely known publications. Like Sutpen an exotic figure in the plantation world of early Mississippi—known as 'Sir' William just as Sutpen was known as 'Colonel'— he too imported into that raw, half-savage world the niceties of European culture: not chandeliers and costly rugs, but books, surveyor's equipment of the finest kind, and the latest instruments of science.

"Dunbar was a Scot by birth, the youngest son of Sir Archibald Dunbar of Morayshire. He was educated first by tutors at home, then at the university in Aberdeen, where his interest in mathematics, astronomy, and belles-lettres took mature shape. What happened to him after his return home and later in London, where he circulated with young intellectuals, what propelled, or led, him out of the metropolis on the first leg of his long voyage west is not known. But whatever his motivation may have been, in April 1771, aged only twenty-two, Dunbar appeared in Philadelphia . . .

"Ever eager for gentility, this well-educated product of the Scottish enlightenment and of London's sophistication—this bookish young *littérateur* and scientist who, only five years earlier, had been corresponding about scientific problems—about 'Dean Swifts beatitudes,' about the 'virtuous and happy life,' and about the Lord's commandment that mankind should 'love one another'—was yet strangely insensitive to the suffering of those who served him. In July 1776 he recorded not the independence of the American colonies from Britain, but the suppression of an alleged conspiracy for freedom by slaves on his own plantation . . .

"Dunbar, the young *érudit,* the Scottish scientist

romancing the shadow 41

229

and man of letters, was no sadist. His plantation regime was, by the standards of the time, mild; he clothed and fed his slaves decently, and frequently relented in his more severe punishments. But 4,000 miles from the sources of culture, alone on the far periphery of British civilization where physical survival was a daily struggle, where ruthless exploitation was a way of life, and where disorder, violence, and human degradation were commonplace, he had triumphed by successful adaptation. Endlessly enterprising and resourceful, his finer sensibilities dulled by the abrasions of frontier life, and feeling within himself a sense of authority and autonomy he had not known before, a force that flowed from his absolute control over the lives of others, he emerged a distinctive new man, a borderland gentleman, a man of property in a raw, half-savage world."*

Let me call attention to some elements of this portrait, some pairings and interdependencies that are marked in the story of William Dunbar. First there is the historical connection between the Enlightenment and the institution of slavery—the rights of man and his enslavement. Second, we have the relationship between Dunbar's education and his New World enterprise. The education he had was exceptional

*Bernard Bailyn, *Voyagers to the West: A Passage in the Peopling of America on the Eve of the Revolution* (New York: Alfred A. Knopf, 1986), pp. 488–492.

42   romancing the shadow

and exceptionally cultivated: it included the latest thought on theology and science, an effort perhaps to make them mutually accountable, to make one support the other. He is not only a "product of the Scottish enlightenment" but a London intellectual as well. He read Jonathan Swift, discussed the Christian commandment to love one another, and is described as "strangely" insensitive to the suffering of his slaves. On July 12, 1776, he records with astonishment and hurt surprise a slave rebellion on his plantation: "Judge my surprise . . . Of what avail is kindness & good usage when rewarded by such ingratitude." "Constantly bewildered," Bailyn goes on, "by his slaves' behavior . . . [Dunbar] recovered two runaways and 'condemned them to receive 500 lashes each at five different times, and to carry a chain & log fixt to the ancle.'"

I take this to be a succinct portrait of the process by which the American as new, white, and male was constituted. It is a formation with at least four desirable consequences, all of which are referred to in Bailyn's summation of Dunbar's character and located in how Dunbar felt "within himself." Let me repeat: "a sense of authority and autonomy he had not known before, a force that flowed from his absolute control over the lives of others, he emerged a distinctive new man, a borderland gentleman, a man of property in a raw, half-savage world." A power, a sense of freedom, he had not known before. But what had he known before? Fine education, London sophistication, theological and scientific thought. None of these, one gathers, could provide him with the authority and autonomy that Mississippi planter life did. Also this sense is understood to be a force that flows, already present and ready to spill as a result of his "absolute control over the lives of others." This force is not a willed domination, a thought-out, calculated choice, but rather a kind of natural resource, a Niagara Falls waiting to drench Dunbar as soon as he is in a position to assume absolute control. Once he has moved into that position, he is resurrected as a new man, a distinctive man—a different man. And whatever his social status in London, in the New World he is a gentleman. More gentle, more man. The site of his transformation is within rawness: he is backgrounded by savagery.

.   .   .

I want to suggest that these concerns—autonomy, authority, newness and difference, absolute power—not only become the major themes and presumptions of American literature, but that each one is made possible by, shaped by, activated by a complex awareness and employment of a constituted Africanism. It was this Africanism, deployed as rawness and savagery, that provided the staging ground and arena for the elaboration of the quintessential American identity.

Autonomy is freedom and translates into the much championed and revered "individualism"; newness translates into "innocence"; distinctiveness becomes difference and the erection of strategies for maintaining it; authority and absolute power become a romantic, conquering "heroism," virility, and the problematics of wielding absolute power over the lives of others. All the rest are made possible by this last, it would seem—absolute power called forth and played against and within a natural and mental landscape conceived of as a "raw, half-savage world."

Why is it seen as raw and savage? Because it is peopled by a nonwhite indigenous population? Perhaps. But certainly because there is ready to hand a bound and unfree, rebellious but serviceable, black population against which Dunbar and all white men are enabled to measure these privileging and privileged differences.

Eventually individualism fuses with the prototype of Americans as solitary, alienated, and malcontent. What, one wants to ask, are Americans alienated from? What are Americans always so insistently innocent of? Different from? As for absolute power, over whom is this power held, from whom withheld, to whom distributed?

Answers to these questions lie in the potent and ego-reinforcing presence of an Africanist population. This population is convenient in every way, not the least of which is self-definition. This new white male can now persuade himself that savagery is "out there." The lashes ordered (500 applied five times is 2500) are not one's own savagery; repeated and dangerous breaks for freedom are "puzzling" confirmations of black irrationality; the combination of Dean Swift's beatitudes and a life of regularized violence is civilized; and if the sensibilities are dulled enough, the rawness remains external.

These contradictions slash their way through the pages of

romancing the shadow 45

American literature. How could it be otherwise? As Dominick LaCapra reminds us, "Classic novels are not only worked over . . . by common contextual forces (such as ideologies) but also rework and at least partially work through those forces in critical and at times potentially transformative fashion."*

As for the culture, the imaginative and historical terrain upon which early American writers journeyed is in large measure shaped by the presence of the racial other. Statements to the contrary, insisting on the meaninglessness of race to the American identity, are themselves full of meaning. The world does not become raceless or will not become unracialized by assertion. The act of enforcing racelessness in literary discourse is itself a racial act. Pouring rhetorical acid on the fingers of a black hand may indeed destroy the prints, but not the hand. Besides, what happens in that violent, self-serving act of erasure to the hands, the fingers, the fingerprints of the one who does the pouring? Do they remain acid-free? The literature itself suggests otherwise.

Explicit or implicit, the Africanist presence informs in compelling and inescapable ways the texture of American literature. It is a dark and abiding presence, there for the literary imagination as both a visible and an invisible mediating force. Even, and especially, when American texts are not "about" Africanist presences or characters or narrative or idiom, the

* Dominick LaCapra, *History, Politics and the Novel* (Ithaca: Cornell University Press, 1987), p. 4.

46   romancing the shadow

shadow hovers in implication, in sign, in line of demarcation. It is no accident and no mistake that immigrant populations (and much immigrant literature) understood their "Americanness" as an opposition to the resident black population. Race, in fact, now functions as a metaphor so necessary to the construction of Americanness that it rivals the old pseudo-scientific and class-informed racisms whose dynamics we are more used to deciphering.

As a metaphor for transacting the whole process of Americanization, while burying its particular racial ingredients, this Africanist presence may be something the United States cannot do without. Deep within the word "American" is its association with race. To identify someone as a South African is to say very little; we need the adjective "white" or "black" or "colored" to make our meaning clear. In this country it is quite the reverse. American means white, and Africanist people struggle to make the term applicable to themselves with ethnicity and hyphen after hyphen after hyphen. Americans did not have a profligate, predatory nobility from which to wrest an identity of national virtue while continuing to covet aristocratic license and luxury. The American nation negotiated both its disdain and its envy in the same way Dunbar did: through a self-reflexive contemplation of fabricated, mythological Africanism. For the settlers and for American writers generally, this Africanist other became the means of thinking about body, mind, chaos, kindness, and love; provided the occasion for exercises in the absence of restraint, the presence of restraint, the contemplation of freedom and of aggression; permitted opportunities for the exploration of ethics and morality, for meeting the obligations of the social contract, for bearing the cross of religion and following out the ramifications of power.

Reading and charting the emergence of an Africanist persona in the development of a national literature is both a fascinating project and an urgent one, if the history and criticism of our literature is to become accurate. Emerson's plea for intellectual independence was like the offer of an empty plate that writers could fill with nourishment from an indigenous menu. The language no doubt had to be English, but the content of that language, its subject, was to be deliberately, insistently un-English and anti-European, insofar as it rhetorically repudiated an adoration of the Old World and defined the past as corrupt and indefensible. In the scholarship on the formation of an American character and the production of a national literature, a number of items have been catalogued. A major item to be added to the list must be an Africanist presence—decidedly not American, decidedly other.

The need to establish difference stemmed not only from the Old World but from a difference in the New. What was distinctive in the New was, first of all, its claim to freedom and, second, the presence of the unfree within the heart of the democratic experiment—the critical absence of democracy, its echo, shadow, and silent force in the political and intellectual activity of some not-Americans. The distinguishing features of the not-Americans were their slave status, their social status—and their color.

It is conceivable that the first would have self-destructed in a variety of ways had it not been for the last. These slaves, unlike many others in the world's history, were visible to a fault. And they had inherited, among other things, a long history on the meaning of color. It was not simply that this slave population had a distinctive color; it was that this color "meant" something. That meaning had been named and deployed by scholars from at least the moment, in the eighteenth century, when other and sometimes the same scholars started to investigate both the natural history and the inalienable rights of man—that is to say, human freedom.

One supposes that if Africans all had three eyes or one ear, the significance of that difference from the smaller but conquering European invaders would also have been found to have meaning. In any case, the subjective nature of ascribing value and meaning to color cannot be questioned this late in the twentieth century. The point for this discussion is the alliance between visually rendered ideas and linguistic utterances. And this leads into the social and political nature of received knowledge as it is revealed in American literature.

Knowledge, however mundane and utilitarian, plays about in linguistic images and forms cultural practice. Responding to culture—clarifying, explicating, valorizing, translating, transforming, criticizing—is what artists everywhere do, especially writers involved in the founding of a new nation. Whatever their personal and formally political responses to the inherent contradiction of a free republic deeply committed to slavery, nineteenth-century writers were mindful of the presence of black people. More important, they addressed, in more or less passionate ways, their views on that difficult presence.

The alertness to a slave population did not confine itself to the personal encounters that writers may have had. Slave narratives were a nineteenth-century publication boom. The press, the political campaigns, and the policy of various parties and elected officials were rife with the discourse of slavery and freedom. It would have been an *isolato* indeed who was unaware of the most explosive issue in the nation. How could one speak of profit, economy, labor, progress, suffragism, Christianity, the frontier, the formation of new states, the acquisition of new lands, education, transportation (freight and passengers), neighborhoods, the military—of almost anything a country concerns itself with—without having as a referent, at the heart of the discourse, at the heart of definition, the presence of Africans and their descendants?

It was not possible. And it did not happen. What did happen frequently was an effort to talk about these matters with a vocabulary designed to disguise the subject. It did not always succeed, and in the work of many writers disguise was never intended. But the consequence was a master narrative that spoke *for* Africans and their descendants, or *of* them. The legislator's narrative could not coexist with a response from the Africanist persona. Whatever popularity the slave narratives had—and they influenced abolitionists and converted antiabolitionists—the slave's own narrative, while freeing the narrator in many ways, did not destroy the master narrative. The master narrative could make any number of adjustments to keep itself intact.

Silence from and about the subject was the order of the day. Some of the silences were broken, and some were maintained by authors who lived with and within the policing narrative. What I am interested in are the strategies for maintaining the silence and the strategies for breaking it. How did the founding writers of young America engage, imagine, employ, and create an Africanist presence and persona? In what ways do these strategies explicate a vital part of American literature? How does excavating these pathways lead to fresh and more profound analyses of what they contain and how they contain it?

.   .   .

Let me propose some topics that need critical investigation.

First, the Africanist character as surrogate and enabler. In what ways does the imaginative encounter with Africanism enable white writers to think about themselves? What are the dynamics of Africanism's self-reflexive properties? Note, for instance, the way Africanism is used to conduct a dialogue concerning American space in *The Narrative of Arthur Gordon Pym*. Through the use of Africanism, Poe meditates on place as a means of containing the fear of borderlessness and trespass, but also as a means of releasing and exploring the desire for a limitless empty frontier. Consider the ways that Africanism in other American writers (Mark Twain, Melville,

Hawthorne) serves as a vehicle for regulating love and the imagination as defenses against the psychic costs of guilt and despair. Africanism is the vehicle by which the American self knows itself as not enslaved, but free; not repulsive, but desirable; not helpless, but licensed and powerful; not history-less, but historical; not damned, but innocent; not a blind accident of evolution, but a progressive fulfillment of destiny.

A second topic in need of critical attention is the way an Africanist idiom is used to establish difference or, in a later period, to signal modernity. We need to explicate the ways in which specific themes, fears, forms of consciousness, and class relationships are embedded in the use of Africanist idiom: how the dialogue of black characters is construed as an alien, estranging dialect made deliberately unintelligible by spellings contrived to disfamiliarize it; how Africanist language practices are employed to evoke the tension between speech and speechlessness; how it is used to establish a cognitive world split between speech and text, to reinforce class distinctions and otherness as well as to assert privilege and power; how it serves as a marker and vehicle for illegal sexuality, fear of madness, expulsion, self-loathing. Finally, we should look at how a black idiom and the sensibilities it has come to imply are appropriated for the associative value they lend to modernism—to being hip, sophisticated, ultra-urbane.

Third, we need studies of the technical ways in which an Africanist character is used to limn out and enforce the invention and implications of whiteness. We need studies that analyze the strategic use of black characters to define the goals and enhance the qualities of white characters. Such studies will reveal the process of establishing others in order to know them, to display knowledge of the other so as to ease and to order external and internal chaos. Such studies will reveal the process by which it is made possible to explore and penetrate one's own body in the guise of the sexuality, vulnerability, and anarchy of the other—and to control projections of anarchy with the disciplinary apparatus of punishment and largess.

Fourth, we need to analyze the manipulation of the Africanist narrative (that is, the story of a black person, the experience of being bound and/or rejected) as a means of meditation—both safe and risky—on one's own humanity. Such analyses will reveal how the representation and appropriation of that narrative provides opportunities to contemplate limitation, suffering, rebellion, and to speculate on fate and destiny. They will analyze how that narrative is used for discourse on ethics, social and universal codes of behavior, and assertions about and definitions of civilization and reason. Criticism of this type will show how that narrative is used in the construction of a history and a context for whites by positing history-lessness and context-lessness for blacks.

These topics surface endlessly when one begins to look carefully, without restraining, protective agenda beforehand. They seem to me to render the nation's literature a much more complex and rewarding body of knowledge.

Two examples may clarify: one a major American novel

romancing the shadow 53

that is both a source and a critique of romance as a genre; the other the fulfillment of the promise I made earlier to return to those mute white images of Poe's.

.   .   .

If we supplement our reading of *Huckleberry Finn,* expand it—release it from its clutch of sentimental nostrums about lighting out to the territory, river gods, and the fundamental innocence of Americanness—to incorporate its contestatory, combative critique of antebellum America, it seems to be another, fuller novel. It becomes a more beautifully complicated work that sheds much light on some of the problems it has accumulated through traditional readings too shy to linger over the implications of the Africanist presence at its center. We understand that, at a certain level, the critique of class and race is there, although disguised or enhanced by humor and naiveté. Because of the combination of humor, adventure, and the viewpoint of the naif, Mark Twain's readers are free to dismiss the critique, the contestatory qualities, of the novel and focus on its celebration of savvy innocence, at the same time voicing polite embarrassment over the symptomatic racial attitude it enforces. Early criticism (that is, the reappraisals in the 1950s that led to the reification of *Huckleberry Finn* as a great novel) missed or dismissed the social quarrel in that work because it appears to assimilate the ideological assumptions of its society and culture; because it is narrated in the voice and controlled by the gaze of a child-without-status—someone outside, marginal, and already "othered" by the middle-class society he loathes and seems never to envy; and because the novel masks itself in the comic, parodic, and exaggerated tall-tale format.

On this young but street-smart innocent, Huck, who is virginally uncorrupted by bourgeois yearnings, fury, and helplessness, Mark Twain inscribes a critique of slavery and the pretensions of the would-be middle class, a resistance to the loss of Eden and the difficulty of becoming a social individual. The agency, however, for Huck's struggle is the nigger Jim, and it is absolutely necessary (for reasons I tried to illuminate earlier) that the term *nigger* be inextricable from Huck's deliberations about who and what he himself is—or, more precisely, is not. The major controversies about the greatness or near greatness of *Huckleberry Finn* as an American (or even "world") novel exist as controversies because they forgo a close examination of the interdependence of slavery and freedom, of Huck's growth and Jim's serviceability within it, and even of Mark Twain's inability to continue, to explore the journey into free territory.

The critical controversy has focused on the collapse of the so-called fatal ending of the novel. It has been suggested that the ending is brilliant finesse that returns Tom Sawyer to the center stage where he should be. Or it is a brilliant play on the dangers and limitations of romance. Or it is a sad and confused ending to the book of an author who, after a long blocked period, lost narrative direction; who changed the serious adult focus back to a child's story out of disgust. Or the ending is a valuable learning experience for Jim and Huck for which we and they should be grateful. What is not stressed is that there is no way, given the confines of the novel, for Huck to mature into a moral human being *in America* without Jim. To let Jim go free, to let him enter the mouth of the Ohio River and pass into free territory, would be to abandon the whole premise of the book. Neither Huck nor Mark Twain can tolerate, in imaginative terms, Jim freed. That would blast the predilection from its mooring.

Thus the fatal ending becomes the elaborate deferment of a necessary and necessarily unfree Africanist character's escape, because freedom has no meaning to Huck or to the text without the specter of enslavement, the anodyne to individualism; the yardstick of absolute power over the life of another; the signed, marked, informing, and mutating presence of a black slave.

The novel addresses at every point in its structural edifice, and lingers over in every fissure, the slave's body and personality: the way it speaks, what passion legal or illicit it is prey to, what pain it can endure, what limits, if any, there are to its suffering, what possibilities there are for forgiveness, compassion, love. Two things strike us in this novel: the apparently limitless store of love and compassion the black man has for his white friend and white masters; and his assumption that the whites are indeed what they say they are, superior and adult. This representation of Jim as the visible other can be read as the yearning of whites for forgiveness and love, but the yearning is made possible only when it is understood that Jim has recognized his inferiority (not as

slave, but as black) and despises it. Jim permits his perse-
cutors to torment him, humiliate him, and responds to the
torment and humiliation with boundless love. The humiliation that Huck and Tom subject Jim to is baroque, endless,
foolish, mind-softening—and it comes *after* we have experienced Jim as an adult, a caring father and a sensitive man. If
Jim had been a white ex-convict befriended by Huck, the
ending could not have been imagined or written: because it
would not have been possible for two children to play so
painfully with the life of a white man (regardless of his class,
education, or fugitiveness) once he had been revealed to us as
a moral adult. Jim's slave status makes play and deferment
possible—but it also dramatizes, in style and mode of narration, the connection between slavery and the achievement (in
actual and imaginary terms) of freedom. Jim seems unasser-
tive, loving, irrational, passionate, dependent, inarticulate (except for the "talks" he and Huck have, long sweet talks we
are not privy to—but what did you talk about, Huck?). It is
not what Jim seems that warrants inquiry, but what Mark
Twain, Huck, and especially Tom need from him that should
solicit our attention. In that sense the book may indeed be
"great" because in its structure, in the hell it puts its readers
through at the end, the frontal debate it forces, it simulates
and describes the parasitical nature of white freedom.

.   .   .

Forty years earlier, in the works of Poe, one sees how the
concept of the American self was similarly bound to Afri-

romancing the shadow   57

canism, and was similarly covert about its dependency. We can look to "The Gold-Bug" and "How to Write a Blackwood Article" (as well as *Pym*) for samples of the desperate need of this writer with pretensions to the planter class for the literary techniques of "othering" so common to American literature: estranging language, metaphoric condensation, fetishizing strategies, the economy of stereotype, allegorical foreclosure; strategies employed to secure his characters' (and his readers') identity. But there are unmanageable slips. The black slave Jupiter is said to whip his master in "The Gold-Bug"; the black servant Pompey stands mute and judgmental at the antics of his mistress in "A Blackwood Article." And Pym engages in cannibalism *before* he meets the black savages; when he escapes from them and witnesses the death of a black man, he drifts toward the silence of an impenetrable, inarticulate whiteness.

We are reminded of other images at the end of literary journeys into the forbidden space of blackness. Does Faulkner's *Absalom! Absalom!,* after its protracted search for the telling African blood, leave us with just such an image of snow and the eradication of race? Not quite. Shreve sees himself as the inheritor of the blood of African kings; the snow apparently is the wasteland of unmeaning, unfathomable whiteness. Harry's destiny and death dream in Hemingway's Africa is focused on the mountain top "great, high, and unbelievably white in the sun" in "The Snows of Kilimanjaro." *To Have and Have Not* closes with an image of a white boat. William Styron begins and ends Nat Turner's journey with a white, floating marble structure, windowless, doorless, incoherent. In *Henderson the Rain King* Saul Bellow ends the hero's journey to and from his fantastic Africa on the ice, the white frozen wastes. With an Africanist child in his arms, the soul of the Black King in his baggage, Henderson dances, he shouts, over the frozen whiteness, a new white man in a new found land: "leaping, pounding, and tingling over the pure white lining of the gray Arctic silence."

If we follow through on the self-reflexive nature of these encounters with Africanism, it falls clear: images of blackness can be evil *and* protective, rebellious *and* forgiving, fearful *and* desirable—all of the self-contradictory features of the self. Whiteness, alone, is mute, meaningless, unfathomable, pointless, frozen, veiled, curtained, dreaded, senseless, implacable. Or so our writers seem to say.

"What's Love Got To Do with It?":
Critical Theory, Integrity, and the Black Idiom

Henry Louis Gates, Jr.

> Rather than being a "linguistic event" or a complex network of linguistic systems that embody the union of the signified and the signifier independent of phenomenal reality, Black creative art is an act of love which attempts to destroy estrangement and elitism by demonstrating a strong fondness or enthusiasm for freedom and an affectionate concern for the lives of people, especially Black people.
>
> Joyce A. Joyce

> It may seem to you that I'm acting confused
> When you're close to me.
> If I tend to look dazed
> I read it someplace, I've got cause to be.
> There's a name for it,
> There's a phrase that fits.
> But whatever the reason
> You do it for me — oh, oh, oh
>
> What's love got to do, got to do with it?
> What's love but a secondhand emotion?
> What's love got to do, got to do with it?
> Who needs a heart when a heart can be broken?
>
> Tina Turner, "What's Love Got To Do with It?"
> lyrics by Terry Britten and Graham Lyle

I HAVE STRUCTURED my response to Joyce Joyce's "The Black Canon" in two parts. The first section of this essay attempts to account for the prevalence among Afro-Americans of what Paul

249

de Man called the "resistance to theory."[1] The second section of this essay attempts to respond directly to the salient parts of Professor Joyce's argument. While the first part of my essay is historical, it also explains why literary theory has been useful in my work, in an attempt to defamiliarize a black text from this black reader's experiences as an African-American. This section of my essay, then, is something of an auto-critography, generated by what I take to be the curiously *personal* terms of Joyce Joyce's critique of the remarkably vague, yet allegedly antiblack, thing that she calls, variously, "structuralism" or "poststructuralism." Apparently for Joyce Joyce, and for several other critics, my name and my work have become metonyms for "structuralism," "poststructuralism," and/or "deconstructionism" in the black tradition, even when these terms are not defined at all or, perhaps worse, not adequately understood. (While Houston Baker generously acknowledges my influence in his remarkable work *Blues, Ideology, and Afro-American Literature*,[2] let me state clearly that our relation of influence is a reciprocal one, in which each stands as "ideal reader" for the other.) These terms become epithets where used as in Joyce Joyce's essay, and mostly opprobrious epithets at that. Just imagine: if Richard Pryor (and his all-too-eager convert Michael Cooke) have their way and abolish the use of the word *nigger* even among ourselves, and black feminists abolish m____, perhaps the worse thing a black person will be able to call another black person will be: "You black poststructuralist, you!" What would Du Bois have said?!

I must confess that I am bewildered by Joyce Joyce's implied claim that to engage in black critical theory is to be, somehow, antiblack. In fact, I find this sort of claim to be both false and a potentially dangerous—and dishonest—form of witch-hunting or nigger-baiting. While it is one thing to say that someone is *wrong* in their premises or their conclusions, it is quite another to ascertain (on that person's behalf) their motivations, their intentions, their *affect*; and then to imply that they do not love their culture, or that they seek to deny their heritage, or that they are alienated from their "race," appealing all the while to an undefined transcendant essence called "the Black Experience," from which Houston Baker and I have somehow strayed. This is silliness.

Who can disagree that there is more *energy* being manifested and good work being brought to bear on black texts by black critics today than at any other time in our history, and that a large part of the explanation for this wonderful phenomenon is the growing critical sophistication of black readers of literature? Or that this sophistication is not directly related to the fact that we are taking our work—

the close reading, interpretation, and *preservation* of the texts and authors of our tradition—with the utmost *seriousness?* What else is there for a critic to do? *What's love got to do with it,* Joyce Joyce? Precisely this: it is an act of love of the tradition—by which I mean *our* tradition—to bring to bear upon it honesty, insight, and skepticism, as well as praise, enthusiasm, and dedication; all values fundamental to the blues and to signifying, those two canonical black discourses in which Houston and I locate the black critical difference. It is merely a mode of critical masturbation to praise a black text simply because it is somehow "black," and it is irresponsible to act as if we are not all fellow citizens of literature for whom developments in other sections of the republic of letters have no bearing or relevance. To do either is most certainly *not* to manifest "love" for our tradition.

Before I can respond more directly to Joyce Joyce's essay, however, I want to examine the larger resistance to (white) theory in the (black) tradition.[3]

I

Unlike almost every other literary tradition, the Afro-American literary tradition was generated as a response to allegations that its authors did not, and *could not,* create "literature." Philosophers and literary critics, such as Hume, Kant, Jefferson, and Hegel, seemed to decide that the presence of a written literature was the signal measure of the potential, innate "humanity" of a race. The African living in Europe or in the New World seems to have felt compelled to create a literature both to demonstrate, implicitly, that blacks did indeed possess the intellectual ability to create a written art, but also to indict the several social and economic institutions that delimited the "humanity" of all black people in Western cultures.

So insistent did these racist allegations prove to be, at least from the eighteenth to the early twentieth centuries, that it is fair to describe the subtext of the history of black letters as this urge to refute the claim that because blacks had no written traditions, they were bearers of an "inferior" culture. The relation between European and American critical theory, then, and the development of the African and Afro-American literary traditions, can readily be seen to have been ironic, indeed. Even as late as 1911, when J. E. Casely Hayford published *Ethiopia Unbound* (the "first" African novel), that pioneering author felt compelled to address this matter in the first two paragraphs of his text. "At the dawn of the twentieth century," the novel opens, "men of light and leading both in Europe and in America had not yet made up their minds as to what place to assign to the spiritual aspirations of the black man; . . . Before this time," the narrative continues, "it had been discovered that the black man was not necessarily the missing link between man and ape. It had even been granted that for intellectual endowments he had nothing to be ashamed of in an *open* competition with the Aryan or any other type."[4] *Ethiopia Unbound*, it seems obvious, was concerned to settle the matter of black mental equality, which had remained something of an open question in European discourse for two hundred years. Concluding this curiously polemical exposition of three paragraphs, which precedes the introduction of the novel's protagonist, Casely Hayford points to "the names of men like [W.E.B.] Du Bois, Booker T. Washington, [Wilmot E.] Blyden, [Paul Laurence] Dunbar, [Samuel] Coleridge-Taylor, and others" (2) as prima facie evidence of the sheer saliency of what Carter G. Woodson once termed "the public [Negro] mind."[5] These were men, the narrative concludes, "who had distinguished themselves in the fields of activity and intellectuality" (2), men who had demonstrated conclusively that the African's first cousin was indeed the European, rather than the ape.

That the presence of a written literature could assume such large proportions in several Western cultures from the Enlightenment to this century is even more curious than is the fact that blacks themselves, as late as 1911, felt moved to respond to this stimulus, indeed felt the need to speak the matter silent, to end the argument by producing literature. Few literary traditions have begun or been sustained by such a complex and curious relation to its criticism: allegations of an absence led directly to a presence, a literature often inextricably bound in a dialogue with its potentially harshest critics.[6]

Black literature and its criticism, then, have been put to uses that were not primarily aesthetic; rather, they have formed part of a larger discourse on the nature of the black and his or her role in the order of things. The integral relation between theory and a literary text, therefore, which so very often in other traditions has been a sustaining relation, in our tradition has been an extraordinarily problematical one. The relation among theory, tradition, and integrity within the black literary tradition has not been, and perhaps cannot be, a straightforward matter.

Let us consider the etymology of the word *integrity*, which I take to be the keyword implied in Dr. Joyce's essay. *Integrity* is a curious keyword to address in a period of bold and sometimes exhilarating speculation and experimentation, two other words which aptly characterize literary criticism, generally, and Afro-American criticism, specifically, at the present time. The Latin origin of the English word *integritas* connotes wholeness, entireness, completeness, chastity, and purity; most of which are descriptive terms that made their way frequently into the writings of the American New Critics, critics who seem not to have cared particularly for, or about, the literature of Afro-Americans. Two of the most common definitions of *integrity* elaborate upon the sense of wholeness derived from the Latin original. Let me cite these here, as taken from the *Oxford English Dictionary:* "1. The condition of having no part or element taken away or wanting; undivided or unbroken state; material wholeness, completeness, entirety; something undivided; an integral whole; 2. The condition of not being marred or violated; unimpaired or uncorrupted condition; original perfect state; soundness." It is the second definition of *integrity*—that is to say, the one connoting the absence of violation and corruption, the preservation of an initial wholeness or soundness—which I would like to consider in this deliberation upon "Theory and Integrity," or more precisely upon that relationship which ideally should obtain between African or Afro-American literature and the theories we borrow, revise, or fabricate to account for the precise nature and shape of our literature and its "being" in the world.

It is probably true that critics of Afro-American literature (which, by the way, I employ as a less ethnocentric designation than "the Black Critic") are more concerned with the complex relation between literature and literary theory than we have ever been before. There are many reasons for this, not the least of which is our increasingly central role in "the profession," precisely when our colleagues in other literatures are engulfed in their own extensive debates about the intellectual merit of so very much theorizing. Theory, as a second-order reflection upon a primary gesture such as "literature," has *always* been viewed with deep mistrust and suspicion by those scholars who find it presumptuous and perhaps even decadent when criticism claims the right to stand, as discourse, on its own, as a parallel textual universe to literature. Theoretical texts breed other, equally "decadent," theoretical responses in a creative process that can be remarkably far removed from a poem or a novel.

For the critic of Afro-American literature, this process is even more perilous precisely because the largest part of contemporary literary theory derives from critics of Western European languages and literatures. Is the use of theory to write about Afro-American literature, we might ask rhetorically, merely another form of intellectual indenture, a form of servitude of the mind as pernicious in its intellectual implications as any other form of enslavement? This is the issue raised, for me at least, by the implied presence of the word *integrity* in Joyce Joyce's essay, but also by my own work over the past decade. Does the propensity to theorize about a text or a literary tradition "mar," "violate," "impair," or "corrupt" the "soundness" of a purported "original perfect state" of a black text or of the black tradition? To argue the affirmative is to align one's position with the New Critical position that texts are "wholes" in the first place.

To be sure, this matter of criticism and integrity has a long and rather tortured history in black letters. It was David Hume, after all, who called the Jamaican poet of Latin verse, Francis Williams, "a parrot who merely speaks a few words plainly";[7] and Phillis Wheatley has for far too long suffered from the spurious attacks of black and white critics alike for being the original *rara avis* of a school of so-called "mockingbird poets," whose use and imitation of received European and American literary conventions have been regarded, simply put, as a corruption itself of a "purer" black expression, privileged somehow in black artistic forms such as the blues, signifying, the spirituals, and the Afro-American dance. Can we, as critics, escape a "mockingbird" relation to theory, one destined to be derivative, often to the point of parody? Can we, moreover, escape the racism of so many critical theorists, from Hume and Kant through the Southern Agrarians and the Frankfurt School?

As I have argued elsewhere, there are complex historical reasons for the resistance to theory among critics of comparative black literature, which stem in part from healthy reactions against the marriage of logocentrism and ethnocentrism in much of post-Renaissance Western aesthetic discourse. Although there have been a few notable exceptions, theory as a subject of inquiry has only in the past decade begun to sneak into the discourse of Afro-American literature. The implicit racism of some of the Southern Agrarians who became the New Critics and Adorno's bizarre thoughts about something he calls "jazz" did not serve to speed this process along at all. Sterling A. Brown has summed up the relation of the black tradition to the Western critical tradition. In response to Robert Penn Warren's line from "Pondy Woods" (1945), "Nigger, your breed ain't metaphysical," Brown replies, "Cracker, your breed ain't exegetical."[8] No tradition is "naturally" metaphysical or exegetical, of course. Only recently have some scholars attempted to convince critics of black literature that the racism of the Western critical tradition was not a sufficient reason for us to fail to theorize about our own endeavor, or even to make use of contemporary theoretical innovations when this seemed either useful or appropriate. Perhaps predictably, a number of these attempts share a concern with that which, in the received tradition of Afro-American criticism, has been most repressed: that is, with close readings of the text itself. This return of the repressed —the very language of the black text—has generated a new interest among our critics in theory. My charged advocacy of the relevance of contemporary theory to reading Afro-American and African literature closely has been designed as the prelude to the definition of principles of literary criticism peculiar to the black literary traditions themselves, related to and compatible with contemporary critical theory generally, yet "indelibly black," as Robert Farris Thompson puts it.[9] All theory is text-specific, and ours must be as well. Lest I be misunderstood, I have tried to work through contemporary theories of literature *not* to "apply" them to black texts, but rather to *transform* by *translating* them into a new rhetorical realm. These attempts have been successful in varying degrees; nevertheless, I have tried to make them at all times interesting episodes in one critic's reflection on the black "text-milieu," what he means by "the tradition," and from which he extracts his "canon."

It is only through this critical activity that the profession, in a world of dramatically fluid relations of knowledge and power, and of the reemerging presence of the tongues of Babel, can redefine itself away from a Eurocentric notion of a hierarchical canon of texts, mostly white, Western, and male, and encourage and sustain a truly comparative and pluralistic notion of the institution of literature. What all students of literature share in common is the art of interpretation, even where we do not share in common the same texts. The hegemony implicit in the phrase "the Western tradition" reflects material relationships primarily, and not so-called universal, transcendant normative judgments. Judgment is specific, both culturally and temporally. The sometimes vulgar nationalism implicit in would-be literary categories such as "American Literature," or the not-so-latent imperialism implied by the vulgar phrase "Commonwealth literature," are extraliterary designations of control, symbolic of material and concomitant political relations, rather than literary ones. We, the scholars of our profession, must eschew these categories of domination and ideology and insist upon the fundamental redefinition of what it is to speak of "the canon."

Whether we realize it or not, each of us brings to a text an *implicit* theory of literature, or even an unwitting hybrid of theories, a critical gumbo as it were. To become aware of contemporary theory is to become aware of one's presuppositions, those ideological and aesthetic assumptions which we bring to a text unwittingly. It is incumbent upon us, those of us who respect the sheer integrity of the black tradition, to turn to this very tradition to create self-generated theories about the *black* literary endeavor. We must, above all, respect the integrity, the wholeness, of the black work of art, by bringing to bear upon the explication of its meanings all of the attention to language that we may learn from several developments in contemporary theory. By the very process of "application," as it were, we recreate, through revision, the critical theory at hand. As our familiarity with the black tradition and with literary theory expands, we shall invent our own theories, as some of us have begun to do—black, text-specific theories.

I have tried to utilize contemporary theory to *defamiliarize* the texts of the black tradition, to create a distance between this black reader and our black texts, so that I may more readily *see* the formal workings of those texts. Wilhelm von Humboldt describes this phenomenon in the following way: "Man lives with things mainly, even exclusively—since sentiment and action in him depend upon his mental representations—as they are conveyed to him by language. Through the same act by which he spins language out of himself he weaves himself into it, and every language draws a circle around the people to which it belongs, a circle that can only be transcended in so far as one at the same time enters another one." I have turned to literary theory as a "second circle." I have done this to preserve the integrity of these texts, by trying to avoid confusing my experience as an Afro-American with the black act of language which defines a text. On the other hand, by learning to read a black text within a black formal cultural matrix, and explicating it with the principles of criticism at work in *both* the Euro-American and Afro-American traditions, I believe that we critics can produce richer structures of meaning than are possible otherwise.

This is the challenge of the critic of black literature in the 1980s: not to shy away from literary theory; rather, to translate it into the black idiom, *renaming* principles of criticism where appropriate, but especially *naming* indigenous black principles of criticism and applying these to explicate our own texts. It is incumbent upon us to protect the integrity of our tradition by bringing to bear upon its criticism any tool of sensitivity to language that is appropriate. And what do I mean by "appropriate"? Simply this: *any* tool that enables the critic to explain the complex workings of the language of a text is an "appropriate" tool. For it is language, the black language of black texts, which expresses the distinctive quality of our literary tradition. A literary tradition, like an individual, is to a large extent defined by its past, its received traditions. We critics in the 1980s have the especial privilege of explicating the black tradition in ever closer detail. We shall not meet this challenge by remaining afraid of, or naive about, literary theory; rather, we will only inflict upon our literary tradition the violation of the uninformed reading. We are the keepers of the black literary tradition. No matter what theories we seem to embrace, we have more in common with each other than we do with any other critic of any other literature. We write for each other, and for our own contemporary writers. This relation is a sacred trust.

Let me end this section of my essay with a historical anecdote. In 1915, Edmond Laforest, a prominent member of the Haitian literary movement called "La Ronde," made of his death a symbolic, if ironic, statement of the curious relation of the "non-Western" writer to the act of writing in a modern language. M. Laforest, with an inimitable, if fatal, flair for the grand gesture, calmly tied a Larousse dictionary around his neck, then proceeded to commit suicide by drowning. While other black writers, before and after M. Laforest, have suffocated as artists beneath the weight of various modern languages, Laforest chose to make his death an emblem of this relation of indenture. We commit intellectual suicide by binding ourselves too tightly to nonblack theory; but we drown just as surely as did Laforest if we pretend that "theory" is "white," or worse—that it is "antiblack." Let scores of black theories proliferate, and let us encourage speculation among ourselves about our own literature. And let us, finally, realize that we must be each other's allies, even when we most disagree, because those who would dismiss both black literature and black criticism will no doubt increase in numbers in this period of profound economic fear and scarcity unless we meet their challenge head-on.

II

That said, let me respond to the salient points in Joyce Joyce's essay. Joyce Joyce's anecdote about the student who could not understand Jimmy Baldwin's essay "On Being 'White' . . . and Other Lies" is only remarkable for what it reveals about her student's lack of reading skills and/or training. Let me cite a typical paragraph of Baldwin's text, since so very much of Joyce Joyce's argument turns upon the idea of *critical language as a barrier of alienation between black critics and "our people"*:

. . . Without further pursuing the implication of this mutual act of faith, one is nevertheless aware that the Jewish translation into a white American can sustain the state of Israel in a way that the Black presence, here, can scarcely hope—at least, not yet—to halt the slaughter in South Africa.

And there is a reason for that.

America became white—the people who, as they claim, "settled" in the country became white—because of the necessity of denying the Black presence, and justifying the Black subjugation. No community can be based on such a principle—or, in other words, no community can be established on so genocidal a lie. White men—from Norway, for example, where they were *Norwegians*—became white: by slaughtering the cattle, poisoning the wells, torching the houses, massacring Native Americans, raping Black women.[10]

We are not exactly talking about the obscure or difficult language of Fanon or Hegel or Heidegger or Wittgenstein here, now are we? Rather than being "trapped by [her] own contradiction and elitism," as Joyce Joyce claims she was, and granting this student her point, Joyce Joyce *should* have done what Anna Julia Cooper or Du Bois would have done: sent the student back to the text and told her to read it again—and again, until she got it *right*. Then, she, a teacher in training, I presume, must serve as an interpreter, as mediator, between Baldwin's text and "our people" out there. (Would the superb and thoughtful editors of *Essence*, by the way, publish an essay their readers could not understand? Perhaps the anecdote is merely apocryphal, after all.) Next time, give the child a dictionary, Joyce, and make her come back in a week.

To use this anecdote to conclude that Baldwin (and, of course, we blankety-blank poststructuralists) has abnegated "the responsibility of the writer to his or her audience" is for a university professor to fail to understand or satisfy our most fundamental charge as teachers of literature: to preach the responsibility of *the reader* to his or her *writers*. Joyce Joyce, rather regrettably, has forgotten that the two propositions are inseparable and that the latter is the basic charge that *any* professor of literature accepts when he or she walks into a classroom or opens a text. *That's* what love's got to do, got to do with it, Joyce Joyce. How hard are we willing to work to meet our responsibilities to our *writers*? What would you have Jimmy Baldwin *do*: rewrite that paragraph, reduce his level of diction to a lower common denominator, then poll the readers of *Essence* to see if they understood the essay? What insolence; what arrogance! What's love got to do with your student's relation to Baldwin and his text? We should *beg* our writers to publish in *Essence* and in every other black publication, from *Ebony* and *Jet* to the *Black American Literature Forum* and the *CLA Journal*.

The relationship between writer and reader is a reciprocal relationship, and one sells our authors short if one insists that their "responsibility," as you put it, is "to be clear." Clear to whom, or to what?

Their "responsibility" is to write. Our responsibility, as critics, to our writers, is to work at understanding *them*, not to demand that they write at such a level that every one of "our people" understands every word of every black writer without working at it. Your assertion that "the first works of black American literature" were "addressed to white audiences" is not strictly true. The author of *Our Nig*, for example, writes that "I appeal to my colored brethren universally for patronage, hoping they will not condemn this attempt of their sister to be erudite, but rally around me a faithful band of supporters and defenders."[11] How much "blacker" can an author get? No, even at the beginning of the tradition, black writers wrote for a double or mulatto audience, one black *and* white. Even Phillis Wheatley, whose poetry was the object of severe scrutiny for those who would deny us membership in the human community, wrote "for" Arbour Tanner, Scipio Moorehead, and Jupiter Hammon, just as black critics today write "for" each other and "for" our writers, and not "for" Derrida, Jameson, Said, or Bloom.

It is just not true that "the most influential critics of black literature have been the creative writers themselves." Rather, I believe that our "most influential critics" have been academic critics, such as W. S. Scarborough, Alain Locke, Sterling A. Brown, Du Bois (a mediocre poet and *terrible* novelist), J. Saunders Redding, Darwin T. Turner, and Houston A. Baker, among others (though both Brown and Baker are also poets). "Most influential" does not necessarily mean whom a white publisher publishes; most influential, to me, means who has generated a critical *legacy*, a critical *tradition* upon which other critics have built or can build. Among the writers that Joyce Joyce lists, Ralph Ellison has been "most influential" in the sense that I am defining it, while Hughes is cited mainly for "The Negro Artist and the Racial Mountain," Wright mostly for his two major pieces, "The Literature of the Negro in the United States" and "Blueprint for Negro Literature," while almost none of us cites Du Bois at all, despite the fact that Du Bois was probably the very first systematic literary and cultural theorist in the tradition. Rather, we *genuflect* to Du Bois.

I am not attempting to deny that creative writers such as Amiri Baraka and Ishmael Reed have been remarkably important. Rather, I deny Joyce Joyce's claim that a new generation of academic critics has usurped the place of influence in the black tradition which creative writers occupied before "the 1960s." The matter is just not as simple as a "shift in black consciousness" in the 1960s, similar to that caused by migration in the 1920s, which Joyce Joyce maintains led to "the merger of a select number of blacks into American mainstream society" and, accordingly, to our "exogamic, elitist, epistemological adaptations." No, I learned my trade as a critic of black literature from a black academic critic, Charles Davis, who made me read Scarborough, Locke, Redding, Ellison, Turner, and Houston Baker as a matter of course.

This is a crucial matter in Joyce Joyce's argument, though it is muddled. For she implies (1) that larger sociopolitical changes in the 1960s led to the crossover of blacks into white institutions (true), and (2) that the critical language that I use, and my firm belief that "race" is not an essence but a trope for ethnicity or culture, both result from being trained into a "class orientation that ironically result[s] from social changes provoked by racial issues."

There are several false leaps being made here. In the first place, what Joyce Joyce erroneously thinks of as our "race" is our *culture*. Of course I "believe in" Afro-American culture; indeed, I celebrate it every day. But I also believe that to know it, to find it, to touch it, one must locate it in its *manifestations* (texts, expressive culture, music, the dance, language, and so forth) and not in the realm of the abstract or the a priori. Who can argue with that? The point of my passage about our language with which Joyce Joyce takes such issue is that for a literary critic to discuss "the black aesthetic," he or she must "find" it in language use. What is so controversial, or aristocratic, about that? As for my "class orientation," the history of my family, whether or not we were slaves or free, black or mulatto, property owners or sharecroppers, Howard M.D.s or janitors, is really none of Joyce Joyce's business. To say, moreover, that because I matriculated at Yale (when Arna Bontemps and Houston Baker taught black literature there, by the way) and at the University of Cambridge, I became a "poststructuralist" is simply illogical.

This claim is crucial to Joyce Joyce's argument, however, because of her assertion that "middle-class black men" adopted "mainstream [white] lifestyles and ideology" with great intensity after the "integration" of the 1960s. This dangerous tendency, her argument runs, culminated in 1979 with my oft-cited statement about a black writer or critic being the point of consciousness of our *language*. I am delighted that Joyce Joyce points to the significance of this statement, because I think that it is of crucial importance to the black critical activity, and especially to the subsequent attention to actual black language use that is apparent in much of our criticism since 1979.

Why has that statement been such an important one in the development of Afro-American literary criticism? Precisely because if our literary critics saw her or his central function as that of a "guide," as Joyce Joyce puts it, or as "an intermediary in explaining the relationship between black people and those forces that attempt to subdue them," she or he tended to fail at both tasks: neither were we as critics in a position to "lead" our people to "freedom," nor did we do justice to the texts created by our writers. Since *when* have black people turned to our critics to lead us out of the wilderness of Western racism into the promised land of freedom? If black readers turn to black critics, I would imagine they do so to learn about the wondrous workings of *literature,* our literature, of how our artists have represented the complex encounter of every aspect of black culture with itself and with the Other in formal literary language. Who reads our books anyway? Who can doubt that *Black Fire,* the splendid anthology of the Black Arts edited by Larry Neal and LeRoi Jones, has sold *vastly* more copies to black intellectuals than to "our people"?[12] Let us not deceive ourselves about our readership.

Joyce Joyce makes a monumental error here, when she offers the following "syllogism":

1. The sixties led to the "integration" of a few black people into historically white institutions.
2. Such exposure to mainstream culture led to the imitation by blacks of white values, habits, and so on.
3. Therefore, black people so educated or exposed suffer from "an individualistic perspective that enables him or her to accept elitist American values and thus widen the chasm between his or her worldview and that of those masses of Blacks whose lives are still stifled by oppressive environmental, intellectual phenomena."

Joyce Joyce arrives at this syllogism all because, I think, we can see important structures of meaning in black texts using sophisticated tools of literary analysis! As my friend Ernie Wilson used to say in the late sixties, "Yeah, but compared to *what?*"!

Let me state clearly that I have no fantasy about my readership: I write for our writers and for our critics. If I write a book review, say, for a popular Afro-American newspaper, I write in one voice; if I write a close analysis of a black text and publish it in a specialist journal, I choose another voice, or voices. Is not that my "responsibility," to use Joyce Joyce's word, and my privilege as a writer? But no, I do not think that my task as a critic is to lead black people to "freedom." My task is to explicate black texts. That's why *I* became a critic. In 1984, I voted for Jesse Jackson for President: if he stays out of literary criticism, I shall let him continue to speak for me in the political realm. (He did not, by the way, return the donation that Sharon Adams and I sent him, so I suppose that being a "poststructuralist" is okay with Jesse.)

And who is to say that Baker's work or mine is not implicitly political because it is "poststructuralist"? How can the demonstration that our texts sustain ever closer and sophisticated readings *not* be political, at a time in the academy when all sorts of so-called canonical critics mediate their racism through calls for "purity" of "the tradition," demands as implicitly racist as anything the Southern Agrarians said? How can the deconstruction, as it were, of the forms of racism itself (as carried out, for example, in a recent issue of *Critical Inquiry* by black and nonblack poststructuralists) not be political?[13] How can the use of literary analysis to explicate the racist social text in which we still find ourselves be anything *but* political? To be political, however, does not mean that I have to write at the level of diction of a Marvel comic book. No, my task—as I see it—is to train university graduate and undergraduate students to think, to read, and, yes Joyce, even to *write* clearly, helping them to expose false uses of language, fraudulent claims and muddled argument, propaganda and vicious lies from all of which our people have suffered just as surely as we have from an economic order in which we were zeroes and a metaphysical order in which we were absences. These are the "values," as Joyce Joyce puts it, which I hope "will be transmitted through [my] work."

Does my work "negate [my] blackness," as Joyce Joyce claims? I would challenge Joyce Joyce to *demonstrate* anywhere in my entire work how I have, even once, negated my blackness. Simply because I have attacked an error in logic in the work of certain Black Aestheticians does not mean that I am antiblack, or that I do not love black art or music, or that I feel alienated from black people, or that I am trying to pass like some poststructural ex-colored man. My feelings about black culture and black people are everywhere manifested in my work and in the way that I define my role in the profession, which is as a critic who would like to think that history will regard him as having been a solid "race man," as we put it. My association with Black Studies departments is by choice, just as is my choice of subject matter. (Believe me, Joyce, almost no one at Cambridge wanted me to write about black literature!)

No, Joyce Joyce, I am as black as I ever was, which is just as black as I ever want to be. And I am asserting my "real self," as you put it so glibly, and whatever influence that my work has had or might have on readers of black literature *establishes a connection between the self and the people outside the self*, as you put it. And for the record, let me add here that only a black person alienated from black language use could fail to understand that we have been deconstructing white people's languages—as "a system of codes or as mere play"—since

1619. That's what signifying is all about. (If you don't believe me, by the way, ask your grandparents, or your parents, especially your mother.)

But enough, Joyce Joyce. Let me respond to your two final points: first, your claim that "the poststructuralist sensibility" does not "aptly apply to black American literary work." I challenge you to refute any of Houston Baker's readings, or my own, to justify such a strange claim. Argue with our readings, not with *your* idea of who or what we are as black people, or with *your* idea of how so very many social ills can be traced, by fits and starts, to "poststructuralist thinking."

Finally, to your curious claims that "black American literary criticism has skipped a whole phase in the evolution of literary theory," that "one school of literary thought [must] be created from the one that goes before," and that "the move in black American literature from polemical, biographical criticism to poststructuralist theories mean[s] that these principles are being applied in a historical vacuum," let me respond by saying that my work arose as a direct response to the theories of the Black Arts Movement, as Houston Baker demonstrates so very well in the essay that you cite. Let me also point out politely that my work with binary oppositions which you cite (such as my earlier Frederick Douglass essay)[14] *is* structuralist as is the work of several other critics of black literature in the seventies (Sunday Anozie, O. A. Ladimeji, Jay Edwards, and the essays in the black journal *The Conch*) and that my work as a poststructuralist emerged directly from my experiments as a structuralist, as Houston Baker also makes clear. No vacuum here; I am acutely aware of the tradition in which I write.

Was it Keynes who said that those who are "against theory" and believe in common sense are merely in the grip of another theory? Joyce Joyce makes a false opposition between theory and humanism, or theory and black men. She also has failed to realize that lucidity through oversimplification is easy enough to achieve; however, it is the lucidity of *command* which is the challenge posed before any critic of any literature. The use of fashionable critical language without the *pressure* of that language is as foolish as is the implied allegation that Houston and I are nouveau ideological Uncle Toms because we read and write theory.

Coda

Neither ideology nor blackness can exist as an entity in itself, outside of its forms, or its texts. This is the central theme of *Mumbo*

Jumbo, for example. But how can we read the text of black ideology? What language(s) do black people use to represent or to contain their ideological positions? In what forms of language do we speak, or write, or *rewrite*? These are the issues at the heart of Joyce Joyce's essay.

Can we derive a valid, *integral* "black" text of ideology from borrowed or appropriated forms? That is, can an authentic black text emerge in the forms of language inherited from the master's class, whether that be, for instance, the realistic novel or poststructuralist theory? Can a black woman's text emerge authentically as borrowed, or "liberated," or revised, from the patriarchal forms of the slave narratives, on one hand, or from the white matriarchal forms of the sentimental novel, on the other, as Harriet Jacobs and Harriet Wilson attempted to do in *Incidents in the Life of a Slave Girl* (1861) and *Our Nig* (1859)?

How much space is there between these two forms through which to maneuver, to maneuver without a certain preordained confinement or "garroting," such as that to which Valerie Smith alludes so pregnantly in her superb poststructural reading of Jacobs's *Incidents in the Life of a Slave Girl?*[15] Is to revise, in this sense, to exist within the confines of the garrot, to extend the metaphor, only to learn to manipulate the representation of black structures of feeling between the cracks, the dark spaces, provided for us by the white masters? Can we write true texts of our ideological selves by the appropriation of received forms of the oppressor—be that oppressor patriarchy or racism—forms in which we see no reflection of our own faces, and through which we hear no true resonances of our own voices? Where lies the liberation in revision, where lies the ideological integrity of defining freedom in the modes and forms of difference charted so cogently by so many poststructural critics of black literature?

It is in these spaces, or garrots, of difference that black literature has dwelled. And while it is crucial to read closely these patterns of formal difference, it is incumbent upon us as well to understand that the quest was lost, in a major sense, before it had even begun simply because the terms of our own self-representation have been provided by the master. Are our choices only to dwell in the quicksand or the garrot of refutation, or negation, or revision? The ideological critique of revision must follow, for us as critics, our detailed and ever closer readings of these very modes of revision. It is not enough for us to show that these exist, and to define these as satisfactory gestures of ideological independence. In this sense, our next set of concerns must be to address the black political signified, and to urge for our writers the fullest and most ironic explorations of manner and matter, of content and form, of structure and sensibility so familiar and poignant to us in our most sublime forms of art, verbal and non-verbal black music, where ideology and art are one, whether we listen to Bessie Smith or to postmodern and poststructural Coltrane.

But what of the ideology of the black critical text? And what of our own critical discourse? In whose voices do we speak? Have we merely renamed the terms of the Other?

Just as we must urge of our writers the meeting of this challenge, we as critics must turn to our own peculiarly black structures of thought and language to develop our own language of criticism, or else we will surely sink in the mire of Nella Larsen's quicksand, remain alienated in the isolation of Harriet Jacobs's garrot, or masked in the received stereotype of the Black Other helping Huck Honey to return to the Raft again, singing "China Gate" with Nat King Cole under the Da Nang moon, standing with the Incredible Hulk as the monstrous split doubled selves of mild mannered white people, or as Rocky's too-devoted trainer Apollo Creed, or reflecting our balded heads in the shining flash of Mr. T's signifying gold chains.

As Tina Turner puts it:

> I've been taking on a new direction,
> But I have to say
> I've been thinking about my own protection
> It scares me to feel this way.
> Oh, oh, oh,
> What's love got to do, got to do with it?
> What's love but a sweet old-fashioned notion. . . .

CORNELL UNIVERSITY

NOTES

1 See Paul de Man, "The Resistance to Theory," *Yale French Studies*, No. 63 (1982), 3–20.

2 Houston A. Baker, Jr., *Blues, Ideology, and Afro-American Literature: A Vernacular Theory* (Chicago, 1984).

3 Fuller versions of this section of my essay appear in my "Criticism in the Jungle," in *Black Literature and Literary Theory*, ed. Henry Louis Gates, Jr. (New York, 1985), pp. 1–24 and "Writing 'Race' and the Difference It Makes," *Critical Inquiry*, 12, No. 1 (Autumn 1985), 1–20.

4 J. E. Casely Hayford, *Ethiopia Unbound: Studies in Race Emancipation* (London, 1911), pp. 1–2; hereafter cited in text.

5 Carter G. Woodson, "Introduction," *The Mind of the Negro as Reflected in Letters Written During the Crisis, 1800–1860* (New York, 1969), p. v.

6 I have traced the history and theory of this critical debate in my *Black Letters and the Enlightenment*, forthcoming from Oxford University Press.

7   David Hume, "Of National Characters," in *The Philosophical Works*, ed. Thomas Hill Green and Thomas Hodge Grose (Darmstadt, 1964), III, 252 n. 1.

8   Sterling A. Brown, Lecture, Yale University, 17 April 1979.

9   Robert Farris Thompson, *Indelibly Black: Essays on African and Afro-American Art* (forthcoming).

10   James Baldwin, "On Being 'White' . . . and Other Lies," *Essence*, April 1984, pp. 90–92.

11   Harriet Wilson, *Our Nig* (Boston, 1859), p. i.

12   *Black Fire: An Anthology of Afro-American Writing*, ed. LeRoi Jones and Larry Neal (New York, 1968).

13   See *Critical Inquiry*, 12, No. 1 (Autumn 1985).

14   Henry Louis Gates, Jr., "Binary Oppositions in Chapter One of *Narrative of the Life of Frederick Douglass, an American Slave, Written by Himself*," in *Afro-American Literature: The Reconstruction of Instruction*, ed. Dexter Fisher and Robert B. Stepto (New York, 1979), pp. 212–33.

15   Valerie Smith, "'Loopholes of Retreat': Architecture and Ideology in Harriet Jacobs's *Incidents in the Life of a Slave Girl*," paper presented at the 1985 American Studies Association meeting, San Diego.

STUART ALAN CLARKE

FEAR OF A BLACK PLANET

race, identity politics, and common sense

 It seems as if everybody's talking about identity politics—and most of what I hear is bad. I suppose I shouldn't be surprised. It's clear that identity politics—political practices and mobilizations that are based on cultural and social identities—have serious limitations. But they also embody possibilities for empowerment that have, of late, received considerably less attention. This is in part because those who would attend to these positive qualities must contend with a formidable hostility—an almost reflexive dismissal of social identity as the basis for political mobilization.

It is important to develop a politically effective, critical perspective on identity politics. Such a perspective must include an account of the broad "common sense" context within which the political and critical work of identity politics take place. This requires recognizing the ways that common sense is socially constructed, and the political significance of those social constructions. More specifically, it requires recognizing that the most powerful constructions of common sense about identity politics—those with formidable mass media backing—are deeply influenced by racial symbols, racial meanings, and racial understandings. This is a common sense which suggests that identity politics, most clearly evidenced in political mobilizations around race, are part of a fundamental attack on the core values of

Stuart Alan Clarke

teaches political science

and American studies at

Williams College.

our political culture. In this manner identity politics are positioned so as to starkly reflect the need for a reassertion of "traditional" liberal values of individualism, privatism, and authoritarian nationalism.

Some of the most compelling examples of common sense about identity politics are constructed using racial mobilizations as reference points. Social representations—narratives, symbols, images—that privilege race as a sign of social disorder and civic decay can be thought of as part of a socially constructed "fear of a black planet" that has traditionally functioned to blunt progressive political possibilities. I am concerned with the extent to which a good deal of our common sense about identity politics can be placed in this tradition.

As Clifford Geertz has pointed out, common sense is not just what anyone clothed and in his or her right mind believes. Rather it is thoroughly constructed, comprising naturalized and consensual definitions.[1] The relationship of common sense to discourses that are more critical will always be somewhat problematic. This is because it is a part of the process of naturalization to co-opt conclusions and ignore analyses, just as it is a part of the forging of consensus to overwhelm careful and considered judgments with casual and colorful assertions. For these reasons there is a strong temptation for "intellectuals" to dismiss "common sense" as a debased form of knowledge. This is a serious mistake. Common sense is the starting point for political calculation, and its construction must be taken into account in any effort to develop a politically effective critical perspective.

Some of the more powerful mechanisms for the construction of a common sense about identity politics are discourses about "political correctness" and, especially, "multiculturalism." In the popular mind, political correctness on college campuses includes at least two elements: the policing of offensive speech in ways that raise serious First Amendment questions, and efforts to dislodge "traditional" works of literature and philosophy from their privileged places in college and university curricula. Although there is no necessary connection between these two elements, the picture of "political correctness" that has been painted in the popular media suggests a natural and logical connection between the two.

This suggestion prepares audiences for a more dubious insistence on the relationship between pedagogical matters and broader questions of civic decorum. When multiculturalism is represented as the manifestation of a "victim's revolution" in our society, discussions of attempts to broaden college curricula can become a way to speak about the dangers of identity politics for the body politic and, in particular, about the dangers of race.

This construction rests on the notion that we are living, in the words of a *Time* magazine cover story titled "Busybodies and Crybabies," in "the age of the all-purpose victim: the individual or group whose plight, condition or even momentary setback is not a matter that needs be solved by individual effort, but constitutes a social problem in itself."[2] In this context multiculturalism—the attempt to make college curricula more inclusive—has vast social significance (beyond the purely "educational" issues at stake) because it exemplifies the political challenge of what C. Vann Woodward calls the "outburst of minority assertiveness" associated with this revolutionary era of victimhood. This political challenge is identity politics.

For Woodward, multiculturalism is the camel's nose of social chaos. "The cult of ethnicity and its zealots," he writes, "have put at stake the American tradition of a shared commitment to common ideals and its reputation for assimilation, for making a 'nation of nations.'"* *Time* magazine also presents the threat that multiculturalism poses in dire terms, implying that, ultimately, it is a threat to democracy:

> Ultimately, multicultural thinking . . . can lead to several regressive orthodoxies. One is the notion that truth is forever encapsulated within collective identities, that what white males or females or blacks or Hispanics or Asians know about their experiences can be communicated only imperfectly to people beyond their pales . . . The authority of any statement is locked within the skin of the speaker.[3]

---

*C. Vann Woodward, "Equal But Separate," *New Republic*, July 15 & 22, 1991, p. 43. Woodward has taken upon himself the task of defending the academic citadel. Also see his "Freedom and the Universities," *The New York Review of Books*, July 18, 1991.

By contrast, the *Time* article goes on to say, the Western tradition insists that "the validity of any statement can be tested independently of, and in no logical way depends upon, the person who makes it." It is this forceful refutation that, in *Time*'s view, "makes democracy possible." By arguing that "radical multiculturalism turns upside down the principles that drew, and continue to draw, people to America: the freedom to create a new personal identity," *Time* uses the "threat" of multiculturalism to illuminate the dangers that identity politics pose for democracy and freedom.

Common sense is an eclectic phenomenon. Its constituent symbols, images, and meanings are loosely assembled from diverse sources of political and popular culture. Partly for this reason it is not monolithic across a society or a culture—it would be a mistake to think about socially constructed common sense in terms of some absolute ideological hegemony. The neoconservative common sense about identity politics is not the *only* common sense about identity politics. There are always counternarratives, alternative perspectives, local and subjugated knowledges that can (and do) contest dominant social constructions.

Nevertheless, ideological productions that are widely and forcefully disseminated do have great potential for unifying these diverse and divergent "streams" of common sense into a dominant perspective. Particular representations of race—images of black men misbehaving—have historically served this function in U.S. political culture. Over time these images have come to play especially powerful roles in our symbolic economy.

As a political culture we have an enormous appetite for images of black men misbehaving.

As a political culture we have an enormous appetite for images of black men misbehaving, an appetite that stretches at least from D.W. Griffith's *Birth of a Nation* to Tom Wolfe's *Bonfire of the Vanities* or Spike Lee's *Do the Right Thing*. I don't pretend to fully understand the sources of this appetite, although the strategic value these images have had in maintaining social control and blunting progressive political change is certainly an important factor.[4] The substance as well as the technology of much popular culture serves to quicken and deepen this historically conditioned desire. Using semiotic technologies that have "spilled over" from rap music and MTV, movies, television and the print media hawk eroticized images of "the bad nigger."

In this context, it is unsurprising that the "multicultural threat" is pictured most compellingly in the public imagination as a black threat. In reviews of two prominent textual pillars in the construction of the "threat of multiculturalism"—Dinesh D'Souza's *Illiberal Education: The Politics of Race and Sex on Campus* and Arthur M. Schlesinger Jr.'s *The Disuniting of America: Reflections on a Multicultural Society*—Woodward notes that in both instances *race* is the privileged sign of the multicultural threat. "While numerous groups have joined in to voice their own grievances and claim redress as victims," he writes, "black Americans, the largest minority with the oldest and most tragic grievances, have been the most prominent."*

UNCLE GEORGE AND UNCLE THOMAS

The construction of a common sense about identity politics is important because the manipulation of race will play a significant role in conservative strategies to reconfigure U.S. politics. Making sense of the process by which "identity politics" has become part of the structure of a renewed neoconservative common sense about race and social order is especially important now, at the beginning of the second decade of the Reagan-Bush debacle. As Republicans move to secure the electoral gains represented by the Reagan-Bush administrations, the political, social, and cultural delegitimation of the political claims and claimants generated in the late sixties and early seventies will continue to be an important tactic for them.[5]

The energy with which Republicans "quota baited" Democrats during the national debate over the 1991 Civil Rights Bill makes it seem likely that GOP strategists expect one of the decisive symbolic battles in the project to consolidate electoral gains to be joined over race. Thomas Byrne Edsall and Harold Meyerson rightly point out that "the race card" remains an indispensable strategy for blunting

---

*Woodward, "Equal But Separate," p. 42. In a largely favorable review of D'Souza's book, Woodward notes: "Women and homosexuals do not receive nearly the proportion of attention suggested by the title of D'Souza's book" (Woodward, "Freedom and the Universities," p. 35).

the possibilities for progressive populist politics.[6] In other words, much of the "struggle for hegemony" in the last decade of the 20th century may well involve contestation over the meanings of race and racial politics. The range of meanings and assessments that commentators left and right assign to "identity politics" will be profoundly implicated in that struggle.

One of the things for which the election of 1988 will be remembered is having made "Willie Horton" a household name—more testimony to our appetite for pictures of bad black boys. Blatant racism is not, however, an especially stable foundation for a political realignment. There is reason to believe the gentler, kinder George Bush has developed a more subtle and effective utilization of an identity politics of race.

Indeed, with the appointment of Judge Clarence Thomas to the U.S. Supreme Court, the significance of Willie Horton as the black male body most immediately associated with the president is rapidly receding into the distant (but strategically recallable) past. With respect to race, Bush has passed the bad-cop baton on to others because doing so allows him a greater flexibility in manipulating identity politics for political gain. If the misbehavior of Willie Horton encouraged an identity politics of white authoritarian populism, the "good behaviors" of Clarence Thomas promised (at least before Anita Hill's allegations of sexual harassment) to encourage both an identity politics of racial pride and a liberal politics of post-civil rights, post-Cold War, American nationalism.

Bush's astute manipulation of the symbolic politics of race posed real problems for black groups like the Urban League and the NAACP. On the one hand, these groups could have supported the Thomas nomination for reasons of racial solidarity. This would have upheld the symbolic significance of race in U.S. politics while undercutting its effective significance, both by isolating these groups from their natural allies on the left and by tacitly supporting the Bush offensive against affirmative action. In this scenario, an identity politics of racial pride becomes an ineffectual coon show. At the unlikely extreme Clarence Thomas could even become a lever by which black folks are maneuvered into a post-Cold War American nationalism.

The NAACP chose instead to oppose the nomination, undercutting the symbolic significance of race by insisting on a *substantive response* to racial claims on the state. Along with Thurgood Marshall, they insisted that "a black snake is just as bad as a white snake." This is a move that most progressives were probably pleased with, but it has two problematic consequences. First, it can confound a black constituency that has grown accustomed to receiving symbolic benefits with black faces and receiving political analyses that begin and end with race. Second, it provides ammunition for the charge that as a political matter blacks are "crybabies" who can never be satisfied ("You said you wanted a Negro, now it's got to be a *particular* Negro!?"), a charge that situates them comfortably in the *Time*-manufactured image of "moral defectives of the schoolyard jumping up and down on the social contract," and revives the "fear of a black planet."[7] Here an identity politics of race becomes a double-edged sword as Bush turns the expectations that it creates to his own advantage.

The advantages that can accrue to the Bush Administration from an identity politics of race are more immediately evident in New York City's Supreme Court-mandated city council redistricting.[8] After the U.S. Supreme Court found the city's Board of Estimate to be unconstitutional, the city set about the difficult task of expanding its city council from 35 to 51 seats. The process of redistricting has proven to be an object lesson in identity politics. The city's 1989 charter revision required that the fifteen-member commission that would draw up the new districts be made up of African-American, Latino, and Asian-American members in proportion to their population in the city. In practice the redistricting process has been nothing short of racial gerrymandering—the drawing of awkward and improbable district lines designed to ensure the election of at least twelve blacks and ten Latinos to the new city council.

Under the preclearance provisions of the Voting Rights Act of 1964 (as amended in 1982), electoral changes like those taking place in New York City must be approved by the U.S. Justice Department. One might think that the Bush Administration would take strong issue with this clear and obvious institutionalization of quotas in the electoral process, insisting on the inappropriateness of structurally mandating black and Latino seats on legislative bodies. On the contrary, the Bush Justice Department has thrown out four redistricting plans this year *because they did not concentrate black and Latino votes enough.*

The New York City case provides a clue to the Justice Department thinking. Recently the Justice Department voided the New York City redistricting plan because it "consistently disfavored" the city's Latino population. This ruling forces a *re*-redistricting that will likely postpone the new council elections that had been scheduled for the fall. At issue, among other things, was whether a black commissioner had included a predominantly black housing project in a mixed white-Latino district in order to ensure that a black would win the resulting council seat. This dispute resulted in the irony of "Latinos invoking the Voting Rights Act before a Republican administration in order to defend themselves against alleged discrimination at the hands of African-Americans."[9]

This irony is, however, perfectly consonant with GOP strategy to isolate race and consolidate Latino support. Throughout the country the Republican Party has offered technical support to black legislators seeking to construct or challenge redistricting plans in order to ensure safe minority seats. The Republicans recognize the concrete electoral benefits of racial isolation: They can concede these Bantustan districts to the Democrats and run much more competitively (often with the use of Willie Horton-type campaigning) in the overwhelmingly white districts that remain.

Up to this point it would seem that all of the negativism about identity politics makes good sense. Socially constructed common sense about identity politics functions to isolate race in the body politic, while the concrete practices of an identity politics of race have consequences that are profoundly problematic for progressive political possibilities.

While the dangers of identity politics are clear and compelling, there are some observers—like Bob Fisher and Joe Kling—who argue that the possibilities for "transformative popular mobilizations" rest, in part, on an *emphasis* on identity politics.[10] Kling and Fisher believe that

> with the shift of the classic forms of industrial production from the central cities of advanced capitalist states to peripheral regions and Third World nations, the structural bases for class-oriented mobilizations literally move out from under organized labor. Social movements related to such issues as race, gender, and the protection of neighborhood enclaves not only find space to emerge but become the primary arenas of defense and insurgency.[11]

While Fisher and Kling might justly be accused of trying to make a virtue out of necessity, there is value in the recognition of this necessity. Identity politics will invariably remain a persistent feature of our political landscape. Given the realities of African-American existence, the persistence of a hard or soft identity politics of race seems especially inevitable. This "hard" identity politics is manifest in the continuing hold that a variety of nationalisms have on a significant portion of African-Americans. The limited but very real appeal of black nationalists like Louis Farrakhan and the Reverend Al Sharpton has vibrant cultural echoes in the identity politics of rap music. Whether it is the color-coded feminism of women rappers like Queen Latifah and M.C. Lyte, the hard-core nationalism of Public Enemy, or the gangster visions of Ice T and NWA, Cornel West is surely at least partly correct to suggest that

> hip hop culture is based on the desire to create an artistic expression of race. It is conceived and conducted by a group of young black Americans rebelling against their marginalization, their invisibility that only became worse during the Reagan and Bush years. They don't have a movement to appeal to for help.*

Of course rappers and figures like Farrakhan and Sharpton cannot be said to speak for all African-Americans. They may only "represent" a small (but significant) minority. Nevertheless, their core

---

*Cornel West, "Charlie Parker Didn't Give a Damn," *New Perspectives Quarterly,* Summer 1991. On Farrakhan's appeal see Playthell Benjamin, "The Attitude Is the Message," *The Village Voice,* August 15, 1989. For an enormously useful discussion of rap and feminism see Tricia Rose, "Never Trust a Big Butt and a Smile," *Camera Obscura,* no. 23.

belief in the fundamental status of racial difference is pervasive throughout the U.S. black population. If Public Enemy and Louis Farrakhan represent a hard identity politics of race, then the much-remarked-upon fealty of black Americans to the Democratic Party surely represents, at least in part, a soft identity politics of race. For all that has been written by social scientists and others about strategic problems with the black allegiance to the Democrats, the phenomenon is best understood in terms of identity politics. For most black folks, Republicans are rich and white. It's really as simple as that.

While Fisher and Kling may be accused of wishful thinking, it seems to me that they are correct to state that in the 1990s local political mobilizations, "while circumscribed by the logic of accumulation," will be based on "race, gender, community and culturally oriented opposition to the encroachment of state and corporate bureaucracies on the quality of life."[12] The key questions raised by this point concern the form those mobilizations will take and the character of the opposition they may foster.

The point of this is to indicate that the complex, even contradictory, character of identity politics must be accounted for in efforts to develop a politically effective critical perspective. Identity politics will remain a persistent feature of our political landscape in part because it produces limited but real empowerment for its participants. Indeed, identity politics can be considered a source of limited but real opposition to "the encroachment of state and corporate bureaucracies on the quality of life." On the other hand, the relationship between race and identity politics is highly charged, and it creates serious symbolic and concrete problems. Our substantial societal appetite for images of black men misbehaving makes it especially easy to deploy instances of racial politics as symbols of social decay. Moreover, the calculations and logics that often underwrite an identity politics of race can unwittingly support strategies to reconfigure U.S. politics in a regressive way. *Given all of this, critical investigations of identity politics must also address questions concerning the construction and contestation of common sense.*

What follows is a brief consideration of a recent, celebrated episode of identity politics: the events surrounding the alleged abduction and sexual abuse of a young black woman, Tawana Brawley, in the fall of 1987. Space does not permit an analysis that will do justice to the complexities of this episode. In particular I will not be addressing the way in which this episode was at least as much about gender as race—its symbolic significance can be read as much in terms of the vulnerable, victimized black woman as in terms of misbehaving black men. The following analysis is intended to be suggestive of the ways in which spectacles of identity politics interact with the construction of common sense, and provocative of other analyses that can help to complete this picture.

NIGGERS OUT OF CONTROL

"Niggers out of control," Professor Mackey was saying at the back table at Edgar's Food Shop, "always have to be watched. The press has to cover them. It's a thing that scares the system more than anything else. It was true of Malcolm X. It's true of Farrakhan. It's true of Sharpton."[*]

On November 28, 1987, a teenage black woman was discovered in a plastic garbage bag in the parking lot of an apartment complex in Wappingers Falls, New York. The young woman had excrement smeared on her arms and legs and in her hair. Her blue jeans had been burned away at the crotch, in the seat, and along the inner thighs. Wads of cotton had been stuffed into her nostrils and her ears and racist and sexist slurs had been written on her chest and torso. Her name was Tawana Brawley.

Brawley's horrific story of abduction and sexual abuse by up to six white men exploded into the none-too-tranquil arena of New York racial politics. Journalists swarmed over the tiny town of Wappingers Falls. Politicians and law enforcement officials scrambled from Dutchess County to Albany to the Federal Bureau of Investiga-

---

[*] Robert McFadden et al., *Outrage: The Story Behind the Tawana Brawley Hoax* (New York: Bantam Books, 1990), p. 141. This quote and those that follow are taken from this account of the Tawana Brawley episode, written by six *New York Times* reporters who covered the story. The melodramatic introductions of the dramatis personae reveal much about the character of the lenses through which these professional observers view political events.

tion laboratories in Washington, D.C. Radical black activists and the region's "traditional" civil rights community sparred for the right to represent this travesty (and its victims) to the nation at large.

> Alton Maddox stood on the doorstep of 4-D Carmine Drive with a little briefcase in his hand. His hair was close-cropped, his face jowly and astute, and behind the glinting, wire-rimmed spectacles were the world's most solemn eyes. He introduced himself as a lawyer from New York City, but he came in like a revolutionary with a satchel of explosives.[13]

There were ugly insinuations that members of the local police force were involved in the abduction, perhaps even in conjunction with the Ku Klux Klan. A diabolical pattern seemed to be emerging. A year earlier, in Orange County, just across the Hudson River from Dutchess County, a twenty-year-old black man, Jimmy Lee Bruce Jr., had been choked to death outside a movie theater by two white off-duty police officers. Just the previous Sunday there had been reports of a police riot in the Orange County Jail. White guards in riot gear had allegedly "swarmed into the cellblock, swinging clubs and shouting racial slurs, blasting inmates with high-powered water hoses and driving them back with a snarling police dog."[14]

And, of course, there were the recent deaths of graffiti artist Michael Stewart and grandmother Eleanor Bumpurs at the hands of New York City police officers. The criminal trials in the infamous Howard Beach case—a black man practically lynched in a predominantly white section of New York City—were in the process of winding down. Under the circumstances it was just common sense for the Brawley family to rely on the men who, in that most recent case, had demonstrated their willingness to stand up to the white power structure and demand justice in the name of their people.

> It was a Saturday, December 5, a strange day, perhaps, to hold a news conference, but Al Sharpton knew that weekends were slow news days and that events on Saturday, in particular, were destined for prominent play in the high-circulation Sunday papers. It was always easy to grab a headline on Saturdays, when skeleton news teams were scratching around for stories. Sharpton had put out the word, and the reporters had dutifully appeared in droves, as they

always had after Howard Beach. From all over New York City, from far up the Hudson Valley, they were there at the United Auto Workers hall to hear what Sharpton had to say.[15]

Once engaged, the Brawley team—attorneys Alton Maddox and C. Vernon Mason, and the Reverend Al Sharpton—employed the tactics that had served them well in the Howard Beach case. They advised the Brawley family to withhold their cooperation in any official investigation until New York's Governor Cuomo consented to appoint a special prosecutor. And they took their case to the people. They organized "Days of Outrage" to protest racism—acts of civil disobedience that applied "protest tourniquets" to major traffic arteries in New York City.[16] They marshaled prominent figures like Bill Cosby and Mike Tyson to show public support for Brawley. They "did" the Phil Donahue Show and the Geraldo Rivera Show, and were omnipresent on New York's black radio station, WLIB. They did all that they could to impress upon the city, the state, and the nation that this was about more than Tawana Brawley. It was nothing less than the revival of "the movement." And they would be taking no prisoners this time.

> Louis Farrakhan stepped out of the automobile into the bright wintry sunlight, and shouts of excitement broke from the people in waves. For a few moments, the crowd outside the Newburgh church forgot Al Sharpton and Tawana Brawley and even the rally. All eyes watched the minister of the Nation of Islam, the black man whites feared like death. He stood there momentarily, slender and elegant, the sunlight glinting on his gold-wire spectacles, while his entourage of icy-eyed bodyguards rushed ahead, clearing the way. The vast throng divided like extras in a Hollywood epic, and the revolution's executioner moved through them.[17]

They intended to focus an unrelenting spotlight on the deadly consequences of the racism endemic in U.S. society. This comported closely with their images of themselves: Sharpton the "transforming" black leader, and Maddox the lifelong opponent of whites and their racist ways. "I think," Sharpton insisted, "that in an era where almost daily black kids are being beaten or killed and no one is doing time for it . . . we have to yell as loud as we can that we are being bru-

279

talized and killed in New York, until somebody comes and makes New York deal with its image."[18] For Sharpton and Maddox, the fact that black lives could be taken with impunity meant that in spite of the Civil War, in spite of the Emancipation Proclamation, in spite of the Civil Rights Act of 1965, blacks in this country were really in no better condition than they had been in 1857, when the Supreme Court of the United States proclaimed that Negroes "had no rights and privileges but such as those who held the power and the government might choose to grant them." This was why Maddox proclaimed, "Every time I go to court, I'm trying to dismantle the Dred Scott decision. All my cases are just camouflaged Dred Scott."[19]

> **Moderate and progressive activists complained that the Brawley theatrics were without practical strategic or tactical purpose.**

These efforts to jump-start a new black movement caused as much frustration and anger as excitement. Everyday New Yorkers were incensed (as only everyday New Yorkers can be incensed) over the disruptions of their intricately patterned rush hours. Moderate and progressive activists complained that the Brawley theatrics were without practical strategic or tactical purpose and diverted attention from the issues that had the most real effect on the quality of life of New York's black residents, issues such as the municipal budget.[20] Progressive journalists, writing in *The Village Voice*, attacked Sharpton as a "hustler" and a "flimflam man" who was attempting a brand of "leadership by television" in which "hype is preferable to history, and rhetoric to theory."[21]

Ultimately the Brawley team's tactics degenerated into ugly, outrageous outbursts. Providing no evidence whatsoever, they accused a Dutchess County assistant district attorney, Steven Pagones, of being one of Brawley's attackers. They compared Mario Cuomo to the notorious Southern segregationists George Wallace and Lester Maddox. They compared State Attorney General Robert Abrams, appointed by Cuomo as special prosecutor in the case, to Adolph Hitler, and they claimed that he had masturbated over pictures of Tawana Brawley.

On October 6, 1988, a New York State grand jury issued a 170-page report concluding that "there is nothing in regard to Tawana Brawley's appearance on November 28 that is inconsistent with this condition having been self-inflicted." In other words, the grand jury had concluded—based on 6,000 pages of testimony from 180 witnesses and on 250 exhibits—that the Tawana Brawley episode was a long, tragic hoax.

There are many in New York who do not now and probably never will accept the grand jury's findings. It is impossible to be certain about what did or didn't happen to Tawana Brawley. We *can* be certain, however, that the consequences of the grand jury's findings for Brawley, New York, and the contested terrain that "race" constitutes in our polity are not easily erased. Images of these events remain etched in memories both individual and collective, and their wide dissemination in the media ensures that they will have lasting implications for the ways in which many Americans think about the relationships between race, gender, crime, justice, and politics in contemporary U.S. society.

The existence of these lasting implications makes it worth pondering the kinds of challenges that these events pose for all of us. There are, of course, direct and obvious challenges of a moral and political character. It is easy and perhaps necessary to denounce both the rhetorical excesses and the brazen cynicism that Sharpton, Maddox, and Mason brought to the task of "representing" Tawana Brawley. Their scurrilous allegations and accusations did real and probably lasting damage to innocent people like Steven Pagones and Robert Abrams. Many would also argue that the general tenor of their campaign did real and lasting damage to the civic culture of New York City. Perhaps more important, the three men quite clearly exploited the very real tragedy of Tawana Brawley for purposes with an at best indirect, tenuous connection to her circumstances.

The measure of success enjoyed by the Brawley advisors in mobilizing black working-class sentiment also poses serious political challenges, principally involving the development of alternatives to racial animus and resentment as the bases for black working-class political mobilizations. Indeed, during the Brawley episode a day-long conference was held at Medgar Evers College in Brooklyn under the auspices of the Center for Law and Social Justice. The conferees were attempting to "reorient" activist pressure away from racial violence and toward fiscal and employment issues. As Peter Williams of the Center said:

> It is more dramatic to speak about police killings or racial violence. People have to understand, however, that the budget is the basis for government and until we make our concerns known, we cannot hope to improve our quality of life.[22]

I think the Brawley episode also poses an important challenge to our capacity to clearly and imaginatively analyze and assess "identity politics." This is a challenge as much to our political imaginations as it is to our political understandings. In a very real sense these vivid scenes of "black leaders behaving badly" *are* identity politics. Political spectacles of race like the Tawana Brawley episode and other Sharptonesque productions play an enormous role in providing the "video at eleven" for our mental narratives about identity politics. Inasmuch as we "see" (as opposed to read, or write, or think) identity politics in this manner, that is to say *as political performances*, we are "*seeing* through political spectacles."

Most people focus on the challenge that these spectacles pose to our political understanding. They think that political performances distort and refract, obscuring, concealing, or exaggerating some *real* play of powers and interests. Many commentators on the Brawley episode took this position. Optimists among these folks believe that we can correct for this distortion. They believe that given the proper framework we can "see *through*" political performances in the sense of demystifying or decoding them. These are the folks for whom "history" is preferable to "hype," and "theory" preferable to "rhetoric."

Less attention is generally paid to the challenge that these spectacles pose to our political *imaginations.* Our political imaginations can become colonized by these vivid images. Powerful spectacles of racial politics can become irresistible metaphors for *all* identity politics, as I've suggested above. When this happens, the limited but important value of identity politics can easily be overshadowed by the mass-mediated bulk of an Al Sharpton.*

---

*Michael Rogin has written persuasively of the power of vivid racial images to colonize our political imaginations. See *"Ronald Reagan," the Movie and Other Episodes in Political Demonology* (Berkeley: University of California Press, 1987).

SEEING THROUGH POLITICAL SPECTACLES

Michael Rogin and Murray Edelman are the political scientists who have done the most useful work on the construction of political spectacles.[23] Edelman has primarily been concerned with the general functioning of political news as a political spectacle, while Rogin has considered the specific function of public spectacles in consolidating U.S. imperial politics.

Both writers focus on the capacity of political spectacles to buttress established concentrations of power. Although neither seriously considers the counterhegemonic possibilities of political spectacles, both provide insights that support such a consideration. Edelman recognizes that there are different spectacles for different groups of people, and that because they are constructions of language they are open to different interpretations.[24] Noting that political language creates an "endless chain of ambiguous associations and constructions that offer wide potentialities for interpretation and for manipulation," Edelman insists that

> political understanding lies in awareness of the range of meanings political phenomena present and in appreciation of their potentialities for generating change in actions and beliefs.[25]

Rogin offers useful thinking on the particular functioning of race in the history of U.S. political spectacles. According to Rogin, political spectacles operate through a process of *displaying* and *forgetting*. They display "enabling myths of American history" that "the culture can no longer unproblematically embrace," including the organization of U.S. politics around racial domination. The display of these myths affords powerful satisfaction of collective social desires for "meaning-giving order." But these myths must also be forgotten because forgetting allows the "repetition of pleasures that, if consciously sustained in memory over time, would have to be called into question." Describing the amnesiac component of political spectacles, Rogin writes that they "open a door the viewer wants to close so that it can be opened again."[26]

Display-and-forget functions through the presentation of practices, symbols, and images that are disconnected from their historical roots.

Political spectacles operate through a process of displaying and forgetting.

In this way political spectacles can operate as covert instruments for the political marshaling and organizing of previously acceptable but currently problematic desires. For example, Rogin shows how during the Reagan presidency and the Bush presidential campaign political spectacles utilizing Willie Horton and Clint Eastwood helped to organize a culturally repudiated but historically and socially potent racism in the service of executive ambitions.

Using Rogin's framework for the functioning of race in political spectacles and Edelman's insights into the range of meanings available through which to interpret spectacles, we can imagine the possibility of there being some counterhegemonic significance in the spectacles of Sharptonian politics.

As "counterhegemonic" spectacles, Sharpton's performances contest dominant social narratives of an ordered political and ethical progress in racial affairs. This assertion of progress is encoded and disseminated in films like Alan Parker's *Mississippi Burning* and shows like the PBS television series "Eyes on the Prize." While these presentations do retail important historical material to historiographically ignorant and/or indifferent audiences, they also tend to underline the *historical* character of this material. They are period pieces, and their depictions of open hatred and violence against blacks are combined with datable cultural artifacts like clothing and architecture to emphasize a fundamental discontinuity between that period and our own.

This discontinuity is understood to result from the "gains of the sixties." According to this account, the Civil Rights Act of 1964 and the Voting Rights Act of 1965 marked the death of the most important forms of racial injustice in the United States. While inequities undoubtedly remain, they are best understood as correctable viruses in an otherwise sound social network.

If hegemonic political spectacles "display and forget" the historical organization of U.S. politics around racial domination, the "counterhegemonic" political spectacles of Sharptonian politics display and remember (indeed, display in order to remember) that same narrative. The display of the *dis*enabling myth of racial domination provokes (and politicizes) social desires within African-American populations for security, solidarity, racial exceptionalism, and revenge-as-justice.

The spectacles of the Tawana Brawley episode displayed-in-order-to-remember the political modalities of the sixties insurgency. Sharpton, Maddox, and Mason framed the events that precipitated those spectacles in terms that focused attention on the continuity of racial injustice and oppression in this country. Hence their comparison of Mario Cuomo to George Wallace and Lester Maddox. Hence Sharpton's insistence that "New York is now the Mississippi and Alabama of the eighties." Hence the comparison of Tawana Brawley to Rosa Parks. Further, under Sharpton's leadership, the spectacles took the form of protest marches and "Days of Outrage" that invite immediate comparison to the most telegenic moments of the civil rights movement.

And, of course, Sharpton and his supporters characterized Brawley's alleged victimization in terms of the history of forcible sexual relations between white men and black women. This history is common knowledge within black communities. The team that reported on the Brawley case for *The New York Times* reported this reaction of an older African-American upon hearing of Brawley's charges: "I'd be a rich man if I had a hundred dollars for every time a white man tried to have sex with one of my sisters. . . . Time and time again this happened all over that South I grew up in."[27] In this context, Tawana Brawley is simply the latest in an unbroken tradition of black female victims of white male lust and violence.

I am not suggesting that any of these stories about the African-American past are historically accurate or politically unproblematic. In counterhegemonic spectacles, the myths and realities of racial domination are contested through countermyths of racial solidarity. The empowering capability of identity politics involves the production of these stories, these counternarratives.

The Brawley episode provided, at best, a brief moment of empowerment. This was a moment of mobilization and opposition, but both were profoundly limited for at least two reasons. First of all, many of the developments supported an especially narrow construction of race and racial leadership. The rhetoric and behavior of

Sharpton, Maddox, and Mason consistently constructed Tawana Brawley in such a way as to effectively foreclose possibilities for public black female agency.

285

Sharpton, Maddox, and Mason consistently constructed Tawana Brawley in such a way as to effectively foreclose possibilities for public black female agency. The tendency to situate Tawana Brawley in a tradition (dating back to slavery) of black women victimized by white men allowed her three advisors to enact a model of political leadership as the assertion of manly prerogatives.

The "moment" of empowerment and opposition was also brief because the political spectacles that helped to generate it were (and are) quite easily contextualized by the dominant constructions of common sense that I referred to earlier. Whatever insurgent energies Al Sharpton and his cronies may generate are quickly overwhelmed when Sharpton's image is used as a part of stories that attempt to reconfigure U.S. politics in a more reactionary direction. Sharpton can be, in other words, a perfect example of the "outburst of minority assertiveness" that, for Woodward, puts "at stake the American tradition of a shared commitment to common ideals."

YO! NYT RAPS

When Professor Mackey says, "Niggers out of control always have to be watched," he is referring to the surveillance activities of the state. "Watching," of course, can refer to consumption as well as surveillance. In this context the phrase can be understood as a reference to our societal appetite for images of black men misbehaving. This is, as I've mentioned, an appetite that is informed by the vocabularies proffered by television and film—the eroticization and commodification of these images on the evening news, television dramatic programs, and, especially, MTV and its spillover into mass advertising. In my description of the Tawana Brawley episode I've included the passages with which the *New York Times* reporters "introduced" Sharpton, Maddox, and Farrakhan in part because these passages exemplify this fetishization of black male misbehavior almost to the point of caricature. Indeed, the following description of Al Sharpton could quite easily be the story board for an LL Cool J video:

> Sharpton was the whole circus—part lion, part barker, part clown, and part Houdini. He loved to roar and bellow, mug for laughs, juggle fact with fancy, and delight crowds with slick illusions and

vanishing acts. Just when exasperated critics thought they had him bound and gagged, padlocked in a steamer trunk at the bottom of a water tank, he would pop up again, waving to his fans, not even wet.[28]

This fetishization can help to illustrate the way in which images of black male misbehavior are (if the *SR* editors will permit me an Althusserian lapse) always already stuffed with social meaning. It is as "natural" to associate these images with the eroticized, commodified images that permeate our popular cultures as it is to associate them with the narratives of disruption that pervade our political history.

Neither association is univocal. The dialogic character of common sense must always be kept in mind. The association, for example, between rap music and black activism is one that black activists attempt to use to their advantage. Indeed, the case of rap music can illustrate the process by which common sense is both constructed and contested. One construction of common sense results from an alignment of identity politics of race with Cornel West's notion of rap music as a "desire to create an artistic expression of race" to combat alienation and disenfranchisement. It is, of course, a quite different common sense about identity politics that gets constructed when the Brawley advisors are aligned with the stupid but seemingly widespread notion of rap as "the blues with a lobotomy."

This begins to suggest the parameters within which dominant constructions of common sense about race are contested. Social constructions with greater social power—the idea of rap as blues with a lobotomy, or that of multiculturalism as portending social decay—contest with social constructions of less social power—the idea of rap as legitimate and important social protest, or that of multiculturalism as an important and sophisticated pedagogical advance—in the effort to contextualize spectacles of identity politics.

The power and reach of these broader social discourses—rap as nihilistic garbage, the mass media assault on multiculturalism and "political correctness"—make it exceedingly difficult for the empowering and oppositional moments of identity politics to expand. Not only do these discourses support concrete political developments—

such as the consolidation of reactionary electoral blocs—that are inimical to empowerment and opposition, but also they discourage the kind of critical interventions that are necessary if the limitations of identity politics are to be overcome.

A critical perspective on identity politics is indispensable. Episodes of identity politics are both inevitable and highly problematic. These episodes can hinder immediate political prospects by disrupting the possibilities for progressive coalitions. They can also inadvertently conspire in the construction of a broad common sense reaction that helps right-wing forces to effect reactionary political configurations. With respect to the construction of this broad common sense, race is especially important. Our broad societal appetite for images of black men misbehaving—as well as our tradition of narratives of racially motivated social disruption—make racial politics an especially magnetic trope for arguments about identity politics. Given the role that strategies of racial isolation are likely to play in efforts to consolidate conservative electoral blocs in the nineties, this "common sense" cannot be ignored.

During the writings of this essay several people—Sam Crane, L.A. Kauffman, George Lipsitz, Rick Matthews, Brian Powers, Mark Reinhardt, and the San Francisco Bay Area *SR* Collective—generously provided critical encouragement. Regina Kunzel did that *and* held my hand through the rougher moments of composition.

NOTES

1   Clifford Geertz, "Common Sense as a Cultural System" in *Local Knowledge: Further Essays in Interpretive Anthropology* (New York: Basic Books, 1983), p. 75.

2   "Busybodies and Crybabies: What's Happening to the American Character," *Time,* August 12, 1991, p. 16.

3   "Who Are We?" *Time,* July 8, 1991, p. 17.

4   See Michael Paul Rogin, *Ronald Reagan, the Movie and Other Episodes in Political Demonology* (Berkeley: University of California Press, 1987) especially chapter 7, "'The Sword Became a Flashing Vision': D.W. Griffith's *The Birth of a Nation*' and Ronald T. Takaki, *Iron Cages: Race and Culture in 19th Century America* (Seattle: University of Washington Press, 1979).

5   On this point see Thomas Byrne Edsall with Mary D. Edsall, "Race," *The Atlantic Monthly,* May 1991, pp. 53-86, and Harold Meyerson, "A Politics in America?: Populism, Race, and Apathy" *Dissent,* Winter 1991, pp. 37-41.

6   See Meyerson, "A Politics in America?"; Edsall and Edsall, "Race"; and Thomas
    Byrne Edsall, "The Hidden Role of Race," *The New Republic*, July 30 & August 6,
    1990.

7   *"Busybodies and Crybabies,"* p. 15.

8   See Charles Lane, "Ghetto Chic," *The New Republic*, August 12, 1991.

9   Ibid., p. 16.

10 Bob Fisher and Joe Kling, "Popular Mobilization in the 1990's: Prospects for the
    New Social Movements," *New Politics*, Winter 1991.

11 Ibid., p. 75.

12 Ibid., p. 76.

13 Robert McFadden et al., *Outrage: The Story Behind the Tawana Brawley Hoax*
    (New York: Bantam Books, 1990), p. 84.

14 Ibid., p. 66.

15 Ibid., p. 115.

16 "Protest Against Racism Disrupts N.Y. Rush Hour," *The New York Times*, Tuesday,
    December 22, 1987, B-10; "11 Held As Rights Protest Halts La Guardia Traffic,"
    The New York Times, Thursday, January 28, 1988, B-3.

17 McFadden, *Outrage*, p. 134.

18 Ibid., p. 109.

19 Ibid., p. 84.

20 Maria Laurino, "Tough or Fluff: Stopping Traffic for Race, Then and Now," *The
    Village Voice*, January 12, 1988, p. 11; Howard W. French, "Minority Groups Are
    Urged to Focus on Economic Issues," *The New York Times*, Sunday, January 31,
    1988, p. 37.

21 William Bastone, Joe Conason, Jack Newfield, and Tom Robbins, "The Hustler:
    How Al Sharpton Conned the Movement, the Media, and the Government," *The
    Village Voice*, February 2, 1988, p. 17; Playthell Benjamin, "Jive at Five: How Big
    Al and the Bully Boys Bogarted the Movement," *The Village Voice*, July 19, 1988,
    p. 25.

22 French, "Minority Groups Are Urged to Focus on Economic Issues," p. 37.

23 Michael Rogin, "'Make My Day!': Spectacle as Amnesia in Imperial Politics,"
    Representations, vol. 29 (Winter 1990); Murray Edelman, *Constructing the Politi-
    cal Spectacle* (Chicago: University of Chicago Press, 1988).

24 Edelman, *Constructing the Political Spectacle*, pp. 94, 110.

25 Ibid., pp. 111, 123.

26 Rogin, "'Make My Day!'" pp. 105-106.

27 McFadden, *Outrage*, p. 69.

28 Ibid., p. 107.

THE REPRESSED COMMUNITY

Locating the new communitarianism

Richard T. Ford

Discussed in this essay

The Spirit of Community: Rights, Responsibilities, and the Communitarian Agenda, Amitai Etzioni, New York: Crown Publishers

The Good Society, Robert Bellah, Richard Madsen, William Sullivan, Ann Swidler, and Steven Tipton, New York: Knopf

Sexy Dressing: Etc., Duncan Kennedy, Cambridge: Harvard University Press

"Join us," implores Amitai Etzioni in *The Spirit of Community*, a book that ends with a "communitarian platform" and an address where interested readers can send their comments and queries. And many have joined. Prominent academics and public officials have signed on to the communitarian platform. Communitarian organizations have sprouted like crabgrass on suburban lawns, advocating an emphasis on responsibility that, they claim, has ethical implications for issues from the homeless to health care. The Clinton administration reflects the influence of communitarian thought: proposals for national service and of course national health care can be seen as a part of a vision of the nation coming together as a community while the emphasis on responsibility (manifested in largely empty rhetoric about "rights with responsibilities" but also in Clinton's Nixon-in-China reform of the welfare system) arguably reflects a vision of a national community defining its ethical boundaries.

That community signifies a normative ideal as much as a tangible reality is not new to Americans. The courts have recognized "community standards" as an appropriate rationale for legal restrictions on speech and behavior, upholding laws judged repressive by more cosmopolitan standards when applied in a small town or rural setting. Distinctive racial and cultural groups refer to themselves as "communities," defined as much by shared identity and social norms as by location. What *is* new is the articulation of community as a concept that stands alone, without any specific physical location or normative boundaries. This is what arguably binds Etzioni's colloquial focus on shared values and "rights and responsibilities" with Robert Bellah's examination of the role of social institutions in *The Good Society* and with Michael Sandel's critique of political liberalism.

Communitarian political philosophy and social theory argues that individuals are not the primary social or moral agents in the world, rather social groups or "communities" are. This ontological insight is descriptive rather than prescriptive: This fact tells us little about what types of communities we ought to have or what consequences communities have for social practice. If communitarianism is to have consequences beyond the world of academic debate, communitarians must begin to define which types of communities are salient and which types are desirable.

This is less a gripe with the political philosophers than with those who would seek to apply communitarianism to questions of policy. To ask philosophical communitarianism, an ideal theory, to identify what types of communities are useful is to demand that it take on a separate project. But popular communitarianism aspires to apply communitarianism to specific problems in the real world: it aspires to be what Margaret Jane Radin calls nonideal theory, "a normative theory that takes into account the uncertainties and complexities of actual practice." We are justified in asking those who claim that community is an ideal which can guide legal and policy reform to provide some framework with which we can begin to define community. Few would argue against the value of community in the abstract. But community as a norm is like freedom or equality—it means something important to almost everyone, but it also means something different to almost everyone.

Like freedom and equality, community comes only at a cost. Communities are by nature coercive and exclusive. If they aspired to be purely voluntary they would be liberal associations (they would also, like liberal associations, never achieve

Amitai Etzioni
Bill Denison

that aspiration), and communitarianism would be a form of liberalism. If they were not exclusive they would not be communities but rather the universe, and communitarianism would be a universalism, a humanism, or a totalitarianism. Popular communitarianism tends to shift between a liberal voluntarism, a variety of exclusive parochialisms, (localism, nationalism, cultural or political solidarism) and a type of universalism. It elides the difficulties of each by shifting to a justification that applies only to a different normative theory: thus communitarianism pretends to be as nurturing as a cultural solidarism or a narrow localism, as non-coersive as liberalism, and as inclusive as humanism.

• • •

Communitarianism emerges at a particular and crucial moment in American history: at the end of the Cold War when a global economic and political order modeled on Western democratic capitalism seems possible, when the enemy that defined America's self-image and its foreign (and much of its domestic) policy like a photographic negative has become merely one of many theaters of conflict. Francis Fukuyama's declaration of the end of history, while premature (who knows what the future holds?) marks an opportunity and a crisis for America. The collapse of the Soviet Union seems to leave the world "safe for democracy" and for capitalism, but at the same time it has left a void with severe economic and existential consequences. Without an emminent threat, the classic justification for large-scale military expenditures and a domestic security apparatus vanishes—the collapse of the Southwestern aerospace economies followed hard on the heels of the collapse of the Eastern bloc. Without an ideological enemy, the role of America abroad and the identity of Americans at home are left undefined.

Communitarianism attempts to respond to the alienation inherent in liberal politics and, as the personal bonds of marriage and family, workplace, church and civic life dissipate, in contemporary society in general. Popular communitarianism is a reaction to political liberalism, but it goes beyond say, Michael Sandel's critique to express a yearning for identity. As Michael Walzer suggests in *What It Means to Be an American*:

Liberalism . . . is a hard politics because it offers so few emotional rewards; the liberal state is not a home for its citizens; it lacks warmth and intimacy. And so contemporary dissatisfaction takes the form of a yearning for political

community, passionate affirmation, explicit patriotism. These . . . desires . . . leave us open to . . . a willful effort to build social cohesion and political enthusiasm from above, as it were, through the use of state power.

The communitarian movement rejects the single-minded pursuit of individual goals to insist that meaningful thought and action must occur within communities. This is an important insight: as Etzioni correctly argues, the democratic experiment cannot succeed without a commitment to collective action on the part of the citizenry, and as Robert Bellah points out in *The Good Society,* the myth that society consists of a series of uncoordinated individual projects that mesh according to the laws of economics has damaged and continues to damage the institutions that make economic well-being and social harmony possible. In place of individualism, popular communitarians would promote an *esprit de corps*, a common cause defined by a set of "core values." (Indeed this focus takes precedent over concrete or tangible collective action. For example, Etzioni laments the breakdown of the family but offers few concrete reforms that might strengthen it, his prescriptions for promoting responsibility emphasize the "moral voice" and a change in individual attitudes more than socially responsible public policy. He spends a chapter outlining a moral education through which children will be taught to respect society's "core values" without ever clearly defining those values.)

Etzioni's communitarianism appeals to the sense that social alienation and fragmentation have reached an apogee, that "community" is an ideal that was recently lost and can therefore be regained:

In the fifties we had a clear set of values that spoke to most Americans. . . . These values were often discriminatory against women . . . and against minorities, from blacks to Jews. . . . In the sixties all these voices and the values they spoke for were deeply challenged—as they ought to have been. . . . The problem is that the waning of traditional values was not followed by a solid affirmation of new values. . . . We do require a set of social virtues, some settled values, that we as a community endorse and actively affirm.

Even as he recognizes the historical need for race- and gender-focused social change, Etzioni here joins a number of mainstream critics who fault "multi-culturalism" or "identity politics" for dividing the nation against itself. He suggests that communitarianism provides an alternative. While multi-cultural identity politics emphasizes the importance of group-based identity (multiculturalism and cultural pluralism stresses race and ethnicity; feminism, gender; and the activist homosexual politics, sexual preference, as the defining and driving force behind a new politics), communitarianism stresses the importance of a community that *transcends* these specific identities, joining the various fragments of the American community. Rather than a politics defined by a shared racial, gender, or sexual *identity,* it is a shared set of normative *values* that define communitarian politics. Communitarianism stresses the need for baseline principles on which we can all agree, shared values which can free us from the swamp of relativism and the tempest of pluralism (those hobgoblins of like minds). But if the community in communitarianism cannot be the black community, the feminist community, the gay com-

munity, if communitarianism is a reaction to identity politics, it may be less a rejection than a reformulation, an identity politics with a different identity.

How different, for example, is the tendency that Cornel West criticizes in *Race Matters* to define an "authentic" and monolithic African-American identity that marginalizes and "attack[s] black women and black gay men and lesbians" from Etzioni's claims about the authenticity of community "core values," claims that necessarily marginalize dissenters from those values? In the case of identity pol-

> **It's not that Afro-centrists must explain away the existence of "westernized" blacks but that they must constantly assert their existence**

itics, it is not the idea of politics based on identity but a wrongheaded definition of identity, the insistence on a singular "authentic" or essential identity, that proves problematic. In order to assert an authentic self, a crude form of identity politics insists on consensus and sameness, often but not always based on a notion of biological or genetic commonality. This insistence involves more than ignoring the claims of dissenters and marginalized subgroups, it requires representing those claims as dishonest or illegitimate. Dissenting or marginalized "sub-groups" are then (re)presented as exceptions that prove the rule of authentic consensus: thus the claims of militant Afro-centrists that non-Afrocentric blacks have sold out or *denied* their true selves, by "difference feminists" that the unique feminine voice exists but has been *repressed* by women seeking status in a patriarchal society. Ultimately, the *authentic* identity is a semiotic illusion made possible by the existence of the marginalized groups: it's not that Afro-centrists must explain away the existence of "westernized" blacks but instead that they must constantly *assert* their existence, as evidence of what Afro-centrists stand against and ultimately as evidence of their relevance.

A lot hinges on the definition of community, as Robert Bellah recognizes in writing that " 'community' can be misunderstood if interpreted too narrowly." Bellah's focus on social institutions provides a pragmatic definition for community. Unlike Bellah, Etzioni never provides a grounded account of what he means by community, conveniently shifting between the idea of a national community and descriptions of small, local communities (such as Palo Alto, California.) Etzioni's attempt to put flesh on the bones of community posits an unlikely consensus around "shared values." On this view, the problem in contemporary politics is not that citizens actually disagree on fundamental questions of the good, as democratic theorists such as James Madison and Isaiah Berlin have believed, instead it is that our fundamental agreement is hidden from us. From the need for shared values Etzioni moves to the *existence* of shared values, neatly eliding the potentially coercive nature of a political community to those who may not share its vision of the good. For Etzioni those of us who share common values constitute a silent *majority*, cowed in the face of vocal few. The spirit of community is not

absent or contested, it is denied or *repressed* by a lunatic fringe of radical individualists, radical "hyphenated Americans" and multiculturalists, radical feminists, and plain old radical radicals who have captured the discourse while most of America either slept or cowered in fear of the label "politically incorrect":

> there is . . . a set of shared core values . . . far from following a few radical leaders, most members of American minority groups strongly favor core American values, despite their European origin . . . this is surprising only to the extremists.

Etzioni argues against a moderate but still dangerous multiculturalism that "suggests there will be many Americas—a black nation, a Hispanic hemisphere, a Native American country, and so on" and a more extreme multiculturalism that proposes "that if there must be a set of overarching values that bind [us] into one society, they need not be Western or European." Etzioni's insistence on *European* values is puzzling unless one understands Europe as *opposed* to multicultural America (indeed he characterizes the core values as "European" only when he discusses multiculturalism). The image of Europe as culturally pure and socially unified is meaningful only as opposed to the image of America as philistine, culturally fragmented, and radically individualist. As Duncan Kennedy points out in the "Radical Intellectuals" essay in *Sexy Dressing*:

> The intellectuals' picture of American culture is very much constructed by way of contrast with Western European culture. . . . When we say the United States is materialist, individualist, and philistine, we mean to contrast it

with Denmark or Italy. We think of Denmark and Italy as relatively spiritual, communal, and cultured. . . . The communal dimension means that Europeans . . . maintain networks of mutual support and caring, familial and geographic.

Here Europe functions as a stand-in, a society against which American multiculturalism is rhetorically placed, to suggest a unifying identity based on historical kinship, a cultural Eden. Although Etzioni must discredit multiculturalism in order to legitimate his community based on shared European values, at the same time he must point to multiculturalism's presence just outside his community in order to give it the illusion of real weight. The existence of this community depends on the groups that it excludes. What Etzioni's community shares is a hostility to multiculturalism and feminism and a belief that American cultural heterogeneity stands between them and a spirit of community. Without these internal/external threats, there would be no community but only Walzer's liberal state and therefore no identity, no sense of belonging or common purpose. The marginal insider/outsider becomes not a minor inconsistency to be explained away but a full-blown obsession whose definition, interrogation, and delegitimation becomes a defining ritual of the community.

• • •

This is not to say that communitarianism is *inherently* riddled with the contradictions that stem from shared values, just as identity politics need not and often does not assert a problematic "authentic" identity. Many articulations of identity politics recognize that identity is contested and unstable but still insist on its salience. Likewise, communitarianism could assert the salience of some notion of community while recognizing its multiple, undefined, and therefore contested nature. But rather than an *alternative* to identity politics that avoids the difficult questions of inclusion and exclusion, communitarianism is, in this sense, a *variant* of identity politics.

Communitarianism is the identity politics of moderate and liberal white America

Communitarianism is (in practice, if not in theory) the identity politics of moderate and liberal white America. Its appeal is to those who cannot unite around a unifying history of subordination and who do not embrace the explicitly reactionary politics of the nationalist new right or the anti-social extremes of white supremacy. In a self-fashioned Greek epic, the communitarian seeks to reestablish order at home and thereby to secure his own identity, while confronted by implacable enemies: by man-hating feminist radicals who threaten the structure of the family and mock romantic love, by militant, race-conscious nationalists who spit on the cultural traditions of America and challenge the laws on which the republic was founded, and by embarrassing reactionaries who confirm the most extreme convictions of the former two groups. Many Americans experience much of contemporary social conflict, especially cultural conflict, as the betrayal of Agamemnon even as they hope for the self affirming victory of Odysseus.

The nostalgia for a pure and centered community, for a civic home, a society that reflects one's own (and ultimately *only* one's own) values and therefore also one's own *identity,* is a powerful impetus for the rhetoric of community. The drive for a type of cultural purity, ultimately a drive for a centered and unified *identity,* lurks in the wings of many contemporary American social and political movements: the nationalist strand of multiculturalism, the millennial political agenda of the religious right, and many of the popular articulations of communitarianism, which replace a call for a dialogue about priorities and policy with an insistence on defining a core of shared values.

The Political Geography of the Global Village

The desire for an authentic community propels a corollary drive to discover an authentic communal location, free from the conflict of contemporary social life. Rather than grounding community in the cities, towns, and neighborhoods in which we live, the quest for pure identity/community is often rooted in a mythical social history and a *symbolic* geography; it is for an identity rooted in a unadulterated homeland. More than for a history, it is the search for a *place* of belonging, the Freudian womb of unmediated visceral connection, the anti-America. The retracing of family lineage is perhaps the most unabashed manifestation of this desire, an innocent enough pastime. But one marvels at how many Americans are descendants of European royalty (at first blush it seems that the royal families stayed in Europe and the peasantry emigrated),

how direct the connection between the democracies of ancient Greece and modern Europe is supposed to be (no one, it seems, wishes to lay claim to the fascism and totalitarianism of painfully recent memory, to say nothing of the centuries of feudalism and monarchy on the continent—except of course, to claim royal blood), how many Americans are descendants of Egyptian and Ethiopian nobility (two nations whose populations escaped the brutalities of the African slave trade). Geography is more than destiny, it is identity as well.

Lower transportation costs and depressed wages make production in the U.S. less expensive than in the third world

This imagery is very much at odds with the complexities of contemporary society, and the tangible landscape of the contemporary world. Demographic projections indicate that, by the turn of the millenium, more of the world's population will live in cities than in rural areas, while the megapolis already dominates the economic and political life of the (so called) first and third worlds. The political-geographic image of first and third worlds does not capture the reality of the international megapolis with its international capital, international culture, and international combination of class and labor demographics: to an increasing degree the conditions of affluence and cultural sophistication associated with the first world and those of poverty, deprivation, and isolation associated with the third exist literally side by side within every major city. As a consequence, the culture of affluence is only tangentially (and decreasingly) that of the West or of any identifiable geographic origin: capital follows its own logic and elites converse in a highbrow internationalist culture, an Esperanto driven by mobile capital and the expanding mass media.

As the mobility of capital and boundlessness of communication threaten to undermine national loyalty (to say nothing of the loyalties of family, race, and religion) we find an equal and opposite reaction in provincialism, the nostalgia of the whole and the one in which the intrusion of the global precipitates the cultural defense of the village. Although the conventional wisdom has it that internationalization will promote a cultural cosmopolitanism across the globe, bringing both commitment to free expression and tolerance and also a breakdown in strong community ties and norms, there are significant counter trends. Worldwide, societies have managed to combine free economic markets with a heavily regulated social sphere: the global mobility of capital and the shared values of a village.

Last year's debate over the North American Free Trade Agreement was perhaps the most public expression of concern over the permeability of American national boundaries. Most economists agreed that the actual impact of NAFTA on the American economy, positive or negative, is likely to be small, yet for weeks we heard little else on the evening news than the giant sucking sound of thousands of hours (many of them paid for with American tax dollars) spent debating the

issue. Ultimately NAFTA's most profound significance was symbolic, not economic; the question that lurked behind every trade unionist's speech, behind the endorsement of five ex-presidents, behind Ross Perot's wearying populist polemics, behind the studied and cautious support of political economists, was that of national integrity: was America, meaning American businesses, American wealth, the American economy, to be for Americans? Didn't we the people have a choice not to enter a brave new world of horizontal exchange on an international level and vertical stratification at home, a world where one could not tell the difference between Los Angeles and Mexico City, between Seattle and Vancouver?

The debate over NAFTA was symbolic because these questions had long since been answered in the negative. The defeat of NAFTA would hardly have slowed the flight of capital to low-wage labor markets and deregulated production sites. Indeed, the disquieting fact that no one on either side of the NAFTA debate acknowledged was that for access to such inexpensive conditions, most American business did not need to head south of the border—such labor markets exist in every large *American* city. Indeed, in some cases, lower transportation costs combined with depressed wages make production in the states less expensive than in the third world. In an essay entitled "It All Comes Together in Los Angeles," urban theorist Edward Soja notes that "local shops in Los Angeles are producing automobile parts which are stamped 'Made in Brazil' and clothing marked 'Made in Hong Kong' enabling them to intervene in foreign delivery contracts." Nor was it much of an issue whether the jobs, however low-wage, would go to American citizens or foreigners; many of the low-wage laborers in such industries as agriculture, janitorial and domestic services, and textiles are foreign-born and many are undocumented: as a pre-NAFTA segment of the *MacNeil/Lehrer Newshour* pointed out, in many cases it is simply a matter of whether it is the jobs or the people that will cross the border.

Still, it was more than just a function of America's collective memory deficit that no one put the controversy over NAFTA together with the controversy over Zoe Baird's domestic help. Despite its minimal tangible consequences, NAFTA's success probably makes a lot of people *feel* worse: a little less grounded, a little less centered, a little closer to the day when being an "American" means little more than living in North America or the Western hemisphere. Al Gore was correct when he said that NAFTA was ultimately about whether the nation would look outward or turn inward, but its success hardly settles the question. Faced with a fractured and devalued national identity, as the nation's population becomes more and more international and the nation's boundaries become more and more permeable, many Americans of every stripe look to ever smaller, more parochial groups, *communities* whose borders are more defensible, whose populations are more manageable.

The drive to restrict immigration and even to expel those immigrants currently in residence is one obvious move to control the definition of a national community. While many European countries simply deny full citizenship to immigrants and safeguard national culture against foreign influences by government mandates, in the United States, a self-proclaimed nation of immigrants, xenophobic measures are defended on a less overt, social welfare, basis. Thus California Governor Pete Wilson, with newfound compassion for the state's indigenous poor, argues that immigrants voraciously consume public services, denying the Golden State's native sons and daughters their share. His solution is not increased public assistance but instead tighter border controls and a constitutional amendment denying citizenship to native-born children of non-citizens. Wilson has taken a first step towards this goal: Proposition 187, which will deny many public services to undocumented immigrants, was approved by a two-to-one margin.

Likewise, the recently successful legislative initiative to split California into three states (don't worry, the measure still has to be approved by the state's electorate, and survive the procedures for new statehood before we'll see different license plates in Los Angeles and San Francisco) is arguably a response to the permeable nature of the borders between California's major cities and Latin America and the Pacific Rim, borders that are rendered more and more permeable by the relentless demands of the low-end labor market (which requires cheaper laborers than the U.S. can provide) and the high-end commercial real estate market (which requires cheaper capital than the U.S. can provide).

These foreign/domestic policy issues demonstrate the plasticity of communitarianism, its oscillation between the images of the small town and the global village. Bill Clinton and Al Gore heralded NAFTA as the key to America's future in the global community of nations while

Ross Perot and organized labor rejected NAFTA as a threat to the American national community. In the increasingly international context of American politics, any norm of community must tackle the thorny issues of multiple national and cultural groups with multiple values and visions of the good life. If community is to provide a normative framework for contemporary social life, one needs a coherent and workable theory of community.

The Design of Community

At one time it might have been reasonable to speak of the localities where people worked, socialized, raised children, and voted, as communities. But in 1990 the census showed that over half of all Americans lived in mega-cities, metropolitan areas of over 1 million inhabitants. Suburban sprawl is no longer peripheral but rather the central urban form, characterized not only by bedroom "communities" but also multiple commercial and industrial centers, what Joel Garreau has dubbed Edge Cities. Fewer and fewer people live, work, and play in one local "community." Meanwhile technology encourages us to shun face-to-face interaction in favor of what might be called the "electronic community." Trend-watchers note that "cocooning" is now the rage in major cities across the nation: for the first time since the mass production of the automobile, young adults are staying home, enjoying access to increasingly varied types of entertainment through the wire. After the Northridge quake, L.A.'s mayor Richard Riordan re-envisioned the nation's second largest city as home to the "virtual office:" employees will interact through cellular telephones, computer modems, and fax machines while physi-

cally remaining at home, thereby avoiding both increased traffic and the dangers of public exposure.

Instead of asking what community might mean in this context, the image of the authentic community conjures an ideal milieu of the culturally unified nation-state or the homogeneous province. Without a functional definition of community, the desire to root a pure identity in space often drives ecological design; as Celeste Olalquiaga writes in *Megalopolis,* "the conquest of space can be seen as the last Romantic dream."

Public policy is a type of meta-design, which promotes a particular vision of the good society. The ideal of the provincial community was made real by public policy in a California suburb called Lakewood. Lakewood, and many independent suburbs to follow it, owe their existence to a Los Angeles County plan that allows new municipalities to contract for public services at prices determined by the countywide economy of scale. The "Lakewood plan" has spread across the nation like wildfire in the Malibu Hills, and is responsible for the proliferation of suburbs that retain independent control over zoning and local tax revenue while enjoying economic interconnections with a large metropolis.

Are the Lakewood plan suburbs communities? Gary Miller, who studied the Lakewood incorporations in *Cities by Contract* reports that the primary reason for the creation of a Lakewood plan city was not like-mindedness among its citizens or even the expression of public choice in local public services but instead the desire to avoid the burden of providing public services to lower-income persons. Lakewood plan cities not only avoid the local tax burdens of the inner cities they surround, but can effectively block the entry of needier persons through "fiscal zoning" (bans on multi-family housing and minimum acreage requirements for detached homes.)

But these small suburban communities are arguably defined by more than pecuniary motivations. In Monterey Park citizens fought the "Chinese take-over" of their community by adopting an "English only" signage law (although the law only requires that signs *include English* translations, thus avoiding certain judicial invalidation on First amendment grounds) and declaring English to be the official

Like the England of L' Morte d' Arthur and the Ethiopia of Rastafarianism, Disneyland is a place both real and imagined

language of the city. Meanwhile, Mike Davis claims that wealthy San Marino adopted a "bedroom ordinance" to stop wealthy but large Asian families from buying into its Anglophilic piece of the California dream.

Today, the preferred approach to community design is the physical barrier to entry. Across the southwest, the "gated community" is the most popular form of new real estate development: private developers build a "community" from the ground up, surround the subdivision with walls and post a sentry at the points of entrance. Non-residents are admitted by invitation only. Inside, the community is organized as a private government with

rules of conduct that often defy principles of democracy and free expression: speech may be limited in ways that would not pass constitutional muster in a public setting, and decision-making power is often distributed according to home purchase price. A rule of one dollar, one vote replaces that of one person, one vote.

Nor is this hyper-localism restricted to the nominally private association. In Los Angeles, residents of self-defined neighborhood enclaves have petitioned the city for the right to wall off access to public streets; only a successful department of transportation lawsuit blocked the proposal, and an appeal is pending. Meanwhile, hundreds of miles north in Sacramento, the city has approved neighborhood taxation, through which tiny enclaves can raise revenue for their own purposes, avoiding the larger democratic process of the city and the necessity to share the wealth with the city's needier residents. If combined, the ability to restrict access to public streets and the ability to raise and spend revenue through neighborhood taxation would allow the recreation of the private gated association in the public sphere. Some argue that such extremes of decentralization represent the only way for the public sector to compete with the private, but these developments represent a pyrrhic victory for the public life of civic democracy. The willingness of local residents to support city-wide taxes will decline in proportion to their ability to tax at decentralized neighborhood levels. One can expect city-wide democratic institutions to atrophy to irrelevance as public functions are performed and public decisions made at the level of parochially defined and economically segregated "communities" that duplicate private associations in every relevant respect.

Thus the contraction of public spaces follows from the move to local homogeneity: the suburb guarded by fiscal zoning and a racially-motivated bedroom ordinance shades imperceptibly into the homeowners association which replicates municipal functions while avoiding the mandates of public accessibility; the *de facto* segregated (and occasionally *de jure* segregated, witness Detroit's "black male" schools and the special district for New York's Satmar Hassid) public school is nudged to become the private academy, funded by public vouchers or tax-deductible fees.

Even the construction of public works and the development of public policy, once the hallmarks of a commitment to collective action, now reflect a relentless privatism and fragmentation. Today the design and physical construction of our environment is as often driven by private concerns as by public vision: the greatest urban "public" works of the past decade involved downtown revitalization designed to attract private development and commercial industry. To be sure, public works have been built with private capital in mind at least since the heady days of the railroad barons, but the railroads, highways, public transportation, dams, and public buildings of the past were the infrastructure of new society of mixed public and private enterprise rather than merely a new corporate headquarters for a privately operated social order.

• • •

Disneyland stands as the most popular trope for a thoroughly designed, totally-privatized consumer community. Like the England of *L' Morte d' Arthur* and the Ethiopia of Rastafarianism, Disneyland is a place both real and imagined. In Disneyland, socially conservative secular humanism and lotus land's sun-baked pseudo-spirituality combine with relentless consumer capitalism to create a middle-American utopia. Disneyland represents in tangible form a certain powerful strain of the ideology of Americana; it rarely fails to provoke a strong reaction in the observant visitor, from the bemused disdain of the European intellectual, to *Spy* magazine's modest proposal that the Disney Corporation be commissioned to run the federal government at a profit, to the obligatory reference by every cultural critic who writes about either Los Angeles or shopping malls, to the "Night Stalker" Richard Ramirez's famous retort/threat after his conviction: "See you in Disneyland!" In *The Good Society*, Robert Bellah and his co-authors Richard Madsen, William Sullivan, Ann Swidler, and Steven Tipton discover geography and identity linked in Disneyland's landscape of late capitalist desire:

> A design gestures toward a future even as it dramatizes a desirable identity. . . . the Disney plan [is] a projection of America's collective unconscious. . . . Main Street and Tomorrowland are tied together by desire, a desire for a future open to limitless material progress but made secure by a fixed moral universe of the sort which Tocqueville thought had once anchored American confidence.

Disneyland's appeal rests in its ability to subsume the anxieties of modernity within its own relentless socio-spatial logic: here one can celebrate the conquest of the

African continent in Adventureland and bask in cultural diversity in a Small World a few hundred yards away; one can gaze wistfully back though rose-colored glass, almost simultaneously, and herald the millennium. But today Main Street mocks more than exalts history, its power is to mark the distance between the past it evokes and the present it embodies, while already the millennial Tomorrowland is less inspiring than amusing, its polished steel and curvilinear architecture speaking of, well, the fifties. Tomorrowland is as nostalgic and improbable a milieu as Main Street U.S.A. Disney's history is a facade, its future already a relic.

Likewise, the communitarian ideal of authentic identity and latent consensus emerges, not from the contemporary world or from history but from an imaginary landscape in which only the names remain the same. The ideal spatial milieu of communitarian thought oscillates between extremes, each of which contains the anxieties of the other: we have a nostalgia for the small town (which was a part of an expanding society that believed its destiny was manifest) and the millenarian dream of the global village (an image that has its roots in the Space Age aesthetic of the fifties), Main Street and Tomorrowland. In the former, communal space contracts to include only like minds, in the latter it expands to encompass everyone, converting difference into totality. The nostalgic and the millennial images of community are at once quaint antiques and fantastic projections, pastiche and science fiction.

In an article for *Wired* magazine, William Gibson describes Singapore as "Disneyland with the Death Penalty." In many ways Singapore's affluent society is not unlike the American fifties of the nostalgic imagination while its technological infrastructure conjures the Space Age city of the future (Gibson marvels at computer-controlled traffic signals that will "green light" emergency vehicles through to their destination). Singaporeans can take pride in a city-state of remarkable economic prosperity in which urban blight and decay have been eliminated through strong central planning and cutting-edge technology. Nor is social harmony a result of ethnic or cultural homogeneity: the clean cut, traditional families that predominate are multi-culturally aware ("[m]odel . . . Chinese, Malay, or Indian families act out . . . the customs of each culture" on television). But culture is strictly controlled and those expressions deemed deviant are not tolerated: Gibson reports that "A scan through available tapes and CDs confirmed . . . that . . . the stock [could have] been vetted by Mormon missionaries"; official government censors guard against cosmopolitan attitudes, ensuring that publications critical of the government or those of prurient interest—a catagory that includes *Cosmopolitan* magazine—are not available to corrupt the *populus*. "Alternative" subcultures are almost non-existent ("I didn't see a single bad girl in Singapore" muses Gibson, "and I missed her"). The technology that aids emergency vehicles is also employed to monitor streets, subways, and public buildings. The alienation (and also the potentially disruptive spontaneity) of modern sexual relationships is eliminated or at least tempered through government-sponsored "mandatory mixers": employers receive a call if their marriageable employees fail to attend. Carrying a kilogram of marijuana is punishable by death.

None of this tightly-controlled and centrally-planned communal spirit hinders Singapore's economic life in the least. Not only is shopping as popular as in the U.S. (and just about as interesting: Gibson complains that "the city's malls all stock virtually the same goods"); but the city-state is actually planning to franchise itself as entrepreneurs work to create a Singaporean annex in Longkou, China. Singapore's heavily policed society has even turned out to be a public relations coup for the city-state. When American Michael Fey received four strokes with a bamboo cane at the hands of Singaporean authority as punishment for petty vandalism, Singapore's well-ordered, crime-free society inspired nostalgia and envy among Americans. The punishment resonated with the traditional family value of discipline—spare the rod and spoil the child. As Fey sought and was denied clemency, the media featured communitarian-styled celebrations of the caning. Ex-Secretary of Education William Bennett stopped just short of endorsing Singaporean rough justice on *Nightline,* arguing that widespread support for the punishment was evidence that Americans wanted a return to traditional values, a society "that once was and that they believe can come again." One letter to the *New York Times* expressed the view that caning would teach the seventeen year-old Fey that with rights come responsibilities, and suggested that Americans, would-be vandals and civil libertarians alike, might benefit from Singapore's example. Numerous letter writers and call-in commentators regretted only that caning had not been adopted in the United States.

• • •

In the context of social policy it matters how you slice it, and it is not clear which way communitarianism will cut. When communitarianism asks us to take a hard and pragmatic look at the direction our society is taking, it provides a valuable perspective. But when it lapses into nostalgia to suggest that "traditional values" should guide us, communitarianism paves the way for scapegoating—social ills are easily blamed on "foreign influences" and "outside agitators." We all too often define our communities negatively, as a reaction to pressures for change which, although represented as alien, are now an integral part of contemporary society. As we blame foreign influences for the internal contradictions of nation-state capitalism, the rhetoric of community may justify jingoism, know-nothingism and out-and-out repression in the name of national community.

And if communitarians fail to articulate a normative vision of community, our efforts to forge community, even *within* the nation, will stifle the dialogue that might create a civic community and identity. Some of today's most innovative policy proposals couch what is arguably a movement towards privatism in the rhetoric of community. As public space contracts, public dialogue is suffocated and a spirit of community atrophies. Thus a narrow vision of community becomes, ironically, individualism with a vengeance: privatization, the complete abstinence from the risks of pluralist politics in favor of the literal unanimity of the community of one. By avoiding or suppressing the social conflict that actually brings a spirit of community into existence and which gives it life, an easy communitarianism, based on the fiction of the repressed community of shared values, produces its practical antithesis.

The Concerned Community

Communitarianism can be seen as a response to a post-Cold War malaise as well as a revamped American ideology for the global village. It has a material "base": the aspirations of global capitalism and the emergence of a new domestic order to replace Cold War anti-communism and the military-industrial complex. Already the aerospace economy of Southern California and Arizona is retooling to become

> ## How, after all, does one cross-examine a voice from the subconscious?

a security and incarceration economy, fueled by the prospect of mandatory government expenditures on prison construction—the likely end result of the new wave of federal and state "truth in sentencing" and "three strikes" requirements—and by the increasing calls for security generated in part by the media's obsession with crime. The emerging security-industrial complex simultaneously provides a replacement for the built-in economic stimulus of military expenditures and legitimates a domestic security and surveillance appartus to rival that of

the Cold War. The Los Angeles Police Department has used military equipment, including tanks and assault helicopters, for years. And can it be a coincidence that a newish form of criminal incarceration, designed especially for young men, has been dubbed "boot camp"?

The link between crime prevention and an ideal of community does not simply reside in the rhetoric of "rights and responsiblities." The interrogation of the criminal defendant and the monitoring of individuals are linked in Michel Foucault's "examination," a mechanism of normalization and exclusion in which:

> *The case is no longer, as in causistry or juris-*
> *prudence, a set of circumstances defining an act*
> *and capable of modifying the application of a*
> *rule; it is the individual as he may be described,*
> *judged, measured, compared with others, in his*
> *very individuality.*

Individuals acquiesce in their own examination through psychoanalysis, hypnosis and even truth serum, all designed to bring to light "inner demons" and "repressed memories." But participation in examination rarely remains volunatary. Parental rights are determined and criminal cases prosecuted and defended on the basis of "testimony" paradoxically made all the more credible by its resistance to verification: how, after all, does one cross-examine a voice from the subconscious, how does one test the credibility of an inner demon or a devil that made the defendant do it? Not only justice, but the goal of self-knowledge may itself be threatened by psychological probing: an increasing number of former patients are now suing, not the perpetrators of crimes revealed through therapy, hypnosis, or truth serum, but their *therapists* for implanting "false memories."

None of this is to deny or trivialize the benefits that may result from the discovery of actual abuses through psychoanalysis; it is only to suggest that another, less beneficent social logic may also be at work in the increasing tendency to locate the roots of social ills in individual psychological narratives. This is especially true when the interrogation of the inner consciousness becomes compulsory. There are now reports of poorly trained or opportunistic analysts who insist that *all* anorexic patients were victims of abuse: it only remains to get them to remember it. This exclusive location of social evils in individual traumas has the perverse side effect of effacing the broader social causes of such disorders: the relentless and unattainable images of beauty that saturate contemporary society can affect children in even the most loving of home environments. Ironically, the medicalization of social problems becomes an alibi for ignoring the pathologically regulative aspect of contemporary culture and simultaneously justifies further regulation of the mind and body.

This tendency also fuels the belief that individuals should be evaluated and *judged* based not on what they do, but on who they are, on their interior identity. Despite the legal rationale for psychological evidence—that the defendant's state of mind may mitigate culpability—psychological evidence is too often subtly used to prove that the defendant is not a "criminal type" or that the victim deserved his or her fate. The flip side of this belief is the belief that evidence of a criminal personality justifies harsh punishment, despite the insubstantial nature of the offense actually committed. The psychologically troubled but morally innocent murderer finds its evil twin in the recidivist, the defendant whose very personality is thought to predispose him to a life of crime. The proliferation of "three strikes and you're out" crime bills (a centerpiece of Clinton's crime bill) reflect the theory of essential recidivism: a life sentence is justified for the third minor felony, not because of the severity of the crime but because of the irredeemable criminal nature of the defendant.

In a *New Republic* article Robert Wright argued that "the best way to keep the brave new world grounded in bedrock American values may be to bring cosmetic pharmacology to the masses." As a part of a national health care plan, Wright suggests, drugs should be dispensed by Uncle Sam in order to promote the American way. This entails some delicate balancing, trading off personal benefits against social values. For example, the author suggests that certain of Prozac's effects may qualify it as a " 'family values' drug." The balance, according to Wright, favors a daily dose of Prozac with a spoonful of sugar when it will help men to stop cheating on their wives but not when it might help women overcome the guilt that keeps them in destructive marriages (these are Wright's gendered examples).

Community and identity are linked through the collective definition of deviance and normalcy, a process in which the individual participates by contributing herself as data to be compared and assimilated to a mean. The individualized examination suggests a social logic that guides the contemporary trend Richard Sennett described in *The Conscience of the Eye* as "interiority:" the belief that truth and self-knowledge are to be found only by looking within a strictly defined space of home, family, perhaps a small community, and ultimately within oneself. The corresponding view is that "outside there is only exposure, disorder, and cruelty"—the outer or public world of metropolitan civic life is like the shadows inside Plato's cave. Interiority values the local and provincial as the source of truth and identity: more than what we can observe at large in the outside world, it is what is hidden deep within, what we keep most privately guarded that is important. It is not how we engage the world, but what we are like inside our own heads that determines who we are.

Interiority requires a retrenchment of borders, the maintenance of an insular space for self-reflection, self-development, and self-preservation. But as a collective practice it also requires an interrogation of the inner lives of others: if we

Surveillance has become the *modus operandi* of the police state, the free press and the private citizen

cannot trust the public persona or the surface experience, we must dig ever deeper in order to truly know those who confront (and in so doing, threaten) us in the world. The "authentic" identity of every community member becomes important: deviants and dissidents are presented as internal threats even as their existence defines the community by uniting it in opposition. And because the community is the source of identity, the identification

and exposure of marginal persons takes on the character of a personal exorcism.

The burgeoning security industry includes not only a proliferation of technologies designed to restrict access, to safeguard against breach, but also a explosion of techniques and devices designed to spy on others. The security camera screens out unwanted visitors but also monitors the movement of invitees, the same store that sells equipment designed to insure privacy also outfits the private investigator or the suspicious spouse. We are obsessed with privacy and the private, a society characterized by compulsive voyeurism and the paranoia of the subject under constant observation.

And even paranoids have enemies. Technology designed to enforce what Foucault calls "compulsary visibility" is not only able to monitor individual movement but also to identify the subject of surveillance, now through electronic recording of credit card and ATM use and soon, urban futurists tell us, through ubiquitous, highly sensitive cameras hidden in public places and incorporated into panoptical surveillance devices. The *Economist* reports that hidden cameras could scan the individually unique retinal pattern from a discreet distance, identifying potential undesirables, while in a "twenty minutes into the future" essay, Mike Davis reports that camera-equipped satellites designed for use in geo-synchronous orbit, already under development for traffic management and for high-tech automobile security, could easily be used to

> surveil the movements of thousands of electronically tagged individuals and their automobiles. . . . it will be entirely possible to put

the equivalent of a electronic handcuff on the activities of entire urban social strata. Drug offenders and gang members can be "bar coded" and paroled to the omniscient scrutiny of a satellite that will . . . automatically sound an alarm if they stray from the borders of their surveillance district.

This Foucauldian examination does not simply reflect an obsession with the interior, the private and the personal which should be balanced with a corresponding concern over the public and exterior world; instead the distinction between the two is increasingly difficult to make intelligibly. A belief in an embattled interior identity and repressed community produces both an obsessive introspection and a pervasive suspicion of internal subversives; interrogation is equally the tactic of the collective Inquisition and the personal therapist; surveillance, the *modus operandi* of the police state, the free press, and the private citizen.

The Urban Community

The emergence of "community" as a normative ideal seems to define a conspicuous absence in contemporary society. Institutions that once sustained a sense of grounded identity—institutions as various as the nation-state, "genetically determined" racial attributes, established sex roles, organized religion and the family—are either in flux, under attack, or simply discredited. Michael Walzer's astute observation about the liberal state applies to the ideology of liberalism in general: liberal institutions by their very nature are incapable of providing a feeling of warmth or a sense of identity. Liberal institutions are premised on voluntariness and thus

explicitly call attention to their inessential and contested nature: they exist for the purposes their members choose and only for as long as they serve their members' purposes.

It is now a commonplace that liberalism depends on illiberal institutions that operate in the background, taken for granted. These are the institutions that provide identity and they do so precisely because they are *not* voluntary and do not pretend to be: at root identity is not and cannot be a choice. Philosophical communitarians such as Michael Sandel recognize this; indeed their theory depends on it. As a critique of political liberalism, communitarianism argues that voluntariness cannot be the basis for justice because our identity, and hence our ability to make choices, is the product of social context and social groups—communities—that we do not choose. This is a powerful critique of liberalism, but it is only a critique. Community as an abstract norm will not suffice any more than will individual liberty; indeed community in the abstract suffers from the same deficit Sandel identifies in the Rawlsian individual subject: its lack of content makes it potentially everything and actually nothing.

In order to develop prescriptive norms one must examine specific social institutions and their role in fostering specific communities. Real communities arise through necessity as often as by design or choice. They exist for tangible purposes, to correct problems their members cannot ignore, to provide things their members cannot do without. They provide a sense of identity through coercion, exclusion, internal debate, interaction with outsiders, and the experience of collective action. But popular communitarians try to have it both ways; they want a communal identity with a liberal escape clause, ties that bind but with no strings attached. The vague ideal of community seduces with this false promise: a community at once voluntary *and* cohesive, a profound commonality that leaves for another time the messy question of its content. Etzioni's insistence on shared values illustrates the impossibility of this position: the shared values that give his community content are not an option but rather a prerequisite.

This is not to say that we should reject the possibility of meaningful collective action and retreat into our individuality—precisely the opposite. Now more than ever the challenge is to *act* in the awareness that our actions shape our identity (and along with it the identity of others) in ways that we do not and cannot choose. The type of collective action that fosters a sense of community does not consist of a series of arms-length deals or freely-chosen relationships; instead, community is forged from the struggle between people who are either born together, forced together or come together for concrete reasons: for the arts, for social causes, for worship, for companionship. Duncan Kennedy recognizes this in his discussion of workplace organizing:

workplace organizing involves long term, multi-issue, emotionally complex relationships, both with allies and with opponents. . . . There is dependence as well as confrontation. Allies are more like family members, with whom you have to work things out against the background of long involuntary association and mutual critique, than like "signers" or "people who agree with our position on x."

As Robert Putnam has recognized, a sense of community that is forged through meaningful collective action may later become the source of the political cohesiveness, shared ethical values, and mutual trust that make civilized life possible and society prosperous—Putnam calls this social capital. But he recognizes that meaningful action is a necessary condition of community. What is dangerous about the vague call to community and the abstract quest for identity is that they distract us from action and its consequences. As we look past what might produce a useful community and fulfilling identity, our world becomes less just, less humane, and less civilized.

Popular communitarianism might learn from the best of identity politics, emphasizing an identity based on the collective experience and action from which ethical precepts flow, rather than both criticize and replicate identity policies at their worst by insisting on an authentic self we do not actually possess or a consensus "we" have not yet come to. At its best, identity politics draws on the experience of a particular group in order to gain ethical and political insight that transcends a narrow and purely oppositional identity and community. In *Race Matters*, Cornel West outlines a politics that recognizes the solidarity of African-Americans, but avoids conjuring a repressed and repressive "black authenticity:"

Blackness is a political and ethical construct. . . . Instead of cathartic appeals to black authenticity a prophetic viewpoint [is based on] . . . the moral quality of black responses to undeniable racist degradation. . . . Instead of a closing ranks mentality, a prophetic framework encourages a coalition strategy that so-

licits genuine solidarity. . . . Such coalitions
are important because they not only enhance
the plight of black people but also because they
enrich the quality of life in America.

Similarly, Kimberle Crenshaw sees race as neither an essence nor a regulatory norm but as the product of struggle, itself a coalition "between men and women of color." On this view, "cultural pluralism" values the dialogue and debate that occurs *within* as well as between cultural groups, just as participatory democrats value the dialogue and debate that occurs within and between different political groups.

City dwellers uncomfortable with the cities in which they live would prefer to identify with some imaginary landscape of uncomplicated sameness and pristine beauty

Thus community could mean that we are ready to confront the challenges of both civic pluralism and post-structuralism, to actually live with difference rather than either flatten and assimilate it or reflexively fret about or celebrate its "irreducibility." As Richard Sennett suggests, "perhaps . . . difference, discontinuity, and disorientation ought to be ethical forces which connect people to one another."

A pragmatic communitarianism that abandoned the nostalgia for pure identity and the myth of repressed consensus might be drawn to a new urbanism: not only is the metropolis dominant (even as it lit-

erally disintegrates from neglect) in American life and becoming more so both in America and world wide, but the city has always been the civilizing influence in society. In *The Good Society,* Robert Bellah identifies cities as "the spaces [in which] conflict can be sublimated into constructive argument." Cities, in both their established and spontaneous social institutions, provide the greatest hope for responsible collective action and political participation among individuals and groups whose goals and values conflict.

It is within the urban milieu (and this includes the growing post-urbanism of the suburb and the multi-nodal metropolis), as antithetical to community as it may seem, that communitarianism may offer its greatest promise. It is communitarianism's singular genius that it strives to create identity from the fragments of contemporary culture: at its best, the communitarian ideal is the community of the contingent, of the provisional, of the many and of the moment. The city is the logical site for a community that can provide a shared dialogue and a shared civic identity, if not shared values and a shared authentic identity. As Lewis Mumford discovered in his classic study of *The City in History,* "the art of building cities" is a collective project that involves the creation of a civic culture and social networks as much as the creation of policy or the construction of public works. Urban life at its best has always been less about omniscient or clairvoyant central planning than about the collective project of the making of virtue from necessity.

Communities that focus on problem solving and collective engagement while embracing difference may seem hard to imagine. Today it seems that few people wish to identify with the city: Afro-centrism, as its name suggests, focuses on a mythical or at best syncretic Africa rather than on the rich urban culture of, say, the Harlem Renaissance; a growing number of women are enamored with the sylvan Goddess rather than the freedom and stimulation of city life that so charmed Simone de Beauvior and Hanna Arendt. Similarly, a good deal of communitarian thought identifies with the small town and the global village but ignores the city. The predominance of the urban breeds an anti-urbanism in popular self-images and visions of community; city dwellers uncomfortable with the cities in which they live (and have helped to create) would prefer to identify with some imaginary landscape of uncomplicated sameness and pristine beauty.

Urban communities exist; they are the groups that make life in many cities and increasingly urban suburbs a living expression of their inhabitants rather than a deadened bureaucracy. Such communities may form spontaneously to address a particular issue, but they have roots in established relationships that predate any single issue, and they help to establish networks of trust that will endure into the future. These communities do not attempt to efface the loyalties of race and ethnicity but instead build on these pre-existing loyalties. In *The Death and Life of Great American Cities,* Jane Jacobs describes the possibility of meaningful collective political action through urban districts that join ethnic enclaves, small neighborhoods and other constituencies too small to achieve their goals or an effective voice alone:

The crucial stage in the formation of an effective district . . . [involves] an interweaving set

of relationships among people, usually leaders, who enlarge their local public life beyond the neighborhoods of streets and specific organizations or institutions and form relationships with people whose roots and backgrounds are in entirely different constituencies, so to speak.

When she wrote *The Death and Life of Great American Cities* in 1961, Jane Jacobs defied common wisdom by suggesting that urban planning should encourage, not segregated uses but mixed uses: "[d]ifferences," she noted, "not duplication, make for . . . a person's identification with an area. . . . Monotony is the enemy . . . of functional unity. . . . nobody outside [a homogenous] Turf can possibly feel an identity with it or what it contains." Jacobs's vision of vibrant neighborhoods emphasized diversity, function, and permeable borders; her vision of an urban community was not of homogenous stasis, the echo of David Riesman's lonely crowd, but rather that of a dynamic crowd that shared a common space—even as the players change the community remains. Change and diversity does not threaten such an urban community; on the contrary, it keeps it alive: "The difference is . . . between dealing with living, complex organisms, capable of shaping their own destinies, and dealing with fixed and inert settlements. . . ."

Mary Ann Glendon's description of the destruction of one urban community illustrates what is lost when a narrow popular imagination is blind to the potential of organic social groups:

Communities are often caught in a pincer between individual rights on the one hand, and reasons of the state on the other. Thus when Detroit's Poletown residents mounted their campaign to prevent the destruction of their neighborhood, they found that they could not find a way to communicate effectively . . . about [the loss of] a rich neighborhood life; shared memories and hopes; roots; a sense of place. When . . . they brought a lawsuit, they were . . . laughed out of court.

Glendon sees the Poletown case as an illustration of the need for communitarian values, but it seems to point instead toward a need for a new urbanism. Small towns fare better with community-based arguments than did Detroit's Poletown. Take the Village of Belle Terre, which prohibited most unrelated persons from living together and convinced the Supreme Court that the prohibition was necessary to preserve its small, family-oriented, community. Poletown, like many other inner-city neighborhoods, was destroyed not because policy makers and judges failed to understand the value of community but because they could not imagine a viable community in an urban setting.

The destruction of viable city communities is often a result of impoverished notions of what a city and a community can be: the effort to create a simplistic vision of community may result in the neglect or the destruction of communities that actually exist and function. Communitarianism may yet fulfill its promise to provide a normative basis for interpersonal connection within the cold institutions of the liberal state, but we must determine who and why "we" are if the spirit of community is to be more than a phantasm. Cities provide a pragmatic location and purpose for communities—if the cities where we currently live fail to satisfy us, we have our fantasies of purity and escape to blame. If we abandon the false dream of a community without conflict, perhaps we can achieve a working, if imperfect and contested, *human* community through our real lives in the big city.

The New Cultural Politics
of Difference*

CORNEL WEST

In the last few years of the twentieth century, there is emerging a significant shift in the sensibilities and outlooks of critics and artists. In fact, I would go so far as to claim that a new kind of cultural worker is in the making, associated with a new politics of difference. These new forms of intellectual consciousness advance new conceptions of the vocation of critic and artist, attempting to undermine the prevailing disciplinary divisions of labor in the academy, museum, mass media, and gallery networks while preserving modes of critique within the ubiquitous commodification of culture in the global village. Distinctive features of the new cultural politics of difference are to trash the monolithic and homogeneous in the name of diversity, multiplicity, and heterogeneity; to reject the abstract, general, and universal in light of the concrete, specific, and particular; and to historicize, contextualize, and pluralize by highlighting the contingent, provisional, variable, tentative, shifting, and changing. Needless to say, these gestures are not new in the history of criticism or art, yet what makes them novel—along with the cultural politics they produce—is how and what constitutes difference, the weight and gravity it is given in representation, and the way in which highlighting issues like exterminism, empire, class, race, gender, sexual orientation, age, nation, nature, and region at this historical moment acknowledges some discontinuity and disruption from previous forms of cultural critique. To put it bluntly, the new cultural politics of difference consists of creative responses to the precise circumstances of our present moment—especially those of marginalized First World agents who shun degraded self-representations, articulating instead their sense of the flow of history in light of the contemporary terrors, anxieties, and fears of highly commercialized North Atlantic capitalist cultures (with their escalating xenophobias against people of color, Jews, women, gays,

---

*   This is a version of an essay that appears in Russel Ferguson, Martha Gever, Trinh T. Minh-ha, and Cornel West, eds., *Out There: Marginalization and Contemporary Cultures*, New York, The New Museum of Contemporary Art; and Cambridge, MIT Press, 1990.

313

lesbians, and the elderly). The thawing, yet still rigid Second World ex-communist cultures (with increasing nationalist revolts against the legacy of hegemonic party henchmen), and the diverse cultures of the majority of inhabitants on the globe smothered by international communication cartels and repressive postcolonial elites (sometimes in the name of communism, as in Ethiopia), or starved by austere World Bank and IMF policies that subordinate them to the North (as in free-market capitalism in Chile), also locate vital areas of analysis in this new cultural terrain.

The new cultural politics of difference are neither simply oppositional in contesting the mainstream (or *male*stream) for inclusion, nor transgressive in the avant-gardist sense of shocking conventional bourgeois audiences. Rather, they are distinct articulations of talented (and usually privileged) contributors to culture who desire to align themselves with demoralized, demobilized, depoliticized, and disorganized people in order to empower and enable social action and, if possible, to enlist collective insurgency for the expansion of freedom, democracy, and individuality. This perspective impels these cultural critics and artists to reveal, as an integral component of their production, the very operations of power within their immediate work contexts (i.e., academy, museum, gallery, mass media). This strategy, however, also puts them in an inescapable double bind — while linking their activities to the fundamental, structural overhaul of these institutions, they often remain financially dependent on them. (So much for "independent" creation.) For these critics of culture, theirs is a gesture that is simultaneously progressive *and* coopted. Yet, without social movement or political pressure from outside these institutions (extra-parliamentary and extra-curricular actions like the social movements of the recent past), transformation degenerates into mere accommodation or sheer stagnation, and the role of the "coopted progressive" — no matter how fervent one's subversive rhetoric — is rendered more difficult. In this sense there can be no artistic breakthrough or social progress without some form of crisis in civilization — a crisis usually generated by organizations or collectivities that convince ordinary people to put their bodies and lives on the line. There is, of course, no guarantee that such pressure will yield the result one wants, but there is a guarantee that the status quo will remain or regress if no pressure is applied at all.

The new cultural politics of difference faces three basic challenges — intellectual, existential, and political. The intellectual challenge — usually cast as a methodological debate in these days in which academicist forms of expression have a monopoly on intellectual life — is how to think about representational practices in terms of history, culture, and society. How does one understand, analyze, and enact such practices today? An adequate answer to this question can be attempted only after one comes to terms with the insights and blindnesses of earlier attempts to grapple with the question in light of the evolving crisis in different histories, cultures, and societies. I shall sketch a brief genealogy — a history that highlights the contingent origins and often ignoble outcomes—of exemplary critical responses to the question.

The Intellectual Challenge

An appropriate starting point is the ambiguous legacy of the Age of Europe. Between 1492 and 1945, European breakthroughs in oceanic transportation, agricultural production, state consolidation, bureaucratization, industrialization, urbanization, and imperial dominion shaped the makings of the modern world. Precious ideals like the dignity of persons (individuality) or the popular accountability of institutions (democracy) were unleashed around the world. Powerful critiques of illegitimate authorities—of the Protestant Reformation against the Roman Catholic Church, the Enlightenment against state churches, liberal movements against absolutist states and feudal guild constraints, workers against managerial subordination, people of color and Jews against white and gentile supremacist decrees, gays and lesbians against homophobic sanctions— were fanned and fueled by these precious ideals refined within the crucible of the Age of Europe. Yet, the discrepancy between sterling rhetoric and lived reality, glowing principles and actual practices, loomed large.

By the last European century—the last epoch in which European domination of most of the globe was uncontested and unchallenged in a substantive way—a new world seemed to be stirring. At the height of England's reign as the major imperial European power, its examplary cultural critic, Matthew Arnold, painfully observed in his "Stanzas from the Grand Chartreuse" that he felt some sense of "wandering between two worlds, one dead/the other powerless to be born." Following his Burkean sensibilities of cautious reform and fear of anarchy, Arnold acknowledged that the old glue—religion—that had tenuously and often unsuccessfully held together the ailing European regimes could not do so in the mid–nineteenth century. Like Alexis de Tocqueville in France, Arnold saw that the democratic temper was the wave of the future. So he proposed a new conception of culture—a secular, humanistic one—that could play an integrative role in cementing and stabilizing an emerging bourgeois civil society and imperial state. His famous castigation of the immobilizing materialism of the declining aristocracy, the vulgar philistinism of the emerging middle classes, and the latent explosiveness of the working-class majority was motivated by a desire to create new forms of cultural legitimacy, authority, and order in a rapidly changing moment in nineteenth-century Europe.

For Arnold (in *Culture and Anarchy*, 1869), this new conception of culture

. . . seeks to do away with classes; to make the best that has been thought and known in the world current everywhere; to make all men live in an atmosphere of sweetness and light . . .

315

This is the *social idea* and the men of culture are the true apostles of
equality. The great men of culture are those who have had a passion
for diffusing, for making prevail, for carrying from one end of society
to the other, the best knowledge, the best ideas of their time, who
have laboured to divest knowledge of all that was harsh, uncouth,
difficult, abstract, professional, yet still remaining the best knowledge
and thought of the time, and a true source, therefore, of sweetness
and light.

As an organic intellectual of an emergent middle class — as the inspector of
schools in an expanding educational bureaucracy, Professor of Poetry at Oxford
(the first noncleric and the first to lecture in English rather than Latin), and an
active participant in a thriving magazine network — Arnold defined and defended a new secular culture of critical discourse. For him, this discursive strategy would be lodged in the educational and periodical apparatuses of modern
societies as they contained and incorporated the frightening threats of an arrogant aristocracy and especially of an "anarchic" working-class majority. His
ideals of disinterested, dispassionate, and objective inquiry would regulate this
secular cultural production, and his justifications for the use of state power to
quell any threats to the survival and security of this culture were widely accepted.
He aptly noted, "Through culture seems to lie our way, not only to perfection,
but even to safety."

For Arnold, the best of the Age of Europe — modeled on a mythological melange of Periclean Athens, late republican/early imperial Rome, and
Elizabethan England — could be promoted only if there was an interlocking
affiliation among the emerging middle classes, a homogenizing of cultural discourse in the educational and university networks, and a state advanced enough
in its policing techniques to safeguard it. The candidates for participation and
legitimation in this grand endeavor of cultural renewal and revision would be
detached intellectuals willing to shed their parochialism, provincialism, and class-
bound identities for Arnold's middle-class-skewed project: "Aliens, if we may so
call them — persons who are mainly led, not by their class spirit, but by a general
humane spirit, by the love of human perfection." Needless to say, this Arnoldian
perspective still informs much of academic practices and secular cultural attitudes today — dominant views about the canon, admission procedures, and collective self-definitions of intellectuals. Yet, Arnold's project was disrupted by the
collapse of nineteenth-century Europe — World War I. This unprecedented war
— in George Steiner's words, the first of the bloody civil wars within Europe —
brought to the surface the crucial role and violent potential not of the masses
Arnold feared, but of the state he heralded. Upon the ashes of this wasteland of
human carnage — some of the civilian European population — T. S. Eliot
emerged as the grand cultural spokesman.

Eliot's project of reconstituting and reconceiving European highbrow culture—and thereby regulating critical and artistic practices—after the internal collapse of imperial Europe can be viewed as a response to the probing question posed by Paul Valéry in "The Crisis of the Spirit" after World War I:

> This Europe, will it become *what it is in reality*, i.e., a little cape of the Asiatic continent? or will this Europe remain rather *what it seems*, i.e., the priceless part of the whole earth, the pearl of the globe, the brain of a vast body?

Eliot's image of Europe as a wasteland, a culture of fragments with no cementing center, predominated in postwar Europe. And though his early poetic practices were more radical, open, and international than his Eurocentric criticism, Eliot posed a return to and revision of tradition as the only way of regaining European cultural order and political stability. For Eliot, contemporary history had become, as James Joyce's Stephen declared in *Ulysses* (1922), "a nightmare from which he was trying to awake"; "an immense panorama of futility and anarchy" as Eliot put it in his renowned review of Joyce's modernist masterpiece. In his influential essay, "Tradition and the Individual Talent" (1919), Eliot stated that:

> Yet if the only form of tradition, of handing down, consisted in following the ways of the immediate generation before us in a blind or timid adherence to its successes, "tradition" should positively be discouraged. We have seen many such simple currents soon lost in the sand; and novelty is better than repetition. Tradition is a matter of much wider significance. It cannot be inherited, and if you want it you must attain it by great labour.

Eliot found this tradition in the Church of England, to which he converted in 1927. Here was a tradition that left room for his Catholic cast of mind, Calvinist heritage, puritanical temperament, and ebullient patriotism for the old American South (the place of his upbringing). Like Arnold, Eliot was obsessed with the idea of civilization and the horror of barbarism (echoes of Joseph Conrad's Kurtz in *Heart of Darkness*), or, more pointedly, the notion of the decline and decay of European civilization. With the advent of World War II, Eliot's obsession became a reality. Again, unprecedented human carnage (fifty million died)—including an indescribable genocidal attack on Jewish people—throughout Europe as well as around the globe put the last nail in the coffin of the Age of Europe. After 1945, Europe consisted of a devastated and divided continent, crippled by a humiliating dependency on and deference to the United States and Russia.

The second historical coordinate of my genealogy is the emergence of the United States as *the* world power (in the words of André Malraux, the first nation to do so without trying to do so). The United States was unprepared for world power status. However, with the recovery of Stalin's Russia (after losing twenty million lives), the United States felt compelled to make its presence felt around the globe. Then, with the Marshall Plan to strengthen Europe, it seemed clear that there was no escape from world power obligations.

The post–World War II era in the United States, or the first decades of what Henry Luce envisioned as "The American Century," was not only a period of incredible economic expansion, but of active cultural ferment. The creation of a mass middle class — a prosperous working class with a bourgeois identity — was countered by the first major emergence of subcultures of American non-WASP intellectuals; the so-called New York intellectuals in criticism, the Abstract Expressionists in painting, and the bebop artists in jazz music. This emergence signaled a vital challenge to an American male WASP elite loyal to an older and eroding European culture.

The first significant blow was dealt when assimilated Jewish Americans entered the higher echelons of the cultural apparatuses (academy, museums, galleries, mass media). Lionel Trilling is an emblematic figure. This Jewish entrée into the anti-Semitic and patriarchal critical discourse of the exclusivistic institutions of American culture initiated the slow but sure undoing of the male WASP cultural hegemony and homogeneity. Trilling's project was to appropriate Matthew Arnold's for his own political and cultural purposes — thereby unraveling the old male WASP consensus while erecting a new post–World War II liberal academic consensus around cold war, anticommunist renditions of the values of complexity, difficulty, variousness, and modulation. In addition, the postwar boom laid the basis for intense professionalization and specialization in expanding institutions of higher education — especially in the natural sciences that were compelled to somehow respond to Russia's successful ventures in space. Humanistic scholars found themselves searching for new methodologies that could buttress self-images of rigor and scientific seriousness. For example, the close reading techniques of New Criticism (severed from their conservative, organicist, anti-industrialist ideological roots), the logical precision of reasoning in analytic philosophy, and the jargon of Parsonian structural-functionalism in sociology helped create such self-images. Yet, towering cultural critics like C. Wright Mills, W. E. B. DuBois, Richard Hofstadter, Margaret Mead, and Dwight MacDonald bucked the tide. This suspicion of the academicization of knowledge is expressed in Trilling's well-known essay, "On the Teaching of Modern Literature":

> . . . can we not say that, when modern literature is brought into the classroom, the subject being taught is betrayed by the pedagogy of the subject? We have to ask ourselves whether in our day too much does not come within the purview of the academy. More and more, as the universities liberalize themselves, turn their beneficent imperialistic gaze upon what is called life itself, the feeling grows among our educated classes that little can be experienced unless it is validated by some established intellectual discipline. . . .

Trilling laments the fact that university instruction often quiets and domesticates radical and subversive works of art, turning them into objects "of merely habitual regard." This process of "the socialization of the anti-social, or the acculturation of the anti-cultural, or the legitimization of the subversive" leads Trilling to "question whether in our culture the study of literature is any longer a suitable means for developing and refining the intelligence." He asks this question not in the spirit of denigrating and devaluing the academy, but rather in the spirit of highlighting the possible failure of an Arnoldian conception of culture to contain what he perceives as the philistine and anarchic alternatives becoming more and more available to students of the '60s — namely, mass culture and radical politics.

This threat is partly associated with the third historical coordinate of my genealogy — the decolonization of the Third World. It is crucial to recognize the importance of this world-historical process if one wants to grasp the significance of the end of the Age of Europe and the emergence of the United States as a world power. With the first defeat of a western nation by a nonwestern nation — in Japan's victory over Russia (1905); revolutions in Persia (1905), Turkey (1908), Mexico (1911 – 12), China (1912); and much later the independence of India (1947), China (1948); and the triumph of Ghana (1957) — the actuality of a decolonized globe loomed large. Born of violent struggle, consciousness-raising, and the reconstruction of identities, decolonization simultaneously brings with it new perspectives on that long festering underside of the Age of Europe (of which colonial domination represents the *costs* of "progress," "order," and "culture"), as well as requiring new readings of the economic boom in the United States (wherein the Black, Brown, Yellow, Red, White, female, gay, lesbian, and elderly working class live the same *costs* as cheap labor at home as well as in U.S. - dominated Latin American and Pacific rim markets).

The impetuous ferocity and moral outrage that motors the decolonization process is best captured by Frantz Fanon in *The Wretched of the Earth* (1906):

> Decolonization, which sets out to change the order of the world, is obviously a program of complete disorder. . . . Decolonization is the meeting of two forces, opposed to each other by their very nature, which in fact owe their originality to that sort of substantification which results from and is nourished by the situation in the colonies. Their first encounter was marked by violence and their existence together — that is to say the exploitation of the native by the settler — was carried on by dint of a great array of bayonets and cannons. . . .
>
> In decolonization, there is therefore the need of a complete calling in question of the colonial situation. If we wish to describe it precisely, we might find it in the well-known words: "The last shall be first and the first last." Decolonization is the putting into practice of this sentence.
>
> The naked truth of decolonization evokes for us the searing bullets and bloodstained knives which emanate from it. For if the last shall be first, this will only come to pass after a murderous and decisive struggle between the two protagonists.

Fanon's strong words describe the feelings and thoughts between the occupying British Army and the colonized Irish in Northern Ireland, the occupying Israeli Army and the subjugated Palestinians on the West Bank and Gaza Strip, the South African Army and the oppressed Black South Africans in the townships, the Japanese police and the Koreans living in Japan, the Russian Army and subordinated Armenians, and others in southern and eastern Russia. His words also partly invoke the sense many Black Americans have toward police departments in urban centers. In other words, Fanon is articulating century-long, heartfelt, human responses to being degraded and despised, hated and hunted, oppressed and exploited, and marginalized and dehumanized at the hands of powerful, xenophobic European, American, Russian, and Japanese imperial countries.

During the late 1950s, '60s, and early '70s in the United States, these decolonized sensibilities fanned and fueled the Civil Rights and Black Power movements, as well as the student antiwar, feminist, gray, brown, gay, and lesbian movements. In this period we witnessed the shattering of male WASP cultural homogeneity and the collapse of the short-lived liberal consensus. The inclusion of African Americans, Latino/a Americans, Asian Americans, Native Americans, and American women in the culture of critical discourse yielded intense intellectual polemics and inescapable ideological polarization that focused principally on the exclusions, silences, and blindnesses of male WASP cultural homogeneity and its concomitant Arnoldian notions of the canon.

In addition, these critiques promoted three crucial processes that affected intellectual life in the country. First is the appropriation of the theories of postwar Europe — especially the work of the Frankfurt School (Marcuse, Adorno, Horkheimer), French/Italian Marxisms (Sartre, Althusser, Lefebvre, Gramsci), structuralisms (Lévi-Strauss, Todorov), and poststructuralisms (Deleuze, Derrida, Foucault). These diverse and disparate theories — all preoccupied with keeping alive radical projects after the end of the Age of Europe — tend to fuse versions of transgressive European modernisms with Marxist or post-Marxist left politics, and unanimously shun the term "postmodernism." Second, there is the recovery and revisioning of American history in light of the struggles of White male workers, African Americans, Native Americans, Latino/a Americans, gays and lesbians. Third is the impact of forms of popular culture such as television, film, music videos, and even sports on highbrow, literate culture. The Black-based hip-hop culture of youth around the world is one grand example.

After 1973, with the crisis in the international world economy, America's slump in productivity, the challenge of OPEC nations to the North Atlantic monopoly of oil production, the increasing competition in hi-tech sectors of the economy from Japan and West Germany, and the growing fragility of the international debt structure, the United States entered a period of waning self-confidence (compounded by Watergate), and a nearly contracted economy. As the standards of living for the middle classes declined — owing to runaway inflation and escalating unemployment, underemployment, and crime — the quality of living fell for most everyone, and religious and secular neoconservatism emerged with power and potency. This fusion of fervent neonationalism, traditional cultural values, and "free market" policies served as the groundwork for the Reagan-Bush era.

The ambiguous legacies of the European Age, American preeminence, and decolonization continue to haunt our postmodern moment as we come to terms with both the European, American, Japanese, Soviet, and Third World *crimes against* and *contributions to* humanity. The plight of Africans in the New World can be instructive in this regard.

By 1914, European maritime empires had dominion over more than half of the land and a third of the peoples in the world—almost 72 million square kilometers of territory and more than 560 million people under colonial rule. Needless to say, this European control included brutal enslavement, institutional terrorism, and cultural degradation of Black diaspora people. The death of roughly 75 million Africans during the centuries-long, transatlantic slave trade is but one reminder, among others, of the assault on Black humanity. The Black diaspora condition of New World servitude—in which they were viewed as mere commodities with production value, who had no proper legal status, social standing, or public worth—can be characterized as, following Orlando Patterson, natal alienation. This state of perpetual and inheritable domination that diaspora Africans had at birth produced the *modern Black diaspora problematic of invisibility and namelessness*. White supremacist practices—enacted under the auspices of the prestigious cultural authorities of the churches, print media, and scientific academics—promoted Black inferiority and constituted the European background against which Black diaspora struggles for identity, dignity (self-confidence, self-respect, self-esteem), and material resources took place.

An inescapable aspect of this struggle was that the Black diaspora peoples' quest for validation and recognition occurred on the ideological, social, and cultural terrains of other non-Black peoples. White supremacist assaults on Black intelligence, ability, beauty, and character required persistent Black efforts to hold self-doubt, self-contempt, and even self-hatred at bay. Selective appropriation, incorporation, and rearticulation of European ideologies, cultures, and institutions alongside an African heritage—a heritage more or less confined to linguistic innovation in rhetorical practices, stylizations of the body as forms of occupying an alien social space (i.e., hairstyles, ways of walking, standing, talking, and hand expressions), means of constituting and sustaining comraderie and community (i.e., antiphonal, call-and-response styles, rhythmic repetition, risk-ridden syncopation in spectacular modes in musical and rhetorical expressions) —were some of the strategies employed.

The modern Black diaspora problematic of invisibility and namelessness can be understood as the condition of *relative lack of Black power to present themselves to themselves and others as complex human beings, and thereby to contest the bombardment of negative, degrading stereotypes put forward by White supremacist ideologies*. The initial Black response to being caught in this whirlwind of Europeanization was to resist the misrepresentation and caricature of the terms set by uncontested non-Black norms and models, and fight for self-recognition. Every modern Black person, especially cultural disseminators, encounters this problematic of invisibility and namelessness. The initial Black diaspora response was a mode of resistance that was *moralistic in content* and *communal in character*. That is, the fight for representation and recognition highlighted moral judgments regarding Black "positive" images over and against White supremacist stereotypes. These images "re-presented" monolithic and homogeneous Black communities in a way that could displace past misrepresentations of these communities. Stuart Hall has discussed these responses as attempts to change the "relations of representation."

These courageous yet limited Black efforts to combat racist cultural practices uncritically accepted non-Black conventions and standards in two ways. First, they proceeded in an *assimilationist manner* that set out to show that Black people were really like White people—thereby eliding differences (in history and culture) between Whites and Blacks. Black specificity and particularity was thus banished in order to gain White acceptance and approval. Second, these Black responses rested upon a *homogenizing impulse* that assumed that all Black people were really alike—hence obliterating differences (class, gender, region, sexual orientation) between Black peoples. I submit that there are elements of truth in both claims, yet the conclusions are unwarranted owing to the basic fact that non-Black paradigms set the terms of the replies.

The insight in the first claim is that Blacks and Whites are in some important sense alike—i.e., in their positive capacities for human sympathy, moral sacrifice, service to others, intelligence, and beauty; or negatively, in their capacity for cruelty. Yet, the common humanity they share is jettisoned when the claim is cast in an assimilationist manner that subordinates Black particularity to a false universalism, i.e., non-Black rubrics and prototypes. Similarly, the insight in the second claim is that all Blacks are in some significant sense "in the same boat"—that is, subject to White supremacist abuse. Yet, this common condition is stretched too far when viewed in a *homogenizing* way that overlooks how racist treatment vastly differs owing to class, gender, sexual orientation, nation, region, hue, and age.

The moralistic and communal aspects of the initial Black diaspora responses to social and psychic erasure were not simply cast into simplistic binary oppositions of positive/negative, good/bad images that privileged the first term in light of a White norm so that Black efforts remained inscribed within the very logic that dehumanized them. They were further complicated by the fact that these responses were also advanced principally by anxiety-ridden, middle-class Black intellectuals (predominantly male and heterosexual grappling with their sense of double-consciousness—namely their own crisis of identity, agency, audience—caught between a quest for White approval and acceptance and an endeavor to overcome the internalized association of Blackness with inferiority. And I suggest that these complex anxieties of modern Black diaspora intellectuals partly motivate the two major arguments that ground the assimilationist moralism and homogeneous communalism just outlined.

Kobena Mercer has talked about these two arguments as the *reflectionist* and the *social engineering* arguments. The reflectionist argument holds that the fight for Black representation and recognition—against White racist stereotypes—must reflect or mirror the real Black community, not simply the negative and depressing representations of it. The social engineering argument claims that since any form of representation is constructed—i.e., selective in light of broader aims—Black representation (especially given the difficulty of Blacks gaining access to positions of power to produce any Black imagery) should offer positive images, thereby countering racist stereotypes. The hidden assumption of both arguments is that we have unmediated access to what the "real Black community" is and what "positive images" are. In short, these arguments presuppose the very phenomena to be interrogated, and thereby foreclose the very issues that should serve as the subject matter to be investigated.

Any notions of "the real Black community" and "positive images" are value-laden, socially loaded, and ideologically charged. To pursue this discussion is to call into question the possibility of such an uncontested consensus regarding them. Hall has rightly called this encounter "the end of innocence or the end of the innocent notions of the essential Black subject . . . the recognition that 'Black' is essentially a politically and culturally *constructed* category." This recognition—more and more pervasive among the postmodern Black diaspora intelligentsia—is facilitated in part by the slow but sure dissolution of the European Age's maritime empires, and the unleashing of new political possibilities and cultural articulations among ex-colonized peoples across the globe.

One crucial lesson of this decolonization process remains the manner in which most Third World authoritarian bureaucratic elites deploy essentialist rhetorics about "homogeneous national communities" and "positive images" in order to repress and regiment their diverse and heterogeneous populations. Yet in the diaspora, especially among First World countries, this critique has emerged not so much from the Black male component of the left, but rather from the Black women's movement. The decisive push of postmodern Black intellectuals toward a new cultural politics of difference has been made by the powerful critiques and constructive explorations of Black diaspora women (i.e., Toni Morrison). The coffin used to bury the innocent notion of the essential Black subject was nailed shut with the termination of the Black male monopoly on the construction of the Black subject. In this regard, the Black diaspora womanist critique has had a greater impact than the critiques that highlight exclusively class, empire, age, sexual orientation, or nature.

This decisive push toward the end of Black innocence—though prefigured in various degrees in the best moments of James Baldwin, Amiri Baraka, Anna Cooper, W. E. B. DuBois, Frantz Fanon, C. L. R. James, Claudia Jones, the later Malcolm X, and others—forces Black diaspora cultural workers to encounter what Hall has called the "politics of representation." The main aim now is not simply access to representation in order to produce positive images of homogeneous communities — though broader access remains a practical and political problem. Nor is the primary goal here that of contesting stereotypes — though contestation remains a significant though limited venture. Following the model of the Black diaspora traditions of music, athletics, and rhetoric, Black cultural workers must constitute and sustain discursive and institutional networks that deconstruct earlier modern Black strategies for identity formation, demystify power relations that incorporate class, patriarchal, and homophobic biases, and construct more multivalent and multidimensional responses that articulate the complexity and diversity of Black practices in the modern and postmodern world.

Furthermore, Black cultural workers must investigate and interrogate the other of Blackness/Whiteness. One cannot deconstruct the binary oppositional logic of images of Blackness without extending it to the contrary condition of Blackness/Whiteness itself. However, a mere dismantling will not do — for the very notion of a deconstructive social theory is oxymoronic. Yet, social theory is what is needed to examine and *explain* the historically specific ways in which "Whiteness" is a politically constructed category parasitic on "Blackness," and thereby to conceive of the profoundly hybrid character of what we mean by "race," "ethnicity," and "nationality." Needless to say, these inquiries must traverse those of "male/female," "colonizer/colonized," "heterosexual/homosexual," et al., as well.

Demystification is the most illuminating mode of theoretical inquiry for those who promote the new cultural politics of difference. Social structural analyses of empire, exterminism, class, race, gender, nature, age, sexual orientation, nation, and region are the springboards — though not landing grounds — for the most desirable forms of critical practice that take history (and herstory) seriously. Demystification tries to keep track of the complex dynamics of institutional and other related power structures in order to disclose options and alternatives for transformative praxis; it also attempts to grasp the way in which representational strategies are creative responses to novel circumstances and conditions. In this way, the central role of human agency (always enacted under circumstances not of one's choosing) — be it in the critic, artist, or constituency, and audience — is accented.

I call demystificatory criticism "prophetic criticism" — the approach appropriate for the new cultural politics of difference — because while it begins with social structural analyses it also makes explicit its moral and political aims. It is partisan, partial, engaged, and crisis-centered, yet always keeps open a skeptical eye to avoid dogmatic traps, premature closures, formulaic formulations, or rigid conclusions. In addition to social structural analyses, moral and political judgments, and sheer critical consciousness, there indeed is evaluation. Yet the aim of this evaluation is neither to pit art-objects against one another like racehorses nor to create eternal canons that dull, discourage, or even dwarf contemporary achievements. We listen to Laurie Anderson, Kathleen Battle, Ludwig Beethoven, Charlie Parker, Luciano Pavarotti, Sarah Vaughan, or Stevie Wonder; read Anton Chekhov, Ralph Ellison, Gabriel García Márquez, Doris Lessing, Toni Morrison, Thomas Pynchon, William Shakespeare; or see the works of Ingmar Bergman, Le Corbusier, Frank Gehry, Barbara Kruger, Spike Lee, Martin Puryear, Pablo Picasso, or Howardena Pindell — not in order to undergird bureaucratic assents or enliven cocktail party conversations, but rather to be summoned by the styles they deploy for their profound insights, pleasures, and challenges. Yet, all evaluation — including a delight in Eliot's poetry despite his reactionary politics, or a love of Zora Neale Hurston's novels despite her Republican party affiliations — is inseparable, though not identical or reducible to social structural analyses, moral and political judgments, and the workings of a curious critical consciousness.

The deadly traps of demystification — and any form of prophetic criticism — are those of reductionism, be it of the sociological, psychological, or historical sort. By reductionism I mean either one-factor analyses (i.e., crude Marxisms, feminisms, racialisms, etc.) that yield a one-dimensional functionalism or a hyper-subtle analytical perspective that loses touch with the specificity of an art work's form and the context of its reception. Few cultural workers of whatever stripe can walk the tightrope between the Scylla of reductionism and the Charybdis of aestheticism — yet, demystificatory (or prophetic) critics must. Of course, since so many art practices these days also purport to be criticism, this also holds true for artists.

The Existential Challenge

The existential challenge to the new cultural politics of difference can be stated simply: how does one acquire the resources to survive and the cultural capital to thrive as a critic or artist? By cultural capital (Pierre Bourdieu's term), I mean not only the high-quality skills required to engage in critical practices, but more important, the self-confidence, discipline, and perseverance necessary for success without an undue reliance on the mainstream for approval and acceptance. This challenge holds for all prophetic critics, yet it is especially difficult for those of color. The widespread modern European denial of the intelligence, ability, beauty, and character of people of color puts a tremendous burden on critics and artists of color to "prove" themselves in light of norms and models set by White elites whose own heritage devalued and dehumanized them. In short, in the court of criticism and art — or any matters regarding the life of the mind — people of color are guilty (i.e., not expected to meet standards of intellectual achievement) until "proven" innocent (i.e., acceptable to "us").

This is more a structural dilemma than a matter of personal attitudes. The profoundly racist and sexist heritage of the European Age has bequeathed to us a set of deeply ingrained perceptions about people of color including, of course, the self-perceptions that people of color bring. It is not surprising that most intellectuals of color in the past exerted much of their energies and efforts to gain acceptance and approval by "White normative gazes." The new cultural politics of difference advises critics and artists of color to put aside this mode of mental bondage, thereby freeing themselves both to interrogate the ways in which they are bound by certain conventions and to learn from and build on these very norms and models. One hallmark of wisdom in the context of any struggle is to avoid knee-jerk rejection and uncritical acceptance.

Self-confidence, discipline, and perseverance are not ends in themselves. Rather, they are the necessary stuff of which enabling criticism and self-criticism are made. Notwithstanding inescapable jealousies, insecurities, and anxieties, one telling characteristic of critics and artists of color linked to the new prophetic criticism should be their capacity for and promotion of relentless criticism and self-criticism — be it the normative paradigms of their White colleagues that tend to leave out considerations of empire, race, gender, and sexual orientation, or the damaging dogmas about the homogeneous character of communities of color.

There are four basic options for people of color interested in re-presentation — if they are to survive and thrive as serious practitioners of their craft. First, there is the Booker T. Temptation, namely the individual preoccupation with the mainstream and its legitimizing power. Most critics and artists of color try to bite this bait. It is nearly unavoidable, yet few succeed in a substantive manner. It is no accident that the most creative and profound among them — especially those with staying power beyond mere flashes in the pan to satisfy faddish tokenism — are usually marginal to the mainstream. Even the pervasive professionalization of cultural practitioners of color in the past few decades has not produced towering figures who reside within the established White patronage system that bestows the rewards and prestige for chosen contributions to American society.

It certainly helps to have some trustworthy allies within this system, yet most of those who enter and remain tend to lose much of their creativity, diffuse their prophetic energy, and dilute their critiques. Still, it is unrealistic for creative people of color to think they can sidestep the White patronage system. And though there are indeed some White allies conscious of the tremendous need to rethink identity politics, it is naive to think that being comfortably nested within this very same system — even if one can be a patron to others — does not affect one's work, one's outlook, and, most important, one's soul.

The second option is the Talented Tenth Seduction, namely, a move toward arrogant group insularity. This alternative has a limited function — to preserve one's sanity and sense of self as one copes with the mainstream. Yet, it is, at best, a transitional and transient activity. If it becomes a permanent option it is self-defeating in that it usually reinforces the very inferiority complexes promoted by the subtly racist mainstream. Hence it tends to revel in a parochialism and encourage a narrow racialist and chauvinistic outlook.

The third strategy is the Go-It-Alone option. This is an extreme rejectionist perspective that shuns the mainstream and group insularity. Almost every critic and artist of color contemplates or enacts this option at some time in his or her pilgrimage. It is healthy in that it reflects the presence of independent, critical, and skeptical sensibilities toward perceived constraints on one's creativity. Yet, it is, in the end, difficult if not impossible to sustain if one is to grow, develop, and mature intellectually, as some semblance of dialogue with a community is necessary for almost any creative practice.

The most desirable option for people of color who promote the new cultural politics of difference is to be a Critical Organic Catalyst. By this I mean a person who stays attuned to the best of what the mainstream has to offer—its paradigms, viewpoints, and methods—yet maintains a grounding in affirming and enabling subcultures of criticism. Prophetic critics and artists of color should be exemplars of what it means to be intellectual freedom fighters, that is, cultural workers who simultaneously position themselves within (or alongside) the mainstream while clearly aligned with groups who vow to keep alive potent traditions of critique and resistance. In this regard, one can take clues from the great musicians or preachers of color who are open to the best of what other traditions offer, yet are rooted in nourishing subcultures that build on the grand achievements of a vital heritage. Openness to others—including the mainstream—does not entail wholesale cooptation, and group autonomy is not group insularity. Louis Armstrong, Ella Baker, W. E. B. DuBois, Martin Luther King, Jr., Jose Carlos Mariatequi, Wynton Marsalis, M. M. Thomas, and Ronald Takaki have understood this well.

The new cultural politics of difference can thrive only if there are communities, groups, organizations, institutions, subcultures, and networks of people of color who cultivate critical sensibilities and personal accountability—without inhibiting individual expressions, curiosities, and idiosyncrasies. This is especially needed given the escalating racial hostility, violence, and polarization in the United States. Yet, this critical coming-together must not be a narrow closing of ranks. Rather, it is a strengthening and nurturing endeavor that can forge more solid alliances and coalitions. In this way, prophetic criticism—with its stress on historical specificity and artistic complexity—directly addresses the intellectual challenge. The cultural capital of people of color—with its emphasis on self-confidence, discipline, perseverance, and subcultures of criticism—also tries to meet the existential requirement. Both are mutually reinforcing. Both are motivated by a deep commitment to individuality and democracy—the moral and political ideals that guide the creative response to the political challenge.

The Political Challenge

Adequate rejoinders to intellectual and existential challenges equip the practitioners of the new cultural politics of difference to meet the political ones. This challenge principally consists of forging solid and reliable alliances of people of color and White progressives guided by a moral and political vision of greater democracy and individual freedom in communities, states, and transnational enterprises — i.e., corporations, and information and communications conglomerates. Jesse Jackson's Rainbow coalition is a gallant, yet flawed effort in this regard — gallant due to the tremendous energy, vision, and courage of its leader and followers; flawed because of its failure to take seriously critical and democratic sensibilities within its own operations.

The time has come for critics and artists of the new cultural politics of difference to cast their nets widely, flex their muscles broadly, and thereby refuse to limit their visions, analyses, and praxis to their particular terrains. The aim is to dare to recast, redefine, and revise the very notions of "modernity," "mainstream," "margins," "difference," "otherness." We have now reached a new stage in the perennial struggle for freedom and dignity. And while much of the First World intelligentsia adopts retrospective and conservative outlooks that defend the crisis-ridden present, we promote a prospective and prophetic vision with a sense of possibility and potential, especially for those who bear the social costs of the present. We look to the past for strength, not solace; we look at the present and see people perishing, not profits mounting; we look toward the future and vow to make it different and better.

To put it boldly, the new kind of critic and artist associated with the new cultural politics of difference consists of an energetic breed of New World *bricoleurs* with improvisational and flexible sensibilities that sidestep mere opportunism and mindless eclecticism; persons from all countries, cultures, genders, sexual orientations, ages, and regions with protean identities who avoid ethnic chauvinism and faceless universalism; intellectual and political freedom fighters with partisan passion, international perspectives, and thank God, a sense of humor that combats the ever-present absurdity that forever threatens our democratic and libertarian projects and dampens the fire that fuels our will to struggle. Yet, we will struggle and stay, as those brothers and sisters on the block say, "out there" — with intellectual rigor, existential dignity, moral vision, political courage, and soulful style.

Race, articulation and societies structured in dominance

by Stuart Hall

The aim of this paper is to mark out a set of emergent questions and problems in the study of racially-structured social formations, and to indicate where some new and important initiatives are developing. In order to do this, it is necessary to situate the breaks which these studies represent from the established field of study; this, in turn, requires a crude characterization of the field. I begin with such a crude sketch, at a very general level of abstraction—offering only passing apologies for the necessary simplification involved. The attempts to deal with the question of 'race' directly or to analyse those social formations where race is a salient feature constitute, by now, a formidable, immense and varied literature, which is is impossible to summarize at all adequately. No justice can be done to this complexity and achievement here.

Something important about this field of inquiry can nevertheless be grasped by dividing many of the varied tendencies represented within it into two broad dominant tendencies. Each has generated a great variety of different studies and approaches. But the selection of these two tendencies is not wholly arbitrary. In many ways, they have come to be understood as opposed to one another. As is often the case with such theoretical oppositions, they can also be understood, in many respects, as inverted mirror images of one another. Each tries to supplement the weakness of the opposing paradigm by stressing the so-called 'neglected element'. In doing so, each points to real weaknesses of conceptualization and indicates, symptomatically, important points of departure for more adequate theorizations. Each, however, I suggest, is inadequate within the operative terms of its present theorization. The break thus constitutes a theoretical rupture, in part or in whole, with each of these dominant tendencies, and a possible restructuring of the theoretical field such as might enable important work of a new kind to begin.

For simplification sake, the two tendencies may be called the 'economic' and the 'sociological'. Let us begin with the first—the economic. A great range and variety of studies must, for convenience, be bundled together under this crude heading. These include both differences of emphasis and differences of conceptualization. Thus, some studies within this tendency concentrate on internal economic structures, within specific social formations (analyses of the economic and racial structures of South Africa would be a good example). Others are more concerned with relations between internal and external economic features, however these are characterized (developed/underdeveloped; imperialist/colonized; metropolitan/satellite, etc.). Or very different ways of conceptualizing the 'economic' are involved, based on radically different economic premises or frameworks. For the purposes of this paper, I shall group together within this tendency—the pertinent differences will be dealt with later—those which are framed by neo-classical 'development' economics (e.g. a dual sector analysis—capitalist and subsistence sectors); those which adopt a modernization or industrialization model (e.g. based on something like Rostow's theory of 'stages of growth'); those, like the 'dependency' theorists of the ECLA school, utilizing a radical theory of the economics of world underdevelopment; or those like Baran or Gunder Frank, who have employed a Marxist orientation (how classical it remains, as shall be seen, is a matter of continuing controversy). What allows of a characterization of these very different approaches as belonging to a single tendency is simply this: they take economic relations and structures to have an overwhelmingly determining effect on the social structures of such formations. Specifically, those social divisions which assume a distinctively racial or ethnic character can be attributed or explained principally with reference to economic structures and processes.

The second approach I have called sociological. Here again—rather tendentiously—a great variety of approaches are placed under a single rubric. Some concentrate on social relations between different racial or ethnic strata. Some deal more exclusively with cultural differences (ethnicity), of which race is only one, extreme case. Some pursue a more rigorously plural theory, derived from Furnivall and M. G. Smith and others of that school. Some are exclusively concerned with forms of political domination or disadvantage, based on the exploitation of racial distinctions. In the vast majority of these studies, race is treated as a social category. Biological conceptions of race have greatly receded in importance, though they have by no means wholly disappeared (for example: the revival of bio-sociology, and the reintroduction of biologically-based theories, through the genetic principle, in the recent work of Jensen and Eysenck. The principal stress in this second tendency is on race or ethnicity as specifically social or cultural features of the social formations under discussion.

Again, what distinguishes the contributors to this school as belonging—for the purposes here alone—to a single tendency, is this: however they differ internally, the contributors to the sociological tendency agree on the autonomy, the non-reductiveness, of race and ethnicity as social features. These exhibit, they argue, their own forms of structuration, have their own specific effects, which cannot be explained away as mere surface forms of appearance of economic relations, nor adequately theorized by reducing them to the economic level of determination.

Here it can be seen how the two paradigms have been counterposed to one another, each correcting the weakness of its opposite. The first tendency, whether Marxist or not, gives an over-all determinacy to the economic level. This, it is said, imparts a hard centre—a materialist basis—to the otherwise soft-centredness or culturalism of ethnic studies. The stress on the sociological aspects, in the second tendency, is then a sort of direct reply to this first emphasis. It aims to introduce a necessary complexity into the simplifying schemas of an economic explanation, and to correct against the tendency of the first towards economic reductionism. Social formations, the second tendency argues, are complex ensembles, composed of several different structures, none of which is reducible to the other. Thus, whereas the former tends to be mono-causal in form, the latter tends to be pluralist in emphasis, even if it is not explicitly plural in the theoretical sense.

It will be seen that this debate reproduces, *in micro*, the larger, strategic debates which have marked out the field of social science in general in recent years. Consequently, developments in the latter, larger, field—whether they take racially-structured social formations as their specific objects of inquiry or not—are bound to have theoretical effects for that region of study. Hence, the consequences of such breaks in the paradigms for the 'sociological theories of race'. The debate is not, however, exclusively a theoretical one. Differences of theoretical analysis and approach have real effects for the strategies of political transformation in such societies. If the first tendency is broadly correct, then what is often experienced and analysed as ethnic or racial conflicts are really manifestations of deeper, economic contradictions. It is, therefore, to the latter that the politics of transformations must essentially be addressed. The second tendency draws attention to the actual forms and dynamic of political conflict and social tension in such societies—which frequently assume a racial or ethnic character. It points to the empirical difficulty of subsuming these directly into more classical economic conflicts. But if ethnic relations are not reducible to economic relations, then the former will not necessarily change if and when the latter do. Hence, in a political struggle, the former must be given their due specificity and weight as autonomous factors. Theory here, as always, has direct or indirect practical consequences.

Political circumstances—while not sufficient to account for the scientific value of these theories—also provide one of the conditions of existence for theory, and have effects for its implementation and appropriation. This has clearly been the case, even if restricted (as is done for a good section of this paper) primarily to the Latin America and the Caribbean. The dual sector model—based on an export-led, import-substitution, foreign investment supported type of economic development—sponsored a long and disastrous period of national economic development, which further undermined the economic position of one country after another in the region. The theory of modernization was for long the economic cutting-edge of alliance-for-progress strategies in the continent.

Versions of the 'dependency' school have been harnessed, under different conditions, to the promotion of anti-imperialist, national-capitalist development of a radical type. The metropolitan/satellite theories of Gunder Frank and others were specifically developed in the context of the Cuban revolution and the strategies of Latin-American revolution elaborated in OLAS—represented, for example, in the resolutions to the 1962 Second Declaration of Havana. The whole field, indeed, provides an excellent case study of the necessary interconnexions between theory, politics and ideology in social science.

Each tendency exhibits something of its own rational core. Thus, it may not be possible to explain away race by reference to the economic relations exclusively. But the first tendency is surely correct when it insists that racial structures cannot be understood adequately outside the framework of quite specific sets of economic relations. Unless one attributes to race a single, unitary, transhistorical character—such that wherever and whenever it appears it always assumes the same autonomous features, which can be theoretically explained, perhaps, by some general theory of prejudice in human nature (an essentialist argument of a classic type)—then one must deal with the historical specificity of race in the modern world. Here one is then obliged to agree that race relations are directly linked with economic processes: historically, with the epochs of conquest, colonization and mercantilist domination, and currently, with the 'unequal exchanges' which characterize the economic relations between developed metropolitical and 'underdeveloped' satellite economic regions of the world economy. The problem here is not whether economic structures are relevant to racial divisions but how the two are theoretically connected. Can the economic level provide an adequate and sufficient level of explanation of the racial features of these social formations? Here, the second tendency enters its caveat. Similarly, the second tendency is surely correct to draw attention to the specificity of those social formations which exhibit distinctive racial or ethnic charactistics. The critique of economic reductionism is also, certainly to the point. The problem here is to account for the appearance of this 'something else'—these extra-economic factors and their place in the dynamic reproduction of such social formations. But these 'real problems' also help us to identify what weaknesses are obscured by the inversions which each paradigm practices on the other. If the dominant tendency of the first paradigm is to attempt to command all differences and specificities within the framework of a simplifying economic logic then that of the second is to stop short with a set of plural explanations which lack an adequate theorization, and which in the end are descriptive rather than analytic. This, of course, is to state the differences in their sharpest, and most oversimplified form. It is worthwhile, now, exploring some of the complex terrain and arguments which are contained by this simple binarism.

The first aspect can be pinpointed by looking at some features of the recent controversies which have arisen in the analysis of the South African social formation. South Africa is clearly a 'limit case' in the theoretical sense, as well as a 'test case' in the political sense. It is perhaps *the* social formation in which the salience of racial features cannot for a moment be denied. Clearly, also the racial structures of South African society cannot be attributed to cultural or ethnic differences alone: they are deeply implicated with the forms of political and economic domination which structure the whole social formation. Moreover, there can be little argument that this is a social formation in which the capitalist mode of production is the dominant economic mode. Indeed, South Africa is the 'exceptional' (?) case of an industrial capitalist social formation, where race is an articulating principle of the social, political and ideological structures, and where the capitalist mode is sustained by drawing, simultaneously, on what have been defined as both 'free' and 'forced' labour.

Now substantial parts of the literature on the South African social formation deal with the racial aspects of the society as accounted for, essentially, by the governing economic relations. These relations are characterized as, for all practical purposes, class relations in the classical sense. The structuring of the South African labour force into black and white strata is therefore analysed as similar to the 'fracturing' of the working class, which one finds in all capitalist social formations—with the single exception that, here, race is the mechanism by which this stratification of the class is accomplished. As Wolpe has observed, these analyses assume that white and black working classes stand in essentially the same relation to capital. Hence, the dynamic of social relations will fall within the basic logic of class struggle which capitalist relations or production classically assume. The racial divisions amount to 'nothing more than the specific form which the fractionalization of the working class, common to all capitalist modes of production, has taken in the South African social formations' (Wolpe: 1976). Such analyses—Wolpe refers to several sources—thus tend to fall into what we have defined as our 'first' paradigm: the subsumption of racial structures under the 'logic' of capitalist economic relations. This approach can then be easily matched by its immediate, and inverted, opposite. These alternative analyses treat economic class formations as largely irrelevant to the analysis of the social and political structures, where race, rather than class, is treated as the pertinent factor, through which the society is socially structured and around which social conflicts are generated. Such a 'sociological' approach can be found in, for example, Kuper (1974) and Van den Berghe (1965).

Much more important—and more difficult to slot easily into either of the two approaches—is the work of John Rex, himself a South African and a distinguished sociologist. Rex has not worked extensively on South African materials. But his writing, though often necessarily programmatic, represents the 'sociological' approach at one of its richest and most complex points. Rex's first essay on the subject, 'South African society in comparative perspective' (Rex: 1973), opens with a critique of the failure of both structural-functionalist and Marxist perspectives to deal effectively with race and ethnicity in South African society. He is equally critical of, though he gives more attention to, the 'Plural' theory of Furnivall and Smith. Smith argued that the different ethnic segments of Caribbean society were 'plurally' distinct, held together only through the monopoly, by one of the segments, of political power: 'the monopoly of power by one cultural section is the essential precondition for the maintenance of the total society in its current form.' Against this, Rex correctly argues that 'the dynamics of the society turn upon the involvement of men of differing ethnic backgrounds in the same social institutions, viz., the slave plantation' (Rex: 1973, p. 261). The same could be said of the attempts to extend the 'plural society' paradigm, with its primacy of attention to cultural segmentation, and its ascription of the factor of cohesion to the instance of political monopoly, to South Africa. However, he is equally critical of any attempt to explain the racial forms in which social conflict appears in such societies as a species of 'false consciousness'.

Rex bases his own approach on a significant historical fact of *difference*. Whereas, 'classically', capitalism has been installed through the expansion of market relations, production for which is based on 'free labour', capitalism in South Africa arose on the basis of conquest (of the Bantu peoples) and their incorporation into the economic relations on the basis of 'unfree labour', 'as part of an efficient capitalist system of production'. This inaugurates the capitalist mode on very different historic 'presuppositions' from those derived from the general account said to be offered by Marx—presuppositions, however, more typical of 'colonial' formations, where conquest and colonization have been central features, and thus pertinent to the appearance, in such societies, of 'not simply the class struggle engendered by capitalist development, but the "race war" engendered by colonial conquest' (Rex: 1973, p. 262). Rex makes a great deal of these differentiating features: the 'capacity of the employers to command the use of coercive violence during and after colonial conquest', and the fact that the 'central labour institution' is not classical free labour but 'migrant labour in its unfree form'.

Taking as the central feature of his analysis this quite atypical 'central labour institution', Rex is able to delineate more precisely the specific economic mechanisms which have served to 'incorporate' the African working class into the capitalist system in ways which *preserve* rather than liquidate its segmentary racial character. The racial structure of the South African social formation is thereby given concrete economic conditions of existence—the link being traceable, precisely, through its 'peculiarity', its deviation from the 'classical' capitalist path. Rex traces historically the various economic forms of this 'unfreedom': the rural reserves, the labour compound, the emergence of the third element of the migrant labour system, the 'urban native location'. 'Nearly all African labour partakes in some measure of the characteristics of the compound worker and the domestic worker's status. All are liable to masters and servants legislation, and none are completely free, even though the development of secondary manufacturing industry may lead to greater flexibility of wages, greater permanence of the labour force and hence greater recognition of the needs of the worker for kinship and community.' (Rex: 1973, p. 278). These 'differences', both in the mode of entry and in the status of African labour, are seen by Rex as operating principally through the means by which African labour supply is recruited to capitalist industry. The economic relations are thus the necessary, but not the sufficient condition of the racial structure of the South African social formation. For this is also preserved by a 'non-normative' element—for example, political and legal factors—which stems from the political domination of the State by the white settler capitalist class, and the 'workable compromise' between this class and the white working class, which leads both to reap the advantages of confining native labour to its subordinate status in the labour market. In the context of the 'classical' line of capitalist development, a capitalism which preserves rather than abolishes such 'irrational' features must be, to say the least, a 'deviant' case.

There is certainly no simple counterposing of 'social' as against 'economic' factors here. Rex cannot be accused of neglecting the level of economic relations, as many 'culturalists' can. Indeed, it is his concern with the specificity of the *forms* of economic relations peculiar to the South African case which enables him to grasp some of the fundamental features of a social formation which is both identifiably 'capitalist', and yet different in structure from 'the capitalist type' of social development—as the latter has been derived from one reading of the Marxist literature. The attention to the 'central labour institutions' of this formation enables him to bring forward what Marx in another context called the 'differentia specifica'—the basis, as he put it, of an adequate historically-specific abstraction: 'just those things which determine their development, i.e., the elements which are not general and common, must be separated out . . . so that in their unity . . . their essential difference is not forgotten.' (Marx: 1973, p. 85.)

Nor is there a neglect of class relations and the class struggle. The segmentary approach of 'Pluralism' is specifically refused. 'If there is division, the divisions can be seen as functionally integrated within an over-all pattern of political conflict generated by the capitalist development of the country since the mineral discoveries of 1867 and 1886.' The 'revision' involved is rather the refusal of any attempt to subsume these into a universal and univocal form— 'capitalist class relations' in general. 'Clearly what we have here is not something which can be adequately interpreted in terms of some universal Marxist law of class struggle but a specific kind of class struggle there undoubtedly is, namely one in which the classes are groups of varying rights and degrees of rightlessness, according to the kind of conquest or unfreedom which was imposed on them in an earlier period. The history, the structure and the forms of social differentiation which South Africa presents [i.e. its 'racial' aspect] are, as in the case of any former colonial society, the product of such conquest and unfreedom.' These two criteria—conquest and 'unfree' labour—are the critical conceptual mechanisms through which Rex's analysis is organized. The 'origin' of the capitalist mode in conditions of conquest, coupled with the 'peculiar institutions' of unfree labour thus preserve, at the economic level, and secure its continuing racially ascriptive features. This is a capitalism of a very specific and distinctive kind: 'there are a number of different relationships to the means of production more subtle than can be comprehended in terms of distinction between owners and non-owners', each of which 'gives rise to specific class situations . . . a whole range of class situations'. The analysis therefore begins with the economic level but differentiates it from the classical type.

In addition, however, there are other relations which are not ascribable within the 'social relations of production'. These include distinctions at the level of culture and values—maintained, for example, by such institutional structures as the system of Bantu education and forms of political power—established through the separation of political and economic power, such as the control of political power by the whites. These generate conflicts between groups distinct from 'control of the means of production'. Here the analysis encompasses the position of social groups—the African 'middle class', the Cape Coloureds, the Indian traders—which cannot be easily assimilated to the earlier analysis of economic relations. From them many ascriptive features of South Africa's 'closed' structure of social relations also arise.

This analysis, while predicated on the 'peculiarity' of the South African system, is not limited to it. Rex has recently proposed a similar sketch as the basis for analysing ethnic relations in Latin America and the Caribbean (Rex: 1978). Here, too, the analysis begins with delineating 'the basic forms of economic exploitation which can arise in colonial conditions', including 'other possible types of capitalist and non-capitalist exploitation and accumulation'. In this instance, the range includes forms of 'unfree' or 'partly-free' labour—the *encomie* slavery and the plantation system, the formation of a 'dependent peasant'. It includes a similar range of social strata—the 'settlers', pariah trader groups, middlemen, the caciques, missionaries, administrators. The general form of the argument is very similar to that employed in the South African case. 'Some of these groups are opposed to one another as classes in a Marxian sense. All of them, however, form relatively close groups with their own distinctive cultural traits and social organization. The over-all effect is of too much overlap and inter-penetration to justify us in calling it a caste system, but too much closure of avenues of mobility for us to call it a system of social stratification. It is much too complex, involving overlapping modes of production, for it to be described as a situation of class struggle in the Marxian sense. All of these aspects need to be kept in mind when we speak of a colonial system of social stratification.' (Rex: 1978, p. 30).

On the broad theoretical plane, we must see this as a model founded on a very specific theoretical revision. Without undue simplification, it combines elements of a Marxist and a Weberian approach. The synthesis is, however, secured on essentially Weberian terrain. I say this, not because Rex constantly counterposes his own approach to what he sees as an inadequate and simplifying application of the 'Marxist law of class struggle'—though he does. Rather, this characterization refers to the conceptual structure of Rex's revisions. The synthesis is accomplished, theoretically, in two different, complementary ways. The first is the distancing of the analysis from what is conceptualized as a 'classical' Marxist approach. Much depends on how this definition is established. 'Classical' Marxism is characterized as a mode of explanation which assumes that all the various instances of conflict are subsumable within and dominated by the class struggle. Classes are defined by economic position—loosely, in terms of the distinction between 'owners and non-owners' of the means of production. They are economic groups 'in themselves' which can be organized, through the pursuit of their distinct class interests in competing market situations, by means of the class struggle, to become 'classes-for-themselves'. The Marxist approach is also identified, here, with a set of propositions as to the form, the path and the logic of capitalist development. The classical form is that in which free labour confronts the capitalist in the labour market. (Capitalism 'can spring to life only when the owner of the means of production and subsistence meets in the market with the free labourer selling his labour power. And this one historical condition comprises a world's history'. (Marx: 1961, p. 170).) The classical path is that which makes this struggle between owners and non-owners the typical, dominant and determining set of relations in all social formations in which the capitalist mode is dominant. The classical logic is that the 'economic rationality' of capitalist market relations sooner or later prevail over and transform those relations stemming from previous, now displaced, modes of production, so that capitalist relations 'net' the latter within their sway. Rex distances himself from this 'classical' account, in terms of the pertinent differences between it and the actual social formations it is required to explain. True, he concedes that where there is capitalism, there will be economic struggles of a capitalist type—class struggles. However, social formations of a colonial type exhibit different forms which take a different path and obey a different logic. In addition, there are in such social formations other structural relations which are not attributable to class relations of a classical capitalist type.

The second feature is a recuperation of these problems within the framework of a 'classical' Weberianism. By this we mean that, contrary to those who have adopted Weber against Marx, as a way of moving decisively from economic-structural to more 'superstructural' features, Rex always works from that often-forgotten side of Weber's work which treats extensively of economic relations including, of course, economic class conflict of a capitalist type, as one among a range of possible types of such relations. This is a distinctive stress, which allows Rex to encompass Marxian analysis of class relations as one, limited case within a more inclusive range of economic relations, defined as a set of 'ideal-types'. This 'one among a range' approach thus also permits the elaboration of other economic relations to explain peculiar features of social formations which do not exhibit Marx's hypostasized classical capitalist structure. For Weber, economic class conflicts were conceptualized as one among a range of possible market situations, in relation to which groups, differently composed, struggled in competition. For Weber, these different market relations do not overlap into anything which can be called the general form of the class struggle. Groups competing in the struggle over prestige or status may not be the same as groups competing over the power over scarce resources. Thus, in his work on immigration and housing, Rex distinguishes, between and within economic groups in terms of the stratification of the housing market—in relation to which, he identifies a set of distinct 'housing classes'. It follows that the groups dominant in each market situation do not cohere into anything so singular as a single ruling class in the Marxian sense. Instead, one must generate, according to each empirical case, a range of ideal-typical market situations, the sum of these plural structures constituting the social formation. This does not mean that the analysis excludes questions of exploitation. This is not, however, a general feature but one which remains to be specified in each individual case. It is, thus, Weber in this 'harder' form—Weber, so to speak, 'corrected for' by Marx— which is the theoretical basis of the synthesis Rex proposes. The solution to a limited, one-sided form of Marxian explanation is the adoption of a powerful and distinctive 'left Weberianism'. It should be pointed out here that this 'solution' is not restricted exclusively to those who are opposed to the 'totalism' of Marxian forms of explanation. It has been noted recently (cf., McLennan: 1976 and Schwarz: 1978) that some Marxist theorists, when required to integrate political and ideological structures into an economic analysis of a Marxist kind, some-times also attempt to deal with these levels by a somewhat untheorized appro-priation of Weberianism. (This, it has been suggested, is sometimes the case with the work of so distinguished a Marxist economic historian as Maurice Dobb.) So what has been pinpointed here is something like a 'theoretical convergence', operated at one time or another from arguments which begin from either the Marxist or the Weberian pole of the debate.

Significantly, there is one point where Rex challenges both Marx and Weber—a point where, incidentally, they both appear to agree. This is the con-tention that 'free labour was the only form of labour compatible in the long run with the logic of rational capitalism' (Rex: 1973, p. 273). This argument— founded, in Weber, by his particular ideal-type definition of 'capitalist rational-ity', and in Marx, by his historical analysis of the 'typical' path of capitalist development, based on the English case—is contested by Rex on both fronts. Instead, Rex argues that historical deviations from this 'modal' type can often be found in social formations of a 'specifically colonial type'. Here, in contrast, conquest, and a variety of forms of 'unfree labour' (based on apparently irra-tional forms of ascriptive relations, such as those founded on racial differences) can be possible conditions of existence for the emergence and development of an 'effective' capitalist mode of production. Lying behind this analytic distinction is, undoubtedly, a theoretical-political point: namely a refusal of the 'Euro-centredness' of Marxism, based as it is on extrapolating to other social forma-tions forms of development, paths and logics peculiar to, and illegitimately generalized from, European cases (especially, of course, the English case, which forms the basis for the analysis in Marx's *Capital*).

With this important qualification, we can now identify the dominant tendency of this synthesis (the following passage may stand for many other in-stances in Rex's work): 'Of course, one problem in adopting terms like "caste" and "estate" . . . is that all of them seem to omit what is essential to the Marxist definition of class, i.e. relationships to the means of production. What we wish to suggest here, however, departs from simple Marxism in a twofold sense. First it recognizes that at the level of relationships to the means of production there are more possible positions and potentialities for class formation than simple European Marxism seems to allow; and second, that over and above the

actual means of production, there are a number of social functions and positions
and that these functions are appropriated by closed groups which, thereafter,
have their own interests and their own power position vis-a-vis society as a whole.'
When this 'Marx plus Weber' theoretical position is then translated to the domain of politics, it yields a 'Marx plus Fanon' sort of argument. (Rex: 1978,
p. 23–24, p. 45.)

The position, the synthesis of which has been outlined here, has of course
been criticized in the context of its application to South Africa. For example,
Wolpe in a recent article (Wolpe: 1976) points out that the distinction between
'free' and 'forced' labour is not an adequate way of conceptualizing the relations
of production of a capitalist social formation, since, for Marx, even in its classical form, 'free labour' is 'free' only in a very specific and formal sense: it is, after
all, subject to economic compulsions to sell its labour power as a commodity.
Thus, in the South African case, the free/unfree couple, while effective in distinguishing the different constraints which structure the availability of black and
white labour in the market, is not theoretically powerful enough to establish,
for black labour, a relation to capitalist production of a conceptually distinct
kind: 'all labour-power is in some way and in some degree unfree, the type,
gradation or continuum of degrees of unfreedom "merely" affect the intensity
of exploitation but not its mode' (Wolpe: 1975, p. 203). Secondly, this distinction
does not encompass what for Marx was central to 'relations of production';
namely, the mode of appropriation of surplus labour. Thirdly, such an approach abstracts the labour market and its constraints from the system of production relations proper, which are in fact the central preoccupation of a
Marxian analysis. Fourth, the absence of an adequate theorization at the mode of
production level leaves us with a political and ideological definition of 'classes'
which are then too easily homogenized with the main racial groupings. However,
a detailed analysis of the position of the black and white working class in South
Africa, in terms both of their complex relations to capitalist production and their
internal stratifications, does not allow us to 'treat racial groups' as 'homogeneous
in their class composition'. Wolpe, indeed, uses Carchedi's recent work on the
identification of social classes to say that the 'functions' of even the white
working class with respect to capital are not homogeneous. Fifth, Wolpe, argues
that political and ideological positions cannot be ascribed as a bloc to classes
defined at the economic level: 'A social class, or fraction or stratum of a class,
may take up a class position that does not correspond to its interests, which are
defined by the class determination that fixes the horizon of the class struggle.'
(Carchedi: 1977.) The example taken is that of the 'labour aristocracy'. This
leads on to a more general argument, that the analysis of classes and class struggle
must begin from the level of the relations of production, rather than from political and ideological criteria; but that the latter have their specific forms of 'relative autonomy' which cannot be ascribed to the place of a class or class fraction
in the relations of production.

I am not concerned to assess in detail the merits of these arguments as
they relate to the South African case. Instead, I want to use the example of this

exchange to establish the basis of a more general argument. Rex's arguments may not be entirely satisfactory in themselves, but undoubtedly they win effective ground from what he calls 'simple Marxism'—as Wolpe is obliged to concede. These represent real theoretical gains, against some of the weaknesses and lacunae in what has become the dominant form in which the classical Marxist paradigm has been applied. These gains are not wholly offset by pointing, correctly, to the ways in which Rex sometimes misrepresents Marx, and distorts Marx's real theoretical effectivity. Secondly, Wolpe's response shows that these weaknesses can only be 'corrected for', while retaining the broad outline of a Marxist approach, by significantly modifying the dominant form in which the Marxist paradigm has been applied: either by means of a more scrupulous or rigorous application of Marx's protocols (which have often, over time, been subject to severe theoretical simplification and impoverishment) and/or by bringing to the fore aspects and arguments which, though they can be shown not to contradict Marx, have not tended to play a very significant part when applied the the peculiar features of post-conquest or post-colonial social formations. This paper's interest in certain new approaches to these problems, from within a substantially new application of Marxist protocols of analysis, arises precisely from a concern to indicate where and how these new emphases are beginning to develop.

Wolpe himself concedes some of the points, at least. He acknowledges that Rex 'was right to insist upon the need for a more comprehensive and more re-fined conceptualization of class than was encompassed by the bare reference to property relations'. This however, he suggests, means moving away from the attention which Rex gives to market relations and constraints on the labour supply, into a fuller analysis of the relations of production and 'modes of pro-duction' analysis. He acknowledges that Rex was correct to draw attention to pertinent differences in the conditions affecting the entry into the labour market of 'black' and 'white' labour: though he would add that the distinction between free/unfree labour is then too sharply and simply applied. Wolpe also recognizes the Rex brings forward a point of great theoretical interest by his reference to the form of the 'political compromise' between the white capitalist and the white working classes, and the consequent 'supervising and policing' functions which white labour exerts over black. It follows from this that some of the more simplistic political recipes based on the call for 'black' and 'white' labour to sink their differences in a common and general class struggle against capital—the famous call to 'unite and fight'—are abstract political demands, based on theoretically unsound foundations, since they do not adequately grasp the structurally different relations in which 'white' and 'black' labour stand in rela-tion to capital.

Indeed, on this point, Wolpe may not have gone far enough. For a larger argument is involved here, even if only implicitly. Rex is arguing that the South African social system shows no strong or 'inevitable' tendencies to be gradually assimilated to the more 'rational' forms of 'free' labour, which Marx suggested was a necessary precondition for the establishment and reproduction of the capitalist mode of production. Hence, he would argue, the racial fractioning of the South African working classes has a real and substantial basis, with pertinent effects at the economic, as well as at the political and ideological, level. Rex thus points to the need for a definition of 'the capitalist mode' which is able to deal with 'other types of capitalist and non-capitalist exploitation and accumulation'—that is, to a 'capitalist' system founded quite securely on forms of labour other than traditionally free and mobile labour. This formulation may be criticized as being, finally, too plurally descriptive. It avoids the necessity to specify the articulating mechanisms, and the modes of dominance, between these different 'types'. But Rex has clearly succeeded, once again, in putting into question an analysis predicated unquestioningly on a general and necessary classical path of capitalist development, with a classical and irreversible sequence of evolutionary stages. To put this more broadly: he opens up the crucial theoretical question of the teleological and evolutionary form in which Marx's work on the necessary preconditions and optimal line of development of the capitalist mode has been interpreted—from the famous assertion, in *The Communist Manifesto*, that 'The bourgeoisie . . . compels all nations on pain of extinction, to adopt the bourgeois mode of production . . . it creates a world after its own image', through to the legendary discussion on the 'sequence of stages' which is often derived from the section on 'Pre-capitalist forms'—the so-called *Formen*—in the *Grundrisse* (Marx: 1964). Against this teleological extrapolation, it must be said that the fact of conquest, and thus the very different conditions in which pre-conquest social strata have been inserted into the capitalist mode, have not, on the whole played a central role in the versions of Marxist theory usually applied to such post-conquest societies. (The difficulty of deciding precisely what was the nature of the American slave systems—clearly inaugurated within yet separate from the expanding mercantile capitalist phase—is an aspect of the same theoretical problem (Genovese: 1965; Hindess and Hirst: 1975).

These, then, represent some of the gains which Rex's critique makes against a too-simple Marxism. What I am concerned to show, now, is how current Marxist theorizings on these questions have begun, through their own internal critique of what earlier passed as 'classical' or orthodox Marxism, to rectify some of the weaknesses correctly pinpointed by the critics of reductionism. These departures are, at once, rich and complex, often only at a rudimentary stage of formulation, and—as is often the case at a critical moment of paradigm-shift—locked in an intricate internal debate. Only certain indications of some of the main directions in this work can be provided in this review.

We might begin, here, by looking at one, very distinctive formulation with respect to the development of the social formations of Latin America, which not only defines itself within 'classical' Marxism, but which develops, in what is held to be a Marxist direction, one of the lines of argument which the critique by Rex and others has put in question: namely, the work of Gunder Frank, and recent critiques of Frank's work from within a transformed Marxist perspective.

One distinctive but seminal application of what is taken to be the Marxist

paradigm is to be found in the work of A. Gunder Frank. Frank's work was itself counterposed to the dominant and formative school of 'dependency'
theorists, grouped around the United Nations Economic Commission for Latin
America (ECLA) which was established in 1948. This school adopted a more
rigorously structural analysis to explain the 'underdevelopment' of the underdeveloped countries of the region. As against earlier developmentalist models,
the ECLA 'school' insisted that development and underdevelopment had to be
treated within the single framework of a world economic system. The 'underdeveloped' countries were the dependent sectors of such a world economy: as
Furtado put it, 'the theory of underdevelopment turns out to be essentially a
theory of dependence' (Furtado: 1971). This starting point within a global economic framework had much in common, in a 'broadly' Marxist way, with those
writers who had attempted to deal with modern aspects of capitalist development
on a world scale in terms of a 'theory of imperialism' (e.g. Lenin, Luxembourg,
Hilferding and Bukharin). The ECLA theorists accepted some such general
framework of imperialism, giving of course greater attention than the classical
theorists did to the effects of this world system at its peripheries. They were not
necessarily Marxist in any other sense. These general relations of dependency,
they argued, had created internal structures promoting a form of what they called
'dependent capitalist development' in those sectors, and among those classes,
closely linked with the imperialist chain, whilst marginalizing other sectors,
including the great mass of the population, especially the peasantry. 'The
differences between the internationalized sector and the non-industrialized or
marginal sector are the direct result of capitalist expansion, and become a form
of structural dualism.' (O'Brien: 1975). However, the 'school' promulgated a
variety of different strategies for overcoming this externally-induced sectoral
imbalance—often of a technical-economic, rather than of a political kind.

Frank certainly shares with the dependency theorists the necessity to
begin from a world capitalist system in which development and underdevelopment were structurally related. However, he explicitly argued against the possibility of a genuine, indigenous programme of economic development, of, say,
a national-bourgeois type, as a possible path for Latin America out of its phase
of dependent development. And this argument was supported by a startling
thesis, which takes us back to the problems posed earlier. Frank argued that
Latin America had been thoroughly incorporated into capitalist world relations
since the period of the conquest by the European powers in the sixteenth
century. Its underdevelopment stemmed from this dependent nature of its early
insertion into the world capitalist market. Implicit in this thesis was the view that
no structural differences remained between the more and the less developed sectors
of these dependent social formations. 'Dependency' he argued, was no recent
phenomenon in the region. It was only the latest form of the long-standing
'satellitization' of the Latin-American economies within the framework of
imperialist economic relations. The 'expansion of the capitalist system over the
past centuries effectively and entirely penetrated even the most isolated sectors
of the under-developed world' (Frank: 1969). The fundamental term for

understanding this penetration and subversion by capitalist relations which had brought about the structural coupling of development and underdevelopment was that of a single continuum—the 'metropolis-satellite polarization' . . . 'one and the same historical process of the expansion and development of capitalism' which continues to generate 'both economic development and structural underdevelopment'. This was the imperialist chain, which 'extends the capitalist link between the capitalist world and the national metropolises to the regional centres . . . and from these local centres and so on to the large land-owners or merchants who expropriate surplus from small peasants or tenants, and sometimes even from these latter to the landless labourers exploited by them in turn' (Frank: 1969).

The most telling critique of Frank's work is offered in Ernesto Laclau's review essay, 'Feudalism and capitalism in Latin America', republished in a recent volume of essays (Laclau: 1977). Laclau's specific criticisms are easily resumed. The object of his critique is Frank's assertion that Latin America has 'been capitalist from the beginning'—a single process, which must, for Frank, be 'identical in all its aspects from the sixteenth to the twentieth century'. Laclau, first, criticizes Frank's conception of 'capitalism'. Frank defines this as a system of production for the market, of which profit forms the driving motive. This, Laclau argues, differs fundamentally from Marx's conception of mode of production in so far as it dispenses with Marx's principal criteria for defining a 'mode'—the relations of production. This 'error' leads Frank to assume that, wherever their is capital accumulation, then Marx's 'law'—the rapid and inevitable transformation of the social formation by capitalist relations—must follow. However, as Laclau shows, for Marx, the accumulation of commercial capital is perfectly compatible with the most varied modes of production and does not by any means presuppose the existence of a capitalist mode of production: e.g. 'However, not commerce alone, but also merchant's capital is older than the capitalist mode of production, is in fact historically the oldest free state of existence of capital' (Marx: 1974, p. 319–21). This leads Laclau to mount a further critique of Frank's lack of historical specificity—exploitative situations as different as the Chilean *inquilinos*, the Ecuadorian *huasipungeros*, West Indian plantation slaves and Manchester textile workers being, for all practical purposes, subsumed into a single relation, declared 'capitalist'. The same can be said in more detail of the troublesome case of plantation slavery in the New World. This is, of course, the site of a protracted, and still unre-solved debate. Phillips (1969)—who, despite his offensive anti-slave viewpoint, Genovese correctly praises for a seminal analysis of the political economy of slavery—argued, long ago, that plantation slavery was a form of capitalism. That was, indeed, the basis of his objection to it (cf. Genovese: 1971). Genovese himself argues that slavery had a distinct set of exploitative relations—a 'seigneurial society . . . [which] created a unique society, neither feudal . . . nor capitalist' (Genovese: 1977). Hindess and Hirst constitute plantation slavery as its own distinctive 'mode', using primarily formal criteria. Williams, early on, subsequently Genovese, and Banaji among others, have concentrated on the

relationship between plantation slavery—whatever its characteristic 'mode'—
and the global capitalist economy. Fogel and Engerman have recently described slavery as a profitable form of 'capitalist agriculture'. (Hindess and
Hirst: 1977; Williams: 1966; Genovese: 1971; Banaji: 1977; Fogel and
Engerman: 1974.)

Frank quotes Marx's observation in the *History of economic doctrines*—
which describes the plantations as 'commercial speculations, centres of production for the world market'—as proof that Marx regarded them, too, as 'capitalist'. Laclau reminds us that Marx, pertinently, added, 'if only in a formal way'.
Actually, Marx seemed to be arguing the opposite to Frank; for he insists the
plantation slavery could only be 'formally capitalist', 'since slavery among the
negroes excludes free-wage labour, which is the base on which capital production rests. However, those who deal in slave-trading are capitalists'. As Beechey
(1978) has recently argued slavery certainly presupposed private property, a class
of owners and a property-less class. However, whereas under capitalism the
worker owns his own labour power which he sells as a commodity to the capitalist, slaveholders owned both the labour power and the slave. 'The slaveholder
considers a Negro, whom he has purchased, as his property, not because the
institution of slavery as such entitles him to that Negro, but because he has
acquired him like any other commodity through sale and purchase.' (Marx: 1974,
p. 776.) However, both the slave trade itself, and the extraction of the commodities so produced, were funded by mercantile capital and circulated within the
global circuits of capital. As Beechey puts it, with great clarity: 'Slaveholders
were both merchants, dealing with the purchase and sale of commodities on the
world market, and slaveholders exploiting their slaves within the plantation
system, which emerged as a specialized agricultural region, a kind of internal
colony within the expanded world market.' (Beechey; 1978.)

What Marx was describing, then, was something radically different from
Frank's interpretation: namely, an articulation between two modes of production, the one 'capitalist' in the true sense, the other only 'formally' so: the two
combined through an articulating principle, mechanism or set of relations, because, as Marx observed, 'its beneficiaries participate in a world market in
which the dominant productive sectors are already capitalist'. That is, the object of inquiry must be treated as a complex articulated structure which is, itself,
'structured in dominance'. Slave plantation owners thus participated in a general
movement of the world capitalist system: but on the basis of an internal mode
of production—slavery in its modern, plantation form—not itself 'capitalist' in
character. This is a revolutionary proposition in the theoretical sense, since it
departs from that very teleological reading of Marx which produced, in Frank,
the indefensible thesis that Latin America has been 'capitalist' since the Conquest. What we have now, in opposition to the thesis of 'inevitable transformation' of pre-capitalist modes and their dissolution by capitalist relations, is the
emergent theoretical problem of an articulation between different modes of production, structured in some relation of dominance. This leads on to the definition of a social formation which, at its economic level, may be composed of

several modes of production, 'structured in dominance' (cf., Althusser and Balibar: 1970; Hindess and Hirst: 1975, 1977; Poulantzas: 1973). This has provided the basis for an immense amount of formative work, especially on 'pre-capitalist modes of production', offering a more rigorous approach to that reading of Marx, rightly criticized—on this very point—by Rex, whilst retaining the systematic terms of a Marxist analysis. This work is, of course, pitched principally at the level of economic relations. Though it has clear consequences for other levels of the structure of social formations (class formations, alliances, political and ideological structures, etc.), these have not been spelled out (for example in Laclau's essay quoted here: though for related developments pertaining to these levels, see Laclau, and others referred to more extensively below). It has, for example, quite pertinent effects for any analysis of the way this articulated combination of modes inserts economic agents drawn from different ethnic groups into sets of economic relations which, while articulated into a complex unity, need not be conceptualized as either necessarily the same or inevitably destined to become so.

This emergent problematic constitutes perhaps the most generative new theoretical development in the field, affecting the analysis of racially-structured social formations. The emergent theoretical position is grounded by its proponents in a certain 're-reading' of the classical Marxist literature. It is part of that immense theoretical revolution constituted by the sophisticated return to the 'reading' of Marx's *Capital* which has had such a formative intellectual impact over the past decade. It is also being currently developed in a range of different theoretical fields. Laclau puts the essential argument in a strong form: 'the pre-capitalist character of the dominant relations of production in Latin America was not only not incompatible with production for the world market, but was actually intensified by the expansion of the latter.' Marx, in a passage less well known than *The Communist Manifesto* 'scenario' quoted earlier, spoke of the fact that: 'the circuit of industrial capital . . . crosses the commodity circulation of the most diverse modes of social production. . . . No matter whether commodities are the output of production based on slavery, of peasants . . . of State enterprise . . . or of half-savage hunting tribes . . . they come face to face with the monies and commodities in which industrial capital presents itself. . . . The character of the process of production from which they originate is immaterial. . . . They must be reproduced and to this extent the capitalist mode of production is conditional on modes of production lying outside of its own stage of development.' (Marx: 1956, p. 109.) Bettelheim who may appear to take a more 'classical' view, argues that the *dominant* tendency is towards the dissolution of other modes by the capitalist one. But this is often combined with a secondary tendency—that of 'conservation-dissolution': where non-capitalist modes, 'before they disappear are "restructured" (partly dissolved) and thus subordinated to the predominant capitalist relations (and so conserved)' (Bettelheim: 1972).

Using this schema, Wolpe shows that certain problems of the South African social formation, referred to earlier, which could not be satisfactorily explained within the older reading, and which Rex among others correctly

criticized, begin to be resolvable through the use of these new theoretical instruments and in a manner which throws significant light on the racial fracturing
of class relations in South Africa. While the detailed outlines of this attempted
'solution' cannot be entered into here (Wolpe: 1975), its broader consequences
are worth quoting. Wolpe suggests, for example, that the reliance of the capitalist sector in South Africa on the non-capitalist sectors in the African areas
for both cheap labour supply and subsistence reproduction enables capital to
pay for labour-power below the cost of its reproduction, whilst having always
available a plentiful labour supply whose costs of subsistence it does not fully bear
(Wolpe: 1972). He employs both the 'articulation' and the 'dissolution-conserva-
tion' variants of the thesis. In South Africa, the tendency of capital accumulation
to dissolve other modes is cross-cut and blocked by the counter-acting tendencies
to conserve the non-capitalist economies—on the basis that the latter are
articulated in a subordinate position to the former. Where capitalism develops
by means, in part, of its articulation with non-capitalist modes, 'the mode of
political domination and the content of legitimating ideologies assume racial,
ethnic and cultural forms and for the same reasons as in the case of imperialism
. . . political domination takes on a colonial form' (Wolpe: 1975). He adds:
'The conservation of non-capitalist modes of production necessarily requires
the development of ideologies and political policies which revolve around the
segregation and preservation and control of African "tribal" societies'—that is,
the relation assumes the forms of ideologies constructed around ethnic, racial,
national and cultural ideological elements.

In short, the emergent theory of the 'articulation of different modes of
production' begins to deliver certain pertinent theoretical effects for an analysis
of racism at the social, political and ideological levels. It begins to deliver such
effects—and this is the crucial point—not by deserting the level of analysis of
economic relations (i.e. mode of production) but by posing it in its correct,
necessarily complex, form. Of course, this may be a necessary, but not a sufficient
starting point. In this respect, Wolpe's term 'requires' may go too far, suggesting a necessary correspondence, of a too-functionalist kind, between the structure of modes of production and the specific forms of political domination and
ideological legitimation. The level of economic analysis, so redefined, may not
supply sufficient conditions in itself for an explanation of the emergence and
operation of racism. But, at least, it provides a better, sounder point of departure than those approaches which are obliged to desert the economic level, in
order to produce 'additional factors' which explain the origin and appearance
of racial structuring at other levels of the social formation. In this respect, at
least, the theoretical advances briefly outlined here have the merit of respecting
what we would call two cardinal premises of Marx's 'method'. The materialist
premise—that the analysis of political and ideological structures must be
grounded in their material conditions of existence; and the historical premise—
that the specific forms of these relations cannot be deduced, *a priori*, from this
level but must be made historically specific 'by supplying those further delinea-
tions which explain their *differentiae sp.*' Both premises are well expressed in one

of the most justly famous passages from *Capital*: 'The specific economic form, in which unpaid labour-surplus is pumped out of direct producers, determines the relationship of rulers and ruled, as it grows directly out of production itself and, in turn, reacts upon it as a determining element. Upon this, however, is founded the entire formation of the economic community which grows up out of the production relations themselves, thereby simultaneously its specific political form . . .' (the materialist premise). But 'This does not prevent the same economic basis—the same from the standpoint of its main conditions—due to innumerable different empirical circumstances, natural environments, racial relations, external historical influences, etc., from showing infinite variations and gradations in appearance, which can be ascertained only by analysis of the empirically given circumstances' (the historical premise), (Marx: 1974, p. 791–2). Both premises are indeed required, if the conditions of theoretical adequacy are to be met: each, on its own, is not sufficient. The first, without the second, may lead us straight back into the *impasse* of economic reductionism; the second, without the first, snares us in the toils of historical relativism. Marx's method, properly understood and applied, provides us with the conditions—though not, of course, the guarantee—of a theoretical adequacy which avoids both. (For a further elaboration of the 'basic premises' of Marx's method, see, Johnson, et al.: 1978; for a condensed version of the argument outlined by Wolpe, as applied to Latin-American and Carribbean social formations, see, Hall: 1978.)

The application of the 'articulation' thesis, briefly outlined here, has had revolutionary theoretical consequences in other fields of inquiry, which can only be shortly noted here since they fall outside of our principal concern. They can be found, in the English context, in the work on 'pre-capitalist modes' and social formations, by Hindess and Hirst (1975, 1977); in Banaji (1977); in the recent work on 'colonial modes of production' (e.g., Alavi: 1975); in recent issues of *The review of African political economy, Critique of anthropology* and *Economy and society*; also, in a related form, in the renewed debate about 'transition', sparked off by the reissue of the formative set of essays on *The transition from feudalism to capitalism* (Hilton: 1976); and in the forthcoming work on Jamaica by Post. In France, it is most noteworthy in the context of the revived interest in the new 'economic anthropology' to which such writers as Godelier, Meillassoux, Terray, Rey and Dupré have made outstanding contributions (cf., the selection by Seddon, 1978). (For interpretive overviews and critiques in English, see, *inter alia:* Clammer, 1975; Bradby, 1975; Foster-Carter, 1978; Seddon, 1978; Wolpe, 1978.) Meillassoux principally deals with 'self-sustaining' agricultural social formations, and their dissolution-transformation, when they have grafted on to them production for external 'capitalist' markets. This has certain theoretical consequences for those articulated social formations where the non-capitalist sector is 'able to fulfil functions that capitalism prefers not to assume in the under-developed countries' (cf., Wolpe's development of this argument, above)—and thus for such societies as the South African one, where (as Clammer extrapolates) 'people who are obliged to become wage-labourers in a neo- and quasi-colonial situation are forced back on the "traditional" sector to obtain precisely those services which the capitalist does not provide'. Clammer correctly points out that this revives the 'dual sector' analysis—though in a radically new form; since (Meillassoux argues) it is precisely the ideological function of 'dual sector' theories to 'conceal the exploitation of the rural community, integrated as an organic component of capitalist production' (Meillassoux: 1972, 1974; for a more extended critique, see Clammer: 1975).

Rey's work deals principally with 'lineage' societies and, like Meillassoux derives from African fieldwork: but wider extrapolations of a theoretical nature have been made from this terrain (Rey: 1971, 1973, 1975; Rey and Dupré: 1973). It differs from other work in the French 'economic anthropology' tradition by being concerned, in part, with problems of extending the 'articulation' argument —as the title of his second book indicates—to the question of class alliances, and thus to the political level. Rey also departs somewhat from the problematic of 'articulation'. He is concerned with the 'homoficence' of capitalism— what Foster-Carter calls the problem of the 'parallelism of action' of capitalism (cf., Foster-Carter: 1978; also for a more substantive review/critique both of Rey and of the 'articulation' literature). A major distinction in Rey's work is, however, the attempt to periodize this 'parallelism of action' as a process, into three principal stages, marked by the character of the articulation in each. These are: (i) the period of the slave trade, where the European market acquires supplies, through relations of exchange, 'essentially by playing on the internal contradictions of the lineage social formations'; (ii) a transitional phase— colonialism in the full sense—where capitalism takes root, grounding itself in the pre-capitalist mode and gradually subordinating it; (iii) a new type of social formation, with the capitalist mode of production internally dominant; frequently, then, dependent on a metropolitan capitalism (neo-colonialism). To each phase a different set of class alliances corresponds. Rey is also much concerned with the way the lineage societies are interrupted and disarticulated by the exterior force of capital—often through violence and what Marx called the 'fact of conquest' (Foster-Carter: 1978). Rey sees the 'rooting' of capitalism in these precapitalist modes as possible only with the implantation of 'transitional modes'— precisely the function of the colonial period. While giving to this phase a seminal role not normally accorded to it, or even distinctly remarked, Rey's approach leaves the history of capital and the mechanism of transition as one largely 'written outside such social formations' and he tends to treat the relations of exchange as the central articulating feature (for a wider critique, see, Clammer: 1975; Foster-Carter: 1978; Terray: 1972; Bradby: 1975).

The term articulation is a complex one, variously employed and defined in the literature here referred to. No clear consensus of conceptual definition can be said to have emerged so far. Yet it remains the site of a significant theoretical rupture (*coupure*) and intervention. This is the intervention principally associated with the work of Althusser and the 'school' of structuralist Marxism. The term is widely employed, in a range of contexts, especially in the *For Marx* essays, and the succeeding volume, with Balibar, in *Reading Capital*

(1965; 1970). At least two different applications are particularly relevant to our concerns here (though, interestingly, the term is not defined in the 'Glossary', prepared by Ben Brewster and sanctioned by Althusser himself, which appeared in the English editions of both books). Aside from these particular usages, the term has a wider reference of both a theoretical and a methodological nature.

Foster-Carter correctly suggests that is is a metaphor used 'to indicate relations of linkage and effectivity between different levels of all sorts of things'—though he might have added that these things require to be linked because, though connected, they are not the same. The unity which they form is thus not that of an identity, where one structure perfectly recapitulates or reproduces or even 'expresses' another; or where each is reducible to the other; or where each is defined by the same determinations or have exactly the same conditions of existence; or even where each develops according to the effectivity of the same conditions of existence; or even where each develops according to the effectivity of the same contradiction (e.g. the 'principal contradiction' so beloved, as the warrant and guarantee of all arguments, by so-called 'orthodox' Marxists). The unity formed by this combination or articulation, is always, necessarily, a 'complex structure': a structure in which things are related, as much through their differences as through their similarities. This requires that the mechanisms which connect dissimilar features must be shown—since no 'necessary correspondence' or expressive homology can be assumed as given. It also means—since the combination is a structure (an articulated combination) and not a random association—that there will be structured relations between its parts, i.e., relations of dominance and subordination. Hence, in Althusser's cryptic phrase, a 'complex unity, structured in dominance'.

Many of the classic themes of the Althusserian intervention are resumed in and through his various uses of this term: for example, his argument that Marx's 'unity' is not the essentialist 'expressive unity' to be found in Hegel, and that, therefore, Marx's dialectic is not merely an inversion, but a theoretical advance over Hegel. This is the critique against conceiving Marx's 'totality' as an 'expressive totality', which grounds Althusser's early critique of the attempts to rescue Marx's work from 'vulgar materialism' by way of a detour through Hegelianism (see Althusser's *For Marx*, expecially the chapter 'On the Marxian dialectic'). It also founds Althusser's critique of the attempt to read Marx as if he meant that all the structures of a social formation could be reduced to an 'expression' of the economic base; or as if all the instances of any historical conjucture moved in a relation of direct correspondence with the terms of the 'principal contradiction' (that of the 'base', between forces and relations of production)—this is Althusser's critique (the opposite of that against Hegelian idealism) against 'economic reductionism'. Marx's 'complex unity', Althusser argues, is neither that in which everything perfectly expresses or corresponds to everything else; nor that in which everything is reducible to an expression of 'the Economic'. It operates, instead, on the terrain of articulation. What we find, in any particular historical conjuncture (his example, in 'Contradiction and overdetermination' in *For Marx*, is Russia, 1917) is not the unrolling of the 'principal contradiction', evenly, throughout all the other levels of the social formation, but, in Lenin's terms, the 'merger', 'rupture', condensation of contradictions, each with its own specificity and periodization—'absolutely dissimilar currents, absolutely heterogeneous class interests, absolutely contrary political and social strivings'—which have 'merged . . . in a strikingly "harmonious" manner' (Lenin, *Letters from afar*, no. 1). Such conjunctures are not so much 'determined' as overdetermined, i.e., they are the product of an articulation of contradictions, not directly reduced to one another.

Althusser and Balibar, then, employ this general theoretical concept in a variety of different contexts. They conceive of a social formation as composed of a number of instances—each with a degree of 'relative autonomy' from one another—articulated into a (contradictory) unity. The economic instance or level, itself, is the result of such a 'combination': the articulation between forces and relations of production. In particular social formations, especially in periods of 'transition', social formations themselves may be an 'articulated combination' of different modes with specified, shifting terms of hierarchical ordering between them. The term also figures in the Althusserian epistemology, which insists that knowledge and the production of knowledge are not directly produced, as an empiricist reflection of the real 'in thought', but have a specificity and autonomy of their own—thought, 'established on and articulated to the real world of a given historical society' (Althusser and Balibar: 1970, p. 42). The scientific analysis of any specific social formation depends on the correct grasping of its principle of articulation: the 'fits' between different instances, different periods and epochs, indeed different periodicities, e.g., times, histories. The same principle is applied, not only synchronically, between instances and periodizations within any 'moment' of a structure, but also, diachronically, between different 'moments'. This connects with Althusser's objections to the notion of a given and necessary sequence of stages, with a necessary progression built into them. He insists on the non-teleological reading of Marx, on the notion of 'a discontinuous succession of modes of production' (Althusser and Balibar: 1970, p. 204), whose combined succession—i.e., articulation through time— requires to be demonstrated. Indeed, 'scientificity' itself is associated with 'the problem of the forms of variation of the articulation' of the instances in every social structure (Althusser and Balibar: 1970, p. 207). The same is said of the relations between the economic and the political and ideological forms of their appearance. This, too, is thought on the analogy of an articulation between structures which do not directly express or mirror each other. Hence, the classical problem for Marxism—the problem of determinancy of the structure, the 'determination in the last instance by the economic' (which distinguishes Marxism from other types of social scientific explanation)—is itself redefined as a problem of 'articulation'. What is 'determined' is not the inner form and appearance of each level, but the mode of combination and the placing of each instance in an articulated relation to the other elements. It is this 'articulation of the structure' as the global effect of the structure itself—or what has been called, by Balibar, the matrix role of the mode of production'—which defines the Althusserian concept of determination: as a structural causality (Althusser and Balibar: 1970, p. 220). It is this conception, on the other hand, which has provided the basis for the critique by Hirst and Hindess (1975) of Althusser's 'determinacy of articulation by the structure' as, itself, an 'expressive totality'—a Spinozian eternity. Dealing with the example of the relation between feudal ground rent and the feudal relation of lordship and servitude, Balibar treats it as a reduced instance of the articulation of *two* different instances, an 'economic' instance and a 'political' instance. Likewise, Balibar defines the concept of mode of production as, itself, the result of a variant combination of elements (object of labour, means of labour, labour-power). What changes, in each epoch, is not the elements, which are invariant (in the definitional sense), but the way they are combined: their articulation. While it is not possible to 'tell' the whole of the Althusserian intervention through the terms of a single concept, like articulation, it must be by now apparent that the concept has a wide and extensive reference in the works of the structuralist Marxists.

Though we cannot go into the theoretical and methodological background to the emergence of the concept, we can at least note in passing, two pertinent provenances. The first is that of structuralist linguistics, which provided the master-model of a substantial part of the whole 'structuralist' venture. Saussure, the 'founder' of this school, who argued that language is not a reflection of the world but produces meaning through the articulation of linguistic systems upon real relations, insists that meaning is no mere 'correlation between signifier and signified, but perhaps more essentially an act of simultaneously cutting out two amorphous masses, two "floating kingdoms" . . . language is the domain of *articulations*' (Barthes: 1967). More pertinent, perhaps is the warrant which Althusser and others have found, in Marx's most extensive 'methodological' text—the 1857 *Introduction to the Grundrisse*—for a theory of the social formation as what Marx himself calls an 'articulated hierarchy' (Gliederung)— or, as Althusser translates him, 'an organic hierarchized whole'. 'In all forms of society' Marx wrote 'it is a determinate production and its relations which assign every other production and its relations their rank and influence' (Marx: 1973). If this represents a slender warrant for the construction of the whole structuralist edifice, it is certainly clear that, in that text, Marx was decisively opposing himself to any notion of a simple identity between the different relations of capital (production, circulation, exchange, consumption). He spoke, at length, of the complexity of determinations between these relations, the sum of whose articulations, nevertheless, provided him (in this text) with the object of his inquiry (adequately constructed in a theoretical sense); and, in *Capital*, with the key to the unravelling of the necessarily complex nature of the relations between the different circuits operating within the capitalist mode (cf., Hall: 1973). This is the real burden of Marx's extensive criticisms in the 1857 *Introduction* against treating the different relations which compose the capitalist mode as a 'regular syllogism'—an 'immediate identity'. 'To regard society as one single subject is . . . to look at it wrongly; speculatively.' 'The conclusion we reach is not that production, distribution, exchange and consumption are identical, but that they all form

the members of a totality of distinctions within a unity.' (Marx: 1973.) In the
same way, there seems to be a clear warning issued against any simple notion
of an evolutionary sequence or succession of stages in that development:
'Their sequence is determined, rather, by their relation to one another in modern
bourgeois society, which is precisely the opposite of that which seems to be
their natural order or which corresponds to historical development. The point
is not the historic position of the economic relations in the succession of different
forms of society.' This last point indicates what we would want to call (in addition to those already signalled) the third premise of Marx's method: the structural
premise. It is, above all, the employment of the structural premise in the later,
mature work of Marx, and the manner in which this has been appropriated and
developed by Althusser and the structuralists, which produces, as one of its
theoretical results, the extensive-intensive concept of articulation.

The term itself is by no means unproblematic, indicating here a certain
approach, rather than providing in itself a theoretical resolution to the problems
it indexes. It has been subjected to a searching critique. In itself, the term has an
ambiguous meaning, for, in English, it can mean both 'joining up' (as in the
limbs of the body, or an anatomical structure) and 'giving expression to' (cf:
Foster-Carter: 1978). In Althusserian usage, it is primarily the first sense which
is intended. There are, in any case, theoretical objections to the notion that one
structure 'gives expression to' another: since this would be tantamount to seeing
the second structure as an epiphenomenon of the first (i.e., a reductionist conception), and would involve treating a social formation as an 'expressive totality'
—precisely the object of Althusser's initial critique of Hegelianism. Some
notion of an 'expressive' link—say, between the economic and political structures
of a society remains, even in Althusserian usage, but this is elaborated by other
terms which break up or break into any residual sense of a perfect and necessary
'correspondence'. Thus, in addition to insisting on the specificity, the non-
reductiveness, the 'relative autonomy', of each level of the society, Althusser
always uses such terms as 'displacement', 'dislocation', 'condensation', in order
to demonstrate that the 'unity' which these different relations form are not univocal, but mislead through 'over-determination'. Another criticism, then, is
that the concept of 'articulation' may simply leave two dissimilar things yoked
together by a mere external or arbitrary connexion: what Marx once called
'independent, autonomous neighbours . . . not grasped in their unity' (Marx:
1973, p. 90). Althusser attempts to overcome this 'mere juxtaposition' by using
the concept of 'over-determination', and by always speaking of 'articulation'
as involving hierarchical as well as lateral relations i.e., relations of dominance
and subordination (cf: Marx's discussion of money in different historical epochs,
which does not 'wade its way through all economic relations' but is defined by
where it plays a 'dominant' or a 'subordinate' role). This, however, leads on to
other criticisms. The schema, constructed around articulation has, often with
justice, been described as too 'formalist'. Thus, in the full-blown 'structural
causality' of Althusser and Balibar's *Reading Capital*, the 'economic' determines
'in the last instance' not substantively but principally by 'giving the index of

effectivity' in the structure to one or another level: i.e., in a *formal* way. (But Althusser retreats from some of these more formalist excesses (Althusser: 1976).) While the whole attempt to develop such an analysis is predicated on the need for an approach which is not reductive, it has been criticized as giving rise to a conception of 'structure' which—since it contains within itself all the conditions of its own functioning—is itself that 'expressive totality' which Althusser seeks to avoid (cf: Hindess and Hirst: 1975; Hirst: 1977). The framework is also open to the criticism that it leaves the internal elements of any 'structural combination' unchanged with change or transition being limited to the variations (different articulations) through which the 'invariant elements' are combined. This weakens the historicity of the approach—contravening what we have called the historical premise of Marx's work (but again see Althusser: 1976). This notion of the variation between invariant elements has resulted in a very formalist way of defining a 'mode of production' (following, especially, Balibar): so that some of the real advances made in attempting to ground analysis in a more developed and sophisticated understanding of modes of production and their combination can easily be vitiated by a sort of formalist hunt for one, separate, 'mode of production' after another. Nevertheless, we would continue to insist on the potentially generative value of the term and its cognate concepts, which give us a start in thinking the complex unity and *differentiae specificae* of social formations, without falling back on a naive or 'vulgar materialist' reductionism, on the one hand, or a form of sociological pluralism on the other.

So far, I have been speaking, exclusively, of the application of the term 'articulation' to the economic structure of complex social formations. But I have also said that the social formation itself can be analysed as an 'articulated hierarchy'. At the economic level, this may involve the articulation of a social formation around more than one mode of production. Some of the political and ideological features of such societies can then be explained with reference to this particular combination. But it is also possible to conceptualize the different levels of a social formation as an articulated hierarchy. Since we must assume no 'necessary correspondence'—no perfect replication, homology of structures, expressive connexion—between these different levels, but are nevertheless required to 'think' the relations between them as an 'ensemble of relations' (marked by what Marx in his 1857 *Introduction*, when dealing with these issues, defined as the 'law of uneven development')—then it is, once more, to the nature of the articulations between them to which we must turn. The attention—of a more detailed and analytic kind—to the nature of modes of production helps to ground these other aspects of the social formation more adequately at the level of the economic structures (the materialist premise). However, we cannot thereby deduce *a priori* the relations and mechanisms of the political and ideological structures (where such features as racism make a decisive reappearance) exclusively from the level of the economic. The economic level is the necessary but not sufficient condition for explaining the operations at other levels of the society (the premise of non-reductionism). We cannot assume an express relation of 'necessary correspondence' between them (the premise of historical specificity).

These are, as Marx put it, 'a product of historical relations and possess their full validity only for and within these relations'. This is an important, indeed a critical qualification. It requires us to demonstrate—rather than to assume, *a priori*—what the nature and degree of 'correspondence' is, in any specific historical case. Thus, through this opening, some of the criticisms which, as was noted earlier, are made from the perspective of 'sociological' explanations—for example the requirement to be historically specific—begin to be met, within the framework of this seminal revision.

Here, however, different positions within the general problematic of 'articulation' can be identified. Some theorists argue that all we can do is to deal with each level, in terms of its own specificity, and the 'conditions of existence' which must be fulfilled for it to function (e.g. the economic relations of the capitalist mode require, as a condition of existence, some extra-economic, juridical framework, which secures the 'contract' between buyer and seller of labour power). But, it is argued, the internal forms and specificities of the extra-economic levels can neither be prescribed nor identified from the economic level which 'requires it', as a formal necessity of its functioning. This is tantamount to a theory of the 'autonomy' (not 'relative autonomy') of the different levels (Hirst: 1977; Cutler, et al.: 1977). This, however, fails to deal with social formations as a 'complex unity' (Marx's 'unity of many determinations').

Other approaches recognize that there may well be 'tendential combinations': combinations which, while not prescribed in the fully determinist sense, are the 'preferred' combinations, sedimented and solidified by real historical development over time. Thus, as is clear from, say, the Latin-American case, there is no 'necessary correspondence' between the development of a form of capitalism and the political forms of parliamentary democracy. Capitalism can arise on very different political foundations. Engels, himself, showed how capitalism can also harness and adapt very different legal systems to its functions. This does not prevent us from arguing that the advent of capitalism has frequently (tendentially) been accompanied by the formation of bourgeois parliamenatary democratic regimes: or even from accepting Lenin's percipient observation that parliamentary democracy provides 'the "best possible" political shell for capitalism'. We must, however, see these 'combinations' as historically specific, rather than specified *a priori*: as 'laws of tendency'—which can be countermanded by 'counteracting tendencies'. To take a pertinent example: in Europe, the rise of capitalism is consequent upon the destruction of feudal ties and the formation of 'free labour'—of 'labour power' as a commodity. It is hard to think of a capitalist formation in which there would be no form of labour-power available to capital in its 'free' form. This, in turn, means that, whatever is the specific legal form with which capitalist development 'corresponds', it must be one in which the concept of the juridical 'contract' between 'free persons' appears, which can legally regulate the forms of contract which 'free labour' require. This 'requirement' is something more than a mere, empty, or formal 'condition of existence'. However, this does not mean that the tendency to combine capitalism with 'free labour' cannot, under specific historical conditions be cross-cut or countermanded by a counteracting tendency: namely, the possibility of certain of the conditions of existence of capitalism being effectively secured by combining 'free labour' with certain forms of 'unfree' or 'forced' labour. Once we move away from European to post-Conquest or post-colonial societies, this combination—free and 'unfree' labour, on the basis of a combination of different modes of production—becomes more and more the paradigm case. This leaves almost everything of importance, still, to be done in developing a better understanding of the 'laws of motion' of capitalist formations which are structured in this alternative manner. Naturally, it has consequences, then, for political and legal structures. In such 'deviant' social formations (deviant only in the sense of departing from the European paradigm-case), there will be political structures which combine (or may combine) forms of parliamentary democracy with other forms of political representation—or legal structures which elaborate more than one form of citizen status. The 'articulation' of 'free' and 'forced' labour, the combination of 'equal' and 'restricted' franchises, the position of the Chiefs and the Bantustan 'internal colonies', and the different legal statuses of 'white' and 'black' citizens, in the South African social formation, perfectly represent the elements of such a 'variant' case—one which is in no sense 'non-capitalist'; provided, that is, we read Marx's 'laws of development and motion' as laws of tendency (and countertendency) rather than as *a priori* laws of necessity.

Where, then, the relations between the different levels of a social formation are concerned, one needs additional concepts, i.e., to supply further determinations, to those which have been mobilized for the analysis of the economic 'mode of production' levels. And one needs to acknowledge that the economic level, alone, cannot prescribe what those levels will be like and how they will operate—even if their mechanisms are not fully specifiable without attending to the level of the economic. Here, the work of Althusser, and of the 'Althusserians'—for example, Poulantzas's work on 'the State'—requires to be supplemented by the work of another Marxist theorist whose elaboration, at this level, constitutes a contribution to the development of a rigorously non-reduction Marxism of the very first importance. This is the work of Gramsci. Gramsci's work is more fragmentary (much of it written in prison, under the eyes of the censor, in one of Mussolini's jails), far less 'theorized' than that of Althusser. Gramsci has been formative for the development of Althusser's problematic: though, since in certain respects Gramsci remained a 'historicist', the relationship between Althusser and Gramsci is a complex one. In a recent review of this relationship, we have expressed it in terms of Gramsci providing the 'limit case' of historicity for Marxist structuralism (Hall, et al.: 1977).

We cannot elaborate in any depth, here, on Gramsci's concepts (for a review, see: Hall, et al.: 1977; Anderson: 1977; Mouffe: 1978). The central concept in his work is that of hegemony. Hegemony is that state of 'total social authority' which, at certain specific conjunctures, a specific class alliance wins, by a combination of 'coercion' and 'consent', over the whole social formation, and its dominated classes: not only at the economic level, but also at the level of political and ideological leadership, in civil, intellectual and moral life as well as at the material level: and over the terrain of civil society as well as in and through the condensed relations of the State. This 'authority and leadership' is, for Gramsci, not a given *a priori* but a specific historical 'moment'—one of unusual social authority. It represents the product of a certain mastery of the class struggle, certainly, but it is still subject to the class struggle and the 'relations of social forces' in society, of which its 'unstable equilibrium' is only one, provisional, outcome or result. Hegemony is a state of play in the class struggle which has, therefore, to be continually worked on and reconstructed in order to be maintained, and which remains a contradictory conjuncture. The important point, for Gramsci, is that, under hegemonic conditions, the organization of consent (by the dominated classes to the 'leadership' of the dominant class alliance) takes precedence (though it does not obliterate) the exercise of domination through coercion. In such conditions, the class struggle tends to assume the form, not of a 'frontal assault' on the bastions of the State ('war of manoeuvre') but of a more protracted, strategic and tactical struggle, exploiting and working on a number of different contradictions (Gramsci's 'war of position'). A state of hegemony enables the ruling class alliance to undertake the enormous task of modifying, harnessing, securing and elaborating the 'superstructure' of society in line with the long-term requirements of the development of the mode of production—e.g. capital accumulation on an expanded scale. It enables such a class alliance to undertake the educative and formative tasks of raising the whole social formation to what he calls a 'new level of civilization', favouring the expanded regime of capital. This is no immediate and direct imposition of the narrow, short-term, 'corporate' class interests of a single class on society. it forges that unity between economic, political and ideological objectives such that it can place 'all the questions around which the struggle rages on a "universal" not a corporative level, thereby creating a hegemony of a fundamental social group over a series of subordinate groups'. This is what Gramsci calls the 'educative and formative role of the State. . . . Its aim is always that of creating new and higher types of civilization; of adapting the "civilization" and the morality of the broadest popular masses to the necessities of the continuous development of the economic apparatus of production'—the formation of a 'national-popular will', based on a particular relationship between the dominant and dominated classes. This, then, depends, not on a presumed, necessary or *a priori* correspondence between (economic) structure and (political and ideological) superstructures but precisely on those historically specific mechanisms— and the concrete analysis of those historical 'moments'—through which such a formative relationship *between* structure and superstructures comes to be forged. For Gramsci, the object of analysis is always the specificity of this 'structure-superstructure' complex—though as a historically concrete articulation. 'It is the problem of the relations between structure and superstructure which must be accurately posed and resolved if the forces which are active in history . . . are to be correctly analysed.' This is a rigorously non-reductionist conception: 'How then could the whole system of superstructures be understood as distinctions within politics, and the introduction of the concept of distinction into a philosophy of praxis hence be justified? But can one really speak of a dialectic of distincts, and how is the concept of a circle joining the levels of the superstructure to be understood? Concept of "historical bloc", i.e. . . . unity of opposites and distincts. Can one introduce the criterion of distinction into the structure too?' Gramsci, clearly, answers these questions in the affirmative. He is especially sharp against any form of vulgar economism: 'It is therefore necessary to combat economism not only in the theory of historiography, but also and especially in the theory and practice of politics. In this field, the struggle can and must be carried on by developing the concept of hegemony.' (All the quotes are from two essays in Gramsci: 1971.)

Gramsci's theoretical contribution has only begun, recently, to be recognized—though his role as an outstanding militant in Italian politics in the 1920s and 1930s has long been acknowledged. His analysis bears, in a specially rich and productive way, on the analysis of the great bourgeois social formations of a developed capitalist type in Europe—Western Europe, where a reductionist economistic analysis, clearly, will not suffice to account for the depth of the transformations involved. Perhaps for this very reason, he has been thought of as, *par excellence*, the Marxist theorist of 'Western capitalism'. His work has, therefore, hardly been applied or employed in the analysis of non-European formations. There are, however, very strong grounds for thinking that it may have particular relevance for non-European social formations—for three, separate reasons. First, Gramsci may help to counteract the overwhelming weight of economism (Marxist and non-Marxist) which has characterized the analysis of post-Conquest and 'colonial' societies. Perhaps because the weight of imperialist economic relations has been so powerfully visible, these formations have virtually been held to be explainable by an application of 'imperialism' as essentially a purely 'economic' process. Second, these societies present problems as to the relation in the 'structure-superstructure complex' equal in complexity to those about which Gramsci wrote. Naturally, no simple transfer of concepts would be advisable here: Gramsci would be the first to insist on historical specificity, on difference. Third, Gramsci viewed the problem of 'hegemony' from within the specific history of the Italian social formation. This gave him a particular, and highly relevant, perspective on the problem. For long periods Italy was marked precisely by the absence of 'hegemony': by an alliance of ruling classes governing through domination rather than through hegemonic class leadership (direction). So his work is equally relevant for societies in which, according to the rhythm and punctuation of the class struggle, there has been significant movements into and out of a phase of 'hegemonic direction'. Moreover, Italy was/is a society brutally marked by the law of uneven development: with massive industrial capitalist development to the North, massive underdevelopment to the South. This raises the question of how the contradictions of the Italian social formation are articulated through different modes of production (capitalist and feudal), and through class alliances which combine elements from different social orders. The problem of the State, and the question of strategic alliances between the industrial proletariat and the peasantry, the 'play' of traditional and advanced ideologies, and the difficulties these provide in the formation of a 'national-popular will' all make his analysis of Italy specially relevant to colonial societies.

Gramsci's work has recently been taken up and developed in a structuralist manner—especially in Althusser's essay on 'Ideological State apparatuses' (Althusser: 1971). This seminal essay differs from Gramsci's work, specifically, in posing the problem in terms of 'reproduction'. But the concerns which underlie this approach are not all that distant from those of Gramsci. The economic relations of production must themselves be 'reproduced'. This reproduction is not simply economic, but social, technical and, above all, ideological. This is another way of putting Gramsci's observation that, to achieve its full development, capitalist social relations require to be coupled with an elaborate development and elaboration at the 'non-economic' levels of politics, civil society and culture, through moral, intellectual and ideological leadership. Althusser then shares with Gramsci a classical concern for the manner in which the 'hegemony' of a ruling class alliance is secured, at these other levels, through a formative and educative class leadership or authority over the social formation as a whole. Both of them argue that this enlarged or expanded hegemony is specific to the institutions, apparatuses and relations of the so-called 'superstructures' of the State and civil society. Both Althusser and Gramsci, then, insist that ideology, while itself a contradictory site and stake in the class struggle, has a specific function in securing the conditions for the expanded reproduction of capital. It is, therefore, a pertinent, and distinctive level of struggle, where leadership is secured and contested: with mechanisms and sites of struggle 'relatively autonomous'. Both also maintain that 'ideology' is not a simple form of false consciousness, to be explained as a set of myths or simple false constructions in the head. All societies require specific ideologies, which provide those systems of meaning, concepts, categories and representations which make sense of the world, and through which men come to 'live' (albeit unconsciously, and through a series of 'misrecognitions'), in an imaginary way, their relation to the real, material conditions of their existence (which are only representable to them, as modes of consciousness, in and through ideology). Althusser sometimes tends to represent ideology as rather too functionally secured to the rule of the dominant classes: as if all ideology is, by definition, operative within the horizon of the 'dominance ideas' of the ruling class. For Gramsci, ideologies are thought of in a more contradictory way—really, as sites and stakes in the class struggle. What interests Gramsci is how the existing ideologies—the 'common sense' of the fundamental classes—which are themselves the complex result of previous moments and resolutions in the ideological class struggle, can be so actively *worked upon* so as to transform them into the basis of a more conscious struggle, and form of intervention in the historical process. Both insist, however, that ideologies are not simply 'in the head', but are material relations—what Lenin called 'ideological social relations'—which shape social actions, function through concrete institutions and apparatuses, and are materialized through practices. Gramsci insists on the process which transforms these great 'practical ideologies' of fundamental social classes. Althusser, for his part, adds that ideologies operate by constituting concrete individuals as the 'social subjects' of ideological discourses —the process of what, following Laclau, he calls 'interpellating subjects'.

These propositions have recently been taken forward in a seminal intervention by Laclau (1977). In the essays on 'Populism' and 'Fascism', Laclau argues that the individual elements of these ideologies (e.g. nationalism, militarism, racism, 'the people', etc.) have, in themselves, no necessary class-belonging 'no necessary class connotation'. We cannot assume, *a priori* that these elements necessarily 'belong' to any specific class, or indeed that a class, as a single homogeneous entity, has a single unitary and uncontradictory 'world view' which, as Poulantzas says, it carries around with it, through history, 'like a number plate on its back' (Poulantzas: 1973). Ideologies, as concrete discursive formations do exhibit a peculiar 'unity' of their own. This unity arises, first, through what Laclau calls 'condensation': where each element 'fulfils a role of condensation with respect to others. When a familial interpellation, for example, evokes a political interpellation, or an aesthetic interpellation, and when each of these isolated interpellations operates as a symbol of the others, we have a relatively unified ideological discourse'. (This has been defined as 'ideological unity' through a process of connotative condensation—cf., O'Shea: 1978.) Secondly, unity is secured through 'the specific interpellation which forms the axis and organizing principle of all ideology. In trying to analyse the ideological level of a determinate social formation, our first task must be to reconstruct the interpellative structures which constitute it'. If separate ideological elements have no necessary class belonging, and classes do not have paradigmatic ideologies assigned or ascribed to them, what then is the relationship between classes and ideologies? As might be assumed, this relation is understood in terms of the way the class struggle articulates the various ideological discourses. 'Articulation requires . . . the existence of non-class contents—interpellations and contradictions—which constitute the raw materials on which class ideological practices operate. The ideology of the dominant class, precisely because it is dominant, interpellates not only the members of that class but also members of the dominated class.' It succeeds to the extent that it articulates 'different ideologies to its hegemonic project by an elimination of their antagonistic character'. Ideologies are therefore transformed 'through the class struggle, which is carried out through the production of subjects and the articulation/disarticulation of discourses'. This follows Gramsci's general line, which argued that ideologies cannot be reduced to the transparent, coherent 'class interests' of their class-subjects, and that ideologies are transformed, not by one class imposing a unitary 'world vision' upon all other classes, but by 'a process of distinction and of change in the relative weight possessed by the elements of the old ideology . . . what was secondary or subordinate or even incidental becomes of primary importance, it becomes the nucleus of a new doctrinal and ideological ensemble' (Mouffe: 1978; see also Mouffe for a seminal elaboration of this argument in relation to Gramsci).

There are problems with Laclau's tentative formulations: for example, what are 'class practices' which can operate to transform ideologies but which are, themselves, presumably, without any specific ideological elements which 'belong' to them? Despite these difficulties, these theorists begin to give us the tentative elements by means of which we can attempt to construct a non-reductionist theory of the super-structural or extra-economic aspects of social formations—once again, powered through the use of the concept of articulation.

What I have tried to do in this paper is to document the emergence of a new theoretical paradigm, which takes its fundamental orientation from the problematic of Marx's, but which seeks, by various theoretical means, to overcome certain of the limitations—economism, reductionism, 'a priorism', a lack of historical specificity—which have beset certain traditional appropriations of Marxism, which still disfigure the contributions to this field by otherwise distinguished writers, and which have left Marxism vulnerable and exposed to effective criticism by many different variants of economistic monism and sociological pluralism. This is a survey of an emergent field, not a comprehensive critical account. It must in no sense be assumed that the solutions attempted have been fully demonstrated, or that they are as yet adequately developed or without serious weaknesses and lacunae. With respect to those racially-structured social formations, which form the principal objects of inquiry in this collection, the problematic has hardly begun to be applied. Thus all that I have been able to do is to indicate certain strategic points of departure in such a potential field of application, certain protocols of theoretical procedure. Specifically, there is as yet no adequate theory of racism which is capable of dealing with both the economic and the superstructural features of such societies, while at the same time giving a historically-concrete and sociologically-specific account of distinctive racial aspects. Such an account, sufficient to substitute those inadequate versions which continue to dominate the field, remains to be provided. Nevertheless, in the hope of sponsoring and promoting such a development, it might be useful to conclude with a brief outline of some of the theoretical protocols which—in my view, of necessity—must govern any such proposed investigation.

This would have to begin from a rigorous application of what I have called the premise of historical specificity. Racism is not dealt with as a general feature of human societies, but with historically-specific racisms. Beginning with an assumption of difference, of specificity rather than of a unitary, transhistorical or universal 'structure'. This is not to deny that there might well be discovered to be certain common features to all those social systems to which one would wish to attribute the designation, 'racially structured'. But—as Marx remarked about the 'chaotic' nature of all abstractions which proceed at the level of the 'in-general' exclusively—such a general theory of racism is not the most favourable source for theoretical development and investigation: 'even though the most developed languages have laws and characteristics in common with the least developed, nevertheless, just those things which determine their development, i.e. the elements which are *not* general and common, must be

separated out . . . so that in their unity . . . their essential difference is not forgotten.' (Marx: 1973.) Racism in general is a 'rational abstraction' in so far as
'it really brings out and fixes the common element and saves us repetition'. Thus
it may help to distinguish those social features which fix the different positions
of social groups and classes on the basis of racial ascription (biologically or
socially defined) from other systems which have a similar social function. However, 'some determinations belong to all epochs, others only to a few. Some will
be shared by the most modern epoch and the most ancient'. This is a warning
against extrapolating a common and universal structure to racism, which
remains essentially the same, outside of its specific historical location. It is only
as the different racisms are historically specified—in their difference—
that they can be properly understood as 'a product of historical relations
and possess . . . full validity only for and within those relations'. It follows that
there might be more to be learned from distinguishing what, in common
sense, appear to be variants of the same thing: for example, the racism of the
slave South from the racism of the insertion of blacks into the 'free forms' of
industrial-capitalist development in the post-bellum North; or the racism of
Caribbean slave societies from that of the metropolitan societies like Britain,
which have had to absorb black workers into industrial production in the twentieth century.

In part, this must be because one cannot explain racism in abstraction
from other social relations—even if, alternatively, one cannot explain it by
reducing it to those relations. It has been said that there are flourishing racisms
in pre-capitalist social formations. This only means that, when dealing with
more recent social formations, one is required to show how thoroughly racism is
reorganized and rearticulated with the relations of new modes of production.
Racism within plantation slave societies in the mercantilist phase of world
capitalist development has a place and function, means and mechanisms of its
specific effectivity, which are only superficially explained by translating it out
from these specific historical contexts into totally different ones. Finley (1969),
Davis (1969, 1970) and others have argued that, though slavery in the Ancient
World was articulated through derogatory classifications which distinguished
between the enslaved and enslaving peoples, it did not necessarily entail the use
of specifically racial categories, whilst plantation slavery almost everywhere did.
Thus, there can be no assumed, necessary coincidence between racism and
slavery as such. Precisely the differences in the roles which slavery played in
these very different epochs and social formations may point us to the necessary
ground for specifying what this specific coincidence between slavery and racism
might secure. Where this coincidence does in fact appear, the mechanisms and
effectivity of its functioning—including its articulation with other relations—
need to be demonstrated, not assumed.

Again, the common assumption that it was attitudes of racial superiority
which precipitated the introduction of plantation slavery needs to be challenged.
It might be better to start from the opposite end—by seeing how slavery (the product of specific problems of labour shortage and the organization of plantation

agriculture—supplied, in the first instance, by non-black, indigenous labour, and then by white indentured labour) produced those forms of juridical racism which distinguish the epoch of plantation slavery. The elaboration of the juridical and property forms of slavery, as a set of enclaves within societies predicated on other legal and property forms, required specific and elaborate ideological work —as the history of slavery, and of its abolition, eloquently testifies. The same point may be made, *in extenso*, for all those explanations which ascribe racism-in-general to some universal functioning of individual psychology—the 'racial itch', the 'race instinct'—or explain its appearance in terms of a general psychology of prejudice. The question is not whether men-in-general make perceptual distinctions between groups with different racial or ethnic characteristics, but rather, what are the specific conditions which make this form of distinction socially pertinent, historically active. What gives this abstract human potentiality its effectivity, as a concrete material force? It could be said, for example, that Britain's long imperial hegemony, and the intimacy of the relationship between capitalist development at home and colonial conquest overseas, laid the trace of an active racism in British popular consciousness. Nevertheless, this alone cannot explain either the form and function which racism assumed, in the period of 'popular imperialism' at the height of the imperialist rivalry towards the end of the nineteenth century, or the very different forms of indigenous racism, penetrating deep into the working class itself, which has been an emergent feature of the contact between black and white workers in the conditions of post-war migration. The histories of these different racisms cannot be written as a 'general history' (Hall: 1978; Hall, et al.: 1978). Appeals to 'human nature' are not explanations, they are an alibi.

One must start, then, from the concrete historical 'work' which racism accomplishes under specific historical conditions—as a set of economic, political and ideological practices, of a distinctive kind, concretely articulated with other practices in a social formation. These practices ascribe the positioning of different social groups in relation to one another with respect to the elementary structures of society; they fix and ascribe those positionings in on-going social practices; they legitimate the positions so ascribed. In short, they are practices which secure the hegemony of a dominant group over a series of subordinate ones, in such a way as to dominate the whole social formation in a form favourable to the long-term development of the economic productive base. Though the economic aspects are critical, as a way of beginning, this form of hegemony cannot be understood as operating purely through economic coercion. Racism, so active at the level—'the economic nucleus'—where Gramsci insists hegemony must first be secured, will have or contract elaborate relations at other instances —in the political, cultural and ideological levels. Yet, put in this (obviously correct) way, the assertion is still too *a priori*. How specifically do these mechanisms operate? What further determinations need to be supplied? Racism is not present, in the same form or degree, in all capitalist formations: it is not necessary to the concrete functioning of all capitalisms. It needs to be shown how and why racism has been specifically overdetermined by and articulated with certain capitalisms at different stages of their development. Nor can it be assumed that this must take one, single form or follow one necessary path or logic, through a series of necessary stages.

This requires us, in turn, to show its articulation with the different structures of the social formation. For example, the position of the slave in pre-emancipation plantation society was not secured exclusively through race. It was predominantly secured by the quite specific and distinctive productive relations of slave-based agriculture, and through the distinctive property status of the slave (as a commodity) and of slave labour-power (as united with its exerciser, who was not however its 'owner'), coupled with legal, political and ideological systems which anchored this relation by racial ascription. This coupling may have provided the ready-made rationale and framework for those structures of 'informal racism' which became operative when 'freed' black labour migrated northwards in the United States or into the 'free village' system in the post-emacipation Caribbean. Yet the 'coupling' operated in new ways, and required their own ideological work—as in the 'Jim Crow' legislation of the 1880s and 1890s (Van Woodward: 1957). The reproduction of the low and ascribed status of black labour, as a specific fraction of the 'free labouring' classes of industrial capitalism, was secured—with the assistance of a trans-formed racism, to be sure: but also through other mechanisms, which accomplished their structured positioning with respect to new forms of capital in new ways. In the latter case, pertinent struggles have developed which exploited the gaps, or worked directly on the contradictions between racial ascription and the official ideologies of 'equal opportunity' which were simply not available to black slaves under a plantation system (Myrdal, 1962). We treat these differences as 'essentially the same' at our peril. On the other hand, it does not follow that because developed capitalism here functions predominantly on the basis of 'free labour' that the racial aspects of social relations can be assimilated, for all practical purposes, to its typical class relations (as does Cox (1970), despite his many pertinent observations). Race continues to differentiate between the different fractions of the working classes with respect to capital, creating specific forms of fracturing and fractioning which are as important for the ways in which they intersect class relations (and divide the class struggle, internally) as they are mere 'expressions' of some general form of the class struggle. Politically and culturally, these combined and uneven relations between class and race are historically more pertinent than their simple correspondence.

At the economic level, it is clear that race must be given its distinctive and 'relatively autonomous' effectivity, as a distinctive feature. This does not mean that the economic is sufficient to found an explanation of how these relations concretely function. One needs to know how different racial and ethnic groups were inserted historically, and the relations which have tended to erode and transform, or to preserve these distinctions through time—not simply as residues and traces of previous modes, but as active structuring principles of the present organization of society. Racial categories alone will not provide or explain these. What are the different forms and relations in which these racial fractions were combined under capital? Do they stand in significantly different relations to capital? Do they stand within an articulation of different modes of production? What are the relations of dissolution/conservation between them? How has race functioned to preserve and develop these articulations? What are the functions which the dominated modes of production perform in the reproduction of the dominant mode? Are these linked to it through the domestic reproduction of labour power 'below its value', the supply of cheap labour, the regulation of the 'reserve army of labour', the supply of raw materials, of subsistence agriculture, the hidden costs of social reproduction? The indigenous 'natural economies' of Latin America and the forms of semi-domestic production characteristic of the Caribbean societies differ significantly, among and between them, in this respect. The same is true even where different ethnic fractions stand in the same sets of relations to capital. For example, the position of black labour in the industrial North of the United States and of black migration to post-war Britain show highly distinctive patternings along racial lines: yet these situations are not explicable without the concept of the 'reserve army of labour'. Yet it is clear that blacks are not the only division within the 'reserve army': hence race is not the only mechanism through which its size and composition is regulated. In the United States, both white immigrants (e.g. European and Mexican) and women, and in Britain, both women and the Irish have provided a significant alternative element (see Braverman: 1975; Castle and Kosack: 1973).

The either/or alternatives, surveyed in the opening parts of this paper, are therefore seriously disabling, at a theoretical level, whether it is 'metropolitan' or 'satellite' formations which are under discussion; and whether it is historical or contemporary forms which are under scrutiny. As I have recently argued (Hall, et al.: 1978), the structures through which black labour is reproduced—structures which may be general to capital at a certain stage of development, whatever the racial composition of labour—are not simply 'coloured' by race: they work through race. The relations of capitalism can be thought of as articulating classes in distinct ways at each of the levels or instances of the social formation—economic, political, ideological. These levels are the 'effects' of the structures of modern capitalist production, with the necessary displacement of relative autonomy operating between them. Each level of the social formation requires its own independent 'means of representation'—the means by which the class-structured mode of production appears, and acquires effectivity at the level of the economic, the political, the ideological class struggle. Race is intrinsic to the manner in which the black labouring classes are complexly constituted at each of these levels. It enters into the way black labour, male and female, is distributed as economic agents at the level of economic practices, and the class struggles which result from it; and into the way the fractions of the black labouring classes are reconstituted, through the means of political representation (parties, organizations, community action centres, publications and campaigns) as political forces in the 'theatre of politics'—and the political struggles which result; and the manner in which the class is articulated as the collective and individual 'subjects' of emergent ideologies—and the struggles over ideology, culture and consciousness which result. This gives the matter or dimension of race, and racism, a practical as well as theoretical centrality to all the relations which affect black labour. The constitution of this fraction as a class, and the class relations which ascribe it, function as race relations. Race is thus, also, the modality in which class is 'lived', the medium through which class relations are experienced, the form in which it is appropriated and 'fought through'. This has consequences for the whole class, not specifically for its 'racially defined' segment. It has consequences in terms of the internal fractioning and division within the working class which, among other ways, are articulated in part through race. This is no mere racist conspiracy from above. For racism is also one of the dominant means of ideological representation through which the white fractions of the class come to 'live' their relations to other fractions, and through them to capital itself. Those who seek, with effect, to disarticulate some of the existing syntaxes of class struggle (albeit of a corporatist or social-reformist kind) and to rearticulate class experience through the condensed interpellations of a racist ideological syntax are, of course, key agents in this work of ideological transformation—this is the ideological class struggle, pursued, precisely, through harnessing the dominated classes to capital by means of the articulation of the internal contradictions of class experience with racism. In Britain, this process has recently attained a rare and general pitch. But they succeed to the measure that they do, because they are practising on real contradictions within and inside the class, working on real effects of the structure (however these may be 'misrecognized' through racism)—not because they are clever at conjuring demons, or because they brandish swastikas and read *Mein Kampf*.

Racism is, thus, not only a problem for blacks who are obliged to suffer it. Nor is it a problem only for those sections of the white working class and those organizations infected by its stain. Nor can it be overcome, as a general virus in the social body, by a heavy dose of liberal innoculation. Capital reproduces the class, including its internal contradictions, as a whole—structured by race. It dominates the divided class, in part, through those internal divisions which have racism as one of its effects. It contains and disables representative class institutions, by neutralizing them—confining them to strategies and struggles which are race-specific, which do not surmount its limits, its barrier. Through racism, it is able to defeat the attempts to construct alternative means of representation which could more adequately represent the class as a whole, or which are capable of effecting the unity of the class as a result: that is, those alternatives which would adequately represent the class as a whole—against capitalism, against racism. The sectional struggles, articulated through race, instead, continue to appear as the necessary defensive strategies of a class divided against itself, face-to-face with capital. They are, therefore, also the site of capital's continuing hegemony over it. This is certainly not to treat racism as, in any simply sense, the product of an ideological trick.

Nevertheless, such an analysis would need to be complemented by an analysis of the specific forms which racism assumes in its ideological functioning. Here, we would have to begin by investigating the different ways in which racist ideologies have been constructed and made operative under different historical conditions: the racisms of mercantilist theory and of chattel slavery; of conquest and colonialism; of trade and 'high imperialism'; of 'popular imperialism' and of so-called 'post-imperialism'. In each case, in specific social formations, racism as an ideological configuration has been reconstituted by the dominant class relations, and thoroughly reworked. If it has performed the function of that cementing ideology which secures a whole social formation under a dominant class, its pertinent differences from other such hegemonic ideologies require to be registered in detail. Here, racism is particularly powerful and its imprint on popular consciousness especially deep, because in such racial characteristics as colour, ethnic origin, geographical position, etc., racism discovers what other ideologies have to construct: an apparently 'natural' and universal basis in nature itself. Yet, despite this apparent grounding in biological givens, outside history racism, when it appears, has an effect on other ideological formations within the same society, and its development promotes a transformation of the whole ideological field in which it becomes operative. It can in this way, harness other ideological discourses to itself—for example, it articulates securely with the us/them structure of corporate class consciousness—through the mechanism previously discussed of connotative condensation. Its effects are similar to other ideologies from which, on other grounds, it must be distinguished: racisms also dehistoricize—translating historically-specific structures into the timeless language of nature; decomposing classes into individuals and recomposing those disaggregated individuals into the reconstructed unities, the great coherences, of new ideological 'subjects': it translates 'classes' into 'blacks' and 'whites', economic groups into 'peoples', solid forces into 'races'. This is the process of constituting new 'historical subjects' for ideological discourses—the mechanism we encountered earlier, of forming new interpellative structures. It produces, as the natural and given 'authors' of a spontaneous form of racial perception, the naturalized 'racist subject'. This is not an external function, operative only against those whom it disposes or disarticulates (renders silent). It is also pertinent for the dominated subjects—those subordinated ethnic groups or 'races' which live their relation to their real conditions of existence, and to the domination of the dominant classes, in and through the imaginary representations of a racist interpellation, and who come to experience themselves as 'the inferiors', *les autres*. And yet these processes are themselves never exempted from the ideological class struggle. The racist interpellations can become themselves the sites and stake in the ideological struggle, occupied and redefined to become the elementary forms of an oppositional formation—as where 'white racism' is vigorously contested through the symbolic inversions of 'black power'. The ideologies of racism remain contradictory structures, which can function both as the vehicles for the imposition of dominant ideologies, and as the elementary forms for the cultures of resistance. Any attempt to delineate the politics and ideologies of racism which omit these continuing features of struggle and contradiction win an apparent adequacy of explanation only by operating a disabling reductionism.

In this field of inquiry, 'sociological theory' has still to find its way, by a difficult effort of theoretical clarification, through the Scylla of a reductionism which must deny almost everything in order to explain something, and the Charybdis of a pluralism which is so mesmerized by 'everything' that it cannot explain anything. To those willing to labour on, the vocation remains an open one.

Bibliography

ALAVI, H. (1975). India and the colonial mode of production. *Socialist register*. Atlantic Highlands, Humanities.

ALTHUSSER, L. (1965). *For Marx*. London, Allan Lane.

—. (1971). *Lenin and philosophy and other essays*. London, New Left Books.

—. (1976). *Essays in self-criticism*. London, New Left Books.

—; BALIBAR, E. (1970). *Reading Capital*. London, New Left Books.

ANDERSON, P. (1977). The antinomies of Antonio Gramsci. *New left review* (London), no. 100.

BANAJI, J. (1977). Modes of production in a materialist conception of history. *Capital and class*, no. 3.

BARTHES, R. (1967). *Elements of semiology*. London, Cape.

BEECHEY, V. (1978). The ideology of racism. Ph.D. Thesis, Oxford. Unpublished.

BETTELHEIM, C. (1972). Theoretical comments. In: EMMANUEL, A. *Unequal exchange*. London, New Left Books.

BRADBY, B. (1975). Capitalist/precapitalist articulation. *Economy and society* (London), vol. 4, no. 2.

BRAVERMAN, H. (1975). *Labour and monopoly capital*. New York, Monthly Review Press.

CARCHEDI, G. (1977). *On the economic identification of social classes*. London, Routledge & Kegan Paul.

CASTLES, C.; KOSAK, G. (1973). *Immigrant workers and class structure in western Europe*. London, Oxford University Press.

CLAMMER, J. (1975). Economic anthropology and the sociology of development. In: OXALL, I.; BARNETT, T.; BOOTH, D. (eds.) *Beyond the sociology of development*. London, Routledge & Kegan Paul.

COX, O. (1970). *Caste, class and race*. New York, Monthly Press Review.

CUTLER, A. et al. (1977). *Marx's Capital and capitalism today*. London, Routledge & Kegan Paul.

DAVIS, D. B. (1969). Comparative approach to American history: slavery. In: GENOVESE, E.; FONER, L. (eds.) *Slavery in the new world*. Englewood Cliffs, Prentice-Hall.

—. (1970). *The problem of slavery in western culture*. Ithaca, N.Y., Cornell University Press.

FINLEY, M. (1969). The idea of slavery. In: GENOVESE, R.; FONER, L. (eds.) op. cit.

FOGEL, R.; ENGERMAN, S. (1974). *Time on the Cross*. Boston, Little, Brown & Co.

FOSTER-CARTER, A. (1978). The modes of production debate. *New left review* (London), no. 107.

FRANK, G. (1969). *Capitalism and underdevelopment in Latin America*. New York, Monthly Review Press.

FURTADO, C. (1971). Dependencia externa y teoria economica. *El trimestre economico* (Mexico), April-June. (Translated by O'BRIEN, P. In: OXALL, I.; BARNETT, T.; BOOTH, D. (eds.) op. cit.

GENOVESE, E. (1965). *The political economy of slavery*. New York, Vintage.

—. (1970). *The world the slaveholders made*. New York, Vintage.

—. (1971). *In red and black*. New York, Vintage.

—. (1977). Reply to criticism. *Medical history review* (New York), winter.

GRAMSCI, A. (1971). *Selections from the prison notebooks*. London, Lawrence & Wishart.

HALL, S. (1973). Marx's notes on method: a reading of 'The 1857 Introduction'. *Working papers in cultural studies 6*. Birmingham.

—. (1977). Continuing the discussion. In: UNESCO. *Race and class in post-colonial society*. Paris.

—. (1978). Pluralism, race and class in Caribbean society. In: UNESCO. op. cit.

—; LUMLEY, B.; McLENNAN, G. (1977). Politics and ideology in A. Gramsci. *Working papers in cultural studies 10*. Birmingham.

—. et al. (1978). *Policing the crisis*. London, Macmillan.

HILTON, R. (ed.) (1976). *The transition from feudalism to capitalism*. London, New Left Books.

HINDESS, B.; HIRST, P. (1975). *Pre-capitalist modes of production*, London, Routledge & Kegan Paul.

—; —. (1977). *Modes of production and social formation*. Routledge & Kegan Paul.

HIRST, P. (1976). Althusser's theory of ideology. *Economy and society* (London), vol. 5, no. 4.

JOHNSON, R. et al. (1978). (a) The problem of 'a-priorism'. (b) 'The histories' in Marx. Centre for Cultural Studies. Birmingham. (Mimeographed papers.)

KUPER, L. (1974). *Race, class and power*. London, Duckworth.

LACLAU, E. (1977). *Politics and ideology in Marxist theory*. London, New Left Books.

MARX, K. (1956). *Capital*. Vol. 2. London, Lawrence & Wishart.

—. (1961). *Capital*. Vol. 1. Moscow, Foreign Languages Publishing House.

—. (1964). *Precapitalist economic formations*. HOBSBAWN, E. (ed.) London, Lawrence & Wishart.

—. (1973). *Introduction to 'The Grundisse'*. London, Penguin.

—. (1974). *Capital*. Vol. 3. London, Lawrence & Wishart.

McLENNAN, G. (1976). Some problems in British Marxist historiography. Centre for Cultural Studies, Birmingham. (Mimeographed.)

MEILLASSOUX, C. (1960). Essai d'interprétation du phénomène économique dans les sociétiés traditionelles d'auto-subsistence. *Cahiers d'études africaines* (The Hague), vol. 4.

—. (1972). From production to reproduction. *Economy and society* (London), vol. 1, no. 1.

—. (1974). Imperialism as a mode of reproduction of labour power. (Mimeographed.)

MOUFFE, C. (1978). Introduction to a selection of essays on Gramsci. In preparation.

O'BRIEN, P. (1975). A critique of Latin-American dependency theories. In: OXALL, I.; BARNETT, T.; BOOTH, D. (eds.) op. cit.

O'SHEA, A. (1978). A critique of Laclau's theory of interpellation. Centre for Cultural Studies, Birmingham. (Mimeographed.)

OXALL, I.; BARNETT, T.; BOOTH, D. (eds.) (1975). *Beyond the sociology of development*. Routledge & Kegan Paul.

POST, K. (1978). *Arise, ye starvelings*. In preparation.

POULANTZAS, N. (1973). *Political power and social classes*. London, New Left Books.

REX, J. (1970). *Race relations in sociological theory*. London, Weidenfeld & Nicholson.

—. (1973). *Race, colonialism and the city*. London, Routledge & Kegan Paul.

—. (1978). New nations and ethnic minorities. In: UNESCO. *Race and class in post-colonial societies*. Paris.

REY, P.-P. (1971). *Colonialisme, neo-colonialisme, et transition au capitalisme*. Maspéro, Paris.

—. (1973). *Les alliances de classes*. Maspéro, Paris.

—. (1975). Reflections on the lineage mode of production. *Critique of anthropology*, no. 3.

—; DUPRÉ, G. (1973). Reflections on the pertinence of a theory of exchange. *Economy and society* (London), vol. 2, no. 2.

ROSE, S.; HAMBLEY, J.; HAYWOOD, J. (1973). Science, racism and ideology. *Socialist register— 1973*. Atlantic Highlands, Humanities.

SCHWARZ, B. (1978). On Maurice Dobb. In: JOHNSON, R.; McLENNAN, G., SCHWARZ, B. *Economy, history, concept*. Centre for Cultural Studies, Birmingham.

SEDDON, D. (1978). Introduction. *Relations of production*. London, Cass.

SMITH, M. G. (1965). *The plural society in the British West Indies*. Berkeley, University of California Press.

TERRAY, E. (1972). *Marxism and 'primitive societies'*. New York, Monthly Review Press.

VAN DEN BERGHE, P. (1965). *South Africa: a study in conflict*. Middletown, C.T., Wesleyan University Press.

VANN WOODWARD, C. (1957). *The strange career of Jim Crow*. London, New York, Oxford University Press.

WILLIAMS, E. (1966). *Capitalism and slavery*. Chapel Hill, Russell.

WOLPE, H. (1972). Capitalism and cheap labour in South Africa. *Economy and society* (London), vol. 1, no. 4.

—. (1975). The theory of internal colonialism. In: OXALL, I.; BARNETT, T.; BOOTH, D. (eds.) op. cit.

—. (1976). The white working class in South Africa. *Economy and society* (London), vol. 5, no. 2.

—. (1978). The articulation of modes of production. Introduction to a selection of essays. In preparation.

New Ethnicities

Stuart Hall

I have centered my remarks on an attempt to identify and characterize a significant shift that has been going on (and is still going on) in black cultural politics. This shift is not definitive, in the sense that there are two clearly discernible phases—one in the past which is now over and the new one which is beginning—which we can neatly counterpose to one another. Rather, they are two phases of the same movement, which constantly overlap and interweave. Both are framed by the same historical conjuncture and both are rooted in the politics of antiracism and the postwar black experience in Britain. Nevertheless I think we can identify two different "moments" and that the difference between them is significant.

It is difficult to characterize these precisely, but I would say that the first moment was grounded in a particular political and cultural analysis. Politically, this is the moment when the term "black" was coined as a way of referencing the common experience of racism and marginalization in Britain and came to provide the organizing category of a new politics of resistance, among groups and communities with, in fact, very different histories, traditions, and ethnic identities. In this moment, politically speaking, "The Black Experience," as a singular and unifying framework based on the building up of identity across ethnic and cultural difference between the different communities, became "hegemonic" over other ethnic/racial identities— though the latter did not, of course, disappear. Culturally, this analysis formulated itself in terms of a critique of the way blacks were positioned as the unspoken and invisible "other" of predominantly white aesthetic and cultural discourses.

This analysis was predicated on the marginalization of the black experience in British culture; not fortuitously occurring at the margins, but placed, positioned at the margins, as the consequence of a set of quite specific political and cultural practices which regulated, governed, and "normalized" the representational and discursive spaces of English society. These formed the conditions of existence of a cultural politics designed to challenge, resist, and, where possible, transform the dominant regimes of representation—first in music and style, later in literary, visual, and cinematic forms. In these spaces blacks have typically been the objects, but rarely the subjects, of the practices of representation. The struggle to come into representation was predicated on a critique of the degree of fetishization, objectification, and negative figuration which are so much a feature of the representation of the black subject. There was a concern not simply with the absence or marginality of the black experience but with its simplification and its stereotypical character.

The cultural politics and strategies which developed around this critique had many facets, but its two principal objects were, first, the question of *access* to the rights to representation by black artists and black cultural workers themselves. Second, the *contestation* of the marginality, the stereotypical quality, and the fetishized nature of images of blacks, by the counterposition of a "positive" black imagery. These strategies were principally addressed to changing what I would call the "relations of representation."

I have a distinct sense that in the recent period we are entering a new phase. But we need to be absolutely clear what we mean by a "new" phase because, as soon as you talk of a new phase, people instantly imagine that what is entailed is the *substitution* of one kind of politics for another. I am quite distinctly *not* talking about a shift in those terms. Politics does not necessarily proceed by way of a set of oppositions and reversals of this kind, though some groups and individuals are anxious to "stage" the question in this way. The original critique of the predominant relations of race and representation and the politics which developed around it have not and cannot possibly disappear while the conditions which gave rise to it—cultural racism in its Dewesbury form—not only persist but positively flourish under Thatcherism.[1] There is no sense in which a new phase in black cultural politics could

1. The Yorkshire town of Dewesbury became the focus of national attention when white parents withdrew their children from a local school with predominantly Asian pupils on the

replace the earlier one. Nevertheless it is true that as the struggle moves forward and assumes new forms, it does to some degree *displace,* reorganize, and reposition the different cultural strategies in relation to one another. If this can be conceived in terms of the "burden of representation," I would put the point in this form: that black artists and cultural workers now have to struggle, not on one, but on *two* fronts. The problem is, how to characterize this shift—if indeed, we agree that such a shift has taken or is taking place—and if the language of binary oppositions and substitutions will no longer suffice. The characterization that I would offer is tentative, proposed mainly to try to clarify some of the issues involved, rather than to preempt them.

The shift is best thought of in terms of a change from a struggle over the relations of representation to a politics of representation itself. It would be useful to separate out such a "politics of representation" into its different elements. We all now use the word "representation," but, as we know, it is an extremely slippery customer. It can be used, on the one hand, simply as another way of talking about how one images a reality that exists "outside" the means by which things are represented: a conception grounded in a mimetic theory of representation. On the other hand, the term can also stand for a very radical displacement of that unproblematic notion of the concept of representation. My own view is that events, relations, structures do have conditions of existence and real effects outside the sphere of the discursive; but only within the discursive, and subject to its specific conditions, limits, and modalities, do they have or can they be constructed within meaning. Thus, while not wanting to expand the territorial claims of the discursive infinitely, how things are represented and the "machineries" and regimes of representation in a culture do play a *constitutive,* and not merely a reflexive, after-the-event, role. This gives questions of culture and ideology, and the scenarios of representation—subjectivity, identity, politics—a formative, not merely an expressive, place in the constitution of social and political life. I think it is the move toward this second sense of representation which is taking place and which is transforming the politics of representation in black culture.

This is a complex issue. First, it is the effect of a theoretical encounter between black cultural politics and the discourses of a Eurocentric, largely white, critical cultural theory which in recent years has focused so much analysis on the politics of representation. This is always an extremely difficult, if not dangerous, encounter. (I think particularly of black people encountering the discourses of poststructuralism, postmodernism, psychoanalysis, and feminism.) Second, it marks what I can only call "the end of innocence," or the end of the innocent notion of the essential black

---

grounds that "English" culture was no longer taught on the curriculum. The contestation of multicultural education from the right also underpinned the controversies around the Bradford headmaster Ray Honeyford. See Gordon 1987.

subject. Here again, the end of the essential black subject is something which people are increasingly debating, but they may not have fully reckoned with its political consequences. What is at issue here is the recognition of the extraordinary diversity of subjective positions, social experiences, and cultural identities which compose the category "black"; that is, the recognition that "black" is essentially a politically and culturally *constructed* category, which cannot be grounded in a set of fixed trans-cultural or transcendental racial categories and which therefore has no guarantees in Nature. What this brings into play is the recognition of the immense diversity and differentiation of the historical and cultural experience of black subjects. This inevitably entails a weakening or fading of the notion that "race" or some composite notion of race around the term "black" will either guarantee the effectivity of any cultural practice or determine in any final sense its aesthetic value.

We should put this as plainly as possible. Films are not necessarily good because black people make them. They are not necessarily "right-on" by virtue of the fact that they deal with the black experience. Once you enter the politics of the end of the essential black subject you are plunged headlong into the maelstrom of a continuously contingent, unguaranteed, political argument and debate: a critical politics, a politics of criticism. You can no longer conduct black politics through the strategy of a simple set of reversals, putting in the place of the bad old essential white subject, the new essentially good black subject. Now, that formulation may seem to threaten the collapse of an entire political world. Alternatively, it may be greeted with extraordinary relief at the passing away of what at one time seemed to be a necessary fiction. Namely, either that all black people are good or indeed that all black people are *the same*. After all, it is one of the predicates of racism that "you can't tell the difference because they all look the same." This does not make it any easier to conceive of how a politics can be constructed which works with and through difference, which is able to build those forms of solidarity and identification which make common struggle and resistance possible but without suppressing the real heterogeneity of interests and identities, and which can effectively draw the political boundary lines without which political contestation is impossible, without fixing those boundaries for eternity. It entails the movement in black politics from what Gramsci called the "war of maneuver" to the "war of position"—the struggle around positionalities. But the difficulty of conceptualizing such a politics (and the temptation to slip into a sort of endlessly sliding discursive liberal-pluralism) does not absolve us of the task of developing such a politics.

The end of the essential black subject also entails a recognition that the central issues of race always appear historically in articulation, in a formation, with other categories and divisions and are constantly crossed and recrossed by the categories of class, of gender, and ethnicity. (I make a distinction here between race and ethnicity to which I shall return.) To me, films like *Territories, Passion of Remembrance, My Beautiful Laundrette,* and *Sammy and Rosie Get Laid,* for example, make it perfectly clear that this shift has been engaged, and that the question of the black subject cannot be represented without reference to the dimensions of class, gender, sexuality, and ethnicity.

Difference and Contestation

A further consequence of this politics of representation is the slow recognition of the deep ambivalence of identification and desire. We think about identification usually as a simple process, structured around fixed "selves" which we either are or are not. The play of identity and difference which constructs racism is powered not only by the positioning of blacks as the inferior species but also, and at the same time, by an inexpressible envy and desire; and this is something the recognition of which fundamentally *displaces* many of our hitherto stable political categories, since it implies a process of identification and otherness which is more complex than we had hitherto imagined.

Racism, of course, operates by constructing impassable symbolic boundaries between racially constituted categories, and its typically binary system of representation constantly marks and attempts to fix and naturalize the difference between belongingness and otherness. Along this frontier there arises what Gayatri Spivak (1987) calls the "epistemic violence" of the discourses of the other—of imperialism, the colonized, orientalism, the exotic, the primitive, the anthropological, and the folkloric. Consequently the discourse of antiracism had often been founded on a strategy of reversal and inversion, turning the "Manichaean aesthetic" of colonial discourse upside down. However, as Fanon constantly reminded us, the epistemic violence is both outside and inside, and operates by a process of splitting on both sides of the division—in here as well as out there. That is why it is a question, not only of "black-skin, white-skin" but of *Black Skin, White Masks*—the internalization of the self-as-other. Just as masculinity always constructs femininity as double—simultaneously Madonna and Whore—so racism constructs the black subject: noble savage and violent avenger. And in the doubling, fear and desire double for one another and play across the structures of otherness, complicating its politics.

Recently I've read several articles about the photographic text of Robert Mapplethorpe—especially his inscription of the nude, black male—all written by black critics or cultural practitioners.[2] These essays properly begin by identifying in Mapplethorpe's work the tropes of fetishization, the fragmentation of the black image, and its objectification, as the forms of their appropriation within the white,

2. Mercer 1987 and various articles in Bailey 1986, an issue on "black experience."

gay gaze. But, as I read, I know that something else is going on as well in both the production and the reading of those texts. The continuous circling around Mapplethorpe's work is not exhausted by being able to place him as the white fetishistic gay photographer; and this is because it is also marked by the surreptitious return of desire—that deep ambivalence of identification which makes the categories in which we have previously thought and argued about black cultural politics and the black cultural text extremely problematic. This brings to the surface the unwelcome fact that a great deal of black politics, constructed, addressed, and developed directly in relation to questions of race and ethnicity, has been predicated on the assumption that the categories of gender and sexuality would stay the same and remain fixed and secured. What the new politics of representation does is to put that into question, crossing the questions of racism irrevocably with questions of sexuality. That is what is so disturbing, finally, to many of our settled political habits about *Passion of Remembrance*. This double fracturing entails a different kind of politics because, as we know, black radical politics has frequently been stabilized around particular conceptions of black masculinity, which are only now being put into question by black women and black gay men. At certain points, black politics has also been underpinned by a deep absence or more typically an evasive silence with reference to class.

Another element inscribed in the new politics of representation has to do with the question of ethnicity. I am familiar with all the dangers of "ethnicity" as a concept and have written myself about the fact that ethnicity, in the form of a culturally constructed sense of Englishness and a particularly closed, exclusive, and regressive form of English national identity, is one of the core characteristics of British racism today (Hall 1978). I am also well aware that the politics of antiracism has often constructed itself in terms of a contestation of "multiethnicity" or "multiculturalism." On the other hand, as the politics of representation around the black subject shifts, I think we will begin to see a renewed contestation over the meaning of the term "ethnicity" itself.

If the black subject and black experience are not stabilized by Nature or by some other essential guarantee, then it must be the case that they are constructed historically, culturally, politically—and the concept which refers to this is "ethnicity." The term "ethnicity" acknowledges the place of history, language, and culture in the construction of subjectivity and identity, as well as the fact that all discourse is placed, positioned, situated, and all knowledge is contextual. Representation is possible only because enunciation is always produced within codes which have a history, a position within the discursive formations of a particular space and time. The displacement of the "centered" discourses of the West entails putting in question its universalist character and its transcendental claims to speak for everyone, while being itself everywhere and nowhere. The fact that this grounding of ethnicity in difference was deployed, in the discourse of racism, as a means of disavowing the realities of racism and repression does not mean that we can permit the term to be permanently colonized. That appropriation will have to be contested, the term disarticulated from its position in the discourse of "multiculturalism" and transcoded, just as we previously had to recuperate the term "black" from its place in a system of negative equivalences. The new politics of representation therefore also sets in motion an ideological contestation around the term "ethnicity." But in order to pursue that movement further, we will have to retheorize the concept of "difference."

It seems to me that, in the various practices and discourses of black cultural production, we are beginning to see constructions of just such a new conception of ethnicity: a new cultural politics which engages rather than suppresses difference and which depends, in part, on the cultural construction of new ethnic identities. Difference, like representation, is also a slippery, and therefore contested, concept. There is the "difference" which makes a radical and unbridgeable separation; and there is a "difference" which is positional, conditional, and conjunctural, closer to Derrida's notion of *différance,* though if we are concerned to maintain a politics it cannot be defined exclusively in terms of an infinite sliding of the signifier. We still have a great deal of work to do to *decouple* ethnicity, as it functions in the dominant discourse, from its equivalence with nationalism, imperialism, racism, and the state, which are the points of attachment around which a distinctive British or, more accurately, English ethnicity have been constructed. Nevertheless, I think such a project is not only possible but necessary. Indeed, this decoupling of ethnicity from the violence of the state is implicit in some of the new forms of cultural practice that are going on in films like *Passion* and *Handsworth Songs.* We are beginning to think about how to represent a noncoercive and a more diverse conception of ethnicity, to set against the embattled, hegemonic conception of "Englishness" which, under Thatcherism, stabilizes so much of the dominant political and cultural discourses, and which, because it is hegemonic, does not represent itself as an ethnicity at all.

This marks a real shift in the point of contestation, since it is no longer only between antiracism and multiculturalism but *inside* the notion of ethnicity itself. What is involved is the splitting of the notion of ethnicity between, on the one hand, the dominant notion which connects it to nation and "race" and, on the other hand, what I think is the beginning of a positive conception of the ethnicity of the margins, of the periphery. That is to say, a recognition that we all speak from a particular place, out of a particular history, out of a particular experience, a particular culture, without being contained by that position as "ethnic artists" or filmmakers. We are all, in that sense, *ethnically* located and our ethnic identities are crucial to our subjective sense of who we are. But this is also a recognition that this is not an ethnicity which is doomed to survive, as Englishness was, only by marginalizing, dispossessing, displacing, and forgetting other ethnicities. This precisely is the politics of ethnicity predicated on difference and diversity.

The final point which I think is entailed in this new politics of representation has to do with an awareness of the black experience as a *diaspora* experience, and the consequences which this carries for the process of unsettling, recombination, hybridization, and "cut-and-mix"—in short, the process of cultural *diasporaization* (to coin an ugly term) which it implies. In the case of the young black British films and filmmakers under discussion, the diaspora experience is certainly profoundly fed and nourished by, for example, the emergence of Third World cinema; by the African experience; the connection with Afro-Caribbean experience; and the deep inheritance of complex systems of representation and aesthetic traditions from Asian and African culture. But, in spite of these rich cultural "roots," the new cultural politics is operating on new and quite distinct ground—specifically, contestation over what it means to be "British." The relation of this cultural politics to the past, to its different "roots," is profound, but complex. It cannot be simple or unmediated. It is (as a film like *Dreaming Rivers* reminds us) complexly mediated and transformed by memory, fantasy, and desire. Or, as even an explicitly political film like *Handsworth Songs* clearly suggests, the relation is intertextual—mediated, through a variety of other "texts." There can, therefore, be no simple "return" or "recovery" of the ancestral past which is not reexperienced through the categories of the present: no base for creative enunciation in a simple reproduction of traditional forms which are not transformed by the technologies and the identities of the present. This is something that was signaled as early as a film like *Blacks Britannica* and as recently as Paul Gilroy's important book *There Ain't No Black in the Union Jack* ([1987] 1991). Fifteen years ago we didn't care, or at least I didn't care, whether there was any black in the Union Jack. Now not only do we care, we *must*.

This last point suggests that we are also approaching what I would call the end of a certain critical innocence in black cultural politics. And here, it might be appropriate to refer, glancingly, to the debate between Salman Rushdie and myself in the *Guardian* some months ago. The debate was not about whether *Handsworth Songs* or *The Passion of Remembrance* were great films or not, because, in the light of what I have said, once you enter this particular problematic, the question of what good films are, which parts of them are good and why, is open to the politics of criticism. Once you abandon essential categories, there is no place to go apart from the politics of criticism and to enter the politics of criticism in black culture is to grow up, to leave the age of critical innocence.

It was not Salman Rushdie's particular judgment that I was contesting, so much as the mode in which he addressed the films. He seemed to me to be addressing them as if from the stable, well-established critical criteria of a *Guardian* reviewer. I was trying, perhaps unsuccessfully, to say that I thought this an inadequate basis for a political criticism and one which overlooked precisely the signs of innovation, and the constraints under which these filmmakers were operating. It is difficult to define what an alternative mode of address would be. I certainly didn't want Salman Rushdie to say he thought the films were good because they were black. But I also didn't want him to say that he thought they weren't good because "we creative artists all know what good films are," since I no longer believe we can resolve the questions of aesthetic value by the use of these transcendental, canonical cultural categories. I think there *is* another position, one which locates itself *inside* a continuous struggle and politics around black representation, but which then is able to open up a continuous critical discourse about themes, about the forms of representation, the subjects of representation, above all, the regimes of representation. I thought it was important, at that point, to intervene to try to get that mode of critical address right, in relation to the new black filmmaking. It is extremely tricky, as I know, because as it happens, in intervening, I got the mode of address wrong too! I failed to communicate the fact that, in relation to his *Guardian* article, I thought Salman was hopelessly wrong about *Handsworth Songs,* which does not in any way diminish my judgment about the stature of *Midnight's Children.* I regret that I couldn't get it right, exactly, because the politics of criticism has to be able to get both things right.

Such a politics of criticism has to be able to say (just to give one example) why *My Beautiful Laundrette* is one of the most riveting and important films produced by a black writer in recent years and precisely for the reason that made it so controversial: its refusal to represent the black experience in Britain as monolithic, self-contained, sexually stabilized, and always "right-on"—in a word, always and only "positive," or what Hanif Kureishi has called "cheering fictions": "the writer as public relations officer, as hired liar. If there is to be a serious attempt to understand Britain today, with its mix of races and colours, its hysteria and despair, then, writing about it has to be complex. It can't apologise or idealize. It can't sentimentalize and it can't represent only one group as having a monopoly on virtue" (Kureishi 1985). *Laundrette* is important particularly in terms of its control, of knowing what it is doing, as the text crosses those frontiers between gender, race, ethnicity, sexuality, and class. *Sammy and Rosie* is also a bold and adventurous film, though in some ways less coherent, not so sure of where it is going, overdriven by an almost uncontrollable, cool anger. One needs to be able to offer that as a critical judgment and to argue it through, to have one's mind changed, without undermining one's essential commitment to the project of the politics of black representation.

Works Cited

Bailey, D. 1986. *Ten.8* (Birmingham) no. 22.

Gilroy, P. 1991. *There Ain't No Black in the Union Jack*. London: Hutchison, 1987. Reprint, Chicago: University of Chicago Press.

Gordon, P. 1987. "The New Right, Race, and Education." *Race and Class* (London) 29, no. 3 (winter).

Hall, S. 1978. "Racism and Reaction." *Five Views on Multi-Racial Britain*. London: Commission for Racial Equality.

Kureishi, H. 1985. "Dirty Washing." *Time Out* (London), 14–20 November.

Mercer, K. 1987. "Imagining the Black Man's Sex." In *Photography/Politics: Two*, ed. P. Holland et al. London: Comedia/Methuen.

Spivak, G. 1987. *In Other Worlds: Essays in Cultural Politics*. London: Methuen.

Toward a Critical Theory of "Race"

Lucius Outlaw

A Need for Rethinking

For most of us that there are different races of people is one of the most obvious features of our social worlds. The term "race" is a vehicle for notions deployed in the organization of these worlds in our encounters with persons who are significantly different from us particularly in terms of physical features (skin color and other anatomical features), but also, often combined with these, when they are different with respect to language, behavior, ideas, and other "cultural" matters.

In the United States in particular, "race" is a constitutive element of our common sense and thus is a key component of our "taken-for-granted valid reference schema" through which we get on in the world.[1] And, as we are constantly burdened by the need to resolve difficulties, posing varying degrees of danger to the social whole, in which "race" is the focal point of contention (or serves as a shorthand explanation for the source of contentious differences), we are likewise constantly reinforced in our assumption that "race" is self-evident.

Here has entered "critical" thought: as self-appointed mediator for the resolution of such difficulties by the promotion (and practical effort to realize) a given society's "progressive" evolution, that is, its development of new forms of shared self-understanding — and corresponding forms of social practice — void of the conflicts thought to rest on inappropriate valorizations and rationalizations of "race." Such efforts notwithstanding, however, the "emancipatory project"[2] has foundered on the crucible of "race." True to the prediction of W. E. B. Du Bois, the twentieth century has indeed been dominated by "the problem of the color line." It will clearly be so for the remainder

384

of the century, and well into the twenty-first. For on one insightful reading, we are now in a period in which a major political struggle is being waged, led by the administrations of Ronald Reagan and George Bush, to "rearticulate"[3] racial meanings as part of a larger project to consolidate the victory of control of the state by those on the Right, control that allows them to set the historical agenda for America, thus for the Western "free" world.

Of course, it *must* be said that the persistence of social struggles—in the United States and elsewhere—in which "race" is a key factor is not due simply to a failure to realize emancipatory projects on the part of those who championed them. While there is some truth to such an analysis, the fuller story is much more complex. Nor has the failure been total. It is possible to identify numerous points in history, and various concrete developments, that were significantly influenced—if not inspired entirely—by emancipatory projects informed by traditions of critical theoretical thought: from the New Deal to the modern freedom (i.e., civil rights), Black Power, and antiwar movements; to the modern women's and environmental movements in the United States and elsewhere; to anticolonial, anticapitalist, antidictatorial, antiracist struggles throughout the so-called Third World and Europe.

Still, the persistence of struggles around matters involving "race" requires that those of us who continue to be informed by leftist traditions of critical thought and practice confront, on the one hand, unresolved problems. On the other, by way of a critical review of our own traditions, we must determine the extent to which those traditions have failed to account appropriately for "race" (i.e., provide an understanding that is sufficiently compelling for self-understanding and enlightening of social reality) in a way that makes practically possible mobilization sufficient to effect social reconstructions that realize emancipatory promises. It may well be that we will need to review what we think will constitute "emancipation" and whether our notions coincide with those of liberation and self-realization indigenous to persons and traditions of various "racial" groups that would be assisted by us, or who wage their own struggles with assistance from leftist traditions.

No more compelling need is required for our undertaking such reviews than that of getting beyond the interminable debate whether "race" *or* "class" is the proper vehicle for understanding (and mobilizing against) social problems with invidiously racial components. The present essay is another installment in this ongoing rethinking.[4] Here the focus will be less on the limitations of traditions of critical theory and practice with respect to the privileging of "class" over "race" and more on rethinking "race." A primary concern will be to question "race" as an obvious, biologically or metaphysically given, thereby self-evident reality—to challenge the presumptions sedimented in the "reference schemata" that, when socially shared, become common sense, whether through a group's construction of its life world and/or through hegemonic imposition.[5]

This rethinking will involve, first, a review of the career of "race" as a concept: the context of its emergence and reworking, and the changing agendas of its deployment. Second, a brief recounting of approaches to "race" within traditions of critical theory will facilitate responding to the central question of the essay: "Why a critical theory of 'race" today?" This question is generated by the need to face a persistent problem within Western societies but, in the United States and European societies in particular, one that today presents a new historical conjuncture of crisis proportions: the prospects— and the concrete configurations—of democracy in the context of historic shifts in the demographics of "racial" pluralism. The centripetal, possibly balkanizing forces of racial pluralism have been intensified during the past quarter-century by heightened group (and individual) "racial" self-consciousness as the basis for political mobilization and organization without the constraining effects of the once dominant paradigm of "ethnicity," in which differences are seen as a function of sociology and culture rather than biology.[6]

According to the logic of "ethnicity" as the paradigm for conceptualizing group differences and fashioning social policy to deal with them, the socially devisive effects of "ethnic" differences were to disappear in the social-cultural "melting pot" through assimilation, or, according to the pluralists, ethnic identity would be maintained across time but would be mediated by principles of the body politic: all *individuals*, "without regard to race, creed, color, or national origin," were to win their places in society on the basis of demonstrated achievement (i.e., merit). For both assimilationists and pluralists, *group* characteristics (ethnicity) were to have no play in the determination of merit; their legitimacy was restricted to the private sphere of "culture." This has been the officially sanctioned, and widely socially shared, interpretation of the basic principles of the body politic in the United States in the modern period, even though it was, in significant measure, a cover for the otherwise sometimes explicit, but always programmatic, domination of Africans and of other peoples.

For the past twenty years, however, "race" has been the primary vehicle for conceptualizing and organizing precisely around group differences with the demand that social justice be applied to *groups* and that "justice" be measured by *results*, not just by opportunities. With the assimilation project of the ethnic paradigm no longer hegemonic, combined with the rising demographics of the "unmeltable ethnics" in the American population (and the populations of other Western countries, including Great Britain, France, and West Germany) and the preponderance of "race thinking" infecting political life, we have the battleground on which many of the key issues of social development into the twenty-first century will continue to be waged. Will "critical theory" provide assistance in this area in keeping with its traditions

—that is, enlightenment leading to emancipation—or will it become more and more marginalized and irrelevant?

On "Race"

There is, of course, nothing more fascinating than the question of the various types of mankind and their intermixture. The whole question of heredity and human gift depends upon such knowledge; but ever since the African slave trade and before the rise of modern biology and sociology, we have been afraid in America that scientific study in this direction might lead to conclusions with which we were loath to agree; and this fear was in reality because the economic foundation of the modern world was based on the recognition and preservation of so-called racial distinctions. In accordance with this, not only Negro slavery could be justified, but the Asiatic coolie profitably used and the labor classes in white countries kept in their places by low wage.[7]

Race theory . . . had up until fairly modern times no firm hold on European thought. On the other hand, race theory and race prejudice were by no means unknown at the time when the English colonists came to North America. Undoubtedly, the age of exploration led many to speculate on race differences at a period when neither Europeans nor Englishmen were prepared to make allowances for vast cultural diversities. Even though race theories had not then secured wide acceptance or even sophisticated formulation, the first contacts of the Spanish with the Indians in the Americas can now be recognized as the beginning of a struggle between conceptions of the nature of primitive peoples which has not yet been wholly settled. . . . Although in the seventeenth century race theories had not as yet developed any strong scientific or theological rationale, the contact of the English with Indians, and soon afterward with Negroes, in the New World led to the formation of institutions and relationships which were later justified by appeals to race theories.[8]

The notion of "race" as a fundamental component of "race thinking"—that is, a way of conceptualizing and organizing social worlds composed of persons whose differences allow for arranging them into groups that come to be called "races"—has had a powerful career in Western history (though such thinking has not been limited to the "West") and continues to be a matter of significant social weight. Even a cursory review of this history should do much to dislodge the concept from its place as provider of access to a self-evident, obvious, even ontologically *given* characteristic of humankind. For what comes out of such a review is the recognition that although "race" is continually with us as an organizing, explanatory concept, what the term refers to—that is, the origin and basis of "racial" differences—has not remained constant. When this insight is added to the abundant knowledge that the deployment of "race" has virtually always been in service to political agendas, beyond more "disinterested" endeavors simply to "understand" the basis of perceptually obvious (and otherwise not obvious, but real nonetheless) differences among human groups, we will have firm grounds for a rethinking of "race." Such a rethinking might profitably be situated in a more sociohistorically "constructivist" framework, namely, one in which "race" is viewed, in the words of Michael Omi and Howard Winant, as a social "formation."[9] But first, something of the career of the concept.

"Race" and Science

The career of "race" does not begin in science but predates it and emerges from a general need to account for the unfamiliar or, simply, to classify objects of experience, thus to organize the life world. How — or why — it was that "race" came to play important classifying, organizing roles is not clear:

> The career of the race concept begins in obscurity, for experts dispute whether the word derives from an Arabic, a Latin, or a German source. The first recorded use in English of the word "race" was in a poem by William Dunbar of 1508. . . . During the next three centuries the word was used with growing frequency in a literary sense as denoting simply a class of persons or even things. . . . In the nineteenth, and increasingly in the twentieth century, this loose usage began to give way and the word came to signify groups that were distinguished biologically.[10]

This nineteenth-century development was preceded by others in earlier centuries that apparently generated a more compelling need for classificatory ordering in the social world and, subsequently, the use of "race" as such a device. First, there were the tensions within Europe arising from encounters between different groups of peoples, particularly "barbarians" — whether defined culturally or, more narrowly, religiously. (And it should be noted that within European thought, and elsewhere, the color black was associated with evil and death, with "sin" in the Christian context. The valorizing power inherent in this was ready-to-hand with Europe's encounter with Africa.) A more basic impetus, intensified by these tensions, came from the need to account for human origins in general, for human diversity in particular. Finally, there were the quite decisive European voyages to America and Africa, and the development of capitalism and the slave trade.[11]

The function of "race" as an ongoing, classificatory device gained new authority and a new stage in the concept's career developed when, in the eighteenth century, "evidence from geology, zoology, anatomy and other fields of scientific enquiry was assembled to support a claim that racial classification would help explain many human differences."[12] The concept provided a form of "typological thinking," a mode of conceptualization that was at the center of the agenda of emerging scientific praxis at the time, that served well in the classification of human groups. Plato and Aristotle, of course, were precursors of such thinking: the former with his theory of Forms; the latter through his classification of things in terms of their "nature." In the modern period the science of "race" began in comparative morphology with stress on pure "types" as classificatory vehicles. A key figure contributing to this unfolding agenda was the botanist Linnaeus.[13]

A number of persons were key contributers to the development of theories of racial types. According to Banton and Harwood, Johann Friedrich Blumenbach provided the first systematic racial classification in his *Generis humani varietate nativa liber* (On the Natural Variety of Mankind, 1776). This was followed by the work of James Cowles Prichard *(Generis humani varietate*, 1808).[14] Georges Cuvier, a French anatomist, put forth a physical-cause theory of races in 1800 in arguing that physical nature determined culture. He classified humans into three major groups along an implied descending scale: whites, yellows, and blacks. As Banton and Harwood interpreted his work, central to his thinking was the notion of "type" more than that of "race": "Underlying the variety of the natural world was a limited number of pure types and if their nature could be grasped it was possible to interpret the diverse forms which could temporarily appear as a result of hybrid mating."[15]

Other important contributions to the developing science of "race" include S. G. Morton's publication of a volume on the skulls of American Indians (1839) and one on Egyptian skulls (1845). His work was extended and made popular by J. C. Nott and G. R. Gliddon in their *Types of Mankind* (1854). Charles Hamilton Smith (*The Natural History of the Human Species*, 1848) developed Cuvier's line of argument in Britain. By Smith's reckoning, according to Banton and Harwood, "The Negro's lowly place in the human order was a consequence of the small volume of his brain."[16] Smith's former student, Robert Knox (*The Races of Man*, 1850), argued likewise. Finally, there was Count Joseph Arthur de Gobineau's four-volume *Essay on the Inequality of Human Races* (1854) in which he argued that, in the words of Banton and Harwood, "the major world civilizations . . . were the creations of different races and that race-mixing was leading to the inevitable deterioration of humanity."[17]

Two significant achievements resulted from these efforts. First, drawing on the rising authority of "science" as the realization and guardian of systematic, certain knowledge, there was the legitimation of "race" as a gathering concept for morphological features that were thought to distinguish varieties of *Homo sapiens* supposedly related to one another through the logic of a *natural* hierarchy of groups. Second, there was the legitimation of the view that the behavior of a group and its members was determined by their place in this hierarchy. "*Homo sapiens* was presented as a species divided into a number of races of different capacity and temperament. Human affairs could be understood only if individuals were seen as representatives of races for it was there that the driving forces of human history resided."[18] These science-authorized and -legitimated notions about "race," when combined with social projects involving the distinguishing and, ultimately, the control of "racially different" persons and groups (as in the case of the enslavement of Africans) took root and grew to become part of common sense. "Race" was now "obvious."

For Banton and Harwood, this science of "race" peaked during the middle of the nineteenth century. By the century's end, however, a variety of racial classifications had brought confusion, in part because "no one was quite sure what races were to be classified *for*. A classification is a tool. The same object may be classified differently for different purposes. No one can tell what is the best classification without knowing what it has to do."[19] The situation was both assisted and complicated by the work of Darwin and Mendel. Social Darwinism emerged as an effort by some (notably Herbert Spencer and Ludwig Gumplowicz) to apply Darwin's principles regarding heredity and natural selection to human groups and endeavors and thereby provide firmer grounding for the science of "race" (something Darwin was reluctant to do). Such moves were particularly useful in justifying the dominance of certain groups over others (British over Irish; Europeans over Africans . . .). On the other hand, however, Darwin's *Origins* shifted the terrain of scientific discourse from morphology and the stability of "pure types" to a subsequent genetics-based approach to individual characteristics and the effects on them of processes of change, thus to a focus on the analysis of variety. In the additional work of Mendel, this development proved revolutionary:

> A racial type was defined by a number of features which are supposed to go together. . . . The racial theorists of the nineteenth century assumed there was a natural law which said that such traits were invariably associated and were transmitted to the next generation as part of a package deal. Gregor Mendel's research showed that this was not necessarily the case. . . . [It] also showed that trait variation *within* a population was just as significant as trait variations *between* populations . . . traits do not form part of a package but can be shuffled like a pack of playing cards.[20]

And, since environmental impacts that condition natural selection, in addition to heredity and the interplay between dominant and recessive traits, are important factors in the "shuffling" of traits, the notion of "pure" racial types with fixed essential characteristics was displaced: biologically (i.e., genetically) one can only speak of "clines."[21]

The biology of "races" thus became more a matter of studying diversities within — as well as among — groups, and, of particular interest, the study of how groups "evolve" across both time and space. To these efforts were joined others from the *social* science of "race": that is, understanding groups as sharing some distinctive biological features—though not constituting pure types—but with respect to which sociocultural factors are of particular importance (but in ways significantly different from the thinking of the nineteenth-century theorists of racial types).

For many scientists the old (nineteenth-century) notion of "race" had become useless as a classificatory concept, hence certainly did not support in any truly scientific way the political agendas of racists. As noted by Livingstone, "Yesterday's science is today's common sense and tomorrow's nonsense."[22] Revolutions within science (natural and social) conditioned transformed approaches to "race" (although the consequences have still not completely supplanted the popular, commonsensical notions of "races" as pure types as the Ku Klux Klan, among others, indicates).

The conceptual terrain for this later, primarily twentieth-century approach to "race" continues to be, in large part, the notion of "evolution" and was significantly conditioned by the precursive work of Mendel and Darwin, social Darwinists notwithstanding. In the space opened by this concept it became possible at least to work at synthesizing insights drawn from both natural science (genetics, biochemistry) and social science (anthropology, sociology, psychology, ethology) for a fuller understanding of "geographical races":[23] studies of *organic* evolution focus on changes in the gene pool of a group or groups; studies of *superorganic* evolution are concerned with changes in the "behavior repertoire" of a group or groups—that is, with the sociocultural development.[24] And it is a legitimate question—though one difficult to answer—to what extent, if at all, superorganic evolution is a function of organic evolution or, to add even more complexity, to what extent, if at all, the two forms of evolution are mutually influential. The question of the relations between both forms of development continues to be a major challenge.

But what is a "race" in the framework of organic evolution and the global social context of the late twentieth century? Certainly not a group of persons who share genetic homogeneity. That is likely only in the few places where one might find groups that have remained completely isolated from other groups, with no intergroup sexual reproductions. Among other things, the logics of the capitalist world system have drawn virtually all peoples into the "global village" and facilitated much "interbreeding." But capitalism notwithstanding, "raciation" (i.e., the development of the distinctive gene pools of various groups that determine the relative frequencies of characteristics shared by their members, but certainly not by them alone) has also been a function, in part, of chance. Consequently:

> Since populations' genetic compositions vary over time, race classifications can never be permanent; today's classification may be obsolete in 100

generations. More importantly, modern race classifications attempt to avoid being arbitrary by putting populations *of presumed common evolutionary descent* into the same racial group. Common descent, however, is inferred from similarity in gene frequencies, and here the problem lies. For . . . a population's gene frequencies are determined not only by its ancestry but also by the processes of natural selection and genetic drift. This means that two populations could, in principle, be historically unrelated but genetically quite similar if they had been independently subject to similar evolutionary forces. To place them in the same racial group would, as a step in the study of evolution, be quite misleading. In the absence of historical evidence of descent, therefore, it is difficult to avoid the conclusion that classifying races is merely a convenient but biologically arbitrary way of breaking down the variety of gene frequency data into a manageable number of categories.[25]

When we classify a group as a "race," then, at best we refer to generally shared characteristics derived from a "pool" of genes. Social, cultural, and geographical factors, in addition to those of natural selection, all impact on this pool, thus on raciation: sometimes to sustain the pool's relative configuration (for example, by isolating the group—culturally or physically—from outbreeding); sometimes to modify it (as when "mulattoes" were produced in the United States in significant part through slave masters of European descent appropriating African women for their—the "masters'"—sexual pleasure). It is possible to study, with some success, the evolution of a particular group over time (a case of *specific* evolution). The prospects for success are more limited, however, when the context of concern is *general* evolution—that is, the grouping of all of the world's peoples in ordered categories "with the largest and most heterogeneous societies in the top category and the smallest and most homogeneous in the bottom."[26] In either case—general or specific evolution—the concern is with superorganic evolution: changes in behavior repertoires. And such changes are not tied to the genetic specificities of "races."

But not all persons (or groups) think so. Although evolutionary—as opposed to typological—thinking, in some form, is at present the dominant intellectual framework for systematic reconstructions and explanations of human natural and social history, it, too, has been enlisted in the service of those who would have "science" pass absolution on their political agendas: that is, to legitimate the empowerment of certain groups, certain "races," over others. Even shorn of the more crude outfittings of social Darwinism's "survival of the fittest" (those in power, or seeking power, over others being the "fittest," of course), the field of the science of "race" is still occupied by those offering orderings of human groups along an *ascending* scale with a particular group's placement on the scale being a function of the level of their supposed development (or lack thereof) toward human perfectibility: from "primitive" to "civilized" (circa the nineteenth century); from "undeveloped" or "underdeveloped" to "developed" or "advanced" (circa the twentieth century).

Such arguments find fertile soil for nourishment and growth now that "evolution" (organic and superorganic, often without distinction), frequently conceived as linear development along a single path which *all* "races" have to traverse, is now a basic feature of our "common sense," Creationists excepted, and as we still face political problems emerging from conflicts among "racial" groups. "Race" continues to function as a critical yardstick for the rank-ordering of racial groups both "scientifically" and sociopolitically, the latter with support from the former. At bottom, then, "race" — sometimes explicitly, quite often implicitly — continues to be a major fulcrum of struggles over the distribution and exercise of power.

Certainly one of the more prominent contemporary struggles has centered on the validity of measurements of the "intelligence" of persons from different "racial" groups that purport to demonstrate the comparative "intelligence" of the groups. This struggle is propelled by the social weight given to "intelligence" as an important basis for achievement and rewards in a meritocratic social order. At its center is the question of the dominant roles played by either the genes or the environment in determining "intelligence" (and, by extension, in determining raciation).

Whichever way the question is answered is not insignificant for social policy. If the genes predominate, some argue, then social efforts in behalf of particular groups (e.g., blacks, women, Hispanics, etc.) intending to ameliorate the effects of disadvantageous sociohistorical conditions and practices are misguided and should be discontinued. It would be more "rational" to rechannel the resources poured into such efforts into "more socially productive" pursuits. On the other hand, if environmental factors dominate, then in a liberal democracy, for example, where justice prevails disparites of opportunities (and results?) among "racial" groups must be corrected, especially when the disparities are the result of years, even centuries, of invidious discrimination and oppression.

The politics of "race" are played out on other fields besides that of "intelligence." Modern science has also been concerned with whether the genes of a "race" determine its cultural practices and/or social characteristics. The findings?

> All the known differences between geographical races in the frequency of genes which affect behavior are . . . quite trivial. Yet in principle it is possible that there may be genetic differences affecting socially, politically or economically significant behaviours and it seems reasonable to expect that the more population geneticists and physical anthropologists look for such genetic differences, the more will they discover. Because, however, of (1)

the relative plasticity of human behaviour, (2) the genetic heterogeneity of all human populations, and (3) the mass of data suggesting the importance of situational determinants (e.g., economic and political factors) in explaining race relations, there is at present little reason to expect that a substantial part of intergroup relations will ever be explicable in genetic terms.[27]

But if not the genes, what about "evolution"? Has it produced differences in behavior and biological mechanisms for survival in different "races"? Is it possible to extrapolate from studies of the evolution of animal behavior to the evolution of human behavior? According to Banton and Harwood, such efforts are inconclusive, the conclusions being at best hypothetical and difficult to test on humans. Moreover:

> . . . the difficulty with generalising about evolution is that it is a process that has happened just once. With relatively few exceptions it is impossible to compare evolutionary change with anything else, or to say what would have happened had one of the components been absent. Therefore everything has its place in evolution. . . . If everything has its place then, by implication, everything is justified.[28]

What, then, after this extended review of the science of "race," are we left with by way of understanding? With the decisive conclusion, certainly, that "race" is *not* wholly and completely determined by biology, but is only partially so. Even then biology does not *determine* "race," but in complex interplay with environmental, cultural, and social factors provides certain boundary conditions and possibilities that affect raciation and the development of "geographical" races. In addition, the definition of "race" is partly political, partly cultural. Nor does the modern conceptual terrain of "evolution" provide scientifically secure access to race-determining biological, cultural, social developmental complexes distributed among various groups that fix a group's rank-ordered place on an ascending "great chain of being." Racial categories are fundamentally *social* in nature and rest on shifting sands of biological heterogeneity.[29] The biological aspects of "race" are conscripted into projects of cultural, political, and social construction. "Race" is a *social* formation.

This being the case, the notion of "evolution" is particularly fruitful for critical-theoretical rethinking of "race." As has been indicated, in the biological sciences it dislodged the nineteenth-century notion of races as being determined by specific, fixed, natural characteristics and made possible better understandings of racial diversities *and* similarities. In addition, as a concept for organizing our thinking about change, "evolution" continues to provide a powerful vehicle for studying human sociohistorical development. It is a notion that is part and parcel of the terrain of critical social thought of the nineteenth and twentieth centuries.

On "Critical Theory" and "Race"

There is some ambiguity surrounding the notion of "critical theory" within traditions of *social* theory—beyond the fact that it is a phrase now used in reference to certain contemporary efforts in literary studies. On the one hand, the phrase is used to refer to a tradition of significantly revised and extended Marxism initiated by a group of theorists often referred to as "the Frankfurt School."[30] In this case "critical theory" is the name Max Horkheimer, an early director of the Institute for Social Research (established in Frankfurt, Germany in the late 1920s, hence the name "Frankfurt School"), gave to what he projected as the appropriate character and agenda for theoretical work directed at understanding—and contributing to the transformation of—social formations that, in various ways, blocked concrete realizations of increased human freedom.[31] This characterization of the nature of social theorizing and its agenda was shared by other members of the Institute (Herbert Marcuse, Theodor Adorno) even though still other members (Erich Fromm, Henryk Grossman) approached matters differently and used different methods in doing so. Further, there were theoretical differences between Horkheimer, Adorno, and Marcuse (and in Horkheimer's own thinking) over time that are masked by the label "critical theory."[32] Still, the label stuck and even today is used to identify a mode of social thought in the Frankfurt School tradition that continues in the work of a number of persons, Jürgen Habermas no doubt being one of the most widely known. Particularly through the influences of Marcuse on many in the generation coming of age in the 1960s during the socially transforming years of the great social mobilizations of the civil rights, black power, and antiwar movements, it is a tradition that has been especially influential in the United States, in part because it brought many of us of that generation to Marx, without question the major intellectual precursor to Frankfurt School critical theory (along with Kant, Hegel, Freud, Lukács, and others). And here lies the ambiguity, for, on the other hand, the phrase is often expanded to include Marx's work, and that in the various currents of Marxism as well, the Frankfurt School included. In the words of Erich Fromm: "There is no 'critical theory'; there is only Marxism."[33] Thus, while the various schools of Marxism, of whatever pedigree, all share important "family resemblances," there are, as well, significant differences among them sufficient to demand that each be viewed in its own right.[34] This is particularly the case when we come to the issue of "race" in "critical theory."

For a number of complex reasons, the Frankfurt School, for all of its influence on a generation of "new" leftists of various racial/ethnic groups many of whom were being radicalized in struggles in which "race" was a key factor, was not known initially so much for its theorizing about "racial" problems and their resolution as for its insightful critique of social domination gener-ally. Although members of the Institute, according to Martin Jay, were over-whelmingly of Jewish origins, and the Institute itself was made possible by funds provided by a member of a wealthy Jewish family expressly, in part, to study anti-Semitism, all in the context of Germany of the 1920s and early 1930s, "the Jewish question" was not at the center of the Institute's work.[35]

This changed in the late 1930s and early 1940s. With the rise of Hitler and the Nazis, the Institute was eventually moved to New York in 1935 (and California in 1941) where its work continued until after the war (when it was reestablished in West Germany in the 1950s). The focus of the Institute's work during this time was the battle against fascism with debates centering on the character of the changed nature of the economy in twentieth-century capitalism; that is, the expression of group sentiments were to be understood in the historical context of the society.[36]

In this, notes Jay, the Institute broke significant new ground. No less so in another major contribution they made to the Marxian legacy, through the work of Fromm especially, that made their studies of anti-Semitism so in-formative: the articulation, later supported by extensive empirical studies, of a social psychology — and of individual psychology and character structure in the context of the social — drawing off the work of Freud (among others), in the context of Marxian social theory. This made possible analyses that linked cultural, political, *and* economic structural and dynamic features of the social world, and the character structure of the person, which helped to il-luminate the de facto conditions of possibility for the emergence and social maintenance of Nazi fascism and anti-Semitism. Here, particularly, is to be found the significance of Frankfurt School critical theory for our discussion of "race."

In the course of the Institute's work during its stay in the United States, the concern with anti-Semitism became less and less the focus as members of the Institute concentrated increasingly on "prejudice" more generally, al-though still fundamentally as related to authority and authoritarianism. Ini-tiated by the American Jewish Committee in 1944 and conducted through its Department of Scientific Research established for that purpose, with the collaboration of the Berkeley Public Opinion Study, the Institute conducted major empirical studies, with critical philosophical analyses of the findings, of "one or another facet of the phenomenon we call prejudice." The object of the studies, it was noted, was "not merely to describe prejudice but to ex-plain it in order to help in its eradication." The sweep of the project involved studies of the bases and dynamics of prejudice on individual, group, institu-tional, and community levels all in the context of the social whole.[37]

The Authoritarian Personality, the result of an integrated set of studies and analyses, was one among a number of volumes that grew out of this project. As Horkheimer notes in its preface, it is a book that deals with "social discrimination," and its authors, in the terms of the *credo* of critical theory, were "imbued with the conviction that the sincere and systematic scientific eluci- dation of a phenomenon of such great historical meaning can contribute directly to an amelioration of the cultural atmosphere in which hatred breeds."[38] It is especially pertinent to this discussion of "race," Daniel Levin- son's chapter on ethnocentric ideology in particular.[39]

Here two conceptual moves are to be noted. First, Levinson substitutes "ethnocentrism" for "prejudice":

> Prejudice is commonly regarded as a feeling of dislike against a specific group; ethnocentrism, on the other hand, refers to a relatively consistent frame of mind concerning "aliens" generally. . . . Ethnocentrism refers to group relations generally; it has to do not only with numerous groups to- ward which the individual has hostile opinions and attitudes but, equally important, with groups toward which he is positively disposed.
>
> A theory of ethnocentrism offers a starting point for the understanding of the psychological aspect of *group* relations. (p. 102, my emphasis)

Equipped with a wider gathering concept, Levinson is able to make yet an- other move, one he thinks crucial to gaining the understanding being sought: "The term 'ethnocentrism' shifts the emphasis from 'race' to 'ethnic group' " (p. 103). What was gained by this?

> . . . apart from the arbitrariness of the organic basis of classification, the greatest dangers of the race concept lie in its hereditarian psychological im- plications and in its misapplication to cultures. Psychologically, the race theory implies, whether or not this is always made explicit, that people of a given race (e.g., skin color) are also very similar psychologically because they have a common hereditary family tree . . . Furthermore, the term "race" is often applied to groups which are not races at all in the technical sense . . . There is no adequate term, other than "ethnic," by which to de- scribe cultures (that is, systems of social ways, institutions, traditions, lan- guage, and so forth) which are not nations . . . From the point of view of sociology, cultural anthropology, and social psychology, the important concepts are not race and heredity but social organization (national, regional, subcultural, communal) and the interaction of social forms and in- dividual personalities. To the extent that relative uniformities in psycholog- ical characteristics are found within any cultural grouping, these uniformi- ties must be explained primarily in terms of social organization rather than "racial heredity." (p. 103)

As noted in the previous section, the conclusion had been reached in con- temporary natural and social science that, at the very least, "something other than "racial heredity, understood as biological homogeneity, had to serve as a basis for understanding group characteristics and intergroup dynamics. Frankfurt School critical theory was distinctive as critical philosophical theory and material, social, analysis (a la Marx), fortified by Freudian psychology, deployed in cultural analyses of authority and mass culture. In the Institute's American sojourn particularly, there developed an explicit concern to bring critical thought to bear on the problems of invidious group-based and group-directed discrimination and oppression. "Race" was viewed as an adequate vehicle for such a task. Conditioned by a commitment to engage in critical praxis as an interdisciplinary venture that drew on the best science available (including that on "race"), these social theorists, through an approach to prejudice cum ethnocentrism fashioned from Hegelian, Marxian, Freudian elements, provided a means for getting at the problems of "race" — more precisely of race-*ism* — that was both critical and radical: within the context of an emancipatory project, it cut through social thought based on a reified, erroneous, even fraudulent philosophical anthropology that derived the culture, psychology, and social position of various groups from the biologizing of their "racial types."

Herbert Marcuse, among all members of the Frankfurt School, is most responsible for conveying this legacy to the "New Left" generation of the United States and Western Europe. In contrast to other members of the Institute, he became the most integrated into the American scene and chose to remain in the country when other members returned to Germany in the 1950s.[40] Influential as a teacher and colleague in a number of institutions, his *One Dimensional Man* inducted many of us into critical theory.[41] Here was an understanding of the social order in a way the necessity of which had been driven home to many of us as, in the context of concrete struggles, we came up against the limits of the idealism fueled by the thought of liberal democracy. For a significant group of persons involved in struggles over the "color line," the limits — and their attempted transcendence — were indicated in the evolution of the struggle for "civil rights" to one seeking "Black Power."[42]

But the Frankfurt School did *not* introduce Marxism to the United States. Nor, consequently, was it the first group of Marxian radical theorists to confront the problems of "race." There were other, much older legacies, in fact.[43] It is this history of multiple legacies that makes for the ambiguity of "a critical theory of race" when "critical theory" covers both the Frankfurt School *and* Marxian traditions in general. For an obvious, critically important question is, "Why, given other Marxian legacies, did the New Left seek guidance in the work of the Frankfurt School which might be applied to the problems of 'race,' among others"?

With respect to what we might call the black New Left, but with regard to many nonblack New Leftists as well, this question has been insightfully probed by Harold Cruse. For him, a crucial reason had to do with what he termed the "serious disease of 'historical discontinuity' ":

. . . since World War I a series of world-shaking events, social upheavals and aborted movements have intruded and sharply set succeeding generations of Negroes apart in terms of social experiences. The youngest elements in the Negro movement today are activists, of one quality or another, who enter the arena unfortified with the knowledge or meaning of many of the vital experiences of Negro radicals born in 1900, 1910, 1920, or even 1930. The problem is that too many of the earlier-twentieth-century-vintage Negro radicals have become too conservative for the 1940ers. Worse than that, the oldsters have nothing to hand down to the 1940ers in the way of refined principles of struggle, original social theory, historical analysis of previous Negro social trends or radical philosophy suitable for black people. . . . All the evidence indicates that the roots of the current crisis of the Negro movement are to be found in the period between the end of World War I and the years of the Great Depression. . . . most of the social issues that absorb the attention of all the Negro radical elements today were prominently foreshadowed in these years. Yet the strands between the period called by some the "Fabulous Twenties" and the current Negro movement have been broken.[44]

The disease of discontinuity affected more than black youth. It was further facilitated by the anti-Communist repression led by Senator Joseph McCarthy, which had "a distinctly deleterious effect" not only on the leadership of black movements at the time, as Cruse notes, but on "radical" leadership in general.[45]

This discontinuity, bolstered by McCarthyism, was institutionalized in the curricula of most American colleges and universities, both black and white: virtually none provided systematically mediated learning regarding the history of previous struggles in which "radicals" had played important roles. Thus, when we remember that the U.S. New Left generation emerged principally on campuses and was forged in the crucibles of the modern civil rights and antiwar movements whose troops and general staff included thousands of students, the availability and attractiveness of Frankfurt School critical theory was *in part* a function of happy historical conjuncture: it was available when members of a generation were in need — and actively in search — of understandings to guide them in the transformation of a society that, when measured by its own best principles, was found seriously deficient. Those who suffered the deficits were no longer willing to do so, and were moving to secure their "freedom." Many others were moved to share in the struggles committed to the realization of what the principles called for. Marcuse, himself a teacher and scholar, was among others a major contributor to the recovery from discontinuity by providing an important linkage with Marxian (and Freudian) critical social thought that aided the conceptualization and understanding of the social order as a whole, within a global, historical context, in which it was possible to situate particular problems that were the focus of struggle, including, to some extent, those of the color line.

But only in part was this a matter of happy coincidence. The linkages between the old and new Lefts were never *completely* broken. Many young whites, in particular, were supported in their efforts by parents and others who themselves had been—and still were—radical activists of previous generations. There was another crucial factor, particularly as experienced by blacks "on the Left," an experience that has been formed into its own legacy: the felt *inadequacy* of Marxian Communist and Socialist projects with respect to "the Negro question," the ultimate test case of the problem of "race." At the core of this legacy is the *other side* of the science of "race": not its scientific, critical conceptualization, but the lived experiences of *real* persons whose experiences are forged in life worlds in part constituted by self-understandings that are in large measure "racial," no matter how "scientifically" inadequate.[46] Other Left theoretical and practical activities, advanced by various groups and parties, ran aground on this reality. Frankfurt School critical theory, unconstrained by dogmatic adherence to "the party line," offered a conceptualization of revolutionary social transformation while, at the same time, it took democratic freedom seriously. Since, at the time, on the black side of struggles involving "race," Black Nationalism was an increasingly ascendant force that even those on the white side had to contend with, and since participants from both "sides" had been forged in large part by liberal democracy, the vision of a new society that decidedly antidogmatic Frankfurt School critical theory helped to shape (particularly by not centering on *class* theory) was potentially more promising as a resolution of racism while preserving black integrity. In this regard there was the promise that the legacy of inadequacy of other traditions of Marxist thought might be overcome.

Oversimplified, the inadequacy had to do with the reductionism in the theorizing about "race" in those Marxian traditions that attempted to confront problems of the color line through approaches that rested on close adherence to a particular reading of the *classic* texts of the "mature" Marx and Engels, a reading sanctified after the Russian Revolution of 1917 by the subsequent Communist Internationals: *class* was the central—indeed, the only—vehicle for fully and properly understanding social organization and struggle. Problems of "race" are to be understood, then, as secondary to the "primary contradiction" of class conflict that is indigenous to social relations in capitalist social formations given the relations of the various classes to the means of production, relations that, at the very least, determine classes "in the last instance." The prospects for progressive social transformation and development, within and beyond capitalism, on this view, are dependent on successful organization and struggle by the international working class, racial differences notwithstanding. Such differences were to be transcended in the brotherhood of class solidarity beyond their opportunistic manipulation by the class of owners and managers, who used them as devices to foster divisions among workers, and by supposedly misguided, chauvinistic blacks (e.g., Marcus Garvey).

The history of Marxian Communist and Socialist organizations in the United States and elsewhere, populated, on the whole, by persons of European descent, is littered with errors, tragedies, and farces resulting from the dogmatic application of this approach.[47] A key source of the difficulty is the inadequate philosophical anthropology presumed by the privileging of "relations to the means of production" as the definitive determinant of groups defined by these relations, thus of the persons in those groups.[48] Aside from problems involving the racism of white workers in the class struggle, and, frequently, the paternalism of the white leadership, for many African-Americans "proletarianism internationalism" was not enough of a basis for forging a new Communist or Socialist world; it disregards — or explicitly treats as unimportant — much that they take to be definitive of African-Americans as a *people*. Identifying and nurturing these characteristics, and the institutions and practices that generate, shape, sustain, and mediate them, constitute a complex tradition of its own, that of "Black Nationalism."[49] It is a tradition that continues to inform approaches to "race" from the black side, within Marxian critical theory as well (though not that of the Frankfurt School). In 1928–29, for example, with impetus from black Communists (Cyril Briggs, Richard B. Moore, and Harry Haywood), who also had roots in the decidedly nationalist African Black Brotherhood, the Communist International took the position that blacks in the "black belt" of the southern United States were an oppressed "nation." The program for their liberation thus called for "self-determination" and "national independence." This was the official position, on and off, for nearly thirty years (1928–57) and was carried out in this country by the Communist Party of the United States of America (CPUSA).[50]

The house of "critical theory" has thus been divided on the issue of "race," sometimes against itself: the approach of the tradition of the Frankfurt School on one side; those of other Socialist and Communist organizations, of many persuasions, on the other, with numerous schools of thought and practice in between: "race" is without scientific basis as an explanatory notion (Frankfurt School); "race," while real, is a factor of conflict secondary to the primary contradiction of class struggle ("classical," "official" Marxism); "race" is the basis of a nation — a group whose members share common history and culture ("official" Marxism of 1928–57). Certainly the divergences have as much to do with social matters as with matters theoretical: the concrete histories of different groups, their agendas, their locations, the personal histories of their members, and so forth. Still, those of us who continue to be informed by legacies and agendas of "critical social theory" must move past this "Tower of Babel" in our own midst if we are to meet the challenges of the present and near future.[51]

Why a Critical Theory of "Race" Today?

Since the Black Nationalist tradition has continued to stress "race" over class, and classical Marxism class over "race," the "class or race" debates have persisted, at great expenditures of paper and ink, not to mention years of interminable struggle, confusion, and failure to conceive and secure the realization of promised emancipation. As we continue to struggle over matters of "race" in the United States and other societies, with very real possibilities for increased conflict, it is not enough to view today's problems as being brought on by the "heightened contradictions" of late capitalism attendant to the policies of neoconservative administrations conflicting with struggles for national liberation and socialism/communism in the "Third World." More is needed, both theoretically and practically.

"Both race *and* class" has been the response of some participants in the debate: "Left Nationalists" such as Manning Marable, on the one hand; theorists of the role of race in market relations and in social stratification (i.e., the social distribution of resources) such as William J. Wilson and Edna Bonacich, on the other.[52] Still others have proposed notions of "people-class," "eth-class," and "nation-class."[53] Yet all of these approaches, mindful of nationalist traditions from the black side, as well as of previous running-agrounds on "race," still presuppose the reality of "race."

But what is that reality? And "real" for whom? Would it be helpful for contemporary critical theory to recover the insights of twentieth-century science of "race" and those of the Frankfurt School regarding "race," "prejudice," and "ethnocentrism" and join them to recently developed critical-theoretic notions of social evolution to assist us in understanding and contributing to the emancipatory transformation of the "racial state" in its present configuration?[54] For, if Omi and Winant are correct: in the United States, the state is *inherently* racial, every state institution is a *racial* institution, and the entire social order is equilibrated (unstably) by the state to preserve the prevailing racial order (i.e., the dominance of "whites" over blacks and other "racial" groups);[55] during the decades of the 1950s through the 1970s, the civil rights, Black Power, Chicano, and other movements assaulted and attempted the "great transformation" of this racial state; however, the assaults were partial, and thus were not successful (as evidenced by the powerful rearticulation of "race" and reforming of the racial state consolidating power and dominance in the hands of a few "whites" in service to "whites" presently under way), because "all failed to grasp the comprehensive manner by which race is structured into the U.S. social fabric. All *reduced* race: to interest group, class fraction, nationality, or cultural identity. Perhaps most importantly, all these approaches lacked adequate conceptions of the racial state"[56] — if they are correct, might this not be case enough (if more is needed) for a new critical theory of "race" cognizant of these realities?

Omi and Winant think so, and propose their notion of "racial formation." It is a notion intended to displace that of "race" as an "essence" ("as something fixed, concrete and objective . . . "), or, alternatively, as a "mere illusion, which an ideal social order would eliminate." Thus, race should be understood as

> . . . an unstable and "decentered" complex of social meanings constantly being transformed by political struggle. . . . The crucial task . . . is to suggest how the widely disparate circumstances of individual and group racial identities, and of the racial institutions and social practices with which these identities are intertwined, are formed and transformed over time. This takes place . . . through political contestation over racial meanings.[57]

Central to their argument is the idea that "race" is socially and historically constructed and changes as a consequence of social struggle. "Race," in a racial state, is thereby irreducibly political.

The discussions and analyses of Omi and Winant, facilitated by their notion of "racial formation," are insightful and informative, particularly for their reading of the "rearticulation" of "race" by the Reagan administration. What these theorists offer is an important contribution to a revised and much needed critical theory of race for the present and near future. And part of the strength of their theorizing lies in the advance it makes beyond the reductionist thinking of other leftist theorists while preserving the sociohistorical constructivist (socially formed) dimensions of "race."

Part of the strength lies, as well, in the resituating of "race" as a "formation." For what this allows is an appreciation of the historical and socially constructive aspects of "race" within the context of a theory of social evolution where learning is a central feature.[58] Then we would have at our disposal the prospects of an understanding of "race" in keeping with the original promises of critical theory: enlightenment leading to emancipation. Social learning regarding "race," steered by critical social thought, might help us to move beyond racism, without reductionism, to pluralist socialist democracy.

Lest we move too fast on this, however, there is still to be explored the "other side" of "race": namely, the lived experiences of those within racial groups (e.g., blacks for whom Black Nationalism, in many ways, is fundamental). That "race" is without a scientific basis in biological terms does not mean, thereby, that it is without any social value, racism notwithstanding. The exploration of "race" from this "other side" is required before we will have an adequate critical theory, one that truly contributes to enlightenment and emancipation, in part by appreciating the integrity of those who see

403

themselves through the prism of "race." We must not err yet again in thinking that "race thinking" must be completely eliminated on the way to eman-
cipated society.

That elimination I think unlikely — and unnecessary. Certainly, however,
the social divisive forms and consequences of "race thinking" ought to be
eliminated, to whatever extent possible. For, in the United States in particular, a new historical conjuncture has been reached: the effort to achieve
democracy in a multi-"ethnic," multi-"racial" society where "group thinking" is a decisive feature of social and political life. A critical theory of "race"
that contributes to the learning and social evolution that secures socialist,
democratic emancipation in the context of this diversity would, then, be of
no small consequence.

NOTES

1. Alfred Schutz and Thomas Luckmann, *The Structures of the Life-World*, trans. Richard M.
Zaner and H. Tristram Engelhardt, Jr. (Evanston, Ill.: Northwestern University Press, 1973),
p. 8.

2. The anticipation of "a release of emancipatory reflection and a transformed social praxis"
that emerges as a result of the restoration, via critical reflection, of "missing parts of the historical
self-formation process to man and, in this way, to release a self-positing comprehension which
enables him to see through socially unnecessary authority and control systems." Trent Schroyer,
The Critique of Domination: The Origins and Development of Critical Theory (Boston: Beacon Press,
1973), p. 31.

3. "Rearticulation is the process of redefinition of political interests and identities, through
a process of recombination of familiar ideas and values in hitherto unrecognized ways." Michael
Omi and Howard Winant, *Racial Formation in the United States: From the 1960s to the 1980s* (London: Routledge & Kegan Paul, 1986), p. 146, note 8.

4. For previous installments in this discussion, see my "Race and Class in the Theory and
Practice of Emancipatory Social Transformation," in *Philosophy Born of Struggle: Anthology of Afro-
American Philosophy from 1917*, ed. Leonard Harris (Dubuque: Kendal/Hunt, 1983), pp. 117–129;
"Critical Theory in a Period of Radical Transformation," *Praxis International*, 3 (July 1983),
pp. 138–46; and "On Race and Class. Or, On the Prospects of 'Rainbow Socialism,' " in *The Year
Left 2: An American Socialist Yearbook*, ed. Mike Davis, Manning Marable, Fred Pfeil, and Michael
Sprinker (London: Verso, 1987), pp. 106–21.

5. On life-world construction see Schutz and Luckmann, *The Structures of the Life-World*, and
Peter L. Berger and Thomas Luckmann, *The Social Construction of Reality* (Garden City, N.Y.:
Doubleday, 1966). "Hegemonic imposition" is a notion much influenced by the ideas of Antonio
Gramsci (e.g., *Selections from the Prison Notebooks*, ed. and trans. Quintin Hoare and Geoffrey
Nowell Smith [New York: International, 1971]), although a now classic formulation of the ba-
sic insight was provided by Marx (and Engels?) in *The German Ideology*: "The ideas of the ruling
class are in every epoch the ruling ideas; i.e., the class which is the ruling *material* force of society,
is at the same time its ruling *intellectual* force" (in *The Marx-Engels Reader*, 2nd ed., ed. Robert
C. Tucker [New York: Norton, 1978], p. 172; emphasis in original).

6. In contrast to biologically oriented approaches, the ethnicity-based paradigm was an insurgent theory which suggested that race was a *social* category. Race was but one of a number
of determinants of ethnic group identity or ethnicity. Ethnicity itself was understood as the result of a group formation process based on culture and descent." Omi and Winant, "The Domi-

nant Paradigm: Ethnicity-Based Theory," in *Racial Formation in the United States* (pp. 14–24), p. 15.

7. W. E. B. Du Bois, "The Concept of Race," in *Dusk of Dawn: An Essay Toward an Autobiography of a Race Concept* (New York: Schocken Books, 1968 [1940]), p. 103.

8. Thomas F. Gossett, *Race: The History of an Idea in America* (Dallas: Southern Methodist University Press, 1963), pp. 16–17.

9. "Our theory of racial formation emphasizes the social nature of race, the absence of any essential racial characteristics, the historical flexibility of racial meanings and categories, the conflictual character of race at both the 'micro-' and 'macro-social' levels, and the irreducible political aspect of racial dynamics." Omi and Winant, *Racial Formation in the United States*, p. 4.

10. Michael Banton and Jonathan Harwood, *The Race Concept* (New York: Praeger, 1975), p. 13.

11. Ibid., p. 14.

12. Ibid., p. 13.

13. "The eighteenth-century Swedish botanist Linneaus achieved fame by producing a classification of all known plants which extracted order from natural diversity. Scientists of his generation believed that by finding the categories to which animals, plants and objects belonged they were uncovering new sections of God's plan for the universe. Nineteenth-century race theorists inherited much of this way of looking at things." Ibid., p. 46.

14. Ibid., pp. 24–25. Both works were closely studied in Europe and the United States.

15. Ibid., p. 27.

16. Ibid., p. 28.

17. Ibid., pp. 29–30. These authors observe that while Gobineau's volumes were not very influential at the time of their publication, they were later to become so when used by Hitler in support of his claims regarding the supposed superiority of the "Aryan race."

18. Ibid., p. 30.

19. Ibid., p. 38.

20. Ibid., pp. 47–49; emphasis in original.

21. "An article by an anthropologist published in 1962 declared in the sharpest terms that the old racial classifications were worse than useless and that a new approach had established its superiority. This article, entitled 'On the Non-existence of Human Races', by Frank B. Livingstone, did not advance any new findings or concepts, but it brought out more dramatically than previous writers the sort of change that had occurred in scientific thinking. . . . The kernel of Livingstone's argument is contained in his phrase 'there are no races, there are only clines'. A cline is a gradient of change in a measurable genetic character. Skin colour provides an easily noticed example." Ibid., pp. 56–57.

22. Ibid., p. 58, quoted by Banton and Harwood.

23. "When we refer to races we have in mind their geographically defined categories which are sometimes called 'geographical races', to indicate that while they have some distinctive biological characteristics they are not pure types." Ibid., p. 62.

24. Ibid., p. 63. "The main mistake of the early racial theorists was their failure to appreciate the difference between organic and superorganic evolution. They wished to explain all changes in biological terms." Ibid., p. 66.

25. Ibid., pp. 72–73; emphasis in original.

26. Ibid., p. 77.

27. Ibid., pp. 127–28.

28. Ibid., p. 137.

29. Ibid., p. 147.

30. For discussions of Frankfurt School critical theory see, for example, Martin Jay, *The Dialectical Imagination: A History of the Frankfurt School and the Institute of Social Research, 1923–1950* (Boston: Little, Brown, 1973); Zoltán Tar, *The Frankfurt School: The Critical Theories of Max Hork-*

heimer and Theodor W. Adorno (New York: Wiley, 1977); David Held, *Introduction to Critical Theory: Horkheimer to Habermas* (Berkeley: University of California Press, 1980); and Schroyer, *The Critique of Domination.*

31. Among Horkheimer's characterizations of critical theory is his now classic essay "Traditional and Critical Theory," reprinted in Max Horkheimer, *Critical Theory,* trans. Matthew J. O'Connell et al. (New York: Herder & Herder, 1972), PP. 188–243.

32. Zoltán Tar, *The Frankfurt School,* p. 34.

33. From a personal telephone conversation with Fromm during one of his last visits to the United States in 1976.

34. For a particularly conversant overview of the various currents of Marxism and their philosophical and historical backgrounds, see Leszek Kolakowski, *Main Currents of Marxism,* 3 vols. (Oxford: Oxford University Press, 1978).

35. "If one seeks a common thread running through individual biographies of the inner circle [of the Institute], the one that immediately comes to mind is their birth into families of middle or upper-middle class Jews. . . . If one were to characterize the Institute's general attitude towards the 'Jewish question', it would have to be seen as similar to that expressed by another radical Jew almost a century before, Karl Marx. In both cases the religious or ethnic issue was clearly subordinated to the social. . . . In fact, the members of the Institute were anxious to deny any significance at all to their ethnic roots." Jay, *The Dialectical Imagination,* pp. 31–32.

36. Ibid., pp. 143, 152.

37. Max Horkheimer and Samuel H. Flowerman, "Foreword to Studies in Prejudice," in *The Authoritarian Personality,* Theodor W. Adorno et al. (New York: Norton, 1950), pp. vi, vii.

38. Ibid., p. ix.

39. The following discussion centers on the fourth chapter in *The Authoritarian Personality,* "The Study of Ethnocentric Ideology," by Daniel J. Levinson. Page references will be included in the text.

40. The significance of the Studies in Prejudice notwithstanding, Martin Jay, for example, has noted the strategic moves adopted by Institute members on their movement to New York (e.g., continuing to publish their works in German, rather than English) that limited their integration into the mainstream of American social science. See *The Dialectical Imagination,* pp. 113–14; and Held, *Introduction to Critical Theory,* p. 36.

41. Subtitled *Studies in the Ideology of Advanced Industrial Society,* the book was published by Beacon Press (Boston) in 1964. His *An Essay on Liberation* (Beacon Press, 1969) was an important—though problematic—sequel that attempted to come to terms with the massive mobilizations of the late 1960s in the United States and Western Europe, Paris (1968) in particular. In the latter case (Paris), during a student-initiated national strike, Marcuse was celebrated as one of the "three 'M's" of revolutionary heroes: "Marx, Mao, Marcuse." For pertinent writings in regard to Marcuse, see, for example: *The Critical Spirit: Essays in Honor of Herbert Marcuse,* ed. Kurt H. Wolff and Barrington Moore, Jr. (Boston: Beacon Press, 1967); Paul Breines, (ed.), *Critical Interruptions: New Left Perspectives on Herbert Marcuse* (New York: Herder & Herder, 1970). *The Critical Spirit* includes a helpful Marcuse bibliography.

42. See Clayborne Carson, *In Struggle: SNCC and the Black Awakening of the 1960s* (Cambridge, Mass.: Harvard University Press, 1981); and Robert Allen, *Black Awakening in Capitalist America* (Garden City, N.Y.: Doubleday, 1969).

43. For important discussions, see T. H. Kennedy and T. F. Leary, "Communist Thought on the Negro," *Phylon,* 8 (1947), pp. 116–23; Wilson Record, "The Development of the Communist Position on the Negro Question in the United States," *Phylon,* 19 (Fall 1958), pp. 306–26; and Philip Foner, *American Socialism and Black Americans* (Westport, Conn.: Greenwood Press, 1977). For discussions by black thinkers, see, among others, Cedric J. Robinson, *Black Marxism: The Making of the Black Radical Tradition* (London: Zed Press, 1983); Henry Winston, *Class, Race and Black Liberation* (New York: International Publishers, 1977); Harry Haywood,

Black Bolshevik: Autobiography of an Afro-American Communist (Chicago: Liberator Press, 1978); James Boggs, *Racism and the Class Struggle: Further Pages from a Black Worker's Notebook* (New York: Monthly Review Press, 1970); Manning Marable, *Blackwater: Historical Studies in Race, Class Consciousness and Revolution* (Dayton: Black Praxis Press, 1981); Oliver Cox, *Caste, Class and Race* (New York: Modern Reader, 1970); and Harold Cruse, *The Crisis of the Negro Intellectual* (New York: Morrow, 1967).

44. Harold Cruse, *Rebellion or Revolution?* (New York: William Morrow, 1968), pp. 127, 130.

45. "The hysteria of the time (which was labeled as McCarthyism, but which ranged far beyond the man) had shaken many persons, cowed others, silenced large numbers, and broken the radical impetus that might have been expected to follow the ferment and agitation of the 1930s and 1940s." Vincent Harding, *The Other American Revolution*, Center for Afro-American Studies Monograph Series, Vol. 4, Center for Afro-American Studies (Los Angeles, Calif.) and Institute of the Black World (Atlanta, Ga. 1980), p. 148.

46. A full exploration of "race" in the context of critical theory from the *black* side, if you will, requires a separate writing. For some of my thinking, see the previous installments cited in note 4, as well as in the writings of persons listed in note 43.

47. In the African context, for example, note Aimé Césaire's protest in his resignation from the Communist Party in 1956: "What I demand of Marxism and Communism. Philosophies and movements must serve the people, not the people the doctrine and the movement. . . . A doctrine is of value only if it is conceived by us and for us, and revised through us. . . . We consider it our duty to make common cause with all who cherish truth and justice, in order to form organizations able to support effectively the black peoples in their present and future struggle— their struggle for justice, for culture, for dignity, for liberty." Cedric Robinson, *Black Marxism*, p. 260, as cited by David Caute, *Communism and the French Intellectuals, 1914–1960* (New York: Macmillan, 1964), p. 211.

48. For a characterization and critique of this philosophical anthropology and its relation to class theory in Marx et al., see my "Race and Class in the Theory and Practice of Emancipatory Social Transformation."

49. Literature on this tradition is abundant. See, for example, John Bracey, Jr., et al. (eds.), *Black Nationalism in American* (New York: Bobbs-Merrill, 1970); Sterling Stuckey, *The Ideological Origins of Black Nationalism* (Boston: Beacon Press, 1970); Alphonso Pinkney, *Red, Black and Green: Black Nationalism in the United States* (New York: Cambridge University Press, 1976); and M. Ron Karenga, "Afro-American Nationalism: Beyond Mystification and Misconception," in *Black Books Bulletin*, (Spring 1978), pp. 7–12. In addition, each of these includes a substantial bibliography.

50. See Cedric J. Robinson, *Black Marxism: The Making of the Black Radical Tradition*, p. 300, and Kennedy and Leary, "Communist Thought on the Negro."

51. "There is a kind of progressive Tower of Babel, where we are engaged in building an edifice for social transformation, but none of us are speaking the same language. None understands where the rest are going." Manning Marable, "Common Program: Transitional Strategies for Black and Progressive Politics in America," in *Blackwater: Historical Studies in Race, Class Consciousness and Revolution*, p. 177.

52. See Marable's *Blackwater: Historical Studies in Race, Class Consciousness and Revolution* and "Through the Prism of Race and Class: Modern Black Nationalism in the U.S.," *Socialist Review*, May/June, 1980; William J. Wilson's *The Declining Significance of Race: Blacks and Changing American Institutions* (Chicago: University of Chicago Press, 1978); and Edna Bonacich's "Class Approaches to Ethnicity and Race," *Insurgent Sociologist*, 10 (Fall 1980), pp. 9–23. For a fuller discussion of approaches to "race" through the prism of the paradigm of class theory, see Omi and Winant, *Racial Formation in the United States*, pp. 25–37.

53. On "nation-class," see James A. Geschwender, *Racial Stratification in America* (Dubuque: Brown, 1978).

82   Lucius Outlaw

54. The recent notions of social evolution I have in mind are those of Jürgen Habermas. See, in particular, his "Historical Materialism and the Development of Normative Structures" and "Toward a Reconstruction of Historical Materialism," in Jürgen Habermas, *Communication and the Evolution of Society*, trans. Thomas McCarthy (Boston: Beacon Press, 1979), pp. 95–177.

55. Omi and Winant, *Racial Formation in the United States*, pp. 76–79.

56. Ibid., p. 107.

57. Ibid., pp. 68–69; emphasis in original.

58. See Habermas, *Communication and the Evolution of Society*.

Acknowledgments

Baldwin, James. "On Being White and Other Lies." *Essence* (April 1984): 90–92. Reprinted by permission of the estate of James Baldwin.

Dyer, Richard. "White." *Screen* 29 (1988): 44–64. Reprinted with the permission of Oxford University Press.

Hooks, Bell. "Representations of Whiteness in the Black Imagination." In *Black Looks: Race and Representation* (Boston: South End Press, 1992): 165–78. Reprinted with the permission of South End Press.

Mullen, Harryette. "Optic White: Blackness and the Production of Whiteness." *Diacritics* 24 (1994): 71–89. Reprinted with the permission of Johns Hopkins University Press.

Omi, Michael and Howard Winant. "By the Rivers of Babylon: Race in the United States." *Socialist Review* 13 (1983): 31–65. Reprinted with the permission of Duke University Press.

Goldberg, Barry. "Slavery, Race and the Languages of Class: 'Wage Slaves' and White 'Niggers.'" *New Politics* 11 (1991): 64–83. Reprinted with the permission of New Politics Associates, Inc.

Guillaumin, Colette. "Race and Nature: The System of Marks." *Feminist Issues* 8 (1988): 25–43. Reprinted with the permission of Transaction Publishers.

Michaels, Walter Benn. "The No-Drop Rule." *Critical Inquiry* 20 (1994): 758–69. Reprinted with the permission of the University of Chicago Press, publisher.

Gordon, Avery and Christopher Newfield. "White Philosophy." *Critical Inquiry* 20 (1994): 737–57. Reprinted with the permission of the University of Chicago Press, publisher.

Butler-Evans, Elliott. "Beyond Essentialism: Rethinking Afro-American Cultural Theory." *Inscriptions* 5 (1989): 121–34. Reprinted with the permission of the University of California, Santa Cruz, Board of Studies in History of Consciousness.

Lloyd, David. "Race under Representation." *Oxford Literary Review* 13 (1991): 62–94. Reprinted with the permission of the *Oxford Literary Review*.

Morrison, Toni. "Romancing the Shadow." In *Playing in the Dark: Whiteness and the Literary Imagination* (Cambridge: Harvard University Press, 1992): 31–59. Reprinted with the permission of International Creative Management.

Gates, Henry Louis, Jr. "'What's Love Got To Do With It?'": Critical Theory, Integrity, and the Black Idiom." *New Literary History* 18 (1987): 345–62. Reprinted with the permission of John Hopkins University Press.

Clarke, Stuart Alan. "Fear of a Black Planet: Race, Identity Politics and Common Sense." *Socialist Review* 21 (1991): 37–59. Reprinted with the permission of Duke University Press.

Ford, Richard T. "The Repressed Community: Locating the New Communitarianism." *Transition* 65 (1995): 96–117. Reprinted with the permission of Duke University Press.

West, Cornel. "The New Cultural Politics of Difference." *October Magazine* 53 (1990): 93–109.

Hall, Stuart. "Race, Articulation and Societies Structured in Dominance." In *Sociological Theories: Race and Colonialism* (Paris: UNESCO, 1980): 305–45. Reprinted with the permission of UNESCO Publishing. Copyright 1980 UNESCO.

Hall, Stuart. "New Ethnicities." In *Black British Cultural Studies*, edited by Houston A. Baker Jr., Manthia Diawara, and Ruth H. Lindeborg (Chicago: University of Chicago Press, 1996): 163–72. Reprinted with the permission of the University of Chicago Press. Copyright 1996, University of Chicago Press.

Outlaw, Lucius. "Toward a Critical Theory of 'Race.'" In *The Anatomy of Racism*, edited by David Theo Goldberg (Minneapolis: University of Minnesota Press, 1990): 58–81. Reprinted with the permission of the University of Minnesota Press.